Mercer Commentary on the Bible

Volume 3

(Wisdom) Writings

Mercer University Press

Mercer Dictionary of the Bible
July 1990; 5th and corrected printing July 1997

Mercer Dictionary of the Bible Course Syllabi
July 1990

Mercer Commentary on the Bible
November 1994

Cover illustration: *Theology* (1509–1511) by Raphael (Raffaello Sanzio, 1483–1520), a ceiling tondo fresco in Stanza della Segnatura, the Vatican, Rome. In 1508, Raphael was commissioned by Pope Julius II to decorate the *Stanze*, the new papal apartment in the Vatican palace. *Theology* is one of four large ceiling tondi in the private library of the pope depicting the four "faculties"—the others are *Philosophy*, *Poetry*, and *Jurisprudence*. (Imaged by Planet Art.)

"The fear of the LORD is the beginning of wisdom, and the knowledge of the Holy One is insight" (Proverbs 9:10 RSV).

Mercer Commentary on the Bible

Volume 3

(Wisdom) Writings

GENERAL EDITORS
Watson E. Mills, Richard F. Wilson

ASSOCIATE EDITORS
Roger A. Bullard, Walter Harrelson, Edgar V. McKnight

MERCER UNIVERSITY PRESS EDITOR
Edmon L. Rowell, Jr.

WITH MEMBERS OF THE
National Association of Baptist Professors of Religion

MERCER UNIVERSITY PRESS
January 2001

ISBN 0-86554-508-1   MUP/P135

Mercer Commentary on the Bible: (Wisdom) Writings
Volume 3 of an 8-volume perfect-bound reissue of
the *Mercer Commentary on the Bible* (©1995)
with articles from the *Mercer Dictionary of the Bible* (1990, 1997)
Copyright ©2001
Mercer University Press, Macon GA 31210-3960
All rights reserved
Printed in the United States of America
First printing, January 2001

The paper used in this publication meets the minimum requirements
of the American National Standard for Information Sciences—
Permanence of Paper for Printed Library Materials, ANSI Z39.48-1984.

Library of Congress Cataloging-in-Publication Data

Mercer commentary on the Bible.
Volume 3. (Wisdom) Writings /
general editors, Watson E. Mills and Richard F. Wilson;
associate editors, Walter Harrelson . . . [et al.].
pp. cm.
1. Bible—commentaries. I. Mills, Watson Early. II. Mercer University Press.
III. National Association of Baptist Professors of Religion.

CIP data available from the Library of Congress.

Contents

Preface vii

Introduction (articles from the *Mercer Dictionary of the Bible*)

Of Philosophers, Poets, and Preachers

Job . . . . *James L. Crenshaw* ix
Job, Targum of . . . . *Joseph L. Trafton* xi
Job, Testament of . . . . . *Joseph L. Trafton* xii
Justice/Judgment . . . . . . *Samuel L. Balentine* xiii
Poetry . . . . *Denise Dombkowski Hopkins* xv
Proverb . . . . *Leo G. Perdue* xx
Proverb/Riddle . . . . *Paul Ciholas* xxiv
Psalms, Apocryphal . . . . *Joseph L. Trafton* xxiv
Sirach . . . . *Heber F. Peacock* xxvi
Solomon, Wisdom of . . . *Heber F. Peacock* xxviii
Suffering in the OT . . . . *E. Luther Copeland* xxx
Wisdom in the NT . . . . *Norm Yance* xxxiii
Wisdom in the OT . . . . . *James L. Crenshaw* xxxiv
Wisdom Literature . . . . . *James L. Crenshaw* xxxviii

(Wisdom) Writings Dictionary Articles

Job, Book of . . . . *Samuel L. Balentine* xlv
Psalms, Book of . . . . . . *Reidar B. Bjornard* xlviii
Proverbs, Book of . . . . *Leo G. Perdue* lii
Ecclesiastes, Book of . . . *Clayton N. Jefford* lv
Song of Songs . . . . *Walter Harrelson* lvii

Commentaries (from the *Mercer Commentary on the Bible*)

Job . . . . *Samuel E. Balentine* 1

Psalms . . . . *Marvin E. Tate* 41

Proverbs . . . . *David Penchansky* 193

Ecclesiastes . . . . *James L. Crenshaw* 229

Song of Solomon . . . . *Mona West* 243

Preface

From the *Mercer Commentary on the Bible* (MCB), this volume includes commentaries on the so-called "Writings" of the Old Testament, also referred to as, for example, the "Books of Wisdom and Poetry." In general this group of writings corresponds to the third rank in the Hebrew Bible, Kethuvim, after Torah and Nevi'im (Prophets). (In the Hebrew Bible, however, Writings also includes Ruth, Lamentations, Esther, Daniel, Ezra, Nehemiah, and 1 and 2 Chronicles.)

Appropriate articles from the *Mercer Dictionary of the Bible* (MDB) make up the introduction section which precedes the commentaries.

This MCB/MDB fascicle is for use in the classroom and for any other setting where study focuses on these Old Testament writings and where a convenient introduction text is desired. This is number 3 in the series of MCB/MDB portions or fascicles.

1. Pentateuch/Torah (Genesis–Deuteronomy)   Isbn 0-86554-506-5 P133
2. History of Israel (Joshua–Esther)   Isbn 0-86554-507-3 P134
3. **(Wisdom) Writings (Job–Song of Songs)**   **Isbn 0-86554-508-1 P135**
4. Prophets (Isaiah–Malachi)   Isbn 0-86554-509-X P136
5. Deuterocanonicals/Apocrypha   Isbn 0-86554-510-3 P137
6. Gospels (Matthew–John)   Isbn 0-86554-511-1 P138
7. Acts and Pauline Writings (Acts–Philemon)   Isbn 0-86554-512-X P139
8. Epistles and Revelation (Heb–Rev)   Isbn 0-86554-513-8 P140

That these divisions and their titles are arbitrary is obvious. These particular groupings originate in the classroom as convenient and provisionally appropriate blocks of text for focused study during a semester-long or quarter-long course of study. Other divisions are possible, perhaps even desirable (combining Acts with the Gospels, for example, rather than with Paul), but the present divisions seem appropriate for most users.

Regarding this "(Wisdom) Writings" division, one may contrast the "Wisdom Literature" grouping in volume 5 of the *New Interpreter's Bible* (Nashville: Abingdon, 1997): Job and Psalms are in a separate "Hebrew Poetry" grouping in *NIB* 4 (1996). But the grouping here coincides with other current scripture divisions, for example, the "Poetical Books or 'Writings' " in the *New Oxford Annotated Bible* (NRSV, 1991) and the "Books of Wisdom and Poetry" in the recent *Learning Bible* (CEV, 2000).

Regarding the use of this and other MCB/MDB portions, please note the following.

A bracketed, flush-right entry at the head of each MDB article and MCB commentary indicates the original page number(s): for example, "Proverbs [MCB 527-49]"; "Proverb [MDB 718-20]." The text from both MDB and MCB is *essentially* that of the original, differing only in format: the text is redesigned to fit a 6x9-inch page (the page size of both MDB and MCB is 7x10 inches). Also, we have taken advantage of the opportunity of this fascicle reprint to make some corrections and very minor revisions.

References to other MDB articles are indicated by SMALL CAPS. In addition, the "See also" sections at the end of the MDB articles indicate other articles that are appropriate for further study.

MDB has introductory articles for every book of the Bible, including those referred to as apocryphal and/or deuterocanonical. For this volume the appropriate introductory articles are reprinted here, but MCB does *not* include small-caps references to these MDB introduction articles unless reference is made to a specific statement in the article. For other fascicles in this series, it is assumed the reader is aware of these MDB introductory articles and will refer to them in MDB as needed.

Notice that small caps are used also for BCE and CE, for certain texts and versions (LXX, KJV, NRSV; CEV), and for the tetragrammaton YHWH.

For abbreviations, see the lists in either MDB or MCB. Regarding the editors and contributors, please see both MDB and MCB. The *Course Syllabi* handbook has a complete listing of original MDB articles (pp. 73-80). MDB includes a complete listing of articles arranged by contributor (pp. 989-93).

We intend that these texts be available, appropriate, and helpful for Bible students both in and out of the classroom and indeed for anyone seeking guidance in uncovering the abundant wealth of the Scriptures. Your critical response to these and other texts from Mercer University Press is welcome and encouraged.

Advent 2000   *Edmon L. Rowell, Jr.*
Macon, Georgia USA   Mercer University Press

Introduction

Of Philosophers, Poets, and Preachers

Job   [MDB 454-55]

•**Job.** [jōb] The name Job is well attested in the ancient Near East, appearing in Egyptian execration texts, the AMARNA tablets, Ugaritic literature, and documents from MARI and Alalakh. Its meaning seems to be "inveterate foe" or "enemy," presumably as an occupation or in the passive sense. The sixth-century prophet Ezekiel mentions Job in connection with Noah and Daniel, each of whom is remembered as having saved others through his intercession. In all probability, this Daniel, cited by Ezekiel, belongs to Ugaritic legend, as the spelling makes clear (*dn'l* rather than *dny'l*). Therefore, Ezekiel implies that a tradition about three ancient worthies circulated in the Exile, in some ways reminiscent of the seven sages in ancient Sumer.

The prominence of the name throughout the Fertile Crescent and the memory of folk heroes suggest that the Job of the Bible was not a historical person. Job is a fictional character, the invention of the author of the book, although by name linked to a figure of legendary fame. This statement also applies to Job's children, the three friends, and the interloper, all fictional characters. The tendency of later readers to treat Job as a real person testifies to the realistic presentation of his struggle.

In a sense, two different kinds of Job make their appearance in the book. The first, patient in the midst of cruel treatment, sat for the portrait that the Epistle of James lifts up for exemplary conduct. The second, impatient to the point of blasphemy, is the disputant with Eliphaz, Bildad, Zophar, and God (he does not respond at all to Elihu). The patient Job in the prose account receives God's badge of honor, in addition to earning the same praise from the narrator. This Job has impeccable credentials. He has personal integrity (*tām*), moral uprightness (*yāšār*), religious fervor (*yĕrē 'ĕlōhîm*), and innocence (*sār mērā'*). The only chinks in his formidable armor are a suspicion about his children and impatience with his wife's solution to his troubles. In his humble faith, he brought nothing into the world and will return naked to mother earth (or Sheol, if *šāmâ* functions euphemistically). Similarly, the Lord gives and takes away, for both of which the proper response is praise. Small wonder that this Job receives God's affectionate title "my servant," and ends his days in enviable style, surrounded by new children and grandchildren.

The other Job bears little resemblance to this one of pious remembrance. From the outset he curses the day of his birth, the nearest thing to cursing God. Until the end he maintains innocence, with the consequence that God must be guilty. Between these two emotional points Job grows increasingly angry, charging his three friends with ineptness as comforters and accusing God of attacking him viciously and of hiding so that Job cannot achieve vindication. Caught in a quandary of his own making, he undercuts the very premise that allows him to complain about his personal condition. In short, if God lacks justice, as Job claims to be the case, then Job has no basis on which to seek redress for wrongs perpetrated against him. This pitiful creature struggles to achieve vindication in the courts, for he knows he is innocent. His plight evokes fleeting thoughts of a powerful advocate who will force God to face Job in a higher court, and in the end Job pronounces an oath of innocence designed to force the deity to answer. Confident that a sinner cannot stand before the creator, Job dares God to appear.

Job's response to the speeches from the tempest indicates that he understands the implications of the rapturous description of nature and its creatures. Not one word is spoken about human beings, whereas God's excitement over these wild creatures seems boundless. No wonder Job recognizes his smallness and abandons titanic ambitions. God's further exuberance over mythic creatures of chaos, Leviathan and Behemoth, evokes yet another admission of finitude. Astonishingly, Job concedes that his prior knowledge of God came indirectly, as if by rumor, and acknowledges that his present knowledge derives from direct vision, which prompts him to submission of some sort. Does he now reject the serious charges against God's manner of running the universe? Or does he abandon his fruitless effort to force a trial in which the Creator appears as defendant?

The former Job, the pious one, gave rise to a devotional text, the *Testament of Job*. Here the hero possesses magical powers to recognize a disguised Satan and passes these powers along to his daughters. This Job also feeds the hungry and protects the dignity of the poor; in addition, he enjoys the love of a wife who sells her hair to feed her sick husband. The defiant Job probably prompted the warning in Ecclesiastes 6:10 against struggling with one who is stronger. This impatient Job has many modern admirers—philosophers, poets, and literary critics.

The biblical Job is probably a non-Israelite, an Arab dwelling in the land of Edom. His friends also represent foreign lands, with the exception of Elihu, who gives voice to traditional Jewish wisdom. The setting for this story about Job appropriately fits the patriarchal period. Although Job's suffering resembles that of Jewish exiles, the reference seems much wider. Job stands for the suffering of extraordinarily virtuous people from every land. He does not represent everyone, however, for few can boast such moral credentials. The religious question posed by this fictional character extends beyond "Why do the innocent suffer?" to an even more penetrating query, "Can religion survive adversity?" The issue of disinterested righteousness, then, is that to which Job lent his name.

See also WISDOM IN THE NEW TESTAMENT; WISDOM IN THE OLD TESTAMENT; WISDOM LITERATURE.

Bibliography. C. Duquoc and C. Floristán, eds., *Job and the Silence of God*; G. Gutiérrez, *On Job: God-Talk and the Suffering of the Innocent*; N. C. Habel, *The Book of Job*; J. G. Janzen, *Job*; M. H. Pope, *Job*; A. de Wilde, *Das Buch Hiob*.

—JAMES L. CRENSHAW

Targum of Job   [MDB 456]

•**Job, Targum of.** The *Targum of Job* is an ancient ARAMAIC translation of JOB, fragmentary manuscripts of which have been found at Qumran in caves 4 and 11. The longer and more important of the manuscripts, *11QtgJob*, consists of twenty-seven large fragments, a number of smaller fragments, and a small scroll. The fragments contain portions of Job 17:14–36:33 in twenty-eight columns. The end of the manuscript, still in scroll form, contains parts of Job 37:10–42:11 in ten columns. A single fragment in two columns, *4QtgJob*, contains parts of Job 3:5-9 and 4:16–5:4. In all, about fifteen percent of the text of Job has survived. Although copied by different scribes, both manuscripts date from the first half of the first century CE. The *Targum* is unrelated to a fifth century CE targum by the same name.

The *Targum of Job* seems to be a generally faithful translation of a Hebrew text which apparently was similar to the MT. The date of the translation (as opposed to the date of the manuscripts) is somewhat problematic. Careful study of the Aramaic indicates that it is closely related to, but later than, the Aramaic of DANIEL and earlier than the Aramaic of the GENESIS APOCRYPHON. Assuming a date for Daniel in the first half of the second century BCE and a date for *1QapGen* in the first century BCE, scholars have generally dated the *Targum* to the second half of the second century BCE. But the Aramaic of Daniel, notoriously difficult to date on linguistic grounds, might be as early as the late sixth century BCE. Thus, an alternate date of 250–150 BCE has been suggested for the *Targum*. In any event, the *Targum of Job* is the oldest known targum.

Nothing in the *Targum* suggests that it is a sectarian composition. Its significance therefore does not lie in shedding light on the peculiar doctrines and practices of the ESSENES, other than that they used it. Rather, its importance is fourfold. First, it is a witness to the Hebrew text of Job at a stage prior to the MT. Thus it contributes to a better understanding of the history of the OT text. Second, it is a witness to the early existence and use of Aramaic translations of the OT. Thus it contributes to a better understanding of the origins and history of the targums. Third, it is a witness to a particular stage in the development of Aramaic. Thus it contributes to a better understanding of the history of the Aramaic language. Fourth, it is a witness to a form of Aramaic still used in Palestine in the first century CE. Thus, it contributes to a better understanding of the language spoken by Jesus.

According to a rabbinic tradition, Rabbi GAMALIEL I (first half of the first century CE) condemned a targum of Job. Certainty is impossible, but it may be that

Gamaliel was shown a copy of the *Targum* being used in Qumran and rejected it because of its association with the Essenes.

See also DEAD SEA SCROLLS.

Bibliography. J. A. Fitzmyer, "Some Observations on the Targum of Job from Qumran Cave 11," *CBQ* 36 (1974): 503-24; T. Muraoka, "The Aramaic of the Old Targum of Job from Qumran Cave XI," *JJS* 25 (1974): 425-43; M. Sokoloff, *The Targum to Job from Qumran Cave XI*.

—JOSEPH L. TRAFTON

Testament of Job   [MDB 456-57]

•**Job, Testament of.** The *Testament of Job* is a retelling, with considerable differences, of the story of JOB, primarily by Job himself. The book takes the form of a testament, that is, a set of final exhortations from an aged father to his children. The story, purportedly told by Job's brother Nereus, begins with Job, ill and desiring to settle his affairs, calling together his seven sons and three daughters. He recounts for them his former wealth and piety; how SATAN had retaliated against him for destroying an idol's temple; the loss of his possessions, children, and health; his wife's subsequent humiliation and eventual death; the coming of the three kings, Eliphas, Baldad, and Sophar, and their interaction with him; Elihu's Satan-inspired insult; and God's response, involving the forgiveness of the three kings, the rejection of Elihu, and the restoration of Job. Job then gives some concluding exhortations and divides his possessions among his sons. To each of his daughters he gives a multicolored cord, a protective amulet of the Father, which changes their hearts and enables them to speak ecstatically in the dialect of angels. Finally, Job's soul is taken away in a heavenly chariot and his body is buried, to the ecstatic blessings of his daughters.

The *Testament of Job* is extant in Greek, Slavonic, and Coptic (in part). Although a semitic original is possible, the strong linguistic affinities between the testament and the SEPTUAGINT version of Job suggest that it was composed in Greek, probably during the first century BCE or CE Whether the author was a Jew or a Christian is debated. An ESSENE or, more likely, Egyptian Theraputae milieu has been suggested, and it is possible that the *Testament* was redacted by Montanists at the end of the second century CE. It may have been known by Tertullian (cf. 20:8-9 and *DePat* 14:5), and it is listed as apocryphal by the so-called Gelasian Decree (sixth century).

The differences between the *Testament* and canonical Job are striking. Satan's attack on Job is seen as retaliation for Job's destruction of an idol's temple. God, in fact, forewarns Job of such retaliation while promising to restore Job if he endures patiently. Thus, Job's suffering does not surprise him, and his patience never wavers. Also, Job's wealth and concern for the poor are described at length. His wife's humiliation and ultimate consolation receive much attention. The role of Job's three friends is greatly diminished, as is that of Elihu, who speaks for Satan.

God's response to Job, so crucial in the canonical Job, is merely alluded to. Finally, the elaborate concern for the multicolored cords and their effect on Job's daughters is unique to the testament, as is the description of Job's death.

Other noteworthy features of the *Testament* include a strong otherworldliness (e.g., 33:3-9; 48–50), a firm hope in the RESURRECTION alongside a body/soul DUALISM (cf. 4:9 and 52:10-11), and a strong interest in women (e.g., female servants and widows, as well as Job's wife and daughters).

See also JOB, BOOK OF; SATAN IN THE OT; TESTAMENTS, APOCRYPHAL.

Bibliography. J. J. Collins, "Testaments," *Jewish Writings of the Second Temple Period*, ed. M. E. Stone; R. P. Spittler, "Testament of Job," *The Old Testament Pseudepigrapha*, ed. J. H. Charlesworth; R. Thornhill, "The Testament of Job," *The Apocryphal Old Testament*, ed. H. F. D. Sparks.

—JOSEPH L. TRAFTON

Justice/Judgment [MDB 482-83]

•**Justice/Judgment.** The range of issues addressed by the terms justice and judgment is broad indeed. As an introduction three important perspectives should be considered: (1) justice/judgment as defined essentially by *law*; (2) justice/judgment as *more than legal definition*; and (3) the quest for *divine justice*, particularly as framed in the issue of theodicy.

Justice and Law. The judicial framework of justice/judgment (Hebrew *mišpāṭ*) is most evident in the association with law or commandment. Thus God's *mišpāṭîm* are those laws given through Moses (Exod 24:3) which the people are to hear (*šm'*, e.g., Deut 5:1; 7:12), keep/obey (*šmr*, e.g., Lev 18:5, 26; Deut 7:11; 11:1; 12:1) and do (*'śh*, e.g., Lev 18:4; Deut 11:32; 26:16). These laws are true (*'ĕmet*, Ps 19:10), good (*tôb*, Ps 119:39), right (*yāšār*, Ps 119:137), and righteous (*sedeq*, Ps 119:75) and thus commend themselves to careful observance, for in living according to God's laws people bring themselves into conformity with God's will. The reward for such obedience is the blessing of God (cf. Deut 28:1-14); the consequence for disobedience, God's punishment (cf. Deut 28:15-68).

A judicial nuance is also present in a number of cases where *mišpāṭ* is appropriately rendered "decision," in the sense of a legal ruling by a judge. One may come before the king (e.g., 2 Sam 15:2, 6) or a judge (e.g., Judg 4:5) for such a decision, or one may appeal the case directly to God (e.g., Num 27:5; Job 13:18; 23:4). In all these cases *mišpāṭ* refers to both the process involved in the decision making (cf. Ps 1:5) as well as the content of the decision rendered. The content is described as positive for those who are innocent and therefore have a legitimate claim, or negative for those who are in the wrong, in which case the decision has the character of legal punishment. When God executes justice (*'āśâ mišpāṭ*) in this latter sense, it is the opponents of God who are punished (e.g., Exod 12:12; Num 33:4). The righteous wait expectantly for such judgments on their enemies (e.g., Pss 119:84; 149:9) and indeed count it as their right (cf. 1 Kgs 8:45, 49, 59; Mic 7:9; Pss 9:4; 140:12;

146:7) for maintaining obedience before the God who is proclaimed in faith as the judge of all the earth (Gen 18:25; cf. Judg 11:27; Isa 33:22; Pss 82:8; 96:13; 98:9).

Justice and Righteousness. While justice-judgment is surely to be understood in a judicial sense, it is clearly the case that in the OT neither idea can be limited simply to a question of legal definition. This is especially clear in the frequent collocations of "justice" (*mišpāṭ*) and RIGHTEOUSNESS (*ṣĕdāqâ*). God is a lover of righteousness and justice (Ps 33:5), characteristics which, when coupled with God's unending love (*ḥesed*) and compassion (*rahămîm*), serve as the cornerstones of God's rule (Ps 89:14; cf. Jer 9:23; Hos 2:19 [MT 2:21]; 12:6 [MT 12:7]). The people of Israel are to follow in the way of God by doing righteousness and justice (Gen 18:19), and their leaders, especially their kings, are charged to implement policies that nurture and secure these qualities in the lives of those for whom they are responsible (2 Sam 8:15; Ps 72:1-2; Jer 22:3; cf. 1 Kgs 3:7-9). Such policies are prominently described with reference specifically to social concerns, namely caring for the poor and the needy (Ps 72:2, 4), securing the welfare of the alien, the orphan, and the widow (Jer 22:3). Faithful attention to these concerns determines God's evaluation of one's true loyalties.

It was primarily the prophets who sounded the charge that Israel's kings (e.g., Jer 22:13-19) and official leaders (e.g., Mic 3:1-12; cf. Jer 2:8; 5:31; 6:13-14; 8:8-12) had failed to live up to this high standard of justice. Certainly the prophetic condemnations focused on the breaking of the Law. This is especially clear in their attacks on such clearly prohibited offenses as bribery, idolatry, and murder (e.g., Jer 7:3-15). But it is also the case that the prophets concerned themselves with behavior which, under the letter of the law, may not have been illegal. They were particularly concerned, for example, with false attitudes that would permit one to observe faithfully the formalities of worship while at the same time plotting to defraud and cheat their neighbors (Amos 8:4-6; cf. 2:6-8; 5:10-12; Mic 3:9-12). Such behavior makes a mockery of justice (Amos 5:7; 6:12), and God will not abide it (cf. Amos 5:21-24; Mic 6:6-8). Gradually the prophets come to look toward the future when the ideal King will at last embody the true justice that is God's (Isa 11:1-4) and toward the new Jerusalem where programs of social reform will assure that justice can be achieved outside the Temple and not only within it (Ezek 45:8-17; 46:16-18).

God's Justice. In a still broader sense, what is at stake in the issue of justice becomes especially clear in those OT texts that raise pointed and probing questions about God's justice. It is evident that there is a standard of justice which is expected of God, in essence that God will faithfully discriminate between the righteous and the wicked (cf. Ps 1), and that God for the most part acts consistently in accordance with this standard, even when external circumstances may raise doubts (e.g., Gen 18:22-25; Ezek 18:1-32). And yet it is also clear that God is in no way bound to human standards of justice. On the one hand this results in magnanimous and undeserved forgiveness from a God whose compassion and mercy override the requirement of justice (e.g., Exod 33:19; Hos 11:8-9; Jonah 4:1-5, 9-11). But on the other hand it leaves many an innocent sufferer groping for answers where none seem available. The OT unashamedly recounts the hard and pressing questions of many of these sufferers, most notably in the significant tradition of lament that runs throughout Israel's encounter with God (e.g., the lament psalms, the confessions of Jeremiah, Job). In their pursuit of relief, or at least understanding, these hurl at God questions and complaints, anger and frustration, even doubt and skepticism, in the hope of finding some clue to the mystery of God's justice. In the end God proclaims, "I am God" (Hos 11:9) and "I am creator" (cf. Job 38–41). Within this proclamation, and within its testimony to God's ultimate sovereignty, the quest for divine justice must find its way.

See also ETHICS IN THE NT; ETHICS IN THE OT; SUFFERING IN THE OT.

Bibliography. R. Adamiak, *Justice and History in the Old Testament: The Evolution of Divine Retribution in the Historiographies of the Wilderness Generation*; J. Barton, "Natural Law and Poetic Justice in the Old Testament," *JTS* 30 (1979): 1-14; H. J. Boecker, *Law and the Administration of Justice in the Old Testament and in the Ancient Near East*; W. Brueggemann, "Theodicy in a Social Dimension," *JSOT* 33 (1985): 3-25; J. Crenshaw, "Popular Questioning of the Justice of God in Ancient Israel," *ZAW* 82 (1970): 380-95; L. Epsztein, *Social Justice in the Ancient Near East and the People of the Bible*; B. Johnson, "מִשְׁפָּט, *mišpāṭ*," *TWAT*; J. Mags, "Justice: Perspectives from the Prophetic Tradition," *Int* 37 (1983): 5-17; P. Miller, *Sin and Judgment in the Prophets*.

—SAMUEL E. BALENTINE

Poetry   [MDB 697-99]

•**Poetry.** Literature in which balanced PARALLELISM and terseness are perceived to be predominant. Biblical poetry lacks features that mark classical verse as poetry, such as quantitative meter and regular rhyme; parallelism within and between lines and words serves as its primary identifying feature. Terseness also identifies biblical poetry; it is a condensing and compressing of the poetic message into brief clauses of often no more than three or four words containing the bare essentials of meaning. Parallelism activates a network of linguistic correspondences within and between lines, thereby increasing the feeling of their connectedness, while terseness creates a correspondence in the number of parts so that the parts and lines appear balanced in length or rhythm. Parallelism and terseness together create the perception of the poetic couplet or brief, two-part sentence form that is the essence of poetry. This form gives poetry the feeling of regularity, closure, and completeness akin to the final "click" of rhyme. Perception is a crucial part of the process of all language. One perceives the dominance of parallelism in poetry not only because of its quantity, but because of its terseness.

Extent. Though it has been argued on the one hand that the entire Bible is written in poetic verse, and, on the other hand, that there is no precise distinction between biblical prose and poetry, Psalms, Proverbs, Job, Canticles, Lamentations, much of the prophets, and portions of the Pentateuch, Daniel, and Ecclesiastes are generally recognized as "poetry" in the OT. Only a few passages are seen as poetry in the NT, e.g., the MAGNIFICAT and prophecy of Zechariah in Luke 1, the NUNC DIMITTIS in Luke 2, the HYMN in Phil 2, and parts of Revelation, along with fragments of poetic lines quoted by NT authors, e.g., 1 Cor 15:33 and Acts 17:28. Poetry also appears in the APOCRYPHA, pseudepigrapha, and the DEAD SEA SCROLLS.

Form and Its Effects. The short, two-part sentence form or couplet is the basic unit of Hebrew poetry. The two parts are separated by a slight stop or pause (indicated by /). The second part is usually a continuation of the first in some way, and ends in a full pause or stop (indicated by //): _____ / _____ //. This binary form is the rule in biblical Hebrew, while the three-part or ternary sentence is the exception. A confusing range of terminology is used to talk about this form. Each part of it is variously called line, stich or stichos (row, line), hemistich (half line), colon (part, member), verset, or A or B. The two parts together are called line, distich (two stichs), stich, bicola, verse, or couplet. This binary form, or line, exhibits a varied correspondence or intensity of parallelism between its two parts (which will be called A and B—so Kugel).

The medial pause in a line has too often been seen as an "equals" (=) sign; it is rather simply a pause or comma, or perhaps better, a double arrow (←——→, so Kugel). That is, B comes after A, adding to it, particularizing, or expanding it (Muilenburg), as well as looks back to A to connect to it; B thus exhibits both "retrospective" and "prospective" qualities. The afterwardness of B gives it its "emphatic" character; it parallels or seconds and reinforces A and gives to the poetic line the feeling of closure and completeness akin to the final "click" of rhyme (Kugel), as for example in Job 3:3.

Sometimes an obvious correspondence exists between A and B, the latter a seeming restatement of the former, as in Ps 146:2. Yet A and B can also be quite unequal in length and seem to be parallel, as in Ps 124:6. Most poetic parallelisms fall somewhere in between these two extremes in varying paralleling intensities. In proverbs and sayings, however, the whole point of the form is finding the precise connection between the seemingly unrelated A and B, as in Eccl 7:1. The "sharpness" of this proverb, that is, "the potential subtleties hidden inside juxtaposed clauses," is the highest form of parallelism (Kugel).

Terseness also contributes to the poetic effect of the binary form or line. Parallelism and terseness together create our perception of "oneness forged out of twoness" (Berlin) and of the regularity of poetry. Terseness constantly presses toward compactness and ellipsis. The most frequent grammatical omissions are the definite article *ha-*, the relative particle *'ašer*, and personal suffixes on nouns, verbs, and prepositions, as for example in Ps 118:22.

The compactness, simplicity, and shortness of A and B, which are usually clauses of only three or four words, forces us to consider their connectedness, particularly when their relationship is left unstated. One cannot reduce the "telegraph style" (Kugel) that is terseness, however, to metrical formulae or statistical analyses of length or syntax because terseness, like parallelism, is variable.

Parallelism. The history of the study of biblical parallelism has been shaped by Bishop Robert Lowth's eighteenth-century *De sacra poesi Hebraeorum* (1753; ET: *Lectures on the Sacred Poetry of the Hebrews*, 1787) and his Isaiah commentary (1778). Lowth identified *parallelismus membrorum* ("the parallelism of the clauses") and distinguished three types of semantic parallelism as the essence of Hebrew poetry: synonymous (interpreted as a restatement or saying the same thing twice), antithetical (a negation or opposite statement), and synthetic (a catchall category of sequence and combination). For more than 200 years, Lowth's work has served as the model that scholars fleshed out and identified. Recently, however, the model has come under attack, particularly from linguists.

Parallelism is the complex network or feeling of correspondence between adjacent lines, parts of lines, and/or words. The nature of this correspondence varies; it cannot be restricted to one level of language or another, although the semantic and grammatical aspects of parallelism are most evident and have historically received the most attention. Parallelism activates all the aspects of language at once: lexical (vocabulary), grammatical (syntax and morphology), semantic (meaning), and phonological (sounds) on the levels of the word and the line (Berlin). Their interplay and integrated effect contribute to the feeling of a pervasive parallelism.

(1) The grammatical aspect of parallelism. Inflection or formation of verbs, nouns, adjectives, and so forth within a line (morphology) and the combination of parts within A and B and of A and B with each other (syntax) mark the grammatical aspect of parallelism. An exact grammatical correspondence in which the syntax and morphology of A and B are the same, or repeated, is rare: see Ps 103:10. Usually B substitutes something morphologically different for what appears in A, as in Ps 33:2, where a pronoun is substituted for a noun.

> Praise *the* LORD with the lyre /
> With the ten-stringed harp sing to [*him*] //

Often, too, verbs from the same root but different conjugations or aspects are paired in A and B, as the *qal/niph'al* in Ps 24:7:

> *Lift up*, O gates, your heads /
> and *be lifted up*, O eternal doors //

Alternation also frequently takes place between *qtl-yqtl* forms (the Hebrew "perfect" and "imperfect") as in Ps 92:4:

> For you, O LORD, *have made me glad* by your work /
> in the works of your hands *I (will) exult* //

Scholars have traditionally viewed these morphological alternations, and others such as shifts from A to B in person, number, gender, definiteness, and case (not in terms of case endings but nouns as nominative or accusative) as simply stylistic devices for variety. Rather, they are examples of morphological parallelism that serve to differentiate and integrate A and B. Kugel argues that the *qtl/yqtl* alternation, for example, indicates an intermeshing of actions in the same way as subordinating phrases function in English.

Common syntactical parallelisms include transformations from A to B of nominal (without a finite verb) to verbal (with a finite verb), as in Mic 6:2b:

For the LORD has a quarrel with [his] people /
and with Israel [he] will dispute //

Also occurring are positive-negative transformations, as in Prov 6:20:

Guard, my son, the commandment of your father /
and do not forsake the teaching of your mother //

Other transformations involve grammatical mood, that is, a contrast of the indicative and interrogative, e.g., Pss 6:6; 73:25. These transformations challenge the emending of texts because of so-called grammatical "inconsistencies."

(2) The lexical and semantic aspects of parallelism. These two aspects are intertwined. The lexical aspect refers to specific words or word groups that are paired in A and B, while the semantic deals with the relationship between the meanings of A and B. Words, of course, affect that relationship. The discovery of the Ugaritic poems at Ras Shamra in 1929 led to the collection by Dahood of "fixed word pairs," that is, parallel terms that occur in both the Bible and Ugaritic texts. It also generated theories about oral composition—poets drew upon a stock of fixed pairs for their oral composition of parallel lines (Culley). This hypothesis finds little support today (Yoder). Rather, word pairs are viewed as the products of normal word associations (Berlin, O'Connor).

Some words are paired frequently with others to make a single merismatic phrase: "day and night" for example, meant "all the time" (Kugel). Further, a word may elicit a parallel word or be paralleled by itself, that is, repeated, as the comparison of 2 Sam 22 and Ps 18 shows. Also, a word may elicit many different associations, depending upon the poet's artistry, the requirements of the context and how stereotyped it has become. One cannot predict word associations in biblical parallelism but can only explain and categorize them according to rules of linguistics.

The semantic aspect of parallelism has received the most attention because of Lowth's tripartite model. But as Kugel argues, "Biblical parallelism is of one sort, 'A, and what's more, B' or a hundred sorts; but it is not three." Scholars today tend to see a more dynamic movement within a line than Lowth did. Parallelism does not always make the semantic relationship between A and B explicit. As Kugel argues: "A is so, and what's more, B." B in its connection to A has an "emphatic, seconding character"; B carries A further, echoing, defining, restating, contrasting it, "it does not matter which."

Alter prefers to speak of the movement of meaning within a line as "heightening," or "intensification." His "rule of thumb" is that a general term occurs in A and is specified or concretized or focused or intensified in B, as in Prov 3:10 (the verbal movement shows intensification, the noun movement specification/concretization):

Then your barns will be filled with plenty /
and your vats will be bursting with new wine //

In this light, ellipsis, which occurs when the subject or verb appears in A but is "gapped" (missing) and only implied in B, is no longer seen as an example of "incomplete" or defective parallelism. Rather, ellipsis is one way in which B "seconds" or "intensifies" A by isolating terms for attention, as in Lam 3:19:

> *Remember* my affliction and my bitterness /
> the wormwood and the gall //

Semantic parallelism is rarely complete or explicit; "language resists true synonymity" (Alter). Not only can B "second" or "intensify" or complete A, but sometimes B can cause us to see A in a new way. Scholars speak of this dual semantic function of parallelism in different ways: as disambiguation (or redundance) and ambiguity (Berlin) or as the perception of disharmony which prompts semantic modifications (Alter). This dialectical tension of semantic parallelism is evident in the "intensification" of numbers, as in Deut 32:30a (cf. Ps 62:12; Gen 4:24):

> How could *one* chase a *thousand* /
> and *two* put *ten thousand* to flight //

The dialectical tension is also evident in the movement from a standard, common, literal term in A to a more literary, figurative, metaphorical term in B (Alter), as in Gen 4:23 (cf. Prov 26:9; Eccl 7:1; Ps 88:12-13; Jer 48:11):

> *Ada and Zilla, hear* my voice /
> *Wives of Lamech, give ear* to my speech //

Parallelism can serve as the vehicle for figurative language and metaphor: cf. Isa 1:9-10.

(3) The phonologic aspect of parallelism. Traditionally, the study of sound parallelism in biblical poetry has been relegated to the secondary status of poetic "technique," that is, alliteration, assonance, onomatopoeia, or paranomasia (wordplay or punning), as in Amos 8:2 ($q\acute{a}yis$/basket, paired with $q\bar{e}s$/end). Contemporary scholars focus upon the repetition and contrast of sounds in parallel lines, and more specifically on sound pairs, that is, "the repetition in parallel words or lines of the same or similar consonants (at least two sets) in any order within close proximity" (Berlin).

Sound may play a part in certain lexical combinations, for example, desert-wilderness (*mdbr-'rbh*) in Jer 2:6. Some sound pairs also show grammatical and semantic correspondence, as in Ps 122:7:

> May there be peace [*šlwm*] in your ramparts /
> Tranquility [*šlwh*] in your citadels //

Other sound pairs show no lexical and/or semantic correspondence, but occur in addition to a word pair or in place of one, as in Job 36:15. This shows that sound pairing is more than coincidental. Most sound pairs are not naturally associated word pairs or automatic responses "but a one-time nexus between sound and sense" (Berlin); the "unexpectedness" of their combination creates their effect.

(4) Summary. Given the different aspects of language that may be activated by parallelism, it is clear that no one formula can account for all possible parallelisms within and between poetic lines. One can identify, however, formal principles that may make parallelism perceptible and interesting to a reader or listener. Parallelism itself does not have meaning; parallelism does, however, help to structure the text and its meaning. Each parallelism fits into its context, and participates in and contributes to the meaning of the text as a whole.

Meter and Poetry. There is no word for "poetry" in biblical Hebrew, yet, ever since Lowth, parallelism has been equated with poetry. Lowth himself argued that meter was the basis of biblical poetry but was lost to us because of the uncertainties of Hebrew pronunciation; its existence and structure, however, could be inferred from parallelism. Since Lowth, scholars have either persisted in the belief that meter characterizes Hebrew poetry (disagreeing over how meter is to be measured), or they have taken parallelism as a substitute for meter and its regularity. Many scholars today argue, however, that the rough equality of lines and the rhythm or meter of poetry are not accidental but also not metrical, that is, not a product of syllable, accent, or word quantities; meter is rather a product of parallelism and cannot be understood apart from it. Textual emendation for the sake of meter is generally rejected today. Terse parallelism, not meter, distinguishes poetry from prose.

See also PARALLELISM.

Bibliography. R. Alter, *The Art of Biblical Poetry*; A. Berlin, *The Dynamics of Biblical Parallelism*; U. Cassuto, *Biblical and Oriental Studies*; T. Collins, *Line-Forms in Hebrew Poetry*; F. M. Cross and D. N. Freedman, *Studies in Ancient Yahwistic Poetry*; P. Craigie, "The Problem of Parallel Word Pairs in Ugaritic and Hebrew Poetry," *Semitics* 5 (1979): 48-58; R. Culley, *Oral Formulaic Language in the Biblical Psalms* M. Dahood, "Poetry," *IDBSupp* and *Psalms I, II, III*; S. Geller, *Parallelism in Early Biblical Poetry*; N. Gottwald, "Poetry, Hebrew," *IDB*; G. B. Gray, *The Forms of Hebrew Poetry*; J. Kugel, *The Idea of Biblical Poetry*; R. Lowth, *Lectures on the Sacred Poetry of the Hebrews* and *Isaiah: A New Translation with a Preliminary Dissertation and Notes Critical, Philological, and Explanatory*; J. Muilenburg, "A Study in Hebrew Rhetoric: Repetition and Style," *VTSupp* 1 (1953): 97-111; M. O'Connor, *Hebrew Verse Structure*; T. H. Robinson, *The Poetry of the Old Testament*; B. H. Smith, *Poetic Closure: A Study of How Poems End*; D. Stuart, *Studies in Early Hebrew Meter*; P. Yoder, "A-B Pairs and Oral Composition in Hebrew Poetry," *VT* 21 (1971): 470-89.

—DENISE DOMBKOWSKI HOPKINS

Proverb   [MDB 718-20]

•**Proverb.** A proverb is a succinct saying that registers a conclusion based on experience and the powers of observation. The proverb is one of the important forms of language used by the teachers who developed the WISDOM LITERATURE of the Bible. The Hebrew word often translated proverb is *māšāl*. *Māšāl* has two meanings: "likeness" (metaphor or simile) and "rule."

"Likeness" refers to the idea that two or more things are similar to each other, or may be understood in relationship to each other. Thus "wealth" is like a "strong city" while "poverty" is like a "desolate ruin" (Prov 10:15); or

> The words of a good person are *like pure silver*,
> but the thoughts of an evil person are *almost worthless*. (Prov 10:20 CEV)

"Rule" expresses the idea that a proverb should take up residence in the mind and form and shape human conduct. Residing behind proverbs is the belief that reality (the world, society, and religion) possesses an order that is just, beautiful, and coherent. By observing this order, putting the observance into sayings and other forms of teaching, and following what is taught, the wisdom teachers believed that people would experience order, well-being, and blessing in life.

Broadly speaking, there are two major categories of proverbs: folk sayings and literary sayings. A folk proverb comes from popular culture. Drawing vivid images from nature and society, it presents a truth that is widely accepted by its culture. Well-known examples include

> Like Nimrod a mighty hunter before the LORD. (Gen 10:9)
> The fathers have eaten sour grapes,
> and the children's teeth are set on edge. (Ezek 18:2 = Jer 31:29)
> A city set on a hill cannot be hid. (Matt 5:14)
> The tree is known by its fruit. (Matt 12:33 = Luke 6:44)

More artistically crafted than folk sayings, literary proverbs are poetic sayings normally expressed in the declarative mood:

> The mouth of the righteous brings forth wisdom,
> but the perverse tongue will be cut off. (Prov 10:31)
> A disciple is not above his teacher,
> nor a servant above his master.
> (Matt 10:24; cf. Luke 6:40a; John 13:16; 15:20)

There are several specific varieties of literary sayings: comparative, better, numerical, riddle, question, and beatitude.

Comparative ("like") proverbs seek to express analogies normally between two things:

> Like a dog who returns to his vomit
> is a fool who repeats his folly. (Prov 26:11)
> Every scribe who has been trained for the kingdom of heaven is like a householder who brings out of his treasure what is new and what is old. (Matt 13:52)

Comparative proverbs occasionally describe the mysterious with images that are better known:

> As the heaven for height, and the earth for depth,
> so the mind of kings is unsearchable. (Prov 25:3)

Sometimes comparative proverbs use the pattern "if here, then how much more there." The inference is drawn that if something is true in one instance, how much more true it is in another:

> Sheol and Abaddon lie open before the LORD,
>> how much more the hearts of people! (Prov 15:11)
> If you then, who are evil,
>> know how to give good gifts to your children,
> how much more will your Father in heaven
>> give good things to those who ask him! (Matt 7:11 = Luke 11:13)

A *better* saying is a type of proverb that makes a value judgment. In comparing two items, the conclusion is that one is preferable to another:

> Better is a little with righteousness,
>> than great revenues with injustice. (Prov 16:8)
> Better is open rebuke,
>> than hidden love. (Prov 27:5)

Numerical proverbs seek to establish relationships between a variety of things. Such sayings point to one feature that is held in common by each thing mentioned. The three-four pattern is the most common, but other patterns do occur:

> Under three things the earth quakes,
>> under four it cannot bear up:
> a slave when he becomes king,
>> a fool when he is filled with food;
> an unloved woman who gets a husband,
>> and a maid when she succeeds her mistress. (Prov 30:21-23)

Another literary saying, the *riddle*, describes something in enigmatic terms. Involving a match of wits between the riddler and the listener, the riddler's intention is to confuse the listeners so that they will not be able to guess what is being described. Often the riddle is more than an intellectual game designed to entertain. A riddle may become the focal point of a contest or initiation that results literally or figuratively in life and death for the participants. There are two well-known riddles in the story of SAMSON. The first is one proposed by Samson to his Philistine opponents during his marriage feast:

> Out of the eater came something to eat,
>> Out of the strong came something sweet. (Judg 14:14)

The answer extorted from Samson's fiancee is the second riddle:

> What is sweeter than honey?
>> What is stronger than a lion? (Judg 14:18)

In the context of the wedding feast, the normal answer to the second riddle, which contains the answer to the first, would be "love." The irony is that the countrymen of the Philistines paid for their treachery with their lives. Proverbs also include questions. Rhetorical questions are sayings that require no answer. The typical use is to support the truth of the teaching, presented in the context of an instruction or disputation. With assent given, the teacher's case is made by analogy, "if this, then that":

Can a man carry fire in his bosom,
    and his clothes not be burned?
Or can one walk upon hot coals,
    and his feet not be scorched? (Prov 6:27-28)
Are grapes gathered from thorns,
    or figs from thistles? (Matt 7:16 = Lk 6:44)
Can the wedding guests fast
    while the bridegroom is still with them? (Mark 2:19 = Matt 9:15)

Impossible *questions* point to the limits of human knowledge, ability, and existence:

Consider the work of God:
    who can make straight
what he has made crooked? (Eccl 7:13)
And which of you by being anxious
    can add one cubit to his span of life? (Matt 6:27 = Luke 12:25)

Finally, *beatitudes* are a declaration of well-being to those who engage in virtuous and righteous behavior: studying and obeying the teachings of the law (Prov 29:18); caring for the poor (Prov 14:21); trusting in God (Prov 16:20); and finding wisdom (Prov 3:13). They normally begin with the word translated "happy" or "blessed."

Blessed is the one who finds wisdom,
    and the person who obtains understanding. (Prov 3:13)

Jesus uses this saying to indicate that those who are victims now will experience well-being in the coming Kingdom of God.

Blessed are you poor,
    for yours is the kingdom of God. (Luke 6:20b = Matt 5:3)

See also PROVERBS, BOOK OF; PROVERB/RIDDLE; WISDOM IN THE OT; WISDOM LITERATURE.

Bibliography. W. Beardslee, *Literary Criticism of the New Testament*; J. L. Crenshaw, *Old Testament Wisdom*; J. L. Crenshaw, "Wisdom," *Old Testament Form Criticism*, ed. J. H. Hayes; C. Fontaine, *Traditional Sayings in the Old Testament*; R. Murphy, *Wisdom Literature*; L. G. Perdue, "The Wisdom Sayings of Jesus," *Forum* 2/3 (1986): 3-35; G. von Rad, *Wisdom in Israel*; J. Williams, *Those Who Ponder Proverbs*.

—LEO G. PERDUE

Proverb/Riddle   [MDB 720]

•**Proverb/Riddle.** Proverbs and riddles belong to the genre of WISDOM LITERATURE and convey oracular or aphoristic truth by means of pithy sayings or statements which are often metaphorical or enigmatic. However, proverbs differ greatly from riddles in purpose and content.

Riddles are intentionally worded in an obscure manner, and their enigmatic form requires elucidation and interpretation. They are infrequent in the NT. The Greek term for riddle (αἴνιγμα *ainigma*) appears only in 1 Cor 13:12 to remind the faithful of the mysterious nature of faith. Elsewhere they are presented as puzzles to be solved (Rev 13:18).

Proverbial sayings are numerous in the NT and can be easily applied to the various situations of the hearers. They embody the knowledge and wisdom of past generations, both Jewish and heathen. In the NT, the technical term for proverb (παροιμία *paroimia*) is used only in the Gospel of John (10:6; 16:25, 29) and in 2 Pet 2:22—one of the most pointed proverbs in canonical writings:

A dog goes back to what it has vomited and
A pig that has been washed goes back to roll in the mud. (TEV)

Gospel authors have sometimes chosen to use the term παραβολή *parabole* to speak of proverbial wisdom (Luke 4:23), but most proverbs are used without semantic qualification. Their listings abound and greatly differ from each other.

Numerous statements in Paul's letters can be characterized as general truths in the form of proverbial sayings (Rom 14:14; 1 Cor 6:12; Gal 6:7; 1 Cor 3:19). Paul's exhortations especially reflect the use of proverbial wisdom (Rom 12:21; Phil 4:8).

Proverbs are more numerous in the NT than RIDDLES. Both forms by their very nature are far less developed than other forms of teaching, but their encapsulated wisdom provides important insights linking everyday experience and universal truth.

See also PARABLES; PROVERB; RIDDLE; WISDOM IN THE OLD TESTAMENT; WISDOM LITERATURE.

—PAUL CIHOLAS

Apocryphal Psalms   [MDB 722]

•**Psalms, Apocryphal.** [sahmz] The Hebrew Bible/Old Testament contains 150 psalms. Some Syriac manuscripts contain five additional psalms, one of which is found in the LXX. The *Qumran Psalms Scroll (11QPs;ka)* includes eight additional psalms, four of which correspond to three of the Syriac psalms, and one of which is related to SIRACH. Thus there exist at least ten known apocryphal psalms. Eight are attributed to DAVID and two to HEZEKIAH, although there is little reason to accept these attributions as historical. These psalms apparently were composed in Hebrew by different authors prior to the first century BCE.

The most widely known of these psalms is Ps 151. It is extant in Hebrew, Greek, and Syriac, as well as in a number of other ancient versions of the Bible. It is clear from the Hebrew that this psalm was originally two psalms, the second of which is almost completely lost in the Hebrew. The Greek and the Syriac have abbreviated these psalms and combined them into a single psalm. Ps 151A is a psalm of praise in which David purportedly recounts his youth and his anointing by SAMUEL (cf. 1 Sam 16:1-13). In Ps 151B, most of which is lost, David tells of his defeat of GOLIATH (cf. 1 Sam 17:4-51). These two psalms were apparently composed no later than the third century BCE. Combined as Ps 151, this psalm was popular among early and medieval Christians and is accepted by Eastern Orthodox churches as being authoritative.

An apparently conflated version appears as Ps 151 in some manuscripts of the LXX; in modern English versions, it appears among the Deuterocanonicals/Apocrypha in the (expanded) RSV, NRSV, and CEV. A translation of a more extensive version (from Qumran) is included in the introduction to Ps 151 in the NOAB/RSV (but not NOAB/NRSV).

The other Syriac psalms are commonly numbered 152 through 155. Pss 152 and 153, extant only in Syriac, are based on 1 Sam 17:34-35. In Ps 152 David asks God to come to his aid when he is attacked by a lion and a wolf while watching his father's flocks. Ps 153 is a hymn of praise to God for delivering him from the two beasts. Pss 154 and 155 are extant in Hebrew and in Syriac. One late Syriac manuscript attributes them to Hezekiah. Ps 154 is a call to the congregation to praise God for the giving of his WISDOM to humanity. Ps 155 is a plea to God for deliverance from the wicked and for cleansing from sin.

The other four apocryphal psalms in the Qumran Psalter are attributed to David. One is a poem to divine Wisdom and is closely related to Sir 51:13-30. Another is, like Ps 155, a plea for deliverance. The third, an acrostic poem, is a hymn to ZION. The fourth is a hymn to God as Creator. The Psalms Scroll also contains a prose supplement concerning David's poetic accomplishments; he is said to have written 4,050 compositions—3,600 psalms and 450 songs.

Works such as the PSALMS OF SOLOMON, the Qumran hymn scroll, and the PRAYER OF MANASSEH are clear testimony to the widespread composition of psalms in Judaism prior to 70 CE. The presence of apocryphal "Davidic" psalms alongside canonical ones, moreover, raises questions about the extent to which the canonical psalms actually constituted a fixed collection in this period.

See also DEAD SEA SCROLLS; MANASSEH, PRAYER OF; HYMN; PSALMS, BOOK OF; SOLOMON, PSALMS OF.

Bibliography. J. H. Charlesworth and J. A. Sanders, "More Psalms of David," *Old Testament Pseudepigrapha*, ed. J. H. Charlesworth; D. Flusser, "Psalms, Hymns, and Prayers," *Jewish Writings of the Second Temple Period*, ed. M. E. Stone; J. A. Sanders, *The Dead Sea Psalms Scroll*.

—JOSEPH L. TRAFTON

Sirach   [MDB 829-30]

•**Sirach.** [si'rahk] A book of the Apocrypha or Deuterocanonicals, also known as *Ecclesiasticus* or the *Wisdom of Jesus the Son of Sirach*; the latter is abbreviated as *Wisdom of Ben Sirach* (son of Sirach) or simply *Sirach*.

Sirach was written in Hebrew by a man named Joshua (Gk. Jesus) ben Sira and was later translated into Greek by his grandson. When he translated the book, the grandson wrote a preface or foreword (printed preceding chap. 1), in which he describes how he translated the book into Greek for non-Hebrew-speaking Jews residing in Egypt. He himself had gone to settle in Egypt in 132 BCE, and he must have begun his work of translation shortly thereafter.

The book was originally composed in Hebrew, probably in Jerusalem, some sixty years or so before the translation was made. This means the book came into existence after 200 BCE. Scholars generally agree it was written between ca. 195 and 165 BCE. The original author seems to have been a scribe and teacher who had traveled widely.

Although written in Hebrew, the book has been transmitted through the centuries in its Greek form. It is only in modern times that Hebrew materials have become available, first in the discovery in 1896 of Hebrew manuscripts and fragments in the storeroom of an ancient synagogue in Cairo (the "Cairo Genizah"). This provides materials in Hebrew for about two-thirds of the book, although many questions can be raised about the character of this late Hebrew text. A few additional pages have come to light more recently from Qumran and Masada. The Greek text itself is preserved in a number of manuscripts, but the task of deciding what is the original text is a complicated one. Most modern translations will provide the reader with some insight into the variations that occur in many places in the book.

Ben Sira wrote at a time when there was great pressure on the Jews of Palestine to adopt Greek manners and customs. The Seleucids had come to power in 198 BCE, and hellenization made rapid inroads, particularly among the upper classes. Antiochus Epiphanes was about to break upon the scene (175–164 BCE), with his efforts to hellenize the Jews by force. The MACCABEES resisted this effort, but Ben Sira was a resistance fighter with his pen—he opposed the hellenization movement by appealing to the ancient traditions of WISDOM and LAW. He remained devoted to the TEMPLE and its liturgy but also appealed to the sacred scriptures as he taught wisdom to all those who would listen.

The book belongs in the mainstream of Jewish WISDOM LITERATURE and follows the pattern of PROVERBS in treating all kinds of subject matter from the standpoint of wisdom. These wisdom messages are often presented in isolated statements that seem to be glued to each other often without any clear indication of how they are connected, although sayings are grouped together more frequently than in Proverbs. The book has been called a "lifetime scrapbook of a lecturer or teacher" (Snaith), and it does contain many sayings in poetic form about all kinds of secular subjects. An outline is hardly possible, but there are some significant discrete sections. Beginning with 42:15, the writer deals with the glory of God as shown in nature (42:15–43:33) and in history (44:1–50:29). This latter section, beginning "Let us now praise famous men [Heb., godly men]" may be one of the best-known parts of the book. Chap. 51, which seems to be an addition, contains a psalm of thanksgiving and an acrostic poem (in Hebrew) on the search for wisdom.

Sirach can provide much information regarding religious thought at the beginning of the second century BCE. The author is clearly devoted to the Law and urges faithful practice of traditional religion (1:25-28; 6:37). The theme of the fear of the Lord is so prevalent (e.g., 2:15-17; 34:13ff.) that some have proposed to take it as the major theme of the book, but it seems rather to be a natural expression for the traditional obedience to the Lord's commands. It is also evident that the fear of the Lord, combining love and obedience, is the basis for the emphasis on prayer that is found in the book. God is to be feared and trusted, and all human beings should learn to depend upon him.

One senses a universal spirit in the author, in spite of his insistence that the true faith is to be found in Judaism. As in other wisdom literature, there are evidences of non-Jewish influence, particularly from Egypt. In the section dealing with famous men from Enoch to the high priest Simon II, a contemporary of the author (chaps. 44–50), and other parts of the book, God is presented as the creator of a perfect creation; he is the controller of the universe and deals with it justly; he is everything (16:17-23; 16:24–17:24; 42:21ff.; 43:27).

Chap. 24, with its personification of WISDOM as a female figure in heaven, is important in emphasizing that Wisdom truly dwells in Israel. Whatever else the other nations may have, the creator has given Wisdom to the Jewish people, who are now called to obey Wisdom, created for eternity.

The opening words of the prologue are important in providing the earliest indication of the division of the Hebrew Bible into the Law, the Prophets, and the (other) Writings. Although Sirach was not finally accepted into the Jewish CANON, it seems to have been quite popular among Jewish readers. It is cited in the Talmud and referred to in Jewish literature until the Middle Ages. It was certainly widely used among early Christian writers (perhaps the name Ecclesiasticus—"The Church Book" supports this). The book is more Sadducean than Pharisean, and that may account for its rejection from the Jewish canon.

See also APOCRYPHAL LITERATURE; HELLENISTIC WORLD; WISDOM LITERATURE.

Bibliography. I. Levi, *The Hebrew Text of the Book of Ecclesiasticus*; J. G. Snaith, *Ecclesiasticus*; T. H. Weber, "Sirach," *JBC*; Y. Yadin, *The Ben Sira Scroll from Masada*.

—HEBER F. PEACOCK

Wisdom of Solomon   [MDB 844-45]

•Solomon, Wisdom of. The Wisdom of Solomon, one of the books of the Apocrypha or deuterocanonicals, is also known simply as the Book of Wisdom. Although the book claims King SOLOMON, known for his wisdom, as its author (see 9:7-8), this is clearly just a literary device, common in Jewish WISDOM LITERATURE. There is abundant evidence that the book was composed in Greek and that the author made use of the OT in one of its SEPTUAGINT versions. The author remains anonymous, but most scholars agree the book probably was written some time between 220 BCE and 50 CE. David Winston argues strongly for the period 37–41 CE, during the reign of Gaius Caligula.

The book was probably written in Egypt, perhaps in Alexandria. In addition to the fact that a major portion of the book (chaps. 11–19) contrasts the blessings of God on Israel and the punishment of God on Egypt, the author is well acquainted with Greek philosophy and its use in Jewish literature. Its origin is clearly in diaspora Judaism, and Alexandria, a major center of Jewish-Greek learning, is a likely place of writing.

The unity of the book was questioned in the eighteenth and early nineteenth centuries and again in the early twentieth century, but there seems to be a growing consensus that the book is a unity in spite of the large differences of style in the first and last parts of the book. A careful examination of language and style leads to the conclusion that the book is by a single author and forms a whole.

The Book of Wisdom certainly belongs with that body of Jewish literature known as wisdom literature, although it differs from other wisdom materials. It does not consist of short pithy sayings that are so familiar from a book like PROVERBS. It is more akin to ECCLESIASTES, and not only in that both are attributed to Solomon. Wisdom is a public discourse that presents an argument in the hope of convincing Jewish people in the diaspora that their faith need not be rejected in favor of the competing religions around them. The author uses the standard forms for such an exhortation, combining philosophy and rhetoric, and trying to show that his position is logical and just.

The book is concerned to strengthen the faith of Jews living in the DIASPORA. The Jewish community living in the HELLENISTIC WORLD, and in intimate daily contact with new ideas and new religions, must not lose heart and suppose that its own faith is no longer valid. It is a time of crisis, and many are tempted to turn away from their faith. Some of the problems that Jews are facing from surrounding philosophical or religious positions can be seen in chap. 2, with its contrast between the wicked and the righteous. The author calls upon fellow Jews to take pride in their religion, which is far superior to what is offered in the world around them. Jews worship the one true God, and all the idolatry of the polytheistic world around them can be rejected as inferior.

The content of the book is not readily outlined or summarized, not because the plan of the book is obscure, but because of recurring themes found at several places in the book. Many outlines have been proposed. A common scheme divides the book into three sections: (1) the practical value of Wisdom (chaps. 1–5); (2) in praise of Wisdom (chaps. 6–9); and (3) Wisdom's guidance of the nations in history (chaps. 10–19). This outline does justice to the main themes of the book but is not entirely convincing as to the points of division. A better solution may be found in the author's use of INCLUSIO, in which the author repeats at the end of a section a key word or phrase from the beginning of that section. In such an approach the book may be divided into two major sections: (1) in praise of Wisdom (chaps. 1–10) and (2) God's use of Wisdom in the Exodus (chaps. 11–19). This may become a threefold division if one wishes to recognize a shift in section (1) at 6:22, where material on the nature of Wisdom and Solomon's search for her begins.

Many of the religious ideas of the book are significant in marking changes from views held at an earlier time. For example, the book gives the clearest and earliest Jewish expression of the idea that the suffering of the innocent in this world has little importance in light of the future life they will enjoy with God; and this future life is strongly affirmed (3:1-9). The preexistence of the soul (8:19) and its IMMORTALITY (1:12f.; 3:1) contrast sharply with earlier views of human wholeness, with an earthly body made alive by the breath of God. Divine providence and future judgment, in this world and the next are everywhere assumed.

As one reads the book, the place of allegory becomes increasingly obvious. In fact, the last section of the book is a kind of allegorical MIDRASH on God's deliverance of his people through wisdom at the time of the Exodus. In 10:7 the pillar of salt stands for disbelief in general. In 10:17 the pillar of cloud or of fire represents wisdom. And one should not overlook the repeated use of a contrast between God's punishment of the Egyptians and his blessing of the Israelites. For example, in 11:4 the author makes use of the contrast between the Nile water turned to blood and the water from the rock provided for the Israelites.

The Book of Wisdom is important for understanding late Jewish thought and should be studied carefully by those interested in Hellenistic Judaism and the NT. It should also be noted that the place of Wisdom in God's plan for the universe has parallels in the NT.

The text of the book is well established as preserved in five Greek uncial manuscripts with Codex Vaticanus and Codex Sinaiticus preserving the text most accurately. Modern editions of the Greek text provide a good critical text with an apparatus showing variants, and most modern translations provide some textual information.

See also APOCRYPHAL LITERATURE; WISDOM LITERATURE.

Bibliography. J. Reider, *The Book of Wisdom*; D. Winston, *The Wisdom of Solomon*; A. G. Wright, "Wisdom" *The Jerome Biblical Commentary*.

—HEBER F. PEACOCK

Suffering in the Old Testament   [MDB 860-62]

•**Suffering in the Old Testament.** Since suffering is a universal phenomenon, all religions must concern themselves with it. It is not surprising, therefore, that suffering occupies a prominent place in the OT. Near the beginning of the first book of the Bible the reality of suffering is introduced. Here it is rooted in the disobedience of the primeval couple, Adam and Eve (Gen 3:1-19).

Suffering in the Context of the OT Thought World. The sufferings described in the OT run the gamut of human experience. There are physical pains associated with diseases, handicaps, and violence. There are the miseries of stressful mental and spiritual states: fear, guilt, shame, bereavement, deprivation, a sense of failure, loneliness, forsakenness, etc.

The means of coping with suffering, likewise, are various and not remarkable except at one point: in the OT there is the highly developed use of lamentation as a ritualistic or liturgical method of registering complaints to God and seeking relief from suffering. Though quite different in literary form, both Job and Lamentations are OT books of this genre. More important for the worship life of Israel were the many laments included in the Psalter. These psalms often articulate a sufferer's sense of being forsaken by God. They describe the plaintiff's sufferings, often graphically, but characteristically end in thanksgiving for relief and affirmation of the greatness of God. Ps 22 is an example of an individual lament, while Ps 10 is a lament on behalf of the poor who suffer at the hands of wicked exploiters.

In ancient Israel there was the inclination to attribute everything to the will or action of God. Therefore, the lament concerning one's pain was first and foremost a complaint to God: "Thou art the God in whom I take refuge; why hast thou cast me off? Why go I mourning . . . ?" (Ps 43:2); or, "Remove thy stroke from me; I am spent by the blows of thy hand" (Ps 39:10); or again, "Fill me with joy and gladness; let the bones which thou hast broken rejoice" (Ps 51:8).

At the same time there was the awareness of many spiritual beings in the environment, some of them malevolent. Israel gradually outgrew its polytheistic environment and renounced superstition and magic, but these are never far in the background. Who knows what awareness of mysterious evil in the environment may have inspired words such as these: "My heart is in anguish within me, the terrors of death have fallen upon me. Fear and trembling come upon me, and horror overwhelms me" (Ps 55:4-5)?

There is also a sense of social solidarity by which people must suffer collectively for the acts of individuals. Thus God is represented as "visiting the iniquity of the fathers upon the children and the children's children, to the third and fourth generation" (Exod 34:7). In one instance, the sin of one man caused Israel to suffer defeat in battle, and the problem was solved by the execution, not only of the individual at fault but of his whole family (Josh 7:1-26). Nevertheless, the sense of individual responsibility arose to modify or contradict this concept of corporate guilt (cf. Deut 24:16; Ezek 18:1ff.; Jer 31:29).

In addition, the people of Israel had a vague view of life beyond death, so that the imbalances of suffering and prosperity could not be deferred to the afterlife (cf. Pss 88:10; 115:17, etc.). Late in the OT period a belief in resurrection and a heavenly existence develops, but even by the time of Jesus it was by no means universal (cf. Mark 12:18 and par.).

The Meanings of Suffering in the OT. In the OT suffering is interpreted variously. The diverse understandings reflect in part developments attending Israel's experiences in history. They are not mutually exclusive but rather tend to be complementary.

(1) Much of human suffering was simply considered ordinary or normal. It was to be borne and not necessarily explained, even as animals suffer uncomplainingly. Minor aches and pains surely were so viewed. Eliphaz remarked that "man is born to trouble as the sparks fly upward" (Job 5:7). Though Job's own miseries were too immense and poignant thus to be ignored, no doubt many suffered minor difficulties, or even more tragic ones, without complaint or questioning. Though by its very nature such a view of suffering would not receive much attention, there are indications that it was present (cf. Pss 37:7; 38:13-14). It is suggested, also, that this stoical method was tried and found wanting: "I was dumb and silent, I held my peace to no avail; my distress grew worse . . . ; then I spoke with my tongue" (Ps 39:2-3).

(2) The most prevalent understanding of suffering in the OT is that it is a recompense for sin. This retributive interpretation is met with in Gen 3 where the origin of suffering is traced to the disobedience of Adam and Eve. The formula is that sin results in suffering while goodness produces success. Both individuals and nations are punished for evil and rewarded for righteousness. This retributive principle is written so large upon the pages of the OT that it is impracticable to cite references. Deut 30:15-20 is an adequate summary statement: "if your heart turns away, . . . you shall perish; you shall not live long. . . . "

While this principle of reaping what one sows is certainly true, it is quite inadequate to explain the mystery of suffering. Many of the psalms take note of the seeming prosperity of the wicked. Ps 73, for example, protests that the unrighteous are "not in trouble" and "not stricken like other men" (v. 5). Although the psalmist satisfies himself that the wicked eventually get their just deserts, such an observation could not stand minute scrutiny. Job is a powerful protest against a naive view of the misery of the wicked and the prosperity of the righteous.

(3) Other interpretations had to emerge, prominent among which is the view that suffering serves a disciplinary or educational purpose. References are numerous. In Lev 26 God promises Israel various blessings for obedience and dire consequences for disobedience. But if in spite of these penalties Israel still will not obey, then God would chastise her sevenfold for her sins (Lev 26:18), and the process would be repeated if necessary (Lev 26:24, 27-28).

Suffering, then, has the disciplinary purpose of returning Israel to God. Proverbs includes the exhortation: "My son, do not despise the LORD's discipline or be weary of his reproof, for the LORD reproves him whom he loves, as a father the son in whom he delights" (Prov 3:11-12; cf. 15:10).

Suffering may lead to repentance and thus to a more mature understanding of God and of one's vocation, as in the experience of Jeremiah (15:19-21). Likewise, after God has chastened the chosen people "in just measure" by their afflictions (Jer 30:11), they will be prepared for restoration and for entering into a new and more profoundly spiritual covenant (31:31ff.). This process of chastening-suffering-restoration is even more graphically described in the speech of Elihu in Job 33:19-28.

(4) Closely related to the disciplinary idea is the concept of suffering as probationary. Character is tried, proved, purified in the crucible of suffering. In several places in the OT God is represented as "trying the hearts" of the righteous: "The crucible is for silver, and the furnace is for gold, and the LORD tries hearts" (Prov 17:3). In the Book of Job the reader is let in on the secret that God had permitted the SATAN to put Job to trial by tragic and inordinate suffering. Job is not informed of this transcendent decision, nevertheless he declares that God "knows the way that I take; when he has tried me, I shall come forth as gold" (23:10). Then there is the well-known story of God testing Abraham in the offering up of Isaac (Gen 22:1-14), with the reiteration, after the test, of God's promise to bless Abraham and his heirs and the world through him.

(5) Some suffering in the OT is viewed as empathic, that is, as the pain of those who identify with the sufferings of others. Such was the suffering of the three friends of Job when they first encountered him in his loathsome and pitiable condition. After observing the customary ritual of mourning, they sat with him on the ground in silence for seven days and nights (Job 2:13). It is sometimes remarked that this empathic ministry of silence was more effective than their wordy and erroneous speeches.

The prophets often suffered with their people. Ezekiel sat "overwhelmed" among the Jewish exiles for seven days (Ezek 3:15). Jeremiah declared, "For the wound of the daughter of my people is my heart wounded, I mourn, and dismay has taken hold on me" (Jer 8:21).

More notable was the awareness that God suffered with the people, an understanding that is expressed frequently in the OT. It was because God knew the afflictions of the Hebrew slaves in Egypt that he determined to deliver them through Moses (Exod 3:7ff.). In fact, the principle of retribution, that suffering is the penalty for sin, is often contradicted by the understanding that the poor were victims, not of their own sins but the sins of others. Throughout the OT God is represented as taking the side of the poor: "If he cries to me I will hear, for I am compassionate," says the Lord (Exod 22:27). The numerous references indicating that God enters into the sufferings of God's people are summed up in the affirmation that "in all their affliction he was afflicted . . . ; in his love and in his pity he redeemed them . . . " (Isa 63:9).

(6) The verse just cited is very close to the insight that it is by God's own suffering that sins may be forgiven and redemption effected. This expiatory role of

suffering is more clearly understood, however, with regard to human suffering. Moses offers to take upon himself the sins of his people (Exod 32:32). Through the sufferings of Israel in the Babylonian Exile, her sins are pardoned: "she has received from the LORD's hand double for all her sins" (Isa 40:2).

Yet it is in the servant songs of Deutero-Isaiah that the expiatory or vicarious meaning of suffering is most clearly expressed. The nations confess that the Servant of the Lord "was wounded for our transgressions" and "bruised for our iniquities," and that "the LORD has laid on him the iniquity of us all" (Isa 53:5-6). The identity of the SERVANT is not clear, whether Israel as a whole, a remnant group or an individual Israelite, and it is not until the servant is identified with Jesus, the Son of God, in the NT that God's involvement in vicarious suffering is understood, according to Christian belief.

(7) In addition, suffering is occasionally interpreted as eschatological; that is, tribulation of unusual intensity may be a harbinger of the end time. This interpretation may be seen in Isa 24–27 and in the Book of Daniel.

(8) An extreme view of suffering as meaningless is found in Ecclesiastes, where a generally pessimistic attitude prevails. The whole round of human life is "an unhappy business" and "all is vanity and a striving after wind" (Eccl 1:13-14). That such an unorthodox and unsatisfying view of life could be included in the canon may testify to the honesty of Israel.

(9) Finally, even if all these various attempts to invest suffering with meaning were fitted together into some integrated whole—which the OT does not attempt to do—suffering would remain vastly mysterious. Perhaps one meaning of the Book of Job is not simply that the sufferings of the righteous are due to some transcendent process of testing, but rather that since human beings are not privy to the counsels of God, suffering is humanly inexplicable. Interpretations of it as retributive, disciplinary, expiatory, etc. are by no means erroneous. They are simply inadequate to fathom the mystery of suffering.

See also DISEASE AND HEALING; EVIL; SIN; SUFFERING IN THE NEW TESTAMENT.

Bibliography. E. S. Gerstenberger and W. Schrage, *Suffering*; W. McWilliams, *When You Walk through the Fire*; H. W. Robinson, *Suffering Human and Divine*; J. A. Sanders, *Suffering as Divine Discipline in the Old Testament and Post-Biblical Judaism*; D. J. Simundson, *Faith under Fire: Biblical Interpretations of Suffering*; E. F. Sutcliffe, *Providence and Suffering in the Old and New Testaments*.

—E. LUTHER COPELAND

Wisdom in the New Testament   [MDB 960-61]

•**Wisdom in the New Testament.** Wisdom in the NT is seen primarily in its relation to Jesus who embodies wisdom in his person and teaching. The prologue of John sets forth the Word/Wisdom in a way similar to Prov 8 and passages in the Apocrypha (Sir 24; Bar 3–4; Wis 7–9). The Word is eternal wisdom personified in Jesus (John 1:1-18; see LOGOS/WORD).

In 1 Cor 1:24, Paul exalts Jesus as eternal wisdom personified, as "the wisdom of God." In Colossians Christ unites in himself the fullness of God in bodily form (Col 1:19). In Col 1:15-20 (cf. Eph 3:8-10), Christ is the creative wisdom of God: "for in him all things were created" and "in him all things hold together" (cf. John 1:3). He is the one "in whom are hid all the treasures of wisdom and knowledge" (Col 2:3). In the Gospel of Matthew, Jesus is Torah personified and equated with divine wisdom, and in Luke 11:49 he is simply the "wisdom of God."

The historical Jesus was a rabbi, a wisdom teacher, whose sayings in Matthew and Luke appear to be influenced by the Hebrew wisdom tradition. A number of the parables are clearly in the wisdom style and substance. Many of the sayings of Jesus are in the wisdom mold even when there is no use of the term. In Matt 11:29, Jesus says, "Take my yoke upon you, and learn from me." In Matt 12:42, he states that one "greater than Solomon is here."

Paul makes extensive use of both the term and concept of wisdom. He cries out, "O the depth of the riches and wisdom and knowledge of God" (Rom 11:33). In 1 Cor 1:18-30, he contrasts the wisdom of the world and the wisdom of God. Paul concludes that faith must rest, not in human wisdom "but in the power of God" (1 Cor 2:5) and "in Christ Jesus, whom God made our wisdom" (1 Cor 1:30). James is the NT book most related to wisdom. Its hortatory nature provides the reader with applied wisdom. Noteworthy is 3:13-18, where earthly wisdom and "the wisdom from above" are illustrated.

This wisdom is a gift to humanity (Rom 12:8). This gift enables the Christian to walk in wisdom as urged in Eph 5:15 and Col 4:5. Because wisdom is spiritual, "from above," believers can have the "mind of Christ" (Phil 2:5). In Rev 5:12 and 7:12, wisdom is a characteristic of the age to come.

See also JAMES, LETTER OF; LOGOS/WORD; WISDOM IN THE OLD TESTAMENT; WISDOM LITERATURE.

—NORM YANCE

Wisdom in the Old Testament   [MDB 961-62]

•Wisdom in the Old Testament. In the Bible wisdom has a wide range of meanings, specific and nonspecific. The root *hkm* can designate technical skill or expertise such as that of a goldsmith, weaver, artisan, navigator, shipbuilder, or entrepreneur. It refers to clever action directed toward a desirable end, even if immoral, and to the ability to manipulate persons into accomplishing one's goal. This use of the word resembles the modern sense of practical knowledge issuing in valuable skill rather than theoretical knowledge about the cosmos and its essential nature.

The noun *hkm* also has a technical meaning, designating a member of a professional group, the wise. This use occurs in the latest section of PROVERBS (1–9), in ECCLESIASTES, and in SIRACH. Its Greek equivalent would correctly identify the instructor responsible for WISDOM OF SOLOMON. The wise consciously reflect on the qualifications for membership in their elite company: one must be receptive to instruction, heed advice, answer appropriately, and possess self-control. Their cardinal virtues include timeliness, restraint, eloquence, and integrity. According to Prov 1:6, the wise occupy themselves with similes, taunts, sayings, and riddles. They direct instruction to persons with varying degrees of experience and sophistication, from the naive "innocent" to the learned adult. Their threefold task as reflected in Eccl 12:9 includes teaching, research, and writing. Various benefits accompany wisdom, in the sages' view, especially life, manifesting itself in health, wealth, honor, longevity, and progeny. The word *ṣdq*, a synonym for the professional use of *ḥkm*, indicates both the religious and moral aspects of the wise. In Northwest Semitic inscriptions, kings boast of wisdom, righteousness, and graciousness.

Over against the wise as a professional group stands another class of people, fools. They lack self-control in the areas of food, drink, sexual appetite, anger, and speech. Fools include the untutored and the aggressively incorrigible, as well as various intervening types. Their deficiency falls in the realm of morals rather than intellect. The wise have little patience with fools, and sages believe that only evil consequences accompany foolish conduct. In their enthusiasm over the power of the intellect, some sages prompted rebuke. For instance, the author of Ecclesiastes cautions against excessive claims about the scope of knowledge, daring to call such wise teachers liars.

In the ancient Near East, wisdom and age go together, although exceptions occur. An old fool can let erotic desire lead to disgrace, and an occasional youth can rise to extraordinary moral and intellectual heights, at least in popular memory. Thus Wisdom of Solomon speaks of God's conferral of wisdom on a young king who had the insight to request competence in ruling a people rather than riches (cf. 1 Kgs 3:9). Ordinarily, wisdom was the product of vast experience. In a Ugaritic text, wisdom is associated with El's gray beard; the biblical anecdote about Rehoboam's act of soliciting advice from young and old characterizes the youth as ruthless and the aged as compassionately wise, at least in this particular instance (1 Kgs 12:1-11).

The act of heeding instruction issued in a technical term for instruction, *leqaḥ* (receiving *da'at*, knowledge). In Egypt "the hearing one" functions as another epithet for a sage, and *The Instruction of Ptahhotep* develops this concept at some length. The locus of the intellect in Israelite thought was the heart, *lēb*. Whoever lacked intelligence suffered from an affliction known as *ḥaṣar lēb* (devoid of sense). Synonyms for wisdom include, among others, understanding (*bînâ*), knowledge (*da'at*), counsel (*'ēṣâ*), and occasionally power (*gēbûrâ*).

Mantic and magical wisdom makes brief appearances in the Joseph narrative and in the legends about Daniel. This type of access to secret information of the gods prevails in Mesopotamian culture, where professional sages consulted omens and examined the livers of sacrificial victims to determine the will of the gods. Some Aramaic-cuneiform tablets link *ḥkm* and medicine, whereas Old South Arabic texts emphasize the mantic aspects of *ḥkm* and modern Arabic, its judicial and medicinal features.

Wisdom eventually achieved poetic personification in the Bible. Depicted as a desirable woman, she addressed young people in the center of daily activity. This caring figure resembles a prophet, uttering threats and warnings, ultimately promising life and wealth (Prov 1). She prepares a feast and summons guests to celebrate a newly built house (Prov 9). Her demands appear strenuous at first, but in the end her yoke becomes light. An ideal wife, she bestows honor on the lucky husband who claims her as bride. Moreover, she nurtures her children like a worthy mother.

Just as professional sages emphasized their distinctiveness by imagining an opposing class—the fools—these teachers also fantasized about a rival to Woman Wisdom. This antagonist embodied the most seductive features of the foreign woman, a popular theme in wisdom literature. Her foreignness may be merely a matter of conduct, that is, she may be an Israelite with wholly unconventional morals. Or she may actually be a foreign woman, perhaps one associated with the ritual worship of a sexual goddess. Regardless, this personification of Folly constitutes a powerful threat to the youth whom the wise hope to entice to a wholly different kind of life. Folly's seduction conceals nothing: she invites young men to her bed, using seductive imagery. "Stolen water is sweet, and bread eaten in secret is pleasant" (Prov 9:17). In contrast to the sages' fondness for silence—"silent one" being another near-surrogate for the technical term "wise" in Egypt—this seductress noisily calls attention to herself and lures the unwary to their destruction. Like SHEOL, she has a ravenous appetite: no mention of a toothed vagina occurs, but the consequence is the same.

The poetic personification of wisdom passes over into mythic symbolism as well. Drawing on the Egyptian figure of Ma'at, the goddess of order, justice, and righteousness, who holds the symbol for life in one hand and riches in the other, biblical *ḥokmâ* boasts of having been present at creation, which not even Job witnessed. She claims to be a source of divine pleasure and an instrument of creation, indeed one of God's initial acts. As a witness of the primordial creation, she rejoiced in the world and its human inhabitants (Prov 8). Such a one boldly invites the untutored to "leave simpleness, and live," which finds its closest approximation in Amos's (5:4, 6) prophetic demand in God's name: "Seek me, and live."

Mythic imagery derived from ancient accounts of creation also enriches the description of Wisdom, now almost a hypostasis. Issuing from the divine mouth, like an oracle or statute, she covers the earth like dew. This wondrous creature spans the universe as God alone can do, and she finds temporary lodging among all peoples, until the Creator assigns a permanent abode for her in Israel. She boasts eternal origin and survival, but willingly ministers before God in Jerusalem's holy place. In this favorable setting she flourishes like well-tended trees and produces pleasant aromas and beautiful flowers. Eager to share her delicious produce, she invites the hungry to eat freely, knowing that they will return to the source again and again. An amazing identification of wisdom and TORAH follows: "All this is the book of the covenant of the Most High God, the law which Moses commanded us as an inheritance for the congregations of Jacob" (Sir 24:24). The author does not abandon mythic imagery at this point, but reverts to the Yahwistic account of four rivers that dispense knowledge, in this case wisdom, understanding, and instruction. Ben Sira concedes that, like the first human creatures, he does not fully fathom wisdom, whose thought is vast and profound, resembling sea and abyss.

Access to wisdom was denied by some. The hymn about wisdom's inaccessibility in Job 28 struck a note that resonated in many hearts. Only God has access to wisdom; humans, like Sheol and Abaddon, come no closer than capturing a rumor about her. The author of Ecclesiastes emphasizes wisdom's remoteness and profundity: "All this I have tested by wisdom; I said, 'I will be wise'; but it was far from me. That which is, is far off, and deep, very deep; who can find it out?" (7:23-24). The author of Baruch concurs with this sentiment: "Who has gone up into heaven, and taken her, and brought her down from the clouds? Who has gone over the sea, and found her, and will buy her for pure gold? No one knows the way to her, or is concerned about the path to her" (Bar 3:29-31). The echo of Deut 30:12-13 becomes audibly distinct as Baruch equates wisdom with the Mosaic Law (4:1).

Wisdom becomes more closely identified with the Creator in the Greek text Wisdom of Solomon. Here one enters an entirely new realm of discourse, although connections with earlier speculation about wisdom linger. The emphasis now falls on Wisdom as an eminent attribute of God. She is God's breath (spirit), power (gĕbûrâ), and glory. A pure reflection of the Creator, Wisdom is also a divine image of goodness. Moreover, she is an initiate into divine knowledge. Therefore Wisdom inspires holy persons and instructs sages. The unknown author, in the guise of Solomon, boasts that she instructs him, indeed that she is his bride. Similarly, in every generation Wisdom instructs holy people, in this way guiding the destiny of the elect nation Israel.

The association of Wisdom with Yahweh came reluctantly (cf. Isa 28:26, where Elohim appears), largely because in some circles it was easily linked with morally questionable conduct, but also because of foreign wisdom's connection with magic. Moreover, the sages normally spoke of Elohim rather than the special god of the Jews. The ancient story about the first sin places a question mark over the human acquisition of knowledge. The desire to possess knowledge carries recognizable negative consequences, according to this story. The use of cunning sometimes produced awful results, as exemplified in the story about Jonadab's assistance to a lusting Amnon. As for the manipulation of the gods by means of knowledge, Israel's prophets in the Babylonian period do not mince words about this practice. In the NT, Paul contrasts the "foolishness of God" with human wisdom.

Perhaps the custom of praising kings for their wisdom assisted in the move to attribute wisdom to Yahweh. In the ancient Near East the widespread tradition of wise kings gave rise to liturgical texts such as Isa 9:6, which introduces throne names (Wonderful Counselor, Mighty God, Everlasting Father, Prince of Peace), and 11:2, which gives voice to the people's hope that their ruler will judge wisely: "And the spirit of the LORD shall rest upon him, the spirit of wisdom and understanding, the spirit of counsel and might, the spirit of knowledge and the fear of the LORD."

Nevertheless, the Israelites did not lose touch with reality, for political experience easily disabused them of thinking that all kings lived up to such high ideals. Even Solomon departed sharply from the ideal, despite traditions extolling his exceptional wisdom.

Israel's sages also manifest a sober awareness of their limits. For this, they did not need lessons from Isaiah, who blasts those who are wise in their own eyes and who quips that Yahweh is also astute (Isa 5:21; 31:2). The struggle to elevate religion over knowledge left its mark on the wisdom corpus, for the fear of the Lord was understood as primary, both in a chronological sense and in an evaluative sense.

In Johannine thought, speculation about the divine word (*logos*) corresponds to earlier ideas about *ḥokmâ*, but also to Stoic thought. Certain hymns in the Pauline corpus owe much to mythic imagery about the creative activity of wisdom, now understood as the Christ who existed in the beginning and functioned as the agent of creation (contrast PIRKE ABOTH 3.14, which refers to creation by torah). The Letter of James and gnomic sayings in the gospels continue the other understanding of wisdom as an effort to cope with reality.

Bibliography. J. L. Crenshaw, *Old Testament Wisdom* and "Wisdom in the Old Testament," *IDBSupp*; G. Fohrer, "Sophia," J. L. Crenshaw, ed., *Studies in Ancient Israelite Wisdom*; B. Lang, *Wisdom and the Book of Proverbs*; H.-P. Müller and M. Krause, "חָכָם *chākham*," *TDOT*; R. E. Murphy, "Hebrew Wisdom," *JAOS* 101 (1981): 21-34; G. von Rad, *Wisdom in Israel*; R. N. Whybray, *The Intellectual Tradition in the Old Testament, BZAW* 135; R. J. Williams, "Wisdom in the Ancient Near East," *IDBSupp*.

—JAMES L. CRENSHAW

Wisdom Literature   [MDB 962-65]

•**Wisdom Literature.** A distinctive intellectual tradition extended throughout the ancient Near East, beginning in the early third millennium and reaching into the Common Era. Modern scholars call this phenomenon Wisdom Literature. The Egyptians classified the dominant type of their wisdom literature as *sebayit* (Instruction), whereas Israel's sages labeled their collections of proverbs *meshalim*. But besides such instructions and sentences (or truth statements), ancient wisdom also included philosophical explanations of life's meaning in light of seemingly senseless suffering and injustice. A third type of wisdom, at least in EGYPT and MESOPOTAMIA, consisted of encyclopedic lists of flora, fauna, and other significant bits of information. In addition, some texts praising the scribal profession at the expense of all other vocations or rebuking lazy students and extolling the learning process round out the wisdom corpus.

Egyptian Wisdom. Three texts of *Instructions* have survived from the Old Kingdom, two of them in fragmentary form. Having reached advanced years, *Ptahhotep* (ca. 2450 BCE) requests permission from the Pharaoh to install his own son in the office of counselor. *Ptahhotep* then proceeds to instruct his son on the means of functioning successfully in government: acquiring eloquence, practicing honesty, using correct etiquette, guarding against lust. *Kagemni* reiterates the advice about proper manners at table, and *Prince Hardjedef* warns against boasting and encourages marriage.

Three *Instructions* derive from the Middle Kingdom. The Pharaoh *Merikare* advises his son, combining ruthlessness and silence but extolling eloquence as well. In his teaching, life's shadow-side lurks nearby, necessitating religious and magical scrupulousness. The slain *King Amen-em-het I* cautions his son about the folly of trusting others. The contents of the fragmentary *Sehetipibre* are not known.

The New Kingdom witnessed a crisis of confidence that resulted in widespread religiosity. Two *Instructions*, *Ani* and *Amen-em-opet*, document this change; *Amennakhte* is too fragmentary to ascertain its contents. *Ani* strikes a note that persists in Israelite wisdom too: watch out for the strange or foreign woman. He also evokes response from his son Khonshotep, who insists that his father's code of ethics is too difficult for the son. *Amen-em-opet* offers thirty "chapters" of advice, at least ten of whose sayings have found their way into the biblical Book of PROVERBS. With *Amen-em-opet*, a heightening of piety takes place, despite an inscrutable God who sails the ship of the faithful safely into harbor.

Two Demotic texts complete the list of Egyptian *Instructions*: *'Onksheshonky* and *Papyrus Insinger*. Both address the populace at large and reflect fatalistic understandings of reality.

The Satire of the Trades, or *The Instruction of Khety, Son of Duauf*, describes miserable working conditions between 2150 and 1750 BCE, asserting that only the scribal profession is worth considering. Similarly, *In Praise of Learned Scribes*, the *Instruction of a Man for His Son*, *Papyrus Sallier*, and *Papyrus Anastasi IV*, 9:4-10:1; V, 8:1-9:1, 9:2-10:2 extol the advantages of being a scribe.

Discussions about life's inequities mark *Neferti*, *Khakheperre-sonbe*, *Ipuwer*, and *The Dispute of a Man with His Soul*. *The Tale of the Eloquent Peasant* examines the powerful effects of governmental abuse, and the *Harper Songs* encourage festive living because of approaching death and society's injustices. These texts belong, if at all, on the periphery of Egyptian wisdom. At its center lies the concept of order (*ma'at*) and the human necessity of bringing one's conduct into line with this principle. By observing the cardinal virtues—timeliness, restraint, eloquence, and honesty—a sage, or silent one, appreciably improved the chance of experiencing the good life.

Mesopotamian Wisdom. Sumerian wisdom texts include both major types of the ancient intellectual tradition, proverbs and reflection on life's mysteries. The latter is the concern of a text about a righteous sufferer, *A Man and his God*; it resembles biblical JOB, although the blame falls on humans who are by nature sinful. *The Instructions of Šuruppak* to his son recall some themes already attributed to Egyptian wisdom, such as the danger of sexual misconduct and the advantages of having a good wife (a fertile field). Texts from the tablet house (*edubba*) characterize the life of a student, and various disputes, noun lists, and satires illuminate scribal interests. A fragmentary text resembles the powerful description of old age and death in ECCLESIASTES 12:1-7.

Babylonian wisdom also includes proverbial instruction and penetrating debate over life's injustices. *The Counsels of Wisdom* urge love of enemies and benevolence or silence; similarly, *Advice to a Prince* offers strong advocacy for subjects despite the exalted view of monarchy in vogue. *I Will Praise the Lord of Wisdom* tells about a righteous individual who struggles to understand the cause of his misery and who eventually is restored to health as reward for faithful conduct. Here, as in the Book of Job, God appears to the victim and rectifies the situation. *The Babylonian Theodicy*, an elaborate acrostic or alphabetic poem, takes the form of a dialogue between a sufferer and an orthodox friend. Both of these texts stress the inscrutability of the gods, who made men and women with a predilection to practice evil. *The Dialogue of Pessimism*, a humorous (?) conversation between a master who has been overcome by ennui and a proverbial yes-man, suggests that nothing commends itself, with the possible exception of suicide.

The few examples of wisdom from MARI derive from popular sayings. The Hebrew Bible also has about a dozen such aphorisms scattered throughout the TORAH and the prophetic books. An Aramaic wisdom text, *The Sayings of Ahiqar*, contains a prose framework like Job and '*Onksheshonky*. Ahiqar advised the Assyrian king SENNACHERIB but became wrongly implicated in a palace revolt. From prison, Ahiqar wrote words of advice in the form of popular proverbs. Canaanite wisdom, barely attested, describes life as a journey on which youth embark and offers advice on how to cope. Edomite wisdom, celebrated in the Bible, has not survived.

To sum up, Mesopotamian wisdom literature resembles its Egyptian counterpart in form, although providing considerably more nuanced discussion of life's injustices. The biblical reflections about unjust suffering and the meaning of life continue this tradition, whereas the Book of Proverbs has closer affinities with Egyptian *Instructions* than with Mesopotamian texts, except for Ahiqar. One significant feature of Mesopotamian wisdom, its magical character, does not occur in the OT.

Biblical Wisdom. Ancient Israel's sages preserved their teachings in two forms: *meshalim* and reflections. The former included both instructions (Prov 1–9, SIRACH) and shorter aphorisms (most of Proverbs). The latter comprised Job and Ecclesiastes. In addition, didactic compositions in PSALMS explore the problem of divine justice (Pss 37, 49, 73), and a midrash-like discussion of the Exodus plus an encomium of sorts conclude WISDOM OF SOLOMON and Sirach (Ecclesiasticus) respectively. The scribal tradition continued in certain respects in RABBINIC LITERATURE, especially PIRKE ABOTH, and some elements of earlier wisdom surface in Jesus' aphorisms, the Epistle of JAMES, and possibly in the LOGOS speculation of Johannine thought.

The Book of Proverbs represents a sort of anthology, a number of collections deriving from premonarchic and postexilic circles of tradition. Perhaps as many as eleven separate collections make up the present book: 1–9 (the latest in date), 10–15, 16:1–22:16, 22:17–24:22, 24:23-34, 25–27, 28–29, 30:1-14, 30:15-33, 31:1-9, and 31:10-31. Several of these collections have superscriptions that betray the sages' awareness that SOLOMON did not write these proverbs, although two collections acknowledge foreign authorship (Agur and King Lemuel's mother), and another shares several sayings with *Amen-em-opet*. Egyptian influence stands out in chap. 16 and in the depiction of wisdom as a woman who has life in one hand and prosperity in the other.

The instructions use imperatives to reinforce their teaching, offering promise of reward for obedient conduct and threatening punishment for disobedience. They sometimes quote an aphorism to make a decisive point. Deeply religious in tone and content, the instructions emphasize religious devotion (the fear of the Lord) as the precondition and essential component of knowledge. Both the instructions and the sentences make sharp distinctions between the wise and foolish. The initial collection, 1-9, seems almost preoccupied with the foreign woman, who poses a threat to innocent youth. It also depicts Wisdom as an agent in the act of CREATION, so that her apparent personification offers comfort to those who find Folly's invitation to stolen water and bread eaten in secret enticing indeed (see WISDOM IN THE OLD TESTAMENT).

These instructions and aphorisms enabled youngsters to master reality, thus securing existence. By examining nature and human experience, teachers drew analogies about various means of coming to grips with almost every eventuality. Life in harmony with the principles governing the universe brought riches, honor, long life, and many children. Still, the sages conceded definite limits to their knowledge and control of things, for Yahweh spoke the last word.

The social setting of the separate collections varied from popular sayings arising among the common people to formal instruction of professional scribes and, in one instance, a king. Between these extremes, parental teaching transmitted a lifetime's experience to young sons. The oldest aphorisms probably antedate the monarchy, although the bulk of the collection derives from the exilic and postexilic period. The putative connection with Solomon, implied in several superscriptions, does not accord with the characterization of his proverbs in 1 Kgs 4:29-34, for the "Solomonic" proverbs do not discuss trees, fish, birds, and reptiles.

In time the optimism undergirding the worldview of these proverbs vanished, leaving behind sober questions about the utility of wisdom and goodness. The Book of Job wrestles with undeniable injustices in the world, as if concentrated in a single individual. Perhaps Job's misery symbolizes that of Israel, but his characterization as an Arab sheik seems to preclude such a reading. Dissonance persists in the book to the end, partly due to the combination of an old folk narrative about disinterested righteousness with a fresh poetic treatment of innocent suffering.

The unusual structure, a prose framework enclosing a poetic dialogue, points to a deeper level where traditional understandings of God shelter explosive ideas, in the end returning to safe beliefs. Job's attack against the principle of reward and punishment presupposes precisely that reality, otherwise he would have no basis for complaint. Furthermore, the eventual resolution of his dilemma, if such it be, derives from conventional Yahwism, which spoke of divine manifestations to special people. This aligning of different religious perspectives in a single literary complex encouraged further amplification through hymnic texts, particularly the exploration of God's impenetrability, orthodox rebuke of Job's blasphemy and his friends' ineptness, and descriptive snippets about awe-inspiring creatures such as the ostrich and the wild horse.

Religious and historical events of the sixth century produced a context for this probing exploration of fundamental presuppositions that had never been seriously challenged. Other poets ventured to ask similar questions, especially Deutero-Isaiah, whose imagery sometimes resembles Job's language. Whether one echoes the other, or both give voice to universal complaint, remains uncertain. In any event, Job signals simultaneously wisdom's bankruptcy and its elasticity. The sages' worldview collapsed, but they boldly enlarged the horizons of knowledge to include theophanic vision.

Movement within the Book of Job is greater on the psychological plane than on the theological. Job and his friends remain adamant throughout the debate, except when confronting the divine inquisitor. The harsh attacks on Job by miserable comforters prompt him to entertain fleeting thoughts of vindication against all odds, a pronouncement of "innocent" in the heavenly court. Unable to count on God's help, Job thinks a champion of his cause will emerge from the void created by God's vicious attacks and active hiding (19:25). Instead, the deity silences Job by reminding him of the real wonders of creation, then offers him a sop in the form of restored wealth and children. The reader cannot resist asking: Has the vision perished? Has conventional orthodoxy co-opted venturesome interrogatives, robbing them of their sting?

The other stunning attack on uncritical thinking in the wisdom corpus, Ecclesiastes, undergoes a similar softening. An unknown epilogist warns against further "bookmaking" (not "writing") because everything has already been heard: "Fear God, and keep his commandments" (12:13), confident that every deed, secret or otherwise, will be judged. The opinion of the author of the main body of the book, often called Qoheleth, regarded such a claim as no secret, for in 8:17 he labels it a lie. In his view, not even professional sages can discover God's deeds. Chance governs human lives, and the deity dwells in remote indifference, insofar as one can tell.

According to another epilogist (Eccl 12:9-11), Qoheleth taught ordinary people (hā'ām). This admirer of the teacher points to painstaking preparation on Qoheleth's part, an attentive listening, penetrating inquisitiveness, and planned presentation. Furthermore, Qoheleth valued the aesthetic dimension of speech, but not at the expense of truth. This epilogist linked Qoheleth's teachings with other sapiential collections, all of which derive from one shepherd, either the king or God. Behind this allusion probably lies the royal fiction of Solomonic authorship—a literary conceit that vanishes after the second chapter. The epilogist acknowledges the sting in Qoheleth's teachings and still insists that they function to orient one's thinking securely.

The book's structure certainly indicates careful deliberation. Two poems envelop the complete sayings of Qoheleth; the first describes nature's ceaseless and monotonous movement, and the second depicts the wintry blast of old age and death. A thematic statement about life's utter futility precedes the former poem and concludes the latter. Between them stand Qoheleth's reflections resulting from exhaustive examination of observable phenomena. Refrain-like phrases and self-reflective expressions contribute a sense of unity to the scattered observations. The author pays attention to everything that takes place, drawing conclusions about nature, human and divine.

This impression of unity competes with an equally powerful dissonance, for the book does not speak with a single voice. Throughout Ecclesiastes, a phenomenon of broken sentences occurs in which the author appears to say, "Yes, but on the other hand." Qoheleth seems at odds with his tradition. Moreover, his unorthodox views so offended certain people that they actually tampered with the text, introducing traditional teachings about a divine judgment and denying ultimate authority to death.

On the other hand, Qoheleth declared life "wanting" precisely because the death angel acted with total disdain for demonstrable virtue. Circumspect behavior did not secure one's existence; indeed, wisdom lacked the power customarily attributed to it. The desirable things in life did not necessarily yield satisfaction, for they lacked permanence. Seven times Qoheleth advocates a life of enjoyment, but he issues solemn reminders that existence passes quickly into oblivion. Sweet is the light, and fleeting. The dark house promises a long residence (your eternal home). Qoheleth faces things with stark realism; his skepticism does not cross over into cynicism, although it becomes profoundly pessimistic. The suffering of powerless individuals at the hands of officials and the absence of any deliverer overwhelmed him. So did the silence of the heavens.

The sentiments of the orthodox epilogist to Ecclesiastes find fuller expression in Sirach, often called Ecclesiasticus. The author, Eleazar Jeshua ben Sira (Sir 50:27b; cf. subscript), lived at the beginning of the second century and ran a school, presumably in Jerusalem. His teaching relies heavily on the proverbial tradition, oblivious to the objections to its worldview raised by the author of Job and Ecclesiastes. For Ben Sira, ancient wisdom retained its cogency, especially when reinforced by conventional Yahwism. Earlier sages had remained silent about specific Israelite traditions, contenting themselves with insights available to all people regardless of their individual histories. Ben Sira abandons this universalism, opting for particularistic teachings of the Jews. His observations frequently incorporate canonical allusions, and the extensive hymn praising Israel's great men derives exclusively from the Bible. Nothing in biblical wisdom prepares the way for such lavish praise of human beings.

Ben Sira's sense of adoration spilled over to include God, for the book has majestic hymns about the creative work of the one who evokes the numinous shout, "He is the All" (Sir 43:27). In fact, the praise of men functions also as celebration of God's activity that raised up such wondrous leaders, particularly cultic figures. The culminating eulogy of the high priest, Simon II, indicates that Ben Sira deeply appreciated religious ritual. Two themes resound through the work: the fear of Yahweh and wisdom. In a suggestive mythical treatment of wisdom's search for a dwelling place, Ben Sira equates torah and wisdom. This subsuming of the intellectual tradition under the broad category of religious duty accords with the elevation of "fear of the Lord," which is roughly translatable as "religion."

The students who attended Ben Sira's house of study faced seduction from Hellenism, which prompted him to reflect seriously about competing values. In his view, the insights transmitted by MOSES and the understanding of reality promulgated by the sages rivaled anything the Greeks could offer. Furthermore, God's compassion renders human doubt somewhat innocuous, for a convincing theodicy must take divine mercy into account. Ben Sira draws on Jewish and Hellenistic arguments for divine justice, introducing two emphases that hardly belong in traditional wisdom: the belief that psychological anxiety results from sin, and the conviction that the universe itself punishes vice and rewards virtue.

Egyptian wisdom made an impact on Ben Sira's thinking, particularly *The Satire on the Trades*, but also various features from *The Insinger Papyrus*. He seems unable to transcend a conventional attitude toward suffering as punishment for sin, although he courageously defends the medical profession. Capable of exquisite poetic imagery, he demonstrates unusual awareness of the complexities involved in social relations. His attitude to women contains certain features that offend modern sensitivities, although the attitudes were widespread at the time.

The unknown author of the Wisdom of Solomon, the only wisdom treatise written in Greek that entered the LXX, explores the erotic relationship of knowledge by imagining a union between Solomon and Wisdom. This thinker functions in a thoroughly Hellenistic environment, for the concepts and rhetoric are Greek. The claim can be substantiated by pointing to the reference to the cardinal virtues, the belief in an immortal soul, the hypostasis of Wisdom as a female figure and the attributes of God which she manifests, the stylistic devices such as sorites, and so forth. Wisdom of Solomon uses an early midrash-like analysis of the Exodus event to satirize the Egyptians among whom the Jewish readers of the book resided. Mockery of idolatry lies at the center of this ridicule, which explains the origins of idol making as the result of grief, aesthetic interests, or veneration of an emperor. Such imaginative treatment of the Exodus exaggerates the psychological consternation that propelled Egyptians to their destruction.

In short, biblical wisdom literature includes instructions and sentences, intellectual debate about the possibility of true virtue and religion, serious reflection on life's futility, and the relationship between traditional Torah and paternal counsel. The ancient Near Eastern transmitters of this literary tradition belonged to several social settings: the home, court, and school. They developed special vocabulary and thematic interests, but in the end Israel's sages reached out to embrace traditions peculiar to the Jews. Their speculation about wisdom and their ethical insights lingered, influencing rabbinism and Christianity.

See also ECCLESIASTES, BOOK OF; JOB; JOB, BOOK OF; PROVERBS, BOOK OF; SIRACH; SOLOMON, WISDOM OF; WISDOM IN THE OLD TESTAMENT.

Bibliography. J. L. Crenshaw, *Old Testament Wisdom, Studies in Ancient Israelite Wisdom*, and *Urgent Advice and Probing Questions*; J. G. Gammie et al., *Israelite Wisdom: Theological and Literary Essays in Honor of Samuel Terrien*; W. G. Lambert, *Babylonian Wisdom Literature*; M. Lichtheim, *Ancient Egyptian Literature*; L. G. Perdue, *Wisdom and Cult*; G. von Rad, *Wisdom in Israel*; J. C. Rylaarsdam, *Revelation in Jewish Wisdom Literature*; R. N. Whybray, *The Intellectual Tradition in the Old Testament*.

—JAMES L. CRENSHAW

(Wisdom) Writings Dictionary Articles

Book of Job   [MDB 455-56]

• AN OUTLINE •

    I. Prologue. God Assents to the Testing of Job (1:1–2:13)
   II. Job's Lament (3:1-26)
  III. Dialogue between Job and His Three Friends (4:1–27:23)
  IV. Poem on the Inaccessibility of Wisdom (28:1-28)
   V. Job's Oath of Innocence (29:1–31:40)
  VI. The Speeches of Elihu (32:1–37:24)
 VII. God's Answer to Job from the Whirlwind (38:1–41:34)
VIII. Job's Response and Repentance (42:1-6)
  IX. Epilogue. Job Is Vindicated and His Fortunes Restored (42:7-17)

•**Job, Book of.** The single word that serves as title to this book in the Hebrew canon is אִיּוֹב *'yōb*, "enemy," a word that provides not only the name of the central character of the book, but also the central theme of Job's relation to GOD. The issue is stated bluntly in 13:24: "Why do you hide your face [from me] and count me as your enemy (*lē' ôyēb*)?" For Job, God seems hidden, painfully absent in a time of crisis and need. It is a response Job understands to be appropriate when directed toward opponents and violators of God's will, but not towards those who, like Job, are "blameless and upright" (1:1; cf. 1:9). Thus Job's anguished cry raises the question that the whole of the book that bears his name strains to answer: "Why?" Why do the innocent suffer? And why does God seem absent when they do?

As if to insist that attention not be diverted from this all-important theological issue to questions of lesser importance, the Book of Job gives little attention to matters of historical detail. Nowhere is the author of the book or the date of its writing identified. It is often suggested that the author belonged to the intellectual elite of the day, perhaps working out of the same wisdom tradition responsible for such books as PROVERBS and ECCLESIASTES. Despite some rather certain connections with this tradition, however, it is clear that both the themes of Job and the literary styles that carry them cannot be restricted to any one tradition. With respect to date, a postexilic setting is usually recommended, thus suggesting that the kinds of questions Job raises are to be associated primarily with the period following the destruction of Jerusalem in 587/6 BCE when the stablizing institutions of society and religion could no longer support the full weight of theological assumptions. Yet it is clear from extrabiblical texts that the problem of innocent suffering did not emerge for the first time either in the Book of Job or in the land of Israel. Texts from Sumeria, Babylonia, and Egypt, the oldest dating to the beginning of the second millennium BCE, suggest that by the time of the writing of Job, considerable attention had been devoted to this most fundamental issue.

The book in its present form consists of five major sections: (1) a prose prologue (1–2); (2) three cycles of dialogue between Job and his friends (3–31); the speeches of Elihu (32–37); (4) Yahweh's speeches (38–42:6); and (5) a prose epilogue (42:7-17). The contrast between the narrative style of the prologue, epilogue, and the poetry that dominates in 3–42:6, and more importantly, the stark contrast in the portrayal of Job, suggest that different authors and differing perspectives have shaped the individual sections. Even so, despite the different influences at work here, it is the arrangement of these chapters into their present order that produces the message of the Book of Job in its most compelling and troubling form.

Taken together, the prologue and epilogue present Job as an exemplary model of faith. He is introduced as "blameless and upright," a God-fearer, and as one who "turned away from evil" (1:1). This assessment is twice affirmed by God in precisely the same terms (1:8; 2:3), thus making it unequivocally clear that Job's innocence is beyond question. The strength of Job's character is further manifest in his passive and pious acceptance of the horrendous calamities described in these opening chaps. For him there is no mystery in these experiences: "Shall we receive good from God and not evil?" (2:10). The question is raised without doubt about the answer, and whenever any response other than the one modeled by Job is suggested, it is rejected and dismissed immediately (2:9-10). The reward for such faithfulness is restoration and divine blessing (42:10-17).

In the poetic chapters (3–42:6) the portrayal of Job is quite different. Job's initial response is to curse the day of his birth and to wish for death's relief from his miserable days (3:3). Three cycles of speeches follow (4–14; 15–21; 22–31) in which one by one Job's friends Eliphaz, Bildad, and Zophar offer explanations for Job's suffering. With a variety of approaches the friends each seek to affirm the conventional wisdom, which understands suffering as always linked to punishment for sin. The Elihu speeches (32–37), though usually understood as interpolations,

offer similar explanations. All of these explanations Job rejects, protesting repeatedly his innocence (e.g., 6:28-30; 9:21; 10:7; 16:17; 23:10, 12; 27:2-6), and lashing
out at his friends for their worthless arguments that turn truth into lie in order to
protect God (e.g. 13:4, 7).

Job's primary struggle, however, is not with the friends but with God, who
through all of Job's suffering remains silent and distant. Job's quest for God leaves
him vulnerable before two contrasting experiences. On the one hand, God seems
nowhere to be found. Job moves forward and backward, in this direction and that,
but God is absent (e.g., 23:8-9). He cries out, but God does not answer (cf. 19:7;
30:20; 31:35). On the other hand, God's presence is all too real for Job, hunting him
like some vicious beast set to ravage its prey (10:16-17; 16:7-15), hemming him in
so that he cannot escape and setting nets for his capture (19:8-12). Before this
stalking God, Job sees himself as both enemy and victim.

The climax of the drama comes with two speeches from Yahweh (38–39; 40:6–
41:34) and accompanying responses from Job (40:1-5; 42:1-6). With the severity
and power of hurricane-force winds (cf. 38:1; 40:6) God comes, not answering the
questions Job had been hurling heavenwards, but with divine interrogations that
overwhelm and silence the sufferer. Job can only acknowledge that before this all-
powerful Creator, he is too small (40:4). Against such a formidable opponent, Job
will press his case no further (40:5; 42:6). In neither response is there any admission
of guilt, only submission to the unparalleled power and sovereignty of God. The
dialogue between Creator and creature ends, yet the troubling "Why?" questions
with which it all began remain unanswered.

Nevertheless, in its final form the Book of Job offers clear counsel and
profound encouragement to those who would dare to follow Job's lead. Job had
demanded justice. What he was granted was communion (cf. 42:5-6). It is
significant that such an unqualified intimacy with God occurred for Job in the midst
of his struggle with suffering. It is the counsel of the epilogue that such intimacy
comes only to those who struggle honestly, who risk pressing the outermost
boundaries of what tradition recommends as appropriate response to God, who dare
question and protest and challenge the sovereign God of the universe. It will be
these who can expect a hearing from God (cf. 42:8), not those who know only how
to parrot answers without understanding the questions (cf. 42:7).

See also JOB; SATAN IN THE OT; SUFFERING IN THE OT.

Bibliography. J. Crenshaw, "Popular Questioning of the Justice of God in
Ancient Israel," *ZAW* 82 (1970): 380-395 and "Job" in *Urgent Advice and Probing
Questions*, 426-98; M. B. Crook, *The Cruel God: Job's Search for the Meaning of
Suffering*; R. Davidson, *The Courage to Doubt*; J. Gray, "The Book of Job in the
Context of Near Eastern Literature," *ZAW* 82 (1970): 251-169; N. Habel, *Job*, OTL;
W. L. Humphreys, *The Tragic Vision and the Hebrew Tradition*; M. Tsevat, "The
Meaning of the Book of Job," *HUCA* 37 (1966): 73-106.

—SAMUEL E. BALENTINE

The Book of Psalms   [MDB 722-24]

• AN OUTLINE •

I. Book One. Psalms 1–41
II. Book Two. Psalms 42–72
III. Book Three. Psalms 73–89
IV. Book Four. Psalms 90–106
V. Book Five. Psalms 107–150.

•**Psalms, Book of.** [sahmz] The Book of Psalms is one of the richest and most widely read books in the OT.

Religious Songs in the Ancient Near East. Archaeology has provided us with a rich treasure of religious songs throughout the ancient Near East. A good sampling of these can be found in Pritchard's *Ancient Near Eastern Texts (ANET).* It appears that the hymn in Babylon sprang from the curse, with flattering praise of the deity as introduction in order to draw the deity's attention. Or, fearing that they had been cursed, persons would pray to Shamash for protection (*ANET* 387). The psalm of lament (which occurs rather often), like the hymn, frequently begins with a description of the worshiper's plight, a petition for deliverance and a promise to pay the vows (*ANET* 386b). In ancient Egypt we find a well-developed hymnody. There was, for instance, a famous hymn sung by Akhenaton to the sun God (*ANET* 369b). There were songs of thanksgiving (*ANET* 380) and didactic poems. These have survived, and many more, because they were chiselled into the walls of tombs. Ancient Ugarit on the Phoenician coast is often considered much closer to Hebrew tradition (cf. esp. Dahood). Here, also, there existed religious poetry of various kinds, showing that when the ancient Israelites sang their songs in God's honor, they were participating in a widespread Near Eastern practice.

Hebrew Poetry. Hebrew poetry is different from our modern poetry. Since Bishop Lowth in the eighteenth century it has been customary to speak of "Parallelismus Membrorum," that is, that each line consists of two half lines that are either alike (synonymous) or contradictory (antithetic). Now Kugel has argued with great force that Lowth's "parallelismus membrorum was not so much a discovery as an invention," and Kugel prefers to speak only of "synthetic parallelism," that is, that indeed the two half lines are structurally there but related much more loosely than Lowth thought (Kugel, 57).

Hebrew poetry does not have rhyme like Western poetry, but it does have rhythm. Again, this is an area where there has been much study and little agreement. Most generally accepted is the theory of accented syllables: a hymn has three of them in each of the half lines (3+3), whereas a lament uses a "halting meter" with three and two (3+2). The psalmists felt free to use other rhythms, and so we speak of "mixed meters." The best-known example of such a "mixed meter psalm" is Ps 23. It has hymnic motifs, and yet it appears with largely a 3+2 meter, which is the meter of the lament. A probable explanation for such a "breach" in form would be that Ps 23 really consists of an extended confidence motif, such as is normally found in lamentation psalms. The final word on the forms of Hebrew psalms has not been spoken.

The Psalms in Ancient Israel. The Hebrew canon is divided into three sections: Law, Prophets, and Writings. The Psalms, almost without exception, have been placed first in the third section, the Writings. In the Writings, they are presented in five "books" (Pss 1–41, 42–72, 73–89, 90–106, 107–150). It has been suggested that they were thus compiled in order to create a fivefold human response to God's fivefold demands in the Pentateuch. This, however, is only a final arrangement. There are numerous witnesses to many other groupings, for example, titles such as "Psalms of David," "Psalms of Korah," "Psalms of Asaph." Psalm 72:20 says that "The prayers of DAVID, son of JESSE, are ended," although there are many psalms ascribed to David later in the Book of Psalms. It is even likely that some of the Psalms (42–83) come from the Northern Kingdom, because they consistently use "Elohim" instead of "Yahweh," and ISRAEL, JOSEPH, and EPHRAIM instead of JUDAH, ZION, and JERUSALEM.

Reading the psalms readily reveaks that they express different moods. On this basis they have been assigned to different groups: hymns, laments, thanksgiving psalms, wisdom psalms, and so forth.

The Hymn opens with an exhortation to praise GOD. Then the body of the hymn gives the reason God should be praised. The conclusion repeats the introduction (e.g., Ps 8).

The Lament is a prayer by a community or an individual in need. It often begins with a cry for help or attention (74), then follows a description of the quandary and a repetition of the prayers spoken. In conclusion there is a promise to pay one's vows before the congregation if one is delivered, and sometimes there is an exhortation to others also to trust in Yahweh.

The Thanksgiving psalm is somewhat like the hymn but it concentrates more on praising God for particular things, such as an abundant harvest (65) or deliverance from illness (116).

The Wisdom psalms are more varied. They are often philosophical in nature and appear to be created for the purpose of teaching. A curious feature is that some of them are alphabetic (acrostic)—each line begins with the successive letter of the alphabet (Ps 111) or (like Ps 119) has clusters of eight lines, each beginning with the same letter of the alphabet, making 176 verses in all. (There are twenty-two letters in the Hebrew alphabet.)

Again, there are many psalms that do not quite fit any of these categories, and scholars continue to search for new and better solutions for classifying and understanding the psalms.

The Psalms in Israel's Worship. A reading of the Psalms readily suggests that they are not only different in nature but that they also were created for different purposes. Mowinckel has argued strongly that the purpose for most of them was to serve the cult of the preexilic Temple, that is, during the royal period. Some psalms were for the ceremonial coronation of a king (2, 110); at least one for the king's wedding (45); and one was for the king's well-being, success, and competence as a ruler (72). It is quite plausible that many of the psalms that appear with the first-person pronoun are psalms originally used by the king, whether they are hymns or laments. Other psalms were clearly used on days of penance and prayer (44). A special group that speaks of Yahweh as King (93, 95–99), Mowinckel calls "Yahweh's Enthronement Psalms," that is, they were used at the New Year Festival when Yahweh was again ceremoniously proclaimed king. The land had been threatened by drought and famine because of the rainless season. It was as if the deity had left them. At the New Year, God was again taking his place on the throne (cf. Ps 24) and a good harvest and prosperity was thus guaranteed.

The Age of the Psalms. Wellhausen suggested that "It is no longer a question of how many psalms are preexilic, but whether *any* psalm is preexilic." R. Pfeiffer also maintained that the psalms were only postexilic and used only late in Judaism. Against this view stands that of Sigmund Mowinckel: "A large part of the psalter is preexilic and used in the Temple services during the reign of the kings" (Mowinckel, 137). And Artur Weiser (25): "Only a comparatively small number of the psalms can, in fact, be proved conclusively to have originated in the postexilic period." Otto Eissfeldt (446-47) brings the origin back as far as the beginning of the settlement in Canaan.

The content of the psalms may, in fact, help to date them, because some of them are constructed with refrains. Consider Ps 46, where vv. 7 and 11 clearly are refrains: "The LORD of Hosts is with us, the God of Jacob is our refuge." (This refrain probably should appear also after v. 3.) Another example is Ps 136 where every last half of the verse is repeated: "For his mercy [Heb. *ḥesed*] endures forever." In such cases we have clear hints of liturgical usage in need of a temple setting: there is responsive singing by either (a) a choir and a congregation or (b) a choir and a single voice. The content of the psalms thus supports the view that indeed many of them were created for use in the temple during the royal period.

Titles and Authors. Many of the psalms have superscriptions of various kinds. Some of them detail the musical instrumentation to be used. One of the most common words appearing in the superscriptions is *lamenaṣṣēaḥ*, generally translated "to the choirmaster." This however is awkward, and Mowinckel suggests it should be read "To dispose (the deity) to be merciful." Many other psalms have names listed: "To the Sons of Korah," "To Asaph," "To Solomon." Most common of these are those that have *ledāwîd*, which, in conformity with the other titles, should be translated "To David." (The Heb. preposition *le* generally means "to, for, at.") The strongest argument is provided by the internal evidence: Ps 24 is a psalm *ledāwîd*, yet the psalm speaks of "the ancient doors" of the temple, which was not built until king Solomon, David's son. In the Septuagint LXX many more psalms have David's name in the title. It is most likely that these psalms were dedicated to David, either because David means king or because he was known as a gifted poet and musician (1 Sam 16:14-23; Amos 6:5). (The NEB omits the titles completely, perhaps a wise choice since the titles often can be confusing; yet the revised NEB, the REB, puts back the original titles. The TEV omits the titles of the original and substitutes titles based on the translators' interpretation of the content; CEV maintains such interpretive titles but also reinstates the original titles. Such vacillation by professional translators points up the general uncertainties of the original titles.)

The Theology of the Psalms. It is only natural that in religious songs like these the faith of the nation should be expressed in a richly varied manner.

First, God is presented as the creator in such psalms as 18:7-15, 19:1-6, and 29 (Ps 29 sounds quite primitive). The most powerful expression is found in Ps 33:6-9, where God creates merely by speaking his word, and there is no hint that there was matter before he created, a view found in Gen 1 and 2:4-5. This psalm is the closest the OT comes to our modern doctrine of *creatio ex nihilo*—creation out of nothing.

Secondly, with all the great things said about God, he is not alone. Ps 82:1 states that he is supreme—"He rules in the midst of the gods"—and, according to Ps 139, even the kingdom of death is under him.

Thirdly, in this way the psalms are presenting the covenant God of Israel. There is a unique relationship between God and his people and this reality permeates most psalms. He is hailed in the hymns, he is implored in the laments; but he is always felt and understood to be *their* God.

Repeatedly Yahweh is presented as holy and righteous. His people rely upon his love (*hesed*) for them. And he is hailed as king, which, according to Pss 93, 95–99, means not only king of his covenant people Israel, but of the whole world that he has created and holds under his sway.

In the Psalms, indeed, one is presented with a very rich view of God, both exalted and intimate.

The psalms come to us in a great variety of forms, and yet each of them follows strict rules for style and language. At the same time we can see that the authors felt free to change the system whenever inspiration demanded it. There is a beautiful balance between form and content, between structure and freedom. There are rules for the presentations, and yet the inspired authors have been able to expand the regulations and express themselves in ways that for all times will be used by people in their personal and congregational devotions.

See also KINGSHIP; POETRY; WORSHIP IN THE OLD TESTAMENT.

Bibliography. B. Ahlstrom, *Psalm 89*; A. A. Anderson, *Psalms*; C. S. Briggs, *A Critical and Exegetical Commentary on the Psalms*, ICC; M. Dahood, *Psalms*, AncB; B. Duhm, *Die Psalmen*; J. Durham, "Psalms," *BBC*; O. Eissfeldt, *The Old Testament: An Introduction*; H. Gunkel, *Ausgewählte Psalmen* and *An Introduction to the Psalms*; A. F. Kirkpatrick, *The Book of Psalms*, CB; H. J. Kraus, *Psalmen*; J. Kugel, *The Idea of Biblical Poetry*; E. A. Leslie, *The Psalms*; S. Mowinckel, *Psalms in Israel's Worship*; J. B. Pritchard, ed., *ANET*; A. Weiser, *The Psalms*, OTL; C. Westermann, *The Praise of God in the Psalms*.

—REIDAR B. BJORNARD

The Book of Proverbs   [MDB 720-21]

• AN OUTLINE •

I. "The Proverbs of Solomon, Son of David, King of Israel":
In Praise of Wisdom (1:1–9:18)
II. "The Proverbs of Solomon": Wise Sayings (10:1–22:16)
III. "The Words of the Wise":
Admonitions to His Son or Pupil (22:17—24:22)
IV. "Also . . . Sayings of the Wise" (24:23-34)
V. "Also . . . Proverbs of Solomon" (25:1–29:27)
VI. "The Words of Agur" (30:1-33)
VII. "The Words of Lemuel" (31:1-9)
VIII. A Poem on the Ideal (Wise) Wife (31:10-31)

•Proverbs, Book of. The Book of Proverbs belongs to the third division of the Hebrew Bible, the Writings, which contains books of a widely different character. This division of the canon was probably not closed until the end of the first century CE. Included among the Writings are the books of wisdom literature: Job, Ecclesiastes, and Proverbs. Two other wisdom books, belonging to the larger canon, are Sirach and the Wisdom of Solomon. These five books of wisdom literature represent the major corpus of an important religious and social tradition extending from the beginnings of Israel well into the Hellenistic period. Rabbinic Judaism continued the development of this tradition into the postbiblical period.

The Book of Proverbs consists of seven major collections, each of which has its own title: (1:1–9:18) "The proverbs of Solomon, son of David, king of Israel"; (10:1–22:16) "The Proverbs of Solomon"; (22:17–24:22) "The words of the wise"; (24:23-34) "These also are the sayings of the wise"; (25:1–29:27) "These also are the proverbs of Solomon which the men of Hezekiah king of Judah copied"; (30:1-33) "The words of Agur son of Jakeh of Massa"; (31:1-9)"The words of Lemuel, king of Massa, which his Mother taught him." In addition there is a concluding poem in 31:10-31 which celebrates the wise woman in Israelite society.

Three of these collections bear the title, "The Proverbs of Solomon," thus leading to the attribution of the entire book to this ruler celebrated for his wisdom (cf. 1 Kgs 3–11). Two other wisdom books suggest an association with SOLOMON: ECCLESIASTES and the WISDOM OF SOLOMON. This does not mean Solomon was the author of these three books: Ecclesiastes, the Wisdom of Solomon, and much of the Book of Proverbs were written well after the death of this king. In all three cases, however, the intent is not to claim Solomon as the author. Patrons of culture are often honored by having their names associated with the materials produced. As the king most renowned for his wisdom and wealth, Solomon was the greatest patron of this literary and social tradition. The Book of Proverbs consists of materials put together over many centuries, from the beginnings of the monarchy in the early tenth century BCE well into the postexilic period.

Those who produced the wisdom tradition, including the Book of Proverbs, were often called "sages" (wise men and women), because of the importance of the term, "wisdom," in this tradition. The "sages" belonged to a variety of social classes in Israel and later Judaism, though the titles of the Book of Proverbs and other texts suggest that many of them worked within two major settings: the royal court during the period of the monarchy and the temple in JERUSALEM in the postexilic period. As servants of the king these sages served in the royal bureaucracy, ranging from positions of political power (e.g., "secretary of the king") to lowly scribes who worked as accountants for royal treasuries and copyists of state documents. After the end of native rule, the sages shifted their locus to the temple, performing similar functions in a nation whose local leadership continued to shift to the high priesthood. Two prominent examples of sages are JOSEPH who became the prime minister to the king of Egypt (Gen 37–50) and EZRA. In addition to writing their own literature, the sages edited many of the books in the Hebrew Bible before these books entered into the official canon.

The initial collection in chaps. 1–9 consists of ten instructions, together with several supplements. The instruction is a form of teaching that provides guidance in moral and religious conduct. It begins with an introduction in which the hearer, "my son" (an ideal student), is exhorted by the teacher, "your father" (the teacher), to give heed to the instruction. This is followed by a main section consisting of admonitions that instruct the hearer to behave in a way deemed to result in life and well-being. Prohibitions warn the student against immoral behavior that leads to tragedy and failure. The conclusion speaks of the results of wise or foolish behavior, and changes from appeal to demonstration, and from address to confirmation. Two personified figures appear often in this collection: Dame Wisdom who represents the wisdom tradition and its code of conduct and Dame Folly who represents ignorance and wicked behavior.

The second major collection (10:1–22:16) consists of 375 individual proverbs or sayings, occasionally grouped together along thematic and/or literary lines (e.g., 16:10-15 concern the king). But most are self-contained units of meaning. Two subsections may be discerned. Common to the first, 10:1–15:33, is the antithetical saying that contrasts the righteous (or wise) with the wicked (or fools). The second subsection, 16:1–22:16, has many themes, including the king and the royal court, respect for proper speech, and appropriate behavior in a variety of social contexts.

The other collections are much shorter. The material in 22:17–24:22 is an instruction based on a well-known Egyptian text, "The Teaching of Amen-em-ope," dating from the thirteenth century BCE. This is one clear example of the international character of the Israelite wisdom tradition. The collection in 24:23-34 is an instruction on diligence in farming and just actions in the judiciary. Chaps. 25–29 comprise a collection that may be subdivided formally and thematically into two sections: 25–27 and 28–29. The first consists of sayings and teachings primarily for youth at court, kings, and sages who conduct royal business. The second section is perhaps a collection for rulers to use in a variety of political and social situations.

The collections in chap. 30 and 31:1-9 derive from the wisdom of Arabia. The "Words of Agur" (chap. 30) in vv. 1-4 echo some of the themes of JOB and ECCLESIASTES: the vain striving for wisdom illustrated by impossible questions. This collection seems to have been countered by a pious editor who added the remaining verses. "The Words of Lemuel" (31:1-9) is an instruction on royal rule, issued to a young Arabian king by his queen mother. The acrostic poem in praise of the wise woman (31:10-31) echoes the poems on Dame Wisdom in 1:20-33 and chaps. 8–9, thus bringing to a fitting close the entire book.

The many topics in the Book of Proverbs find their center in one dominating theme: the origins and maintenance of "order" in creation, society, and individual life. For the sages, God permeated creation with a just and beneficent "order" in which everything has its place, time, and function. The major social institutions also owe their origins to God and have their proper "order," that is, rules and functions that are just and life sustaining. The task of the sages was to observe this "order," place their observations into teachings (sayings and instructions), and transmit them to youths who sought to enter government and temple service. Eventually the teachings were democratized and used as moral instruction for people in various social groups.

The sages specified the norms and appropriate behavior for the institutions of kingship, marriage, economic production and trade, law, education, and religion. These made up the social order that was believed to be grounded in the larger order of creation. Proper decorum within these institutions led to well-being, while unruly and undisciplined behavior led to misfortune, for the individual but also for the larger community. While an occasional "voice" questioned the validity of this understanding and pointed to the limits of wisdom (e.g., Agur), most of the teachings of the Book of Proverbs affirm the goodness of life and the possibility of living in harmony with God, the world, and other persons.

See also PROVERB; WISDOM IN THE OLD TESTAMENT; WISDOM LITERATURE.

Bibliography. J. Blenkinsopp, *Wisdom and Law in the Old Testament*; C. V. Camp, *Wisdom and the Feminine in the Book of Proverbs*; J. L. Crenshaw, *Old Testament Wisdom* and "Proverbs" in *Urgent Advice and Probing Questions*, 355-425; J. G. Gammie and L. G. Perdue, *The Sage in Ancient Israel*; B. Lang, *Wisdom and the Book of Proverbs*; W. McKane, *Proverbs: A New Approach*; D. Morgan, *Wisdom in the Old Testament Traditions*; R. E. Murphy, *Wisdom Literature and Psalms*; L. G. Perdue, *Wisdom and Cult*; R. B. Y. Scott, *The Way of Wisdom*; R. N. Whybray, *The Book of Proverbs*.

—LEO G. PERDUE

The Book of Ecclesiastes [MDB 227-28]

• AN OUTLINE •

I. Theme of the Book: Human Life Is Vain (1:1-11)
II. Illustrations of the Theme (1:12–2:26)
   A.Wisdom is vanity (1:12-18)
   B. Pleasure and labor are vanity (2:1-11)
   C. Life itself is vanity (2:12-17)
   D. Vanity itself is vanity (2:18-24)
   E. Religion too is vanity (2:25-26)
III. A Time for All Things (3:1-15)
IV. The Fate of Righteous and Wicked Is the Same (3:16–4:16)
V. The Author's Wisdom Collection (5:1–11:10)
VI. Old Age and Death Portrayed (12:1-8)
VII. Conclusion (12:9-14)

•Ecclesiastes, Book of. [i-klee'zee-as"teez] One of five *Megilloth*, or "festival scrolls," read in the synagogue during the Festival of Tabernacles or DEDICATION.

The author of the text, though not named, is called "Qoheleth" ("speaker in an assembly"; 1:1-2, 12; 7:27-28; 12:8-10), a Hebrew term translated into Greek as *ekklēsiastēs* ("member of an assembly") and rendered via the Vulgate into the English title for the work. Early rabbinic tradition attributed the book to Solomon, since the author is described in the superscription as "the son of David, king in Jerusalem" (1:1) and later in the text as the "king over Israel in Jerusalem" (1:12). The reputation for wisdom that was associated with Solomon by popular tradition in Israel (1 Kgs 3:12) thus gave a certain authority to the book, as it also did for works such as Proverbs, the *Psalms of Solomon*, the Wisdom of Solomon, and the Song of Solomon, and ultimately assisted Ecclesiastes in its quest for acceptance into the canon.

Several elements of the book suggest that the work in fact derives from an anonymous wisdom teacher (cf. 12:9) during the third century BCE, and thus had only a short history prior to its canonization. The text was composed in a late, transitional form of the Hebrew language that reflects numerous premishnaic idioms, Aramaisms, and Persian loanwords. Early manuscripts of the text are relatively free of the type of errors that arise from the transmission of texts over a period of several generations, and there are few divergencies between the Hebrew text and other early versions, including the quite literal translation found in the LXX. Finally, the concerns of the writing are those of the postexilic period, and the author appears well acquainted with thought patterns that were common to the Hellenistic age.

It is doubtful the text comes from a single author, since several passages reflect redactional tendencies, such as repetitions, contradictions, and irregularities, and since third-person references to the author occur throughout the writing (1:1-2a; 7:27; 12:8-10). These references probably represent additions by a student of the text or, more likely, the concerns of divergent elements within the Jewish wisdom schools of the period, many of which were located in Alexandria, Phoenicia, and Jerusalem. The rationalistic approach of the book and its attack upon traditional religious structures caused anxiety for the adherents of ancient Hebrew orthodoxy, and despite contemporary claims of Solomonic authorship and the acceptance of the book by the sectarian community at Qumran, the rabbinic school of Shammai refused to recognize the book as holy scripture through the end of the first century CE. Subsequent debate concerning the status of Ecclesiastes in its relationship to scripture continued among Jewish authorities well into the second century (*Yad* 3.5).

With respect to literary form, the book is a compilation of negative exhortations and two-part proverbs, the organization of which is parallel to the genre of early Egyptian "royal testaments." There is a high degree of verbal repetition, and individual discussions are linked through catchword associations. The book contains a marked prologue (1:2-11) and an epilogue (12:9-14), the latter of which probably is not original to the work. The body of the text contains three major sections, which are broadly oriented around the themes of vanity (1:12–6:9), wisdom (6:10–11:6), and age (11:7–12:8). While numerous attempts have been undertaken to determine unifying or cohesive structures and literary patterns within the work, no clear rhetorical schema is readily apparent for the book.

As the primary focus of the book, Qoheleth seeks through empirical observation and deliberation to determine the meaning and role of humanity in existence. There is no appeal to any recognized authority, whether tradition, scripture, or divinity, as a justification for the observations or arguments found in the work. Instead, the author relies upon the perception of life provided by cumulative experience and the self-perceived superiority of personal wisdom. The human situation is the subject of great skepticism, and in many respects the book reflects a form of early existentialism that is without parallel elsewhere in the Bible.

The reader is led through an examination of life that proceeds from and returns to the realization that "all is vanity" (1:2; 12:8). The pursuits and toils of humanity, whether for pleasure (2:1-11), wisdom (2:12-17), or wealth (5:10-17), have no ultimate value. Wickedness resides in the places of justice (3:16–4:3) and government (5:18), and death cancels the meaning of righteous endeavors. In many respects the book is an account of the struggle between good and evil—the righteous and the wicked—though no uniform ethical construct ever is established, and it is the very structures of cult and ritual that appear to elicit the greatest despair. The text is dominated by the systematic application of wisdom categories to an investigation of the traditional institutions of ethics and religion. Qoheleth recognizes that all of life exists under the aegis of God, though this God is a rather inaccessible deity whose structuring of reality is incontrovertible, but whose structures are subject to the vagaries of human whim. Otherwise, no divine purpose for human existence or philosophy of history is forthcoming. In the light of these observations concerning reality, life is to be lived for its own benefits: the enjoyment of existence (2:24; 3:22; 8:15); the pleasures of companionship (4:9-12;

9:9); the satisfaction of honest labor (5:12). One detects throughout the book that Qoheleth has intermittently inserted traces of the contemporary doctrine that God is the author of just retribution, much like that belief espoused by the "friends" of Job. Since this doctrine flagrantly contradicts the mood of the book, one is led to consider that such passages are designed to show the foolishness of such a doctrine, or are insertions by a later hand. Instead, Qoheleth concludes that where wisdom and righteousness fail, one must live life on its own terms.

See also WISDOM IN THE OLD TESTAMENT; WISDOM LITERATURE.

Bibliography. G. A. Barton, *A Critical and Exegetical Commentary on the Book of Ecclesiastes*; E. Bickerman, *Four Strange Books of the Bible*; J. L. Crenshaw, *Ecclesiastes, A Commentary* and "Ecclesiastes (Qoheleth)" in *Urgent Advice and Probing Questions*, 499-585; R. Gordis, *The Word and the Book*; R. B. Y. Scott, *Proverbs. Ecclesiastes*; C. F. Whitley, *Koheleth: His Language and Thought*; J. G. Williams, "What Does It Profit a Man?: The Wisdom of Koheleth," *Judm* 20 (1971): 179-93.

—CLAYTON N. JEFFORD

The Song of Songs   [MDB 848]

• AN OUTLINE •

I. Superscription (1:1)
II. Exchanges between Lovers (1:2–2:3)
III. Reflections on Love by the Lovers (2:4–3:11)
IV. Further Exchanges between the Lovers (4:1–8:7)
V. Closing Reflections and Exchanges (8:8-17)

•**Song of Songs.** A collection of love poems attributed to Solomon, but probably coming from a period considerably later than Solomon. The Hebrew title, "Song of Songs," is a superlative (like "holy of holies") and means "the greatest song," or "the most excellent song." In English translation, the title appears variously as "Song of Songs" (or "Canticle of Canticles") or simply as "Songs" ("Canticles") and as "Song of Solomon."

Contents. The book contains perhaps as many as twenty-five lyric and erotic love poems in which the speakers are a man, a woman, and a chorus. The man and the woman in turn praise the beauty and charms of the other, using language more suggestive and affective than descriptive. No clear pattern of development can be traced in the poems as presently arranged. The figures of king and shepherd and of queen and shepherdess recur frequently.

Interpretations. Early interpretations of the collection saw the imagery of bride and groom allegorically or typologically, as representing Israel and God or the Church and Christ. Such interpretations arose, no doubt, because of the symbolism of bride and groom in texts such as Hos 1–3 and Ezek 16 and 23 in the OT, and Eph 5 in the NT.

Critical studies suggest more probable settings for the Song of Songs. Studies of ancient Near Eastern religions reveal the significance of the sacred marriage in the great festivals, where the joining of the Gods Ishtar and Tammuz, for example, symbolize and realize the renewal of the natural world. This sacred marriage was enacted in the practices of worshipers at the shrines. It seems probable, however, that any such background in ancient fertility religion is considerably far removed from the love poetry of the Song of Songs.

The poetry belongs to daily life, to the world of courtship, betrothal, and marriage. It is lyric poetry, stressing the mood of erotic relationships, earthily and also with vivid and gripping uses of imagery and the natural world. Egyptian love poetry of the Late Kingdom offers close analogies to the poetry found here, although there are also rather close parallels with the much later Arab poetry belonging to the celebration of the beauty of bride and groom at betrothal time.

Interpretations of the Song of Songs today stress this affirmative attitude toward the sexual life, toward physical beauty and its attractions. Biblical religion goes far toward demystification of the sexual dimensions of existence, placing sex in the world of God's good creation, a gift to be enjoyed and affirmed.

The Song of Songs and the Canon. The Song of Songs came to be attached to the Passover celebration, offering balance to the somber elements of Passover, with its recollections of bondage in Egypt and of the death of the firstborn sons there. Solomon's many wives and his reported literary activity (1 Kgs 4:29-34) probably led to the attribution of the Song of Songs to Solomon. The Song of Songs came to be very popular in patristic and medieval church life, interpreted, of course, as an allegory of Christ and the Church.

Love and Death. One special connection of the love poetry needs to be mentioned. In Cant 8:6, it is said that "love is strong as [or stronger than] death." Does this reference to death suggest, as some have maintained, that this erotic love poetry belongs beside the grave? (Acts of celebration and festivity in ancient Israel accompanied the burial of the dead and regularly offered ceremonies for keeping death at bay.) It is not impossible that such an affirmation of life and love and beauty would have been found eminently suitable for inclusion, along with acts of lamentation, in ritual and ceremonial acts on the occasions of death.

The Songs of Songs does not strike the reader as serving instrumental purposes, however. It is affirming delight in human love, in human beauty, in the natural world that supports human love. Its character as lyrical, affective poetry also makes it particularly suitable for making human love into an analogy for the love of the community and the individual for God, and of God for the community and the individual.

See also LOVE IN THE NEW TESTAMENT; LOVE IN THE OLD TESTAMENT.

Bibliography. R. Gordis, *The Song of Songs and Lamentations*; M. H. Pope, *Song of Songs*, AncB.

—WALTER HARRELSON

Job

Samuel E. Balentine

Introduction

In one sense the Book of Job requires little introduction. With its focus on innocent suffering, faith, and the justice of God, this book addresses universal concerns. Most persons have some personal experience with these concerns; they do not need a commentary to understand the struggle for meaning in a life broken inexplicably by pain and loss.

From another perspective, however, it is remarkable that despite the universal sympathy with this book, so little of the complexity and the candor of Job's engagement with God is appropriated by the community of faith. Too often the message of the book is reduced to a conventional slogan: the patience of Job (cf. Jas 5:11). As with all slogans, this one distorts by oversimplifying. The full picture of Job and the God before whom he presents his case is both more demanding and more honest.

Authorship, Date, and Setting

Introductions to commentaries normally address traditional questions about a book's author, its date, and its setting. The Book of Job, however, provides little or no information about such matters.

The identity of the author or authors of the book is not known. One may speculate that the author was an Israelite, perhaps someone belonging to the same intellectual tradition that produced such wisdom books as Proverbs and Ecclesiastes, but the evidence is circumstantial.

The date of the book is equally uncertain. Most would date the final composition somewhere between the seventh and fourth centuries BCE, although it is clear that the motif of the innocent sufferer was important in Near Eastern literature from at least the second millennium. Similarities in form and content between Job and Jeremiah (e.g., Job 3:3-10; Jer 20:14-18) and Job and Second Isaiah (Isa 40–55), particularly with reference to the matter of innocent suffering, suggest a linkage to the exilic period. The book itself, however, provides no explicit historical information that ties it definitively to a particular period in Israelite history. Indeed, historical ambiguity is an essential aspect of the book's merit. Israel's experience of suffering, it might be argued, cannot be adequately explained by specific historical causes (cf. Penchansky 1990, 32-34).

The setting for the story in Job is also unclear. The introduction sets the action in *the land of Uz* (1:1), perhaps a reference to the region of Edom (cf. Lam 4:21), but more likely simply a general reference to a distant place somewhere east of Israel. Job himself is described as *the greatest of all the people of the east* (1:3). On balance, geographical location is unimportant for the story of Job. The world of Job is depicted instead as a "heroic world" (Habel 1985, 39), a world that cannot be identified with any specific place or time.

The name "Job" (*'iyyôb*) is curiously ambiguous. The only other reference to Job in the Hebrew Bible ranks him, along with NOAH and Danel (a legendary Canaanite king), as one of the ancient religious heroes (Ezek 14:14, 20). Within Hebrew the etymology of the word "Job" connects it with the passive participle of the verb *'āyab*, "to hate", thus "the hated one" or "the enemy." There may be a play on the words "Job" and "enemy" (*'ōyēb*) in Job 13:24. In second millennium West Semitic texts, an earlier form of the name, *'ayya- 'abum*, means "Where is the (my) father?" (Pope 1965, 6).

Both of these nuances may inform the presentation of the biblical Job. He is one whose life is marked by both invocation ("Where is God?") and accusation ("You count me as your enemy"); his stance before God is that of both the suppliant and the persecuted one (cf. Janzen 1985, 34).

Composition

The Book of Job was not "authored" or "published" in the modern sense. Rather, it is a composite, a collection of parts brought together through a history of transmission. Although the major pieces of the book can be discerned rather easily, the specifics of when and how the parts were combined into a whole remain unclear.

The Frame and the Center. The frame of the book, chaps. 1–2 and 42:7-17, is a narrative about the legendary character Job. This narrative is likely based on an ancient tale that in oral or written form provides the starting point for the present book. The account is written in relatively simple prose, and utilizes a combination of speech and action to convey a coherent account of Job's suffering and restoration.

The center of the book, chaps. 3:1–42:6, consists of a lengthy series of dialogues between Job and his friends and between Job and God. These chapters are written in poetry, not prose, and are dominated by the speech of the characters, not their actions. The speeches are drawn primarily from the genrés of lament and disputation. It is likely that a later transmitter of the Job tradition utilized the existing tale of Job the righteous sufferer, and supplemented it with these dialogues to expand and elaborate on the issues of suffering and retribution.

Chapter 28. The Poem on Wisdom. Within the center of the book, chap. 28 presents a self-contained poem that differs significantly from the surrounding dialogues. It contains neither lament nor disputation; it is addressed to no one directly, and it receives no direct response from other speakers. Its subject, mining, metallurgy and the technological capacities for attaining wisdom, does not fit easily with the issues that dominate the preceding discussion between the friends. Rather, the poem presents a typical wisdom reflection on a proverbial question: "Where then does wisdom come from?" (vv. 12, 20; cf. Westermann 1981, 135-38). The poem is generally regarded as a later addition that, although intrusive, contributes nevertheless in significant ways to the overall argument of the book.

Chapters 32–37. The Elihu Speeches. The speeches of Elihu are commonly thought to be a further later addition to the poetic center. Elihu is not mentioned elsewhere in either the frame or the center of the book. His speeches appear to contribute little to the advancement of the friends' arguments against Job. They constitute, rather, a monologue that many scholars regard as stylistically inferior to preceding speeches. Even as a later interpolation, however, the speeches of Elihu function within the book as a whole as a dramatic interlude that prepares in significant ways for the impending appearance of God.

The Book of Job in Its Present Form

When the several parts of Job are fused together, a new whole results. The framing tale is split in two, forming a prologue (Job 1–2) and an epilogue (Job 42:7-17). The poetic center, with its additions and insertions, divides into dialogues between Job and his friends (Job 3–37) and between Job and God (Job 38:1–42:6). In this complex whole the portraits of both Job and God emerge as multidimensional.

Job's piety is portrayed as a complex fusion of both submission and rebellion (cf. Brenner 1989, 37-52; Penchansky 1990, 44-50, 78-80). In the prologue and epilogue Job exemplifies piety through his willing submission to the inscrutable decisions of God. He accepts affliction without questioning or complaining. God gives and God takes away. In this one-sided relationship with God, the correct response of faith is to worship and to remain a silent recipient of divine decrees.

In the dialogues Job insists that inexplicable misfortune puts God, not the victims, on trial. As victim, Job's piety takes on new forms. Truth and justice require that he assert his innocence, even when established religious tradition presumes his guilt. Faith requires that he hold on to God, even if God is the agent of his injustice. Thus Job curses, complains, questions, and resists *in faith*. This expression of piety insists that in the relationship with the Almighty, the human is no silent partner.

The Book of Job encourages the understanding that these are reciprocal, not opposite or contradictory, expressions of piety. Job is both reverent and rebellious, both accepting of God's mysterious ways and resistant to the notion that God cannot be questioned.

The portrait of God that emerges from this composite is also complex (cf. Penchansky 1990, 74-78; Mettinger 1992, 39-49). In the prologue and epilogue, and in the divine speeches God is wholly sovereign, wholly powerful, and unquestionably just. God afflicts and restores at will, without cause. God speaks and acts; Job listens, acknowledges, and receives. There are hints that God may be manipulated (e.g., by "the Satan") and that God can respond to human challenge with petulance (e.g., in the "whirlwind" speeches). But the primary characteristics on display in this portrait are God's majesty and God's purposive rule of the world.

The dialogues between Job and the friends offer different understandings of God's character. The friends' God is sovereign, but no longer free. In their view God's actions are determined by a rigid system of rewards and punishments. If there is guilt, God will punish; if there is innocence, God will reward appropriately. Their God is more predictable than compassionate, more consistent than gracious.

Job's understanding of God, however, is still different. Throughout the arguments with the friends, Job insists that pain and suffering force a changed perception of the divine-human relationship. To the innocent sufferer God may seem more an enemy than a companion, more an assailant than a savior, and most troubling of all, more absent than present. In Job's experience, the faithful and deserving cry for help often addresses a distant and silent God.

The reader might well wish that these portraits of both Job and God were less complex, that one view could be championed to the exclusion of others. Uniformity is indeed more manageable than diversity. The popular construal of the "patient Job" is only a small case in point. But the Book of Job resists easy solutions to ultimate questions about faith and God. That is both the problem and the invitation of the book.

For Further Study

In the *Mercer Dictionary of the Bible*: JOB; JOB, BOOK OF; JOB, TESTAMENT OF; JUSTICE/JUDGMENT; SATAN IN THE OT; SUFFERING IN THE OT; WISDOM IN THE OT; WISDOM LITERATURE.

In other sources: D. J. A. Clines, *Job 1–20*, WBC; J. L. Crenshaw, *Old Testament Wisdom: An Introduction*; C. Duquoc and C. Floristan, eds., *Job and the Silence of God*; E. M. Good, *In Turns of Tempest. A Reading of Job with a Translation*; R. Gordis, *The Book of God and Man: A Study of Job*; G. Gutiérrez, *On Job. God-Talk and the Suffering of the Innocent*; N. C. Habel, *The Book of Job*, OTL; W. L. Humphreys, "The Tragic Vision and the Book of Job," *The Tragic Vision and the Hebrew Tradition*, OBT; J. G. Janzen, *Job*, Interpretation; D. Penchansky, *The Betrayal of God: Ideological Conflict in Job*; L. G. Perdue and W. C. Gilpen, eds., *The Voice From the Whirlwind. Interpreting the Book of Job*; M. H. Pope, *Job*, AncB; H. H. Rowley, *Job*, NCB; D. Simundson, *The Message of Job*; C. Westermann, *The Structure of the Book of Job*.

Commentary

An Outline

I. Prologue: The Affliction of Job, 1:1–2:13

II. Job's Lament, 3:1-26

III. Dialogue between Job and His Three Friends,
4:1–27:23

  A. First Cycle: God's Moral Governance
of the World, 4:1–14:-22

  B. Second Cycle: The Place of the Wicked
in a Moral World, 15:1–21:34

  C. Third Cycle: The Breakdown
of the Dialogue, 22:1–27:23

IV. Meditation on Wisdom, 28:1-28

V. Job's Summation, 29:1–31:40

  A. Declaration of Past Integrity, 29:1-25

  B. Acknowledgement of Present Misery,
30:1-31

  C. Oaths of Innocence, 31:1-40

VI. Speeches of Elihu, 32:1–37:24

  A. Introduction of Elihu, the "Answerer,"
32:1-22

  B. The Case against Job, 33:1-33

  C. Defense of God's Justice, 34:1–35:16

  D. A Second Defense of God's Justice:
The Majesty and Order of Creation,
36:1–37:24

VII. Dialogue between Job and God, 38:1–42:6

  A. God's First Address:
The Order of the Cosmos, 38:1–40:2

  B. Job's First Response: "I Am Small," 40:3-5

  C. God's Second Address:
The Just Governance of the Cosmos,
40:6–41:34 (MT 41:26)

  D. Job's Second Response: "I Relent," 42:1-6

VIII. Epilogue: The Restoration of Job, 42:7-17

Prologue: The Affliction of Job, 1:1–2:13

The prologue introduces the life journey of the legendary character Job. He is the model of the righteous person, exemplifying piety by his faithfulness along the journey from prosperity to affliction, from joy to pain. He seeks steadfastly to avoid *evil* (*rā '*, 1:1, 8; 2:3), yet is victimized by *evil* (*rā '*, 2:11). His stature (literally, his "greatness") is defined initially by possessions (1:3), but ultimately by pain and anguish (2:13). His journey into suffering inexplicable is decided in God's heavenly court where conversations between God and *hasatan* (1:6-12; 2:1-7a) result in calamity on earth for Job and his family (1:13-22; 2:7b-10). Job's submission to heavenly decisions beyond his knowledge and control affirms his willing commitment to a one-sided relationship with the God who both gives and takes away (1:21).

1:1-5. Job's piety. Job is presented as an exemplary model of faith. Both the beginning and ending of this initial presentation focus on his unparalleled piety. He is *blameless* and *upright*, i.e., a person of integrity and complete honesty, and he is one who *feared God* and *turned away from evil* (v. 1). He is the epitome of the righteous person as portrayed in the wisdom tradition (e.g., Prov 3:7; 16:6, 17) and in the Psalms (e.g., 25:21; 37:27). This cluster of superlatives, reinforced by its verbatim repetition in 1:8 and 2:3, makes clear the Hebraic affirmation of the essential connection between morality and piety. Further, his concern is not limited to himself but extends to his family, for whom he offers preemptive sacrifices just in case they should sin against God in their heart (v. 5).

Sandwiched between the framing descriptions of his faithfulness, vv. 2 and 3 report that Job is blessed with a full family and a contingent of servants and possessions. The numbers *seven, three,* and *ten* are formulaic indicators of the completeness of Job's life. The position of these verses anticipates a crucial question in the Book of Job. What is the connection between Job's piety and his prosperity? Is piety the precondition for prosperity? Or is prosperity the motivation behind one's piety?

1:6-12. First scene in heavenly court. A series of alternating scenes in heaven and on earth explore the causal connection between Job's piety and his prosperity. A heavenly council gathers to discuss God's governance of the world. Among the divine messengers present is one called *hasatan,* "the Satan". The term refers not to the devil or to Satan as known in Christianity, but to one who functions as a kind of prosecuting attorney for God (cf. Zech 3:1-2), probing the veracity of human claims for integrity and faithfulness. There is nothing in the function of this "Prosecutor/Adversary" to suggest that he is God's opponent or that his intentions are in some way evil or contrary to God's purposes. To the contrary, the dilemma posed by the Book of Job is that this one may only act in response to divine initiatives.

God initiates the discussion by asking whether in his rovings "the Satan" has considered *my servant Job* (v. 8). God affirms Job's piety with the same unqualified praise offered in v. 1, adding the assessment that *there is no one like him on the earth.* This evaluation, normally reserved as a description of God's own distinctiveness (only here, in 2:3, and in 1 Sam 10:24 with reference to humans; cf. Clines 1989, 24), heightens the portrayal of Job as righteous beyond comparison.

"The Satan" responds by questioning Job's motivation for loyalty to God. Is it not the case that Job is faithful because he is blessed? Has not God so protected him from the fires of adversity that Job's faith has never really been tested? Suffering, "the Satan" implies, will change the calculus between God and humans. Without the reward, would there be the loyalty?

God concedes that the question is worthy of consideration. Does God know already the answer or is God perhaps asking, with "the Satan," about the real possibilities of disinterested piety? The reader may find it more comfortable to presume that it is the former of these options rather than the latter, but the text itself leaves the question open. Without hesitation God hands Job over for the testing that is to decide the case. There is but one proviso: "the Satan" is to stop short of afflicting Job's person.

1:13-22. Calamity on earth. In rapid succession a series of calamities befalls Job as a consequence of the heavenly debate. Lost are *the oxen, the donkeys,* and the attendant "boys" (vv. 13-15), *the sheep* and the shepherd "boys" (v. 16), *the camels* and the caravan "boys" (v. 17). The loss of Job's family, though not explicitly stated, is indicated by the final allusion to the "children/boys" (v. 19). In all of these instances the NRSV renders the term "boys" (or "children/boys") with *the servants* (or *the young people*).

Throughout it all Job remains unquestioning and unwavering in his commitment to God. He assumes the posture of mourning and worship by falling on the ground in willing submission to the God who both gives and takes away (vv. 20-21). *In all this* Job did not sin or express contempt for God.

2:1-6. Second scene in heavenly court. A second round of discussion between God and "the Satan" repeats almost verbatim the previous debate in heaven, including God's affirmation of Job who persists in holding fast to his integrity. There is, however, one interesting addition to this scene.

Verse 3 reports that God has been *incited* by "the Satan" against Job for the purpose of destroying him *for no reason*. The verb "incite" or "provoke" (*swt*) normally carries negative connotations (cf. Deut 13:6 [MT 13:7]; Josh 15:18; 1 Sam 26:19; 2 Kgs 18:32). When used with reference to God's being provoked, the word invites consideration of God's susceptibility to manipulation. Such consideration is further merited by the concession from God that Job's calamities are without cause (*hinnām*). The admission from God is both candid and troubling. If God acts *for no reason*, without cause, what then is the connection between human behavior and divine action?

"The Satan" heightens the challenge by suggesting that if God will permit a closer scrutiny of Job, i.e., a deeper affliction that reaches to Job's very bone and flesh, it can be shown that his integrity is lacking. Again God agrees to the proposal, offering Job into "the Satan's" hand, with only the condition that his life be spared (vv. 4-6).

2:7-10. Calamity on earth. The second round of discussions in the heavenly council effect calamity on earth similar to the first. Job has already suffered the loss of all his possessions, now he is afflicted with *loathsome sores* that cover all his body, *from the sole of his foot to the crown of his head* (v. 7). Sitting in the ashes, Job assumes the position of the mourner who feels worthless and abandoned.

The question posed by Job's wife contributes indirectly to Job's affliction. The first part of her question recalls the words of God: Are you still "holding on to your integrity" (author trans.; cf. 2:3). The second part of her question echoes the words of "the Satan:" *Curse God and die* (v. 9; cf. 1:11; 2:5; see Clines 1989, 51). Thus does she articulate the contrasting expectations of God and "the Satan" regarding Job.

The dilemma that Job faces is magnified by his wife's urging that he should curse God. The Hebrew text has the word *brk*, "bless," thus, literally, "bless God. . . ." The word *brk* occurs throughout the prologue with a curious ambiguity. Sometimes it conveys its normal meaning, "bless" (1:10, 21), while in other instances it appears to have an opposite meaning, "curse" (1:5, 11; 2:5, 9). In the latter cases interpreters usually understand the word euphemistically, as a scribal substitute intended to tone down the text. If *brk* in v. 9 is read with its normal meaning "bless," rather than its presumed meaning "curse," then the wife's question takes on added significance. Can Job hold to his integrity and *bless* God? (Clines

1989, 52). Or will one commitment have to be sacrificed in order to retain the other?

Job's response hints at the quandary that he faces. On the one hand he rebukes his wife abruptly, suggesting that her option is no option. On the other hand, he moves from the positive declaration of 1:21 to an assertion now framed as a question: *Shall we receive the good at the hand of God, and not receive the bad?* (v. 10). The question is rhetorical, and yet the tremor of Job's ambiguity begins to surface (Janzen 1985, 51).

2:11-13. The arrival of the friends. Having heard of the *troubles* (*rā '*, "evil") that has fallen on Job, the three friends come to *console and comfort* (v. 11) him. The language suggests a dual intent. The verb "console" (*nwd*) means "to move back and forth," and by extension, "to show grief with," or "to identify in mourning with," by moving the head back and forth (e.g., Jer 15:5; 22:10). The form of the verb "to comfort" (*nhm*) used here means "to show sorrow/compassion," hence it conveys the friends' intent to act pastorally towards Job. The same verb, however, in a different form is the standard term for "to repent, change one's mind about." With the ensuing dialogues it will become clear that this second meaning of *nhm* is primary for the friends. Their view of consoling Job is to convince him to repent, i.e., to change his mind about the charges he will lodge against God. Only in this way can he be truly comforted.

But first, they engage in traditional acts of mourning, sitting in silence with Job for *seven days and seven nights* (v. 13). It is a gesture that both recognizes Job's great pain and at the same time isolates the friends from him, for the ritual they observe is one that treats Job as if he were already dead.

Job's Lament, 3:1-26

Job breaks the silence of pain with the voice of anguish. Pain must be spoken, even if, as these opening words of Job make clear, it drives one to curse. This speech is structured in two parts: vv. 1-10, a curse directed at the day of Job's birth and the night of his conception; and vv. 11-26, a lament that thunders a repeated question about the "Why?" of existence. From first word to last there is a steady deterioration into a bitterness of soul marked by rage and agony (v. 26).

3:1-10. Damn the day, damn the night. Job's wife had urged him to *curse God and die* (2:9). Now Job curses, not God directly, but rather the day of his birth (vv. 3-5) and the night of his conception (vv. 6-9). The intent of such cursing is to set in motion the very action the curse itself articulates. From this opening curse to Job's final summoning of God in 31:35-37, the outcome of Job's response to suffering hangs in the balance. Will his cursing unleash the forces of his ultimate demise, as his wife anticipates? Or will Job's harangue against the heavens finally lead to the dialogue with God that he so desperately desires?

Job's curse parodies the language of Gen 1 with a series of incantations that call for a reversal of the created order (cf. Fishbane 1971, 151-67). Verse 3 sets forth the general curse of *day* and *night*, with vv. 4-5 offering an elaboration of the former ("that day, let it be darkness" [author trans.]; cf. Gen 1:1), and vv. 6-9, an extended development of the latter (*that night, let thick darkness seize it*). In sum, Job expresses a preference for darkness over light, death over life. The reason is set forth in v. 10: life outside the womb brings nothing but trouble (cf. Jer 20:18). It is a measure of Job's anguish that his death wish is more than a temporary lapse into despair. It is a recurring theme throughout his speeches (e.g., 7:15-16; 9:21; 10:1; cf. Westermann 1981, 67-70).

3:11-26. Why? why? why? Job's lament is a weaving together of both self-lament, i.e., mournful interior reflection (vv. 11-19, 24-26) and God-lament (vv. 20-23; see further Westermann 1981, 37-38). In both foci the operative word is "Why?" (vv. 11, 12, 20; also implied in vv. 16, 23). A number of Hebrew terms convey this question, but the repetition of the word *lāmmāh* in vv. 11 and 20, a word typically conveying a strong note of protest, gives to the lament a tone of angry despair.

The self-lament (vv. 11-19) expresses Job's wish that he had died at birth, for as a stillborn (v. 16) the sleep of death would offer *quiet* and *rest* (vv. 13, 17). In death there would be a levelling of all that yields inequality and oppression. Royalty (vv. 14-15) and commoner, *the wicked* and *the weary* (v. 17), *prisoners* and *the taskmaster* (v. 18), *the small and the great* (v. 19), all would be as one. But it is not so for Job (vv. 24-26). He has no *ease*, no *quiet . . . no rest*. There is only life, and from his perspective life brings only *trouble* (v. 26, *rōgez*, lit. "raging").

Job's self-lament cannot be resolved on the horizontal plane alone. Ultimately his lament is directed to God for God is the only one who can respond effectively. Thus Job hurls the "Why?" question to God (vv. 20-23). Why does God give light and life to one for whom it means only misery and bitterness? For Job life is no gift. It is a dark form of divine constriction, a "hedge" (v. 23; cf. 1:10) that God places around him to block his escape to the peace of the grave.

Dialogue between Job and His Three Friends, 4:1–27:23

First Cycle: God's Moral Governance of the World, 4:1–14:22

4:1–5:27. Eliphaz. Eliphaz' first response to Job is patient and encouraging, not accusatory. He praises Job for the instruction he has offered in the past to those who have suffered. Now Job himself must heed his own counsel (vv. 2-5). The basis for Job's *confidence* and *hope* is his own piety, his *fear of God* and his *integrity* (v. 6), virtues that Eliphaz, with God (cf. 1:8; 2:3), does not dispute.

The critical question that Eliphaz urges Job to explore is put in v. 7: *Who that was innocent has ever perished? . . . where have the upright been destroyed?* The truth to which Eliphaz summons Job is not that the innocent do not *suffer*, but that they do not ultimately *perish* in their sufferings.

The validation of this truth is drawn from two sources. First, Eliphaz' own experience and observations confirm that God sustains in the world a reliable moral connection between deed and consequence. Those who sow *iniquity* and *trouble* reap the same (vv. 8-11). Second, Eliphaz has been granted a special revelation about the nature of the human condition (vv. 12-21). There is a fundamental distinction between Creator and creature such that it is impossible for mortals of *clay* and *dust* (v. 19) ever to be wholly *righteous* and *pure* before their maker (v. 17). Even God's heavenly servants are blemished and flawed (v. 18); how much more so then a human like Job.

On the basis of these two sources of wisdom, Eliphaz concludes that Job's troubles do not place him outside the meaningful order of God's world. They are but the logical consequence of creaturely imperfection (5:1-7).

Eliphaz extends his observations on God's moral governance of the world with a hymn of praise affirming God's reliable discrimination between the innocent and the needy and their powerful, devious oppressors (5:9-16). To such a God Job should willingly entrust his cause (v. 8), even though it means submitting to a transcendent, often mysterious justice (v. 9). Before such a God the poor always have hope, because ultimately injustice will be silenced (v. 16).

Suffering is more than just an inherent necessity of the human condition. It is evidence of God's positive plan for insuring the full development of human nature. Indeed, Job should be happy for the discipline of divine reproval since it is a demonstration of God's love for him (vv. 17-27). If Job will but follow Eliphaz's counsel to seek God, he will *know* (vv. 24, 25, 27) that the God who *wounds* and *strikes* can be trusted to "bind up" and *heal* (v. 18). Job need have no *fear* (vv. 21, 22) from temporary misfortune. By life's end, when God's correcting love has achieved the intended results, Job will be restored (vv. 22-26).

6:1–7:21. Job. Job's response comprises an indictment of the friends (chap. 6) and a lament to God (chap. 7). The indictment of the friends begins and ends with an emphasis on Job's *calamity* (*hawwāh*, vv. 2, 30). His anguish is heavy and real (vv. 2-3). It is not the contrived imaginations of a fool, as Eliphaz had suggested (5:2-7). And it is this very anguish that keeps him honest in his assessment of the situation (vv. 28-30). The truth is that God has targeted him for destruction, without cause (v. 10), and any effort to comfort that does not acknowledge this fact is repulsive, like rotten food (vv. 4-7).

The friends, Job charges, do not admit the truth of his calamity (vv. 14-27). What despairing ones need from friends in times of crisis is loyalty (*hesed*), even if they have lost faith in *the Almighty* (v. 14; cf. NEB, NIV). Job's friends, however, are like the wadis whose water is only seasonal. When the heat comes they disappear and disappoint all who look to them for sustenance. Job has not asked them for a *gift* or a *bribe* for the judge (v. 22). He has not asked them to rescue him from the hands of the adversary. He has only expected them to stand by him, not to haggle over the worth of his friendship.

From the portrayal of false friends, Job returns once more to speak of his own misery. He compares the human condition to the life of the slave (7:1-6; cf. 3:17-19). He labors in harsh, debilitating compulsory service for the reward of an existence that is meaningless and void of hope.

In 7:7-21 Job addresses God directly for the first time. He laments that God has searched him out like a "seeing eye" (v.8) and a *watcher of humanity* (v.20). God targets him as an opponent to be terrorized and subdued (v. 14), as if he were Yamm (*Sea*) or Tannin (*Dragon*), the primordial enemies of the created order (v. 12). In the bitterness of his soul, Job cries out with anguished imperative *Let me alone* (v. 16).

Such misery turns doxology to accusation. In vv. 17-21 Job utilizes the words of Ps 8:5-6, not to praise God for humanity's exalted status, but to challenge God for being unreasonably preoccupied with so frail an opponent as the human creature. Job asks hypothetically, *If I sin . . .* why should this be of such concern to God? Even if Job were to admit to sin, which he does not do, why should God not let the matter pass? Job's existence on earth is only brief. Surely there can be no harm to God if God suspends the assault until Job lies down in death and is no more (cf. vv. 7, 16, 21).

8:1-22. Bildad. Bildad raises for the first time the question of *justice* (*mišpāt*, vv. 1-7) and then appeals to an ancient parable to support his defense of God's reliable discrimination between the righteous and the wicked (vv. 8-19). On this basis Job can be sure that the truly upright person will not be rejected by God (vv. 21-22).

Bildad begins with a rhetorical question that makes explicit the concern that to this point has been only implied in Job's accusations: *Does God pervert* (lit., "bend," or "twist") *justice* (*mišpāt*) *. . .or the right* (*sedeq*)? (v. 3). For Bildad, the proven moral order of God's world means that God and injustice are mutually incompatible. For every consequence there is a cause, behind every misfortune a sin. If Job is innocent (a claim Bildad does not dispute), there must be a failing elsewhere. Bildad suggests the sin can be traced to Job's children. The same retributive view of justice informs Bildad's counsel. *If* Job will seek God, and *if* Job is pure and upright, *then* God will reward him with such blessings that the former days of affliction will pale by comparison (vv. 1-7).

To buttress this argument, Bildad appeals to the wisdom of the ages (vv. 8-19). He cites a parable of two plants to reiterate the respective fates of the wicked and the righteous: the *papyrus* and *reeds* (v. 11) that wither and then die for lack of water, and another unidentified plant whose shoots thrive and spread beyond the boundaries of its garden (vv. 16-19).

Finally, Bildad applies his teaching to Job, in effect answering the question he himself had posed in v. 3: *Does God pervert justice?* No, the blameless person (*tām*, v. 20; cf. 1:1, 8; 2:3) will not be rejected, and the wicked (*rěšā 'îm*, v. 22) will not survive.

9:1–10:22. Job. In his dispute with Bildad, Job takes up the question of divine justice (chap. 9), and considers the case he can make before the heavenly tribunal (10:1-17). Recognizing both the necessity and the futility of winning a verdict against the sovereign judge of the universe, Job succumbs once more to mournful lament (10:18-22).

In chap. 9 Job offers a critique of God's justice that responds to both Eliphaz and Bildad. Job 9:1-12 addresses Eliphaz' argument that human frailty makes it impossible to be righteous (*sdq*) before God (4:12-21). Job agrees that it is impossible to be *sdq* before God, but his affirmation is different, and it is made on other grounds. Job interprets *sdq* in a legal sense rather than a religious or moral sense, i.e., with reference to innocence rather than righteousness. It is true that mortals cannot be innocent before God, not because they are flawed creatures, but because in God's court "might makes right." Subverting doxological affirmations, Job charges that God uses divine powers to overturn and destroy (vv. 5-9). Such destructive force prompts bewilderment, not praise. It serves to conceal God and baffle humanity. It is a mystery that leads not to wonder and awe (v. 10; cf. 5:9), but to anxious uncertainty (vv. 10-12).

The second strophe of chap. 9 (vv. 13-24) challenges Bildad's contention that God does not pervert justice (cf. 8:3). Job charges that in God's justice there is no differentiation between the blameless and the wicked; they are both marked for destruction (v. 21). Job offers himself as a prime example of divine justice that operates "*without cause* (v. 17). Job is *innocent* (*sdq*, vv. 15, 20) and *blameless* (vv. 20, 21), yet God *mocks* (v. 23) his misfortune and forces him into the submission of the guilty as if he were the primordial chaos monster (vv. 13, 17-18). If justice is a matter of power, then who indeed can contest the verdict of the sovereign Judge?

Job ponders a number of options for his situation (vv. 25-35). He could forget his complaint and try to twist his countenance from sadness to cheerfulness, but this would not relieve his suffering or restore his innocence (vv. 27-28). He could wash himself with potent cleansing agents, but God would still submerge him in filth (vv. 30-31). Or he could appeal for an arbitrator who would lay his hand on both parties, restraining God to a fair legal process and protecting Job from unjust intimidation (vv. 33-35). In the MT v. 33 is prefaced with a negative: "There is no arbitrator." The NRSV renders the phrase *There is no umpire between us*. Other versions preface the statement with a particle suggesting a wish: "If only there were someone to arbitrate. . ." (NIV). Both translations are consistent with Job's dilemma as conveyed in the MT. He wishes for an option that he does not believe exists. Even so, it is a possibility he will continue to pursue (cf. 16:19-21; 19:23-27).

In chap. 10 Job rehearses the case he would make before God, if he only had the chance (vv. 1-17). He reviews and disputes traditional affirmations about God's purposive creation of humanity. God's own hands have fashioned individuals from the womb, knitting them together, bone and flesh, supposedly with a providential care directed towards life and love. Yet from Job's perspective God's intentions seem sinister, not benevolent. God shapes humans only to *destroy* them (v. 8). God creates humans out of *clay* only to facilitate their reduction to *dust* (v. 9). God's motive in watching over the maturation process of humans (like a cheese maker [v. 10] and a clothier [v. 11]) is to search for human flaws (vv. 10-14). If Job were guilty, he would deserve such punishment, but he is innocent (*sdq*, v. 15; cf. 9:15,

20). Now he cannot lift his head, because his shame and his affliction already pronounce him guilty. Indeed, even if he attempted to restore his integrity, God would hunt him down like a lion (v. 17).

Job closes this speech (vv. 18-22) by returning to the painful question "Why?" with which he began in chap. 3. The question is addressed to God: *Why did you bring me [out of] the womb?* (cf. 3:11). Life under God's scrutiny has become abhorrent for Job (10:1; cf. 7:16; 9:21). If he had to be born to such misery, could not God now leave him alone (v. 20; cf. 7:16, 19) so that he might pass quickly to the grave? There, in the presence of death's darkness and gloom, he might at last smile a little (NRSV *find a little comfort*).

11:1-20. Zophar. Zophar assumes the role of a teacher whose instruction is meant to enlighten Job on the matter of God's justice (vv. 1-12) and to direct him to the appropriate response (vv. 13-20).

The instruction begins with a rebuke of Job's claim to be *pure* and *clean* in God's eyes (vv. 1-6). The *secrets of wisdom* are inaccessible to human understanding. There is a surface dimension to God's ways in the world, which ordinary mortals like Job might challenge. But there is also a transcendent dimension to God's wisdom (vv. 8-9: a depth, a height, a length, a breadth) that Job cannot know and should not question (vv. 7-12). Zophar presumes to know this hidden dimension of God's justice, and affirms that on this level God most certainly does discern who is worthless and deceitful. The truth of God's unfathomable justice is that Job has received less than he deserves for his guilt (v. 6).

Zophar's counsel (vv. 13-20) is couched in the same if-then terms that Bildad offered in 8:1-7. *If* Job directs his heart to God, stretches out his hands in humble prayer, removes iniquity from his life, and does not let wickedness reside in his abode (vv. 13-14), *then* God will restore him (vv. 15-19). Whereas Bildad offered such counsel in the presumption of Job's innocence, Zophar assumes Job's need of repentance. Job's *hope* and *confidence* are conditional rewards, not inherent qualities; they are inextricably linked to his return to God (cf. Bildad's discussion of hope in 8:13-14).

12:1-14:22. Job. This complex speech brings to conclusion the first cycle of discourses between Job and the friends. A number of rhetorical themes connect the speech to Job's opening lament in chap. 3 (e.g., *trouble*, in 3:17, 26; 14:1 and *deep darkness* in 3:5; 12:22; see further Janzen 1985, 101-102), and yet the tenor of the language suggests that both Job's anguish and his resolve to protest have escalated dramatically.

The speech is a disputation, comprised of three major parts, which is directed against the friends and against God. The first unit, 12:1-13:12, contests the friends' wisdom and integrity. A crucial transition in 13:13-19 signals Job's decision to address God directly, no matter the cost. The final unit, 13:20-14:22, is Job's challenge to God.

Job disputes the friends' claim to superior wisdom. Job has wisdom of his own, equal to theirs (12:2-3; 13:1-2), and both his intellect and his experience lead him to refute their contention that God is just. Why would a truly wise being make a laughingstock of an innocent and blameless man who seeks only honest dialogue with God? Job concludes that such mockery is the product of the friends' insulation from suffering: "in the thinking of those who are at ease there is contempt for calamity" (12:5, author trans.).

Job appeals to creation itself for his knowledge of God (12:7-12). The *animals*, the *birds of the air*, the *fish of the sea*, *the earth*, all serve as teachers for those who will listen. They declare that every living creature is in the hand of God, including the innocent sufferer.

Such a declaration moves Job to a "doxology of terror" (Perdue 1991, 153), a painful praise in honor of God's destructive purposes in creation (12:13-25). *Wisdom* and "power" (*strength*) are the trademarks of God's work in the world (12:13, 16), not justice, and God uses these virtues to destroy rather than to nourish. God tears down the structures of society, without rebuilding; deprives the created order of sustenance, without replenishing; limits, overthrows, and removes the possibility of human leadership; and in general returns the created order to chaos (see esp. 12:22, 24).

In 13:1-12 Job continues his disputation against the friends by attacking their integrity. They are "lie spreaders" and "quack doctors" (v. 4, author trans.) whose so-called wisdom is as worthless as dust and crumbling clay (v. 12). With a series of rhetorical questions (vv. 7-9, 11) Job implies that the friends have spoken falsely and deceitfully for God. By defending God against Job's truth claims, they hope to curry favor with the sovereign judge. They do not realize that covering up the truth about suffering and injustice is never an adequate defense of God. If they choose to be false witnesses in the case that Job will bring against God, they run the risk of being investigated themselves.

Job 13:13-19 represents a crucial transition point in the speech as Job turns away from the friends and prepares to address God directly. He has prepared his case against God; he knows that he is *sdq*, a fact that should secure his acquittal (v. 18). But he has no misgivings about his chances against so powerful an opponent. God will slay him; he has no hope, yet he must argue his cause before the very face of God (v. 15), even if the effort destroys him (v. 14). Only in daring confrontation with God can Job salvage his integrity (v. 16).

In 13:20–14:22 Job turns with "the courage of absolute vulnerability" (Janzen 1985, 107) to address God. Two questions set the agenda for the radical dialogue with God that Job seeks: *How many are my . . . sins?* (v. 23) and *Why do you hide your face and count me as your enemy?* (v. 24). The answer to these questions requires the mutual participation of God and Job. The contribution of one partner in this relationship without the other will be inadequate for the task. Either God can present the case against Job and Job will defend himself, or Job is prepared to challenge God and await God's defense. Either way there must be dialogue. Job has derided the friends for failing to realize the legitimacy of his request for interchange with God (12:4). Surely God does not condone a stifling of honest discourse.

Having laid the groundwork for his discourse with God, Job yields once more to the realization of the futility of his quest. Mortals have no real hope of contesting God. Their lifespans are set by divine decree, and there are boundaries beyond which they must not pass (14:1-6). There may be hope (*tiqwāh*, v. 7) for a tree to bud again after it is cut down (14:7-12), and perhaps, Job muses, there may be for humans some respite from suffering even after they descend to Sheol (14:13-17). But in truth there is no such hope (*tiqwāh*, v. 19). Mortals ultimately pass away into nothingness, like the dust of the earth that is washed away by the flood waters (14:18-22).

Second Cycle: The Place of the Wicked in a Moral World, 15:1–21:34

15:1-35. Eliphaz. Job had asked the friends to be quiet and listen to his case against God (13:13, 17). They do not cooperate. Instead they become more strident and accusatory in their approach to Job. In his second speech Eliphaz moves from exhortation (chaps. 4–5) to rebuke, reprimanding Job for his so-called *wisdom* (vv. 1-16) and lecturing him on the destiny of the *wicked* (vv. 17-35).

Eliphaz characterizes Job's speeches as a blustery sabotage of true religion (vv. 1-6). His so-called wisdom is tainted as much by his unacknowledged guilt as by his cleverness (v. 5). Job's assessment of his experience is not only inaccurate; it is dangerous. To argue with God as Job has dared to do destroys true piety (*yir 'āh, fear of God*; cf. 1:2, 8; 2:3) and diminishes contemplation of religious truths (v. 4).

To reinforce his charge Eliphaz appeals to the accumulated wisdom of the ages (vv. 7-16). Does Job propose that he has the wisdom of the Primal Human, the firstborn mortal who is privileged to God's primordial decisions (v. 7)? Does Job contend that he has stood in the divine council, where heavenly beings participate with God in the mysterious design of the cosmos (v. 8)? Even such holy ones are not entrusted with full comprehension of the divine plan (vv. 15-16); how then dare Job, a mere mortal, claim to be in the right against God (v. 14)? In his first speech Eliphaz had only briefly addressed God's treatment of the wicked (5:13-14).

In this speech the fate of the wicked is the subject of lengthy discourse (vv. 17-35). Appealing once more to the wisdom of the ancestors (vv. 17-19), Eliphaz asserts that the life of the wicked is filled with pain, terror, and deprivation (vv. 20-25). Their future is charted for a darkness and an emptiness that are unrelieved (vv. 28-31). Their final demise will come abruptly, like a vine that drops its grapes before they are ripe or an olive tree that loses its buds before they bear fruit (vv. 32-35).

The lesson for Job in this dissertation lies in recognizing the cause of the wicked person's ruin. Because they *stretched out their hands against God* and contest God as if they were a mighty warrior (vv. 25-28), they are doomed to the fortunes of an overmatched combatant. In Eliphaz' view, to challenge God is to rebel against God, and rebels, Job should note well, cannot escape the consuming justice of God (cf. v. 30).

16:1–17:16. Job. There is a disjointedness in this speech that yields a portrait of Job reeling back and forth between his disappointment in his friends (16:1-5;

17:6-10), his complaint against God (16:6-17), his hope in the midst of despair (16:18-22), and his steady descent towards death which, even if a respite from his troubles, still offers no hope for restitution (17:1-2, 11-16). The gradual diminishing of Job's direct address to God contributes to this portrait. In contrast to the lengthy address in 13:20–14:22, here Job speaks directly to God only in 16:7b-8a and 17:3-5.

Job rebukes the friends as comforters who cause trouble rather than assuage it. If he had the luxury of their freedom from suffering, perhaps he too might be content with shallow reassurance (16:1-5). The friends content themselves with the conventional position of the righteous. They look at Job's suffering and they retreat to their self-protecting theological certainties: Job is suffering; he must be godless. Job sees that there is not a truly wise person among any who insist on confirming their righteousness by denying his innocence (17:6-10).

As painful as the friends' scorn is for him, it is God who confronts Job as the real enemy (16:6-17). Eliphaz argued that it is the wicked who mount an assault against God (15:24-27). Job counters that it is God who wages war on the innocent. It is God whose teeth tear and grind the flesh like a savage beast (v. 9), who breaks and shatters (v. 12), splits open and *pours out* a person's guts without mercy (v. 13). Such ferocity against one who is gaunt and worn out (vv. 7-8) is incomprehensible. Such violence against one in whom there is no violence, whose cries to be heard are pure, is unconscionable (v. 17).

God's attack on Job is likened to murder. As when Cain murdered Abel and the spilled blood cried out to God for vengeance (Gen 4:8-10), so Job calls on the earth not to cover up the evidence of God's crimes against him (16:18-22). It is a desperate hope for a hearing that reaches to the heavens, where Job believes there is yet a *witness* who will stand in the breach between himself and God.

The identity of this witness is unclear. Is it God? If so, then Job in essence appeals to God *against* God. It is more likely that Job is looking to a third party (cf. 9:33), perhaps a heavenly counterpart to "the Satan," whose task is to search out the good as well as the evil (Habel 1985, 274-75). Perhaps the plea should be interpreted less literally, not for some specific person as witness, but as a hope that Job's own protests of innocence would ultimately be the witness that God could not ignore (e.g., 16:20: "My own lament is my advocate with God," JB; cf. Clines 1989, 390). In either case, it is clear that Job despairs of realizing such a witness. God has attacked him. The inevitable outcome is death. Job has cried out to the earth and the heavens for a justice in which only faith can believe (cf. Janzen 1985, 125).

With this mournful hope, Job surrenders once more to the pressing reality of his impending death (17:1-2, 11-16; cf. 7:17-21; 10:18-21; 14:18-22). He manages but a brief address to God (17:3-5). Abandoned by friends, and with no discernible hope of a witness in heaven, Job offers himself as the only guarantee he has of his innocence (17:3: "take my pledge to you; for who else will give their hand on my behalf?" [author trans.]).

18:1-21. Bildad. Like Eliphaz, Bildad begins his second speech to Job with a rebuke (vv. 2-4) which in turn prepares for a lengthy lecture on the fate of the wicked in a moral universe (vv. 5-21).

Bildad chides Job for insinuating that the friends are dumb cattle (cf. 12:7). It is Job, not God, who is tearing himself apart (v. 4; cf. 16:9). Should the moral order of the *earth* be abandoned, the *rock* of God's impenetrable governance be removed from its place, all because of Job's skewed assessment of things? Bildad knows well that governing ideologies, such as the belief in retributive justice, can sustain their corporate effectiveness only if they remain indifferent to the specifics of individual complaints.

The treatise on the wicked (vv. 5-21) focuses on the certain calamity that awaits them in God's design for the world. In their *tent* (abode) light is extinguished, their stride is shortened, they fall prey to their own schemes, their vitality is consumed by affliction and death (vv. 5-13). They are torn from their *tent* and marched off to the *king of terrors* (v. 14), a reference to Mot (*Death*), the god of the underworld in Canaanite mythology (vv. 14-21). From first to last the destiny of the wicked is portrayed as the inexorable consequence of a self-regulating moral universe. There is but one reference to God in Bildad's entire lecture (v. 21), a single, pointed reminder that it is God who sanctions the system Bildad is defending (cf. Clines 1989, 413).

19:1-29. Job. For the first time since chap. 3, Job does not address God. His anguished questions *How long?* (v. 2) and *Why?* (v. 22), ostensibly intended for God's unresponsive ears, are now directed to the friends. His speech remains focused on complaint (vv. 7-20) and the hope of vindication (vv. 23-27).

Job begins, as usual, by rebuking his friends (vv. 2-6). They have tormented him and broken him apart with arguments that reach to the very center of his existence (*nepeš*, v. 2; NRSV *me*), going beyond the abuse that even "the Satan" was permitted to inflict (cf. 2:5-6). Even if he has strayed, a possibility he does not concede (v. 4; cf. 7:20), his wanderings lodge only within himself; they do not reside with the friends that they should consider themselves the real victims in this ordeal. Job is the victim, and it is none other than God who has "bent" him (v. 6: *put me in the wrong*) with a perverted display of justice (against Bildad, cf. 8:3).

Job's complaint is that he has been violated, and when he has cried out for help, neither the friends nor God proved to be agents of justice for him (vv. 7-20). On the one hand, God and the troops of heaven have laid siege to him (vv. 8-12; cf. 16:9-14). They have surrounded his fragile "tent" as if it were a mighty fortress, blocking all escape routes as if Job were the enemy. Stripped of his *glory* and *crown* (v. 9), like a king imprisoned in his own city, Job is strategically demolished on all sides, until at last every vestige of hope is destroyed (cf. 14:7-9, 14-19).

On the other hand, God has also broken down Job's network of communal support (vv. 13-20). God has alienated everyone from Job: kinsfolk and acquaintances, intimate friends and guests at his table, servants, even his wife and young children. He calls to them, but they do not answer (v. 16). They shun and abandon him like a stranger and an alien. What Job needs from all who would truly befriend him is loyalty (cf. 6:14), especially now that *the hand of God has touched* him (v. 21). What he gets from his so-called friends, instead, is the same kind of relentless abuse that he receives from God.

With no sign of help in heaven or on earth, Job reaches out to a figure called *redeemer* (vv. 23-27). He *know(s)*, i.e., he firmly believes, that his *redeemer* lives. The traditional capitalization of this word in most versions (e.g., NRSV) has influenced a decidedly Christian interpretation of Job's hope as an appeal to a divine Savior, i.e., Jesus (cf. Rouillard 1983, 8-12). The Hebrew *gō 'ēl*, however, refers to the next of kin who has the responsibility of helping a family member in danger of losing possessions (Lev 25:25-34; Jer 32:6-15),their freedom (Lev 25:47-54), or life itself (Num 35:12, 19-27; Deut 19:6, 12; Josh 20:2-5, 9).

The identity of Job's *gō 'ēl* is much debated. Interpreted within the context of Job's previous references to an *umpire* ("arbitrator," 9:33) and a "witness" (16:8), the *redeemer* would appear to be someone whom Job hopes will at last rise on earth to speak in his defense (v. 27). It is possible that Job is appealing to God, even as his enemy and his assailant, to be at the same time his defense attorney. Given the larger context, however, it is likely that Job appeals to a third party to stand in the breach between God and himself, one who would stand at his side, not as adversary, but as ally.

Job's closing words return to a condemnation of the friends (vv. 28-29). They *persecute* (or "pursue") him, aping God's misdirected aggression towards him (cf. v. 22), as if he were the cause of his own misery (v. 28: *the root of the matter is found in him*). They should be afraid, because *there is a judgment* (v. 29) when all who stand in opposition to an innocent victim will suffer the consequences.

20:1-29. Zophar. Zophar begins conventionally with a rebuke of Job and an appeal to corrective wisdom (vv. 2-5). Like the other friends in this cycle, Zophar focuses on the fate of *the wicked* in a moral universe. His thesis, argued at length in vv. 6-29, is enveloped by two summarizing statements (vv. 5, 29): whatever the apparent prosperity of *the wicked*, their ultimate inheritance is determined by God.

With Bildad (8:8) and Eliphaz (15:18-19), Zophar appeals to ancient tradition as his source of corrective wisdom (v. 4). If Job *knows* (cf. 19:25) the truth about God's moral governance of the world, then Job must *know* that the euphoric shouts and joys of *the wicked* are fleeting (v. 5).

To substantiate his argument, Zophar employs a variety of images in order to enlighten Job on the fate of the evildoer. Although their pride and loftiness may extend to *the heavens* (v. 6), their final resting place is *in the dust* of the earth (v. 11). They simply vanish into nothingness, *like their own dung* (v. 7) or a bad *dream* (v. 8), leaving no trace of their haughty existence behind them (v. 9).

Verses 12-23 center on the imagery of eating. *Wickedness* is depicted as food that, although savory and *sweet*, is poisonous and induces vomiting. The focus is on the inherent consequences of eating spoiled goods, although Zophar makes it clear that God is the true source of the sick person's misery (v. 15). The appetite that causes sickness is linked to the wicked's abuse of *the poor* (vv. 19-23). Their greed for possessions not their own will stretch their bellies to the breaking point. While the interval between ingestion, or acquisition (on this correlation see Janzen 1985, 152-53), and pain is not immediate, Job may rest assured that God has filled their stomachs with divine *fierce anger* (v. 23).

The imagery of vv. 24-29 focuses on the violent nature of the wicked's defeat. Their downfall is inevitable. If they escape weapons of *iron*, they will be struck down with arrows of *bronze* that pierce their insides. If they manage to retract the arrow, they will eviscerate themselves. If they survive even this, they will be devoured by supernatural fire, and heaven and earth will rise up against them.

21:1-34. Job. In this last speech of the second cycle, Job turns from the focus on his own suffering (chaps. 16–17, 19) to dispute directly the friends' theology of retribution. He begins (vv. 1-6) and ends (v. 34) by assailing the friends' misguided efforts to offer *consolation* (v. 1). His arguments against them are prefaced with three questions (vv. 7, 17, 28), each of which challenges some previous claim of the friends, and to which Job responds with his own contradicting witness (vv. 7-16, 17-26, 27-33). In keeping with the steady deterioration in the divine-human dialogue that has characterized this cycle of speeches, Job does not address God.

Job implores the friends to *listen carefully* to his words (v. 2) and to *look* squarely at his suffering (v. 5). If they are to speak meaningfully to his pain, they must weep with his eyes and understand calamity through his experience. If they would really look at Job, rather than only speak *at him*, they would be appalled, and his shuddering flesh would silence their empty words. Job's complaint is with God. It is God's justice, not a mortal's failings, that is called into question when an innocent person is victimized.

Job begins his counterattack by challenging Zophar's contention that the wicked enjoy only temporary prosperity (cf. 20:5-11). If Zophar is right, why then do the wicked live long and happy lives (vv. 7-12) and go to their graves in peace (v. 13)? In contrast to Job who has suffered the loss of family, home, and possessions, the wicked enjoy the blessing of children, the security of their houses, and the fertility of their flocks. Their lives are accompanied by the music of unrestrained joy and celebration. They are confident in their powers to control their own destinies. They scoff at the idea that piety has anything to do with the rewards that one can attain in life (v. 14-15). Verse 16 may be read as an affirmation of the friends' certitude: "Indeed our prosperity is not in His hands" (Gordis 1965, 91; cf. Habel 1985, 321; Janzen 1985, 156).

Job's second challenge (vv. 17-26) centers on Bildad's claim that the *lamp of the wicked [is] put out* (cf. 18:5-6). How often, in truth, does calamity come to the wicked? In reality, it is the innocent, like Job, who are driven *like chaff* before the wind of God's anger, not the wicked (v. 18; cf. 13:25). The explanation that God's judgment is stored up for the wicked's children (v. 19) is meaningless. As far as the wicked are concerned, when persons die the question of their innocence or guilt goes to the grave with them (vv. 21-26). The silence of death mutes all questions of injustice on earth.

Job's third challenge (vv. 27-33) continues the argument against the claim that calamity befalls the wicked. The specific focus is on *the house of the* "great one" (NRSV *prince*) and the *tent [of] the wicked* (v. 28). The friends have repeatedly asserted that the houses of the wicked would not survive the destruction God has prepared for them (cf. 8:14-15; 15:28, 34; 18:15-21; 20:26-28). Job counters that *those who travel the roads* (v. 29) know better. The wicked do not receive what they deserve. Instead, their houses are spared the day of calamity, and when they die, their earthly estates are replaced by guarded memorials (v. 32).

In sum, Job turns the theology of the friends upside down. God does not cause the righteous to prosper; God does not punish the wicked. Reality affirms exactly the opposite. Theology that does not square with the facts of life is *hebel*, empty as air (v. 32; cf. the repeated use of this term in Ecclesiastes, e.g., 1:2). Worse still, when empty words of theology are foisted on the suffering, it is an act of fraud.

Third Cycle: The Breakdown of the Dialogue, 22:1–27:33

<u>22:1-30. Eliphaz.</u> In his last speech Eliphaz begins by posing a series of rhetorical questions designed to persuade Job of the undeniable linkage between his mortality and his sinfulness (vv. 2-5). These questions introduce two specific indictments against Job (vv. 6-11, 12-20) and a concluding summons to repentance (vv. 21-30).

In his previous speeches Eliphaz had stressed the fundamental distinction between God and humanity: God is incomparably righteous; humanity is inherently flawed and blemished (cf. 4:17-19; 15:14-16). Now Eliphaz pushes this observation to the extreme (vv. 2-5). Can mortals do anything to profit God? Does God derive any pleasure from a person's righteousness? Is God so concerned with the piety of individuals (or, to imagine the opposite, their impiety) that God stoops to enter into a lawsuit either for or against them? The prologue has made clear that God is in fact concerned with such matters. But Eliphaz' attention here is directed towards what separates God from humanity, not towards the exploration of whatever in the divine economy might bind them together. He concentrates on what for him is a more important issue: Job's sinfulness.

His first accusation (vv. 6-11) cites a number of moral crimes of which Job is allegedly guilty. Job has oppressed the weak and the poor and favored the powerful. No evidence is offered in support of the charges, either by Eliphaz or elsewhere in the Book of Job, and the reader must therefore consider them to be false. For Eliphaz, however, the immediate need is to press ahead with the guilty verdict (vv. 10-11).

The second accusation (vv. 12-20) attributes to Job theological error. Eliphaz presumes to quote Job's views on God's transcendence, namely, that God is so far removed *in the heavens*, God cannot know or judge accurately the affairs of humanity on earth (vv. 12-14). Such a misinterpretation of God's mysterious otherness places Job in the company of the wicked who revel in their misdeeds while asking *What can the Almighty do to us?* (v. 17). Again, Job's guilt is determined quite apart from the evidence of his own words, which consistently affirm God's ability to see and know humanity's deeds (cf. 7:19-20; 14:3; 16:9).

For Eliphaz the solution to Job's separation from God is clear. Job must yield to God and thus secure his peace and restoration (vv. 21-30). Yielding to God means accepting a contractual relationship with the deity (cf. 8:5-7; 11:13-20). *If* Job returns to God; *if* he removes deceit from his life; *if* he learns to replace his own lesser treasures with those of greater value God has in store for him (vv. 23-25); *then* Job will be restored. He will have pleasure in God (v. 26); his prayers will be answered (v. 27); and he will be rescued from the fate that awaits the wicked (vv. 29-30).

23:1-24:25. Job. Job abandons the failed dialogue with the friends and withdraws to the kind of interior reflection that characterized his words in chap. 3 (cf. Janzen 1985, 164-65). He longs for the presence of the absent God, with both confidence (23:3-7) and fear (23:8-16). His hope, however, begins and ends with lament (23:2, 17).

For Job, God's absence is the causal link to the injustices of *the wicked*. They freely abuse the poor and the powerless, and God pays no attention (24:1-12). They work their evil ways by day and by night (24:13-17). Job knows the argument that they will not finally succeed (24:18-20), but the evidence is that their success is assured by none other than God (24:21-25).

Eliphaz had summoned Job to submission before God. In his view, when one suffers, the only proper response is to pray for forgiveness (cf. 22:21-30). But when Job stretches out his hand in prayer it is heavy with a groaning that will not yield, and in his piety he offers rebellion and defiance (23:2: "my complaint is defiant" [cf. NRSV mg.]).

Job's compelling hope and lingering fear is that he might yet find God. On the one hand he eagerly awaits the encounter, because he remains confident that in God's presence an upright person (*yāšār*, v. 7; cf. 1:1) will be given the chance to argue without impunity. God would not use divine power to prosecute Job, but would pay attention to a just cause (23:3-7).

On the other hand, Job searches the far corners of the world, but God remains ever hidden (23:8-9). Job persists in believing that if he could find God's hiding place, his claim to be innocent would be vindicated (23:10-12). Yet in hiddenness, God retains exclusive control over divine decisions. "God is one" (23:13, NRSV *he stands alone*), and in this absolute oneness, God's desires effect decisions that are irrevocable (23:13-14). Before such overwhelming power, Job is terrified. The "face" from which he seeks justice (23:4; literally, "to his face"), is the "face" that strikes fear in the one who seeks a fair trial (23:15-16).

From the lament about the hiddenness of God, Job turns to the consequences of the absence of divine justice for the righteous and the wicked. Why do those who know God never see God's days of judgment? (24:1) When the timetable for the realization of justice on earth is as hidden as God, then injustice rules without restraint. The wicked snatch and seize at will. Like wild asses they prey on the defenseless, stripping them of the basic necessities of life. Victims are left to die, their only resource a wounded cry for help to a God who does not see that anything is wrong (24:2-12).

When there is no timetable for the execution of divine justice, then the governing cycles of the world are reversed. The wicked rebel against the light and embrace darkness as their accomplice in crime. Day's light is shut out; darkness of night beckons evildoers to their missions (24:13-17).

The relation of 24:18-25 to the speech as a whole is disputed. Because the content of these verses, particularly vv. 18-20, appears to contradict Job's position elsewhere, a number of commentators suggest that they comprise part of the missing speech of Zophar in the third cycle (cf. Pope 1965, 168-74; Rowley 1970, 210-13; Habel 1985, 358). If Job is the speaker, the verses likely represent a quotation of the friends' position (cf. Gordis 1978, 533; Janzen 1985, 169).

25:1-6. Bildad. In the final speeches of cycle three (chaps. 25–27) the steady alternating exchange between Job and the friends ends. Bildad's speech is disproportionately short (25:2-6); Job's response is long (chaps. 26–27), and in several places inconsistent with his previous positions (26:5-14; 27:13-24); and Zophar's final speech appears to be missing altogether. Many scholars attempt to restore order to these chapters by rearranging the text in order to lengthen Bildad's speech (by adding 26:5-14) and to reconstruct Zophar's speech (from 27:13-24; e.g., Pope 1965; Gordis 1978; Habel 1985). The option favored here, however, is to interpret the disarray of the text as a clue that the dialogue between Job and the friends has broken down (Janzen 1985, 171-86; cf. Good 1990, 281-90).

Bildad's words in 25:2-6 return to themes that have been well rehearsed in previous speeches. God is incomparably powerful, making peace in the cosmos with "awesome dominion" (NRSV *dominion and fear*, vv. 2-3; Gordis 1978, 274). If the luminescence of the moon and the stars cannot match the purity of God, how can a mere mortal, a maggot, a worm, expect to measure up? (vv. 4-6).

26:1-14. Job. To Bildad's affirmation of God's power, Job responds sarcastically by asking how such a claim can offer any comfort to him (vv. 2-4). He does not dispute his powerlessness and vulnerability before God. But how can a defense of God's incontestable power be construed as "help" or "assistance" or even "counsel" to one innocently victimized by God's prowess? What can possibly be the inspiration for such words?

Verses 5-14 comprise a hymn about divine power. On the surface they appear to be an elaboration on the theme of God's "awe" and "dominion" that is consistent with Bildad's argument in 25:2-6 (cf. Habel 1985, 370-75). Thus these verses are often reassigned as the completion of Bildad's speech. Yet the present configuration of the text attributes the words to Job and thus invites us to interpret them as indicative of his impatience with arguments he has heard already too often.

Job too can affirm God's control over the cosmos, but from his perspective divine dominion elicits cowed submission, not adoration and reverence (cf. Good

1990, 285). The "shades of the dead writhe" before God's power (v. 5, author trans.); *Sheol*—and its parallel identification, *Abaddon*—are exposed (v. 6). The heavenly canopy yields to God's stretching and hanging and wrapping and circum-scribing (vv. 7-10). The pillars of heaven "tremble" (v. 11), and the primordial opponents of God are smitten and defeated (v. 12-13). Indeed, such evidences of God's complete subjugation of the cosmos are but a whisper compared to the thunder of God's limitless power (vv. 13-14).

27:1-23. Job again. On the heels of his paean to God's dominating power, Job pauses, as if awaiting the retort of Zophar (note the modified introduction to the speech in v. 1). The text preserves no response from Zophar, and the third cycle is brought to conclusion with Job continuing to push his own position. He begins with an oath of innocence (vv. 2-6), followed by a curse against his enemy (vv. 7-12). Verses 13-23 conclude the speech with a description of the destiny of the wicked.

Job swears to his innocence by taking an oath on "the life of God" (vv. 2-6, author trans.). The oath is a potential self-curse that calls on God to bring down on him unspoken calamity if what he swears is not true. It is a "catalytic action" (Habel 1985, 380) designed to force a response from the one whose name has been invoked. Paradoxically, Job swears by the life of the one who has denied him justice and embittered his soul. Thus even in this act of desperation, Job remains true to his sense that God is both enemy and ally. The substance of the oath (vv. 4-6) asserts that if Job is guilty of falsehood or deceit, may God be vindicated and Job's punishment be as God decrees. But until his guilt is established, Job will not relinquish his claim to integrity and righteousness.

Job follows his oath with a curse upon his *enemy* (vv. 7-12). While in vv. 11-12 the address is to *you* (pl.), presumably meaning the friends, the reference to *enemy* in v. 7 is singular. The logical referent is God whom Job has repeatedly claimed was his real adversary (cf. 13:24; 16:9; 19:11). In his imprecation Job calls for his enemy (God, and to the extent that they side with God, the friends) to be accorded the same treatment as the wicked. With astonishing audacity Job dares to imagine that if his adversary could know the hopelessness of one whose cries for justice are not heard, then perhaps at last the way would be open to a fair resolution of his case.

Verses 13-23 describe the fate of the wicked in a fashion very similar to the speeches of the friends in cycle two. Because an affirmation of the wicked's downfall seems so out of character for Job, these verses are often reassigned to Zophar as his missing speech in the third cycle. The only attribution in the chapter, however, names Job as the speaker. If we follow this clue, then it is suggestive to imagine that Job has grown so weary of hearing the standard line on the punishment of the wicked that he preempts Zophar's anticipated tired rendition by delivering the speech himself (cf. Janzen 1985, 185-86).

Meditation on Wisdom, 28:1-28

This hymn on the inaccessibility of wisdom has been the focus of enormous scholarly scrutiny, but as yet there is no real consensus on important questions. Who is the speaker, Job, one of the friends, or God? Who is the author of the poem, and is the author the same one responsible for the rest of the book? Does the poem date to the earliest stages of the book, or is it an independent and later insertion? And what is the function of the poem in the Book of Job? To each of these questions there are multiple answers and speculations.

In the absence of consensus on the poem's authorship and date, it is wise to concentrate on its function in the present context. And lacking any definitive indication of a change in speaker, it is plausible to attribute the poem to the last mentioned speaker in the book, namely, Job.

The poem serves as a fitting end to the dialogue between Job and the friends, and a key transition towards what will be explored in the rest of the book. As a closure to the dialogues, the poem ends with a reaffirmation of the importance of the *fear of the Lord* and turning away *from evil* (v. 28), virtues the prologue has repeatedly assigned to Job (cf. 1:1, 8; 2:3). These virtues are then further identified as the key to wisdom and understanding. But if the poem serves to reaffirm Job's piety, it also challenges the simple identification of piety with justice. Job *fears God* and *turns away from evil* (1:8), yet Job is suffering. Clearly there must be more to come before a critical challenge to the traditional understanding of wisdom's rewards can be resolved.

The poem divides into three major sections, vv. 1-14, 15-22, and 23-28, each of which explores the *place* of wisdom (vv. 1, 6, 12, 20, 23) and the *path* (or "way," vv. 7-8, 13, 23) towards its acquisition (cf. Habel 1985, 392-94). Two questions provide the refrain that guides the search for wisdom (vv. 12, 20) and points in the direction of the right answer: God understands the "way" and knows the "place" of wisdom (v. 23).

28:1-14. Wisdom's inaccessibility. The poem begins with an affirmation (vv. 1-6) but ends with a question that negates the possibilities of finding wisdom (vv. 12-14). There is a *mine* (lit., a "coming out place") and a *place* where the earth hides its precious metals of *silver, gold, iron,* and *copper* (vv. 1-2). Although the path to these precious stones cannot be discerned by the sharpest vision of any *bird* or the rovings of even the mightiest of beasts (vv. 7-8), the ingenuity of human miners can achieve relative success (vv. 1-6, 9-11). Miners can open shafts, suspend themselves in the bowels of earth's deep darkness, overturn mountains by their roots, and cut channels to reveal precious things ordinary eyes can never behold.

But even with such skills, mortals cannot discern the *place* of *wisdom* (vv. 12-14). They may know the way to the depths of the earth, but when they arrive at the end of their probe, they hear the primordial sources of the watery abyss say, wisdom is not here.

28:15-22. Wisdom's incomparable value. A catalogue of thirteen precious materials is listed in vv. 15-19. Before each item there is a negative particle (seven times), indicating that whatever the value of this particular treasure, it cannot equal the greater worth of wisdom.

If wisdom cannot be found through human ingenuity, and if it cannot be acquired through buying and selling precious commodities, where then is wisdom to be found? (vv. 20-22).Once more the question introduces a negative response. Wisdom is not only inaccessible and incomparable; it is also hidden. Even *Abaddon* (i.e., *Sheol*, cf. 26:6) and Death (*māwet*, an allusion to the Canaanite God Mot, the god of the underworld; cf. 18:13) have only hearsay knowledge of this most prized possession.

28:23-28. The way to wisdom. The final section offers the answer to the questions posed by the refrains of vv. 12 and 20. God *understands* and *knows* the *way* (or "path") to wisdom. Surprisingly, this answer does not affirm that wisdom is an inherent attribute of God. Rather, just as mortals "dig out" (*ḥqr*, 28:3) the treasures hidden in the depths of the earth, so God "digs out" (*ḥqr*, v. 27; NRSV *searches out*) wisdom as the primordial ordering principle of the world. In the act of weighing the wind, measuring the waters of the cosmos, decreeing the limits of rain and thunder, God searches out and establishes the place of wisdom in governing the whole of the created order. Thus wisdom both precedes God (cf. Prov 8:22-31) and is employed by God in the primordial creative act.

God attains wisdom through direct experience. Mortals, however, possess wisdom only derivatively. God alone discloses (*'mr*, v. 28, "say") what the *deep*, *the sea*, *Abaddon*, and *Death* can never make known (*'mr*, vv. 14, 22, "say"). Wisdom as revealed by God consists not in striving for hidden knowledge, but in piety, specifically in *fearing God* and in *turning away from evil*, the very qualities that, according to God, define Job (cf. 1:8; 2:3).

The reader knows from the prologue that, by God's definition, Job is unfailingly innocent. Now the reader is instructed to understand that, by God's definition, Job is a recipient of the divine gift of wisdom. Job is innocent and wise, yet besieged by God. God is unassailably righteous and unfathomably wise. Given these truths that the book has brought to the fore, what is to be the relationship between God and this suffering servant? The dialogue with the friends over this dilemma has ended. But the dialogue that will push the dilemma to its farthest extremes is yet to begin.

Job's Summation, 29:1–31:40

Job closes the dialogues as he began them, in internal deliberation. But much has transpired since Job's opening soliloquy. In chap. 3 his pain had driven him to despair of life and to long for the relief of death. In these closing chapters Job refuses to relinquish the truth about either his integrity (chap. 29) or his pain (chap. 30). Integrity and pain are now forged into a renewed oath of innocence (chap. 31;

cf. 27:2-6) that challenges God to appear at last for the trial which Job has sought (cf. 23:3-7).

Declaration of Past Integrity, 29:1-25

29:1-10. Past status. Job opens with a declaration that reaffirms his past status with God (vv. 2-6) and in the community (vv. 7-10). He remembers his "autumn days" when he enjoyed both the presence and the friendship of God (v. 4). Under the "lamp" and the "light" of God's protection and sustenance, Job experienced the blessing of children all around (v. 5) and prosperity abundant (v. 6). His honored status was acknowledged by the community. When Job took his place at the city gate to adjudicate the disputes of his peers, they would rise in recognition of his stature, and their words would cease in willing submission to his authority (vv. 7-10).

29:11-17. Administration of justice. His recognized authority was confirmed in his administration of justice in the community (vv. 11-17). Every ear that heard of Job's decisions blessed him, and every eye that witnessed his counsel encouraged him. Contrary to Eliphaz's charge (cf. 22:6-11), Job never failed to respond to the cries of the needy and the disenfranchised. His justice was directed specifically to those who are vulnerable to abuse: *the poor, the orphan, the widow* (vv. 12-13), *the blind, the lame* (v. 15). Even the cause of those whom Job did not know was investigated (v. 16). Indeed, Job did not merely dispense justice, he embodied it, clothing himself with *righteousness* (*sdq*), so that *justice* (*mišpāt*) was like his *robe* and his *turban* (v. 14).

29:18-20. Hope. His devotion to justice became a reason for hope. He had thought that he would be granted the blessing of dying in his nest, and like the immortal *phoenix* (on this imagery see Gordis 1978, 320-21), his honored reputation (NRSV *glory*) would be ever secure.

29:21-25. Leadership and compassion. Job's position in the community was tied not only to his administration of justice. It was also the result of his unfailing compassion and concern for his neighbors' general welfare. The community looked to him with the same need they had for the spring rains. Job smiled upon them with favor. Even when they would not believe, they could not extinguish the guiding light of his countenance. Rather than abandon them to their own resources, Job chose their course for them. *Like a king among his troops* (v. 25), Job was their leader and their comforter.

Job's declaration of integrity serves in the interest of more than just self-flattery. It also continues indirectly his challenge to God. Job asserts with unmitigated confidence that he has been the ideal judge. He has heard the cries of those who look to him for justice, and he has responded by breaking the stranglehold of the wicked on their helpless prey. Can God claim as much? Job has faithfully presided over the welfare of those entrusted to him, providing for their needs and comforting them when they mourn. Can God claim to have offered the same faithfulness to those who look to the heavens for their guidance and consolation? Job has been both judge and king for his community. Who will be judge and king for Job?

Acknowledgment of Present Misery, 30:1-31

30:1-8. Public scorn. If once Job had been among the honored of society (chap.29), now he is the object of public scorn. To add insult to injury, those who now find him contemptible are themselves outcasts of society. They are compared to animals who, driven out from their community, live in caves and bray in the bushes. Job refers to them as the children of the "foolish" and the "nameless" (v. 8). As fools (*nābāl*), they share the moral and religious blindness (cf. Ps 14:1) attributed to Job's wife (cf. 2:10). As nameless ones, they have no identity, no recognized value in society.

30:9-15. Public hostility. The perspective shifts from the character of Job's antagonists to their actions. Job is the "butt of their jokes" (v. 9), like one ostracized from the community and spit upon whenever he breaches the strictures of their alienation. Not content with ridicule, these opponents add all-out attack (vv. 12-15). With the efficiency of an army they build roads for the siege, they break through Job's defenses, and they put him to rout. Such abuse is possible, Job charges, because God has in fact loosened his "cord" (perhaps "tent cord," cf. 4:21; perhaps *bowstring* [as NRSV]; cf. Ps 11:2), leaving him defenseless before his attackers (v. 11).

30:16-19. God, the assailant. Job's real enemy, however, is God. Days of affliction take hold of Job, and pain chews on his bones throughout the night without relief, but it is God who seizes him with power beyond resistance (v. 18, reading God as the implied subject; cf. Pope 1965, 195). God has flung him into the mud, and he has been reduced to nothingness, *like dust and ashes* (v. 19).

The phrase *dust and ashes* recalls Job's previous posture of mourning (2:8). On that occasion Job accepted his suffering as the incomprehensible consequence of God's sovereignty. Now his assignment to *dust and ashes* is interpreted as an act of divine violence, as senseless as the wanton abuse heaped on him by the rogues of society. Job will make one further reference to his position in *dust and ashes* (42:6), a final response to the nothingness that defines his life.

30:20-31. Cry for justice. These verses focus on Job's cry for justice (*šw '*, vv. 20, 24, 28). Job cries to God (vv. 20-23), but there is no answer. God has become the *cruel one* (v. 21: *'akzār*), raging against him with the same ferocity attributed to *Leviathan*, the primordial monster (*'akzār*; cf. 41:10 [MT 41:2]). In contrast to God's cruelty, Job recalls his own compassion for those who cried for help in a time of need (vv. 24-27). Now Job cries for justice *in the assembly*, but his cries are as futile as the doleful sounds of *jackals . . . ostriches* (vv. 24-28). In a world where cries for justice go unheeded both by God and the sanctioned system, evil replaces good, darkness preempts light (v. 26), and instruments for happy occasions accompany mourning and weeping (v. 31; cf. 21:12).

Oaths of Innocence, 31:1-40

31:1-4. Declaration of covenant fidelity. Job's declaration of innocence derives from the *covenant* he has made with his *eyes* (v. 1). It is a covenant pledge that Job has sworn to avoid even the appearance of wrongdoing. He will not even *look on a virgin*, though to do so would in itself be no crime. His decision to master not only his actions but also his attitudes was based on his conviction that there is indeed a fixed destiny for the wicked. The rhetorical questions of vv. 3-4 both state this conviction and hint at Job's uncertainty about whether it continues to apply.

31:5-34, 38-40. Oaths of innocence. In support of his assertion of innocence, Job lists a catalogue of sins from which he insists he is free. The exact number of sins that he disavows is difficult to determine (proposals range from eleven to sixteen), in part because a variety of different literary forms are mixed together throughout the list: questions (vv. 14-15); statements (vv. 6, 11-12, 18, 23, 28, 30, 32); and self-imprecations.

The imprecations proper follow two patterns. The traditional form consists of an "if (not)" (*'im*) phrase (protasis), which presents a crime or sin, followed by a "result" clause (apodosis), which stipulates the punishment expected. In other words, "If I have done A . . . then let B happen to me." This pattern is followed in vv. 7-8, 9-10, 21-22, and 38-40. A variation of the traditional pattern has an "if" clause without the "result" clause. In these cases the conditional statement about sin/crime is assumed to be false. Thus the incomplete statement "If I have done A . . . " is an emphatic way of saying "I have *not* done A." This pattern is more frequent in Job's speech, occurring in vv. 5, 13, 16-17, 19-20, 24, 25, 26-27, 29, 31, 33-34.

The sins stipulated in these two patterns cover a wide range of both actions (e.g., adultery, vv. 9-10; withholding food from the poor, vv. 16-17; exploiting the land, vv. 38-40) and attitudes (e.g., rejoicing in the calamity of others, v. 29; hypocrisy, v. 33). Interlaced with these disclaimers of sin are a number of personal statements that express Job's abhorrence of the sins he is denying (v. 11), his intimate friendships with the disadvantaged whom he insists he has not abused (v. 18), and his understanding that his ethical purity is fundamentally an extension of his relationship with God (vv. 6, 14-15, 23).

Job's oaths of innocence portray him as the epitome of the ethical person. While the prologue affirms that Job is *blameless and upright, one fearing God and turning away from evil* (1:1, 8; 2:3), this summation of his innocence defines in concrete ways how these virtues manifest themselves in Job's life.

31:35-37. Final plea. Job affixes his signature to these oaths of innocence with a final plea that God will address his case in court (vv. 35-37). His plea begins with the formula "Oh, that" (*mi yitten*), an expression used more frequently in Job than in any other book. It is an expression that introduces Job's most important hopes (e.g., 6:8; 14:13; 19:23; 23:3; 29:2; cf. Habel 1985, 347). In this final plea Job's hope is that God, his *adversary* at law (*'iš rîb*, v. 35; Habel 1985, 438), will not only hear and answer him, but will also submit to the court a written document.

The content of this document is not specified. It may constitute a formal indictment (Gordis 1978, 355; Fohrer 1974, 3) or a writ of acquittal (Pope, 1965, 209; Habel 1985, 439). This document Job will wear as a "paper crown" (Habel 1985, 439) when he at last meets God in court. He will come with his own self-assertion of innocence and with this formal attestation, which will either exonerate him or be proven once and for all as an empty indictment.

He will address *the Almighty*, not as the guilty one who must relinquish all arguments before an inscrutable judge (as the friends would have him do), but as *a prince* (v. 37; cf. 29:11-17, 21-25) whose royal status emboldens him to approach God as an equal (cf. Good 1990, 316; Perdue 1991, 193). Although God may number all his steps (v. 4), Job will assume a joint responsibility for "numbering" (*spr;* NRSV *give an account*) his own steps before the God who sits in judgment over him. As a measure of his courage in demanding this appearance before God, Job places these strong statements within the context of the self-imprecations that have defined the center of his speech. *If* Job does not/cannot approach God (cf. v. 36, *'im lō '*, lit. "If I do not...") as one who has joint responsibility for accounting for his ways, *then* may he suffer the consequences that God has in store for him.

Speeches of Elihu, 32:1–37:24

Introduction of Elihu, the "Answerer," 32:1-22

32:1-5. Introduction. With Job's words ended, the narrative anticipates the long-awaited answer from God. An answer is offered in chaps. 32–37, but it comes from Elihu, not from God. The speeches commence with a lengthy "throat-clearing introduction" (Good 1990, 321). Not until 33:1 will Elihu address Job directly.

Although the introduction provides more information about Elihu than has been given about the other friends, it is not really family credentials that define him. It is his anger (four times in vv. 2-5) and his concern with the *answer* (three times in vv. 1, 3, 5) that must be obtained in the case against Job. Ten of the sixty occurrences of the root *answer* in Job appear in this chapter (cf. Habel 1985, 445). Elihu is angry with Job because Job thought himself more righteous than God (v. 2). Elihu is angry with the friends because they could offer no convincing answers to Job, thus making it appear God, not Job, was guilty (vv. 3, 4).

32:6-10. Elihu's claim to knowledge. Elihu commences with an admission of the discrepancy between his youth and the age of the friends. Normally, with many years comes wisdom. But upon listening to the friends, Elihu concludes that wisdom and understanding are not synonymous with advanced age. It is rather the spirit, *the breath of the Almighty* (v. 8), within a person that discloses understanding. Elihu claims to possess this spirit (cf. v. 18). He will speak; the imperative to listen now falls to others (v. 10).

32:11-16. Elihu's impatience. These verses begin and end with a reference to Elihu's "waiting" futilely for the friends' wisdom. Elihu has listened to their *words* and their *wise sayings* (v. 11), and he has found them lacking. The friends do not have the necessary wisdom to serve as the "arbiter" of Job's case (v. 12, *mōkiāh*; NRSV *one that confutes*). When Job had sought someone to arbitrate, he had envisioned someone who would lay hands on both God and himself in order to facilitate a fair and just legal proceeding (cf. 9:33). What Elihu intends, however, is one who will answer Job (v. 12b; cf. 14, 15, 16), that is, prove him wrong.

32:17-22. Elihu's compulsion to speak. Elihu describes himself as so full of *spirit* (or "wind," v. 18; cf. v. 8) that his belly is bloated. The only relief is to belch forth words. Such enthusiasm for speaking, however, identifies him more closely with the fool than the wise person. Ironically, belching forth windy words is precisely the criticism that Eliphaz used to challenge Job's claim to wisdom (cf. 15:2). That Elihu claims a status he will not demonstrate is further indicated by his pretended impartiality (vv. 21-22). Despite his assertion, his speech thus far is replete with references to his undisguised anger at the friends and at Job, and his conclusion that neither has any answer that is worth listening to.

The Case against Job, 33:1-33

33:1-7. The challenge to Job. Elihu reasserts his legitimacy as Job's "Answerer" (vv. 3-4), and challenges Job to enter into a disputation with him. He summons Job to prepare his case and take his stand *before him* (v. 5). Job had summoned God to appear in court to hear the case he had prepared, and had challenged God to speak so that Job might refute the charges against him (cf. 13:17-28). Now Elihu presumes to stand in for God, and at the same time he reverses the ground rules for the confrontation Job has sought. Elihu will issue the summons to Job to appear in court; Elihu will be the prosecutor (and judge), Job the defendant.

33:8-13. The charges against Job. Elihu cites two charges that Job has levelled against God: Job is innocent, yet God treats him as an enemy (vv. 8-11); and God does not answer Job (vv. 12-13). Elihu counters that *in this* Job is not right, and as refutation he states simply that God is greater than humans (v. 12; the issue of God's justice will be addressed more fully in chaps. 34–37). The focal point of Elihu's challenge is Job's accusation that God does not answer him (v. 13; cf. 9:2-4).

33:14-30. Defense of God's answering. Elihu offers a lengthy defense of God's multiple ways of answering people, even if they do not discern what God is saying. First, God speaks through dreams that warn against pride and seek to turn people from their misdeeds (vv. 15-18). Second, God speaks through pain and suffering (vv. 19-22) that serve to "chasten" (*hûkah*) and put one on trial (*ryb*, v. 19; NRSV *with continual strife*). Further, for those tested by suffering, there is an *angel* (lit. "messenger," *mal 'āk*), an "interpreter" (NRSV *mediator*, *mēlîs*), who gives instructions about morality (v. 23), and obtains for the afflicted a ransom and a restoration (vv. 23-26).

These multiple ways of divine communication are framed by an ascending numeration (v. 14, *in one way, and in two*; v. 29, *twice, three times*), which serves to emphasize God's persistence in seeking to speak to people (cf. Good 1990, 324). The purpose of God's efforts is to redeem humanity *from the Pit*, that is, from death (v. 30; cf. vv. 18, 24, 28).

33:31-33. Summation. Elihu extends an apparent invitation to Job to respond. But it is more instruction than invitation. Three times he orders Job to *listen* or *pay heed* to him; twice the instruction is *be silent*. Although Job is given an opening, it is a small one, and it closes quickly as Elihu makes it clear that *he* will address the issue of what is Job's "right" (*sdq*, v. 32).

Defense of God's Justice, 34:1–35:16

The superscriptions at 34:1 and 35:1 introduce these chapters as two separate speeches of Elihu. In terms of their content, however, these chapters share a common concern: the defense of God's justice. In chap. 34 the focus is on Job's charge that he is innocent and that God is in the wrong. Chapter 35 centers on Job's claim that whether he is innocent or guilty, it makes no difference to God. Elihu disputes these charges with lengthy and often entangled theological argumentation, and concludes that in both accusations Job has spoken *without knowledge* (34:35; 35:16).

34:1-9. Summons. Elihu opens with a summons to his peers, the wise and learned ones (vv. 2, 10, 34), to heed his words. Together they will choose what constitutes *justice* (*mišpāt*) and what is *good* (*tôb*) or "legally defensible" (Habel 1985, 481). To put the matter before this tribunal, Elihu cites two of Job's allegations against God (vv. 5-9): Job is innocent, and yet God has denied him justice (*mišpāt*; vv. 5-6); and there is no profit in being in God's favor (v. 9).

Elihu's prejudice in making the case against Job, however, is only thinly disguised. His representation of Job's position borders on being caricature rather than quotation. The first citation seems to be a reference to Job's argument in 27:2, although in Job's mouth the charge is set within the context of an "if-then" self-imprecation. The citation in v. 9 connects with several places in Job's argument (cf. 9:22; 21:7-12); however, the words that Elihu uses are closer to what Eliphaz has said (22:2; cf. Gordis 1978, 244; Good 1990, 142). Adding further to the impression that Elihu is anything but impartial is the insertion in vv. 7-8 of unsubstantiated allegations against Job.

34:10-30. Defense of God's justice. God is not wrong (v. 10), Elihu announces, and God does not pervert the cause of justice (*mišpāt*, v. 12). Two virtues of the divine judge, justice (v. 11) and incomparable power (vv. 13-15), become the center of Elihu's defense in vv. 16-30.

God is both "just" (*sdq*) and powerful (*kabbîr*, v. 17; NRSV *righteous, mighty*). God is certainly just, because God sees all the deeds of humans and faithfully enacts the justice of retribution where it is needed (vv. 21-22, 25-28). And God is just as certainly a judge with inscrutable power, because God's decisions do not require/permit the consultation of others (vv. 23-24). Who will say that God is wrong? When God is absent, who will be able to discern anything different? (v. 29).

34:31-37. Summons to confession. It is Job who must reassess his position, not Elihu, and the court awaits his response. Once more the invitation for Job to speak is more formal than substantive (cf. 33:31-33). As Elihu rushes on to say, the verdict against Job is already in (vv. 34-37). The intelligent and the wise in Elihu's audience will certainly have already concluded that Job's accusations are *without knowledge* (34:35; 35:16).

35:1-4. The advantages and disadvantages of piety. Elihu rehearses Job's position on the advantages and disadvantages of piety. Again Elihu's representation of Job's words is skewed. Job had not argued that he was "more righteous than God" (v. 2, author trans.); rather, he had asked rhetorically (and despairingly), *How can a mortal be just before God?* (9:2). It is Eliphaz who comes closest to the words Elihu assigns to Job (cf. 4:17). And Job had not asked specifically, "How does it benefit you, what do I gain if I avoid sin?" (v. 3, author trans.). It is Eliphaz who uses the language that Elihu cites, and he does so to deny that Job's righteousness makes any difference to God (22:2-4).

35:5-16. Defense of God's relationship with humanity. Elihu offers two observations concerning God's relationship with humanity. First, he appeals to God's transcendence (vv. 5-8). As high as the heavens and the clouds are above the earth, so God is above anything that humans do or do not do in their creaturely ways. God is not affected personally by any individual's actions for good or evil. Goodness and evil redound to the virtue or the disgrace of humans, but God gains or loses nothing either way.

Secondly, Elihu explores the allegation that divine transcendence masks God's sinister silence (vv. 9-13). That some cry out to God for relief but receive no answer does not constitute evidence against God's concern for humanity. The truth of divine silence is that human entreaties are often unauthentic. God will not reward deceit masquerading as piety. On what ground then does Job dare equate God's silence with injustice? Job's arguments are empty and his accusations against God are *without knowledge* (vv. 14-16).

A Second Defense of God's Justice:
The Majesty and Order of Creation, 36:1–37:24

36:1-15. The pedagogy of divine affliction. Elihu returns to the theme of God's incomparable power (cf. 34:10-30). God is *mighty* (*kabbîr*, twice in v. 5), a virtue that he equates with divine justice (vv. 5-15). God governs by giving death to the wicked and justice (*mišpāt*) to the oppressed. If some are *bound in fetters* and *caught in the cords of affliction* (v. 8), it is only the corrective discipline of God who seeks to instruct them about the error of their ways (cf. 33:19-22). Espousing the same kind of contractual relationship with God that the friends have advanced (cf. 8:4-7; 11:13-20; 22:21-30), Elihu contends that the afflicted are afforded two options: *if* they listen and serve God, they can complete their lives in prosperity and pleasantness; *if not*, they will die in ignorance (vv. 11-12).

36:16-25. Warning and summons. It is these two options that Job has before him. Elihu suggests that Job is tilting toward the latter rather than the former (vv. 16-21). He is obsessed with his case and his pursuit of justice, as if by the strength of his own efforts he could remedy his distress. Elihu warns that such misplaced passion will turn Job toward evil, not toward God.

It is to God that Job is summoned (vv. 22-25). It is God who is exalted in power; God who has no peer either as teacher or as judge. Before such incontestable power, the proper response is submission (cf. 36:11 *'ābad*, *serve*) and praise, not rebellion.

36:26–37:13. Praise of God's cosmic governance. The praise of which Elihu speaks is defined in terms of the majesty and order of God's creation. The testimony to God's governance is *in rain* (vv. 27-29), and in the thunder and *the lightning* (36:30–37:4) through which God both judges the people and sustains the created order. It is in the winter storms, the snow, the rains, the frost, which serve as signs for all to see, humans and animals alike, that God is at work regulating the habitable world in keeping with divine purposes (vv. 5-13).

37:14-22. Closing challenge. Elihu addresses Job with a series of questions that seek his compliance with the praise he has modelled. Does Job know how to bring forth the lightning or how to balance the clouds in the sky? Can Job stretch out the heavens? The certain answer to these questions is "No." If Job would consider the wondrous witness to God's control of the world, he would realize that his pretensions toward equality with God are ridiculous.

37:23-24. Summation. Elihu returns to the themes he has emphasized: God's power, justice, and righteousness. To these he adds the affirmation, consistent with Job's own charge, that God remains inaccessible to humans. For Elihu, as for the friends, these virtues summon mortals like Job to fear or reverence (*yir'eh*, v. 24).

Fear and reverence do indeed characterize Job, according to the prologue (cf. 1:1, 8; 2:3); however, with the conclusion of the dialogues, it is clear that the friends define these qualities very differently than Job. The debate has ended, but the resolution concerning the true definition of piety before God is still pending.

Dialogue between Job and God, 38:1–42:6

God's First Address: The Order of the Cosmos, 38:1–40:2

38:1-3. God's appearance and summons. The God who addresses Job is now called "the LORD" (Heb. YHWH), rather than *Shaddai* or *El*, the names used throughout the dialogues with the friends. On the one hand, the encounter with YHWH indicates that Job, like Moses at Sinai, will be granted a personal appearance of God. On the other hand, the imagery accompanying this revelation of presence suggests that YHWH confronts Job with the force of one who comes to do battle. Before the one who speaks with hurricane-force winds, Job is to "gird his loins like a hero," that is, he is to prepare like a warrior for the encounter that is coming. The hopelessness of Job's position, however, is apparent from the outset. In the contest that looms ahead, the one who is *without knowledge* (v. 2) is summoned to "give knowledge" (v. 3; NRSV *declare*).

The agenda for YHWH's initial confrontation with Job is set with the first question (v. 2). Job had charged that God's design, or purpose, for the world was chaotic and destructive (12:13-25; cf. 9:5-9; 10:8-14). YHWH rebuts this accusation by asking, *Who is this* who in ignorance has cast darkness over divine intentions?

The question centers not on Job's identity, but on his pretense to having a knowledge commensurate with God's about the purpose of the world (cf. Good 1990, 343). Thus Job is summoned, not to receive answers (cf. 13:22), but to be interrogated.

38:4-38. The design of the physical world. With a rhetorical sweep across the far regions of the universe, YHWH summons Job to consider the divine plan for the world: *the foundation of the earth* (vv. 4-7); the waters of the sea (vv. 8-11); the *morning* light (vv. 12-15); the watery depths of the netherworld (vv. 16-18); light and darkness (vv. 19-21); the meteorological mysteries of heaven (snow and hail, vv. 22-25; rain, vv. 25-27; dew, frost, and ice, vv. 28-30); the constellations (vv. 31-33); and *the clouds* (vv. 34-38). YHWH questions not only whether Job was present at the beginning of creation (vv. 4-7, 8-11) but also whether Job can demonstrate power over and knowledge of the intricacies of the created order. The intended, yet unspoken, answer to these questions is "No, I cannot," "No, I do not know."

It is clear from this survey of the complexities of the world that God's perspective on order differs from that of the friends and Job. The world is stable, secured by divinely established foundations (v. 4), *measurements* (v. 5), boundaries (vv. 8, 10), places (vv. 12, 19), times (v. 23), and *ordinances* (v. 33). Within this order, the forces of chaos and evil are controlled, but not eliminated (vv. 8-11; 12-15). Light and darkness, good and evil, regularity and randomness, are held together in unyielding tension (cf. Habel 1985, 534; Good 1990, 348). In the midst of such precision and ambiguity, the created order both celebrates (v. 7) and submits (e.g., v. 35) to the divine plan.

38:39–39:30. The design of the animal kingdom. Five groups of animals are cited, along with the characteristics of each that bind them to God: *the lion* and *the raven* and their need for food (38:39-41); *the mountain goats* and *the calving . . . deer* and their reproductive cycles (39:1-4); *the wild ass* and *the wild ox* and their freedom from domestication (39:5-12); *the ostrich* and *the horse* and their speed (39:13-25); and *the hawk* and *the eagle* and the wisdom by which they soar to the heights (39:26-30).

In the animal world, as in the physical world, God embraces disparity within a divine symbiosis. There are *wisdom* (39:26) and stupidity (39:17), courage (39:22) and timidity (39:1-4), domestication (39:19-25) and wildness (e.g., 39:5-8). And within the whole there is an acknowledged dependency on God (38:41) and a submission to the authority of the master designer (39:9).

Again God questions both Job's knowledge of this design and his power over its details. Again the answers expected are "No, I do not know," and "No, I cannot display such power."

40:1-2. Closing summons. God ends this defense of the world's design by resuming the opening challenge to Job. Will the one who is bringing suit against *the Almighty* "instruct" (the verb may also mean "chastise") God in the ways of the world? The time has come for the one who would argue with God (*môkîah*; cf. 13:3, 15) to answer.

Job's First Response: *I Am . . . Small*, **40:3-5**

Job's response to God's lengthy discourse is not to join with creation in submission and celebration, but to retreat to silence. His opening words are curiously ambiguous. The translation, *I am . . . small* is often interpreted as an indication that Job has been humbled, and therefore, in recognition of his insignificance, he will not attempt to instruct the creator of the world (e.g., Rowley 1970, 326; Gordis 1978, 466).

The verb employed here, however, may just as easily convey complaint rather than confession (e.g., Habel 1985, 549). To be *small* is to be "trivial," "of little weight," or in a more disparaging sense, "to be held in contempt" by another person. When interpreted as complaint, Job's response is consonant with his previous posture toward God. Job has repeatedly complained that he is no match for God's incontestable power (e.g., 12:13-25). He may now be understood to complain further that since his encounter with God has only proven that God despises him, there is no point in proceeding with a mock dialogue.

Whether an indication of defiance or humility, Job's response is certainly not a simple "I have sinned" or "I am wrong," as the friends and Elihu have prescribed. Job claps his hand to his mouth in amazement at what he has beheld in this encounter with God (cf. 21:5; 29:9). He has had his say. God has interrogated him into silence. From Job's perspective, there is little point in proceeding further.

God's Second Address:
The Just Governance of the Cosmos, 40:6–41:34 (MT 41:26)

40:6-14. The summons to govern like God. Once more from the whirlwind, YHWH summons Job to prepare for confrontive interrogation (vv. 7-8). The issue is no longer the design of the cosmos but instead its governance. The initial question states the matter in stark either-or terms: "Will you annul my justice (*mišpāṭ*), make me guilty in order that you may be innocent?" The question implies that Job has understood justice to require a clean differentiation between guilt and innocence. If Job is innocent, as he claims, then God must be guilty. The friends share this assumption about justice; however, in Job's case they interpret the situation differently: If God is innocent, as they insist, then Job must be guilty. The question that YHWH now puts to Job (and we may assume to the friends as well) focuses on this latter assumption. In order for there to be justice, must there be a guilty party and an innocent one, a wrong that is countered by a right, evil that can be, and is, clearly separated from good?

From the question about guilt and innocence, YHWH turns to a second question that sets the issue of justice within the context of power (vv. 9-14). Can Job match God's power, can he exert authority comparable to God's own *arm* and *voice*? God summons Job to clothe himself in the regalia of a king and administer the justice that he claims is God's responsibility. He is invited to unleash his anger on the wicked, to humble them, subdue them, and trample them where they stand. Having intervened directly to judge them, he is to complete the swift processes of justice by delivering them to the netherworld where they will be bound forever. If Job can execute his own standard of justice on *all* the world's wicked (cf. vv. 11, 12), then YHWH will acknowledge Job's authority, and concede that indeed Job's own right hand has won a victory.

Is this a sarcastic invitation on God's part, a rhetorical taunting of Job's presumption of royal status (29:21-25; cf. Janzen 1985, 244), or a serious offer to recognize Job's authority? Is it a concession from God that stamping out wickedness in the world is indeed a difficult and unfinished agenda, even for God (cf. Brenner 1981, 133)? Is the whole scenario merely hypothetical (cf. Good 1990, 358)? The tone of God's speech is unclear. Yet within the context of the remainder of the address, there is little doubt that in the matter of power, God has no equal.

40:15-24. Behemoth. The remainder of God's address focuses on the creatures *Behemoth* (40:15-24) and *Leviathan* (41:1-34 [MT 40:25-41:26]), mythical monsters of the land and sea who symbolize the primordial forces of chaos and evil. *Behemoth*, like Job, is one of God's creatures (v. 15), and hence shares with Job a common status before the creator of the world (cf. Habel 1985, 565). What distinguishes this creature from Job, however, is its power (vv. 16-19) and its dominion over the forces of nature (vv. 20-24). With bones like *tubes of bronze* and limbs like *bars of iron* (v. 18), *Behemoth* reigns supreme in the kingdom of the wild. The mountains bring forth tribute (v. 20), the mighty Jordan gushes toward its mouth (v. 23).

But even *Behemoth*, with all its power and dominion, is no match for God. God is creator; *Behemoth*, the creature (v. 15). God and God alone dares to bring the sword against the mighty Behemoth (v. 19). And it is God who subjugates and controls this otherwise unstoppable monster (v. 24).

41:1-34 (MT 40:25–41:26). Leviathan. *Leviathan*, like *Behemoth*, is a creature of strength and ferocity that is beyond the control of humans like Job (vv. 1-11). One cannot fish for it or hunt it. One cannot domesticate it as a servant or play with it as a pet. Those who might try to capture this monster of the deep would be undone by the mere sight of it.

The remainder of the address details the terrible and awesome characteristics of *Leviathan* (vv. 12-32). Its skin is covered with impenetrable rows of shields, like a warrior's armor (vv. 13-17). It sneezes fire and spews forth smoke like a boiling pot (vv. 18-21). It is hard like rock, immovable by external force (vv. 22-24), yet when it rouses itself up, even the gods tremble in fear (v. 25). No weapons can prevail against it (vv. 26-29). It resides in the primeval deep, and thrashes about leaving a wake in its trail (vv. 30-32). In sum, *Leviathan is a creature without fear*, a king in his own realm (vv. 33-34).

Throughout these descriptions of *Behemoth* and *Leviathan* there is no mention of justice, no explicit linkage of God's treatment of these representatives of chaos with the requirements of justice that God has urged Job to demonstrate (cf. 40:11-14). Job is invited to look and listen. What is he to learn from the lessons of *Behemoth* and *Leviathan* about God's justice? The forces of evil are part of the world God has made. God has power sufficient to combat them, to subjugate and control them, but God does not eliminate them.

Job's Second Response: "I Relent," 42:1-6

42:1-2. Concession and complaint. Job begins where God left off, with the matter of divine power (v. 2). He concedes that God indeed has the power to do everything, that no plan God proposes is impossible (*bsr*). In his concession, however, there remains the hint of complaint.

The word used in 38:2 to describe God's plan, or design, is *'esāh* . The word Job uses is *mĕzimmāh*, which may refer both to good and righteous purposes and to evil schemes (e.g., Job 21:27; Jer 11:15; Pss 10:2; 21:11). That Job perhaps tilts toward the latter meaning—God's schemes—is suggested by the close parallels between this verse and Gen 11:6 (cf. Perdue 1991, 234-35). In Gen 11 it is humans who plot against the heavens, evoking from God the response: "nothing they plan (*zmm*) to do will be impossible (*bsr*) for them." In addition to using the same root word for plan, or scheme, that occurs in Job 42:2, Gen 11:6 also uses the very same verb for "to be impossible" (*bsr*). In Gen 11:6 it is God who complains that humans seek to determine their own destinies by scheming against the heavens. Job concedes—complains—that God has the power to plan, or scheme, against humans with devious purposes that are not dissimilar to those on display at Babel.

42:3-6. Concession and relinquishment. Job continues by quoting portions of God's previous challenge to him: *Who is this that hides counsel without knowledge?* (v. 3a, cf. 38:2); *I will question you, and you shall declare to me* (v. 4b, cf. 38:3b=40:7b). Job responds to the first of these challenges by conceding that he is the one who has spoken of things he did not understand, of "wondrous things" he could not comprehend (cf. 5:9; 9:10; 37:5, 14). Job was also challenged to "declare" to God what he would. To this challenge Job turns in vv. 4-5.

Job acknowledges that something has changed since he first launched his quest to find God. To the knowledge of God that he had gained through hearing, he is now privileged to add the insight of personal encounter. He has seen God, an experience he shares with only a select few in Hebraic faith (e.g., Moses, Exod 3:1-6; 24:9-11; 33:23). That God has granted Job a direct revelation of the divine presence is a vindication of Job's integrity, for the godless cannot expect a personal audience with the deity (cf. 13:16). So Job has been specially prepared for a response that will reflect his new experience with God.

Job's final words represent the crux of the book. It is a frustration in the extreme that the response remains unclear despite enormous scholarly efforts to penetrate its ambiguity. What is clear is that the conventional translation *I despise myself* (v. 6) misses the mark. The verb *m 's* is active, not reflexive. In the Hebrew Bible it occurs both with and without a direct object. With an object it has the meaning "despise" or "reject" (e.g., Amos 5:21: "I despise your festivals"; Hos 4:6: "you have rejected knowledge"). Without an object the meaning is "protest" (e.g., Job 34:33: "Should he pay back on your terms because you protest?").

In 42:6 the verb *m 's* is not followed by an object, hence a plausible translation would be "I protest." A number of scholars have argued that an object should be supplied for the verb. Two proposals merit consideration: "I reject/despise the *case* against God" (Habel 1985, 576); and "I reject/despise *God*" (Curtis 1979, 503). Whether Job is merely giving up his case, or, more radically, giving up on God, he is not simply agreeing that he is guilty as charged.

The meaning of Job's declaration is further dependent on the interpretation of v. 6b. The traditional translation—*repent in dust and ashes*—has encouraged the understanding that at long last Job confesses his sins and assumes the posture of penitence. Not only does this interpretation contradict every other affirmation of Job's innocence in the book, including the affirmations of God in the prologue, it also depends on a misreading of the Hebrew text. The Hebrew is "repent of (i.e., concerning [*'al*]) dust and ashes." The expression suggests that Job changes his mind about his position as mourner and relinquishes his litigation against God.

What is left unspoken is what Job would say to God now that he has decided to proceed no further with protest and lamentation. If the text had continued Job's response beyond v. 6, would his next words offer praise (cf. Patrick 1976, 369-71; Perdue 1991, 236-37)? Would he give up his isolation as a sufferer and return to the community prepared to accept suffering as an inevitable part of God's inscrutable design for the world (cf. Habel 1985, 582-83)? Would he remain defiant to the end, giving up on God and rejecting the religious system that enthrones God on the misery of innocent sufferers (cf. Curtis 1979, 503; Good 1990, 378)?

One comes to the end of Job's declaration with these questions still awaiting a definitive answer. Perhaps in the ambiguity of the responses *I am . . . small* and "I relent" there remains yet a further invitation, one directed to the recipients of this anguished testimony to the difficulty of life in relationship with God (cf. Janzen 1985, 258). What does it mean to be faithful to God in the midst of inexplicable pain? The friends argue that it means to submit to God and confess sin. Job insists, before the friends and before God, that he will deny neither his pain nor his innocence. God has spoken of the design of the cosmos and its intricate governance, but has neither affirmed nor denied that Job has been wronged.

There is one scene in this drama yet to come. In the epilogue God will have a further word to speak to the situation. It is this word that provides a final clue to understanding what has preceded.

Epilogue: The Restoration of Job, 42:7-17

42:7-9. God's verdict. The epilogue returns the story to the opening scene where God is assessing human character and dispensing judgment from on high. Two divine verdicts are offered here. The first is a judgment *against* the friends to whom God now speaks in anger. The second is a judgment *for* Job whom God identifies four times as *my servant*. The basis for God's judgment in each case is that Job, not the friends, has spoken truth. The term *truth* (*nĕkônāh*, vv. 7, 8) points to that which is correct, not merely in an intellectual sense, but with reference to facts that are established and consistent with reality.

What is striking in this verdict is that it focuses on the truth *about God*. In the prologue Job affirms that God is the sovereign dispenser of both good and evil (2:10). Before this one who both *gives* and *takes away* (1:21) Job bows in willing submission. In the dialogues Job insists, against the conventional views of the friends, that God is often an enemy, whose inexplicable absence is not only unjust but also destructive. Job has spoken truth about God.

For Job, God is both present and absent, and true piety, therefore, is by necessity a risky combination of devotion and confrontation. God's verdict is that only the prayers of one who speaks truth like Job will be effective against the "foolishness" (NRSV *folly*) of those who, like the friends (v. 8), and his wife (cf. 2:10), champion a less honest understanding of God.

42:10-17. The restoration of Job's fortunes and family. Following Job's intercession for others, God restores both his fortunes and his family. A central part of his restoration, however, is effected by the community of *brothers and sisters and* "friends" (v. 11) who gather round to impart solidarity and companionship. It is they who finally extend to Job the "consolation" and "comfort" that Eliphaz, Bildad, and Zophar could not, or would not, offer (cf. 2:11). They comfort him for *all the evil that God has brought upon him*, not with words or theology, but with active communion. They offer fellowship through the sharing of a meal, and they demonstrate their compassion with tangible gifts that contribute to Job's material needs.

And so it was, the narrative concludes (vv. 16-17), that Job lived and died. The one introduced as *blameless* and *upright* (1:1) departs life *full of days* (v. 16). For all who will be instructed by his journey from the ash heap to the communion table of family and friends, the expression *full of days* becomes an invitation to a larger understanding of what it means to be in relationship with God.

Works Cited

Brenner, A. 1989. "Job the Pious? The Characterization of Job in the Narrative Framework of the Book," JSOT 43, 37–52. 1981. "God's Answer to Job," VT 31, 129–37.

Clines, D. J. A. 1989. *Job 1–20*, WBC.

Curtis, J. B. 1979. "On Job's Response to Yahweh," JBL 98:497–511.

Fishbane, M. 1971. "Jer. 4 and Job 3: A Rediscovered Use of the Creation Pattern," VT 21:151–67.

Fohrer, G. 1974. "The Righteous Man in Job 31," *Essays in Old Testament Ethics (J. Philip Hyatt, In Memoriam)*, ed. J. L. Crenshaw and J. T. Willis.

Good, E. M. 1990. *In Turns of Tempest. A Reading of Job with a Translation*.

Gordis, R. 1965. *The Book of God and Man: A Study of Job*. 1978. *The Book of Job: Commentary, New Translation, Special Studies*.

Habel, N. C. 1985. *The Book of Job*, OTL.

Janzen, J. G. 1985. *Job*, Interpretation.

Mettinger, T. N. D. 1992. "The God of Job: Avenger, Tyrant, or Victor?" *The Voice From the Whirlwind. Interpreting the Book of Job*, ed. L. G. Perdue and W. C. Gilpen.

Patrick, D. 1976. "The Translation of Job 42.6," VT 26:369–71.

Penchansky, D. 1990. *The Betrayal of God: Ideological Conflict in Job.*

Perdue, L. G. 1991. *Wisdom in Revolt, Metaphorical Theology in the Book of Job.*

Pope, M. L. 1965. *Job. Introduction, Translation, and Notes,* AncB.

Rouillard, P. 1983. "The Figure of Job in the Liturgy: Indignation, Resignation, or Silence," *Concilium* 169.

Rowley, H. H. 1970. *Job,* NCB.

Westermann, C. 1981. *The Structure of the Book of Job. A Form-Critical Analysis.*

Psalms

Marvin E. Tate

Introduction

Understanding the Psalter requires some awareness of the literary and historical contexts that shape it. The history of research of the Book of Psalms and its interpretation, however, is unfinished work. This introduction is supplemented by a selected bibliography that may guide further study.

Terminology

Three designations are commonly used for the Psalms. The Hebrew title *tᵉhillim* means "songs of praise" or "hymns." Not all of the psalms are "songs of praise," thus the title probably represents a stage in Israel's past when the psalms were used as a general hymnal, suitable for all occasions.

Two other terms appear in the Book of Psalms. The Hebrew word *mizmor*, fifty-seven times as a title for individual psalms, means a "song that may be accompanied by stringed instruments." *Tᵉphilloth* ("prayers") appears at the end of Ps 72: *The prayers of David son of Jesse are ended.* "Prayers" is an appropriate title for the collection, even though not all of the psalms are specifically prayers.

Two other titles, derived from Greek manuscripts, are well known in English: "Psalms," from a Greek word that meant "playing a stringed instrument," is found in *Codex Vaticanus*; and "Psalter," which also refers to a stringed instrument, is found in *Codex Alexandrinus*. *Codex Sinaiticus* lacks a title for the collection, but has "psalms of David" at the end. The oldest Hebrew manuscripts have no title for the whole book.

Titles of the Psalms

Superscriptions (i.e., titles) appear on 116 of the 150 psalms in the Hebrew Psalter including eighty-seven of the first 100. In addition to the titles, the term *selah* occurs seventy-one times (cf. Hab 3:3, 9, 13). The ancient Greek translations provided all of the psalms with titles except Pss 1 and 2 (see Pietersma 1980, 213–26).

Such a large number of titles would seem to offer assistance in interpretating the psalms. Unfortunately, this is true only to a limited degree. The titles are ancient (how old is uncertain), but they are still later additions and, therefore, give little information regarding the original meaning and use of the psalms to which they are attached.

Some psalm headings refer to the literary form of a psalm and contain various notes on its rendering, for example, the general terms for "psalm" (*mizmor*), "song" (*shir*), and "prayer" (*t'phillah*). These represent early attempts to classify the psalms according to their literary-cultic types.

Many titles contain technical notes relating to the occasion and method of recitation, for example, *to the leader: with stringed instruments* (e.g., Ps 4), *to the leader: for the flutes* (e.g. Ps 5), and so forth. Some of the instructions are relatively clear, such as *with stringed instruments* (e.g. Ps 4), *a song for the dedication of the temple* (Ps 30), *for the memorial offering* (Ps 38), *for the Sabbath Day* (Ps 92), or *a prayer of one afflicted . . .* (Ps 102). Other titles remain conjectural at best, such as "according to a silent dove of distant ones" (Ps 56, author trans).

Such titles are commonly assumed to refer to the tune names used when the psalm was sung or chanted, but proof is lacking. In some cases, the parts of the titles that suggest technical performance matters may have originally been postscripts for preceding psalms and incorporated into the superscriptions of following psalms by later copyists (cf. Pss 3/4; 17/18; 87/88; 108/109; 138/139; 148/149). The most obvious case in support of the theory is found in Pss 87/88 (see comment on Ps 88). The postscripts at the end of the psalms in Hab 3, Ps 72, and the end of a Dead Sea Scroll text of Ps 145 (*11QPs^a* adds "this is for a memorial") provide important data for this interpretation.

Other titles identify psalms with a person or group of persons. The most common of these is DAVID (seventy-three psalms), ASAPH (twelve psalms), and the Sons of KORAH (eleven psalms). SOLOMON (two psalms), Heman, Ethan, and MOSES (one each) also occur. Traditionally it was assumed that the names were of the authors of the psalms. Today, however, it is generally recognized that the titles provide little or no certain indication of authorship (e.g., David would hardly have written Ps 18:49-50). There is no certainty about the meaning of the "of" in such titles as "a psalm of David." The Hebrew construction is a flexible one that can mean "for" or "in relation to" as well as "of." Therefore, "of" may refer to the collection to which the psalm belongs or to its use.

One text from the caves of Qumran (where the DEAD SEA SCROLLS were found) credits David with 4,050 psalms, while a letter from the Nestorian Patriarch Timotheus I in the eighth century CE refers to a discovery of scrolls near Jericho including more than 200 psalms of David—compared with seventy-three in MT. The Davidization of the Psalms is also reflected in the increased number of Davidic titles in the LXX (e.g., Pss 33, 42, 43, 67, 91, 93–100, 104). The Davidization of the Psalms was accompanied by an increased emphasis on the tradition of Davidic authorship.

The matter of authorship in postexilic Israelite life is without clear resolution. However, it is highly probable that authorship became more crucial as texts became

more authoritative and fixed as scripture. Throughout the history of usage, the traditional authority of texts required supplementation by reference to authorship by
persons endowed by God. Thus the *11QPs^a* prose insert on David's composition of
psalms concludes with: "All these he spoke in prophecy which was given him from
the presence of the Most High." David's authorship of Psalms (as was Moses' of
the Pentateuch) was elevated to the status of "prophecy" (Kugel 1986, 134–36).

Few biblical writings have any definite indication of authorship. Such
anonymity may be disturbing to the modern reader. The psalms, however, come
from a different world. Ancient people generally had a sense of history that lacked
precision (by modern standards). Before the Hellenistic period, at least, readers had
relatively little interest in the actual personalities of authors, except when the content
of texts became authoritative (or canonical) as scripture, relatively fixed in text
forms, and no longer subject to being freely modified (when texts became "fixed"
new "noncanonical" compositions emerged).

When personalities were linked to written material, it was done either by
naming the individual writings after the principal character found in them (e.g., the
Pentateuch was ascribed to Moses) or by assigning songs or recitations to famous
people in particular situations. For example, a psalm is put in the mouth of
Hezekiah in Isa 38:1-20 (which is missing from the parallel account in the Books
of Kings) and David appoints a thanksgiving song in 1 Chr 16:7-36 to be sung by
Asaph and his brother (which is made up of material from Pss 96, 105, 106).

A similar process probably lies behind the headings of several psalms that
contain references to the details of some historical situations in the career of David
(see Pss 3, 7, 18, 34, 51, 52, 54, 56, 57, 59, 60, 63, 142). The historical value of
these notes must be decided in each case on its own merits. The only value of such
headings is to show what situations ancient Jewish scribal commentators thought to
be appropriate for them.

One of the best-known words in the Psalter is SELAH, a scribal notation found
seventy-one times in Psalms (and three times in Habakkuk). While there is widespread agreement that the term marked an interlude or interruption in the recitation
of the psalm, its exact meaning is uncertain. Perhaps the best conjecture is the one
that interprets it as marking a pause during the recitation of the psalms when the
congregation fell prostrate in homage and submission to God, probably with shouts
of praise. The action may have been signalled by trumpet blasts from the priests,
and the recitation by the people of a refrain such as "Praise the Lord, for he is
good; for his steadfast love endures forever." Another approach is to think of a
"recitative" or "cantillation" in the pause that recalled a major story or tradition in
Israel's history. Frequently, the *selah* seems to serve as an intensifier coming just
before some climactic statement or between such statements.

The Collections of the Psalter

The present Hebrew Psalter includes 150 psalms. The numbering of these
psalms is not as fixed as it may seem at first. There is a marked variation between

Protestant translations and those of the Roman Catholic and Orthodox traditions. The variations arise at Pss 9–10 (separate in Protestant translations; as one psalm in others); Pss 114–115 (113 in Catholic translations); Ps 116 (114–115 in Catholic translations); and 147 (146–147 in Catholic translations). These differences develop from following the Hebrew texts on the one hand (Protestant) and the Greek and Latin texts (Roman Catholic and Orthodox) on the other. There are other cases where the present numbering of separate psalms is doubtful (see the commentary on Pss 9–10, 32–33, 42–43, 70–71, 117, 150), while other separate psalms may be composed of originally independent units (see Pss 19, 40, 108, 144). Psalm 14 is essentially the same as Ps 53; and Ps 70 repeats the conclusion of Ps 40. Thus the numbering of the psalms must not be considered immutable.

The number 150 as the total of psalms in the Psalter is subject to some variation also. The Greek-text SEPTUAGINT version of the Psalter contains 151 psalms. Psalm 151 (known also in Latin and Syriac translations) has been described as a kind of poetic *midrash* on 1 Sam 16:11-13, and the text of the psalm in Hebrew has recently become known from a psalms manuscript from Cave 11 at Qumran on the Dead Sea *(11QPsᵃ)*. The Syriac Psalter contained 155 psalms (of which 154 and 155 also appear in *11QPsᵃ*). The psalms scroll from Qumran has been dated to the first half of the first century CE.

The Psalter is, of course, a collection of psalms. In the present state of the Hebrew Psalter there are five books or divisions: 1–41, 42–72, 73–89, 90–106, 107–150. Each one of the first four books ends with a similar section of praise or doxology: 41:13; 72:18-19 (to which v. 20 has been added); 89:52; 106:48. The fifth book closes with five psalms that are characterized by a tenfold *Praise the LORD* ("Hallelujah!") and ends with Ps 150, which contains a thirteenfold praise of Yahweh. While this division of the Psalter is deliberate, the exact purpose of the editors is disputed. The fivefold division corresponds to the fivefold division of the Pentateuch (the TORAH) and becomes, in a way, the response of Israel to the Torah of Moses.

The exact date of the present arrangement of the Psalter is not known. It probably should be placed in the postexilic period of Israel's history, and may be as late as the first century CE. The Psalter contains several earlier collections of psalms that have been taken up into the present arrangement. For example, there is a change in the dominant usage of the name of God in Pss 42–83. The name "Yahweh" (read as LORD in most English translations), is usual in Pss 1–41, while "Elohim" ("God" in English translations) predominates in 42–83; "Yahweh" appears again in most cases in 84–150. There can be little doubt that an Elohistic collection (that cuts across present divisions) was made at some point. This conclusion is strengthened by the obvious substitution of "Elohim" for "Yahweh" in such places as Pss 43:4; 45:7; 50:7; 53. This collection may have originated from circles in postexilic Israel when the reluctance to pronounce the divine name *Yahweh* led to the substitution of *Elohim*, before the practice began (common later) of pronouncing Yahweh as *adonai (Lord)*.

The note attached to the end of Ps 72—"The prayers of David son of Jesse are ended"—probably marked the end of an earlier collection. The reader will notice that in the first book of the Psalter (1–41) only four psalms (1, 2, 10, 33) are without a title, while all the others are ascribed to David. Since Pss 1 and 2 are introductory psalms (Ps 2 was probably interpreted as a Davidic psalm when placed in its present position because of its references to the king) and Ps 10 belongs to Ps 9, only Ps 33 is a real exception. It may be that Ps 33 should be linked with Ps 32 (cf. 32:11 and 33:1) or it may be that Ps 33 was placed in its present position to mark the end of some prior collection. In other sections of the Psalter the Davidic psalms are grouped together (51–65, 68–70, 108–110, 138–145), although some are isolated (86, 101, 103, 122, 124, 131). The obvious conclusion is that there was a Davidic collection (or collections) of the psalms at some earlier date.

As noted above, the significance of the preposition "for" or "to" David in the titles is uncertain. It probably indicates psalms that were originally intended (or later so interpreted) for the use of the Davidic king, or were designed to evoke memories of David and his career in the minds of those who read or heard the psalms. David would have been considered to be the speaker in the psalms. After the end of the monarchy (if not before), such psalms were "democratized" and used by ordinary people, while retaining their Davidic associations. In the course of time, conventional idiom associated *all* the psalms with David, similar to the association of *all* the Torah with Moses, and *all* the wisdom works with Solomon.

There are some indications Pss 90–150 may have been compiled from four smaller collections: 90–104 (with 105–107 added); 108–110 (with 111–118 added); 120–134 (the Songs of Ascent or Pilgrimage with 135–136 added); 138–145 (to which the concluding five-psalm doxology of 146–150 was attached). Finally, the royal psalms (2, 20, 21, 45, 72, 89, 101, 110, 132) are now scattered through the Psalter. They probably formed a separate collection in preexilic Israel and their positions in the present Psalter are not accidental.

The history of the Psalter is still impossible to formulate in precise detail, but there is some measure of agreement on its general outline. There is no reason to doubt POETRY was used by the Israelites from the earliest periods of their history, some of which may have been indigenous, while much was borrowed from neighbors. The content of the present psalms, indicates that most of them come from the time in Israel's history when life was centered in the Temple in Jerusalem.

It is difficult to date any psalm within narrow limits; direct historical statements are few. The psalms were probably developed at the worship centers of the Israelite tribes after their settlement in Palestine, although we cannot be certain that we have any of these psalms in the present Psalter. The establishment of the monarchy and center of worship in Jerusalem by David undoubtedly brought a new stimulus for the writing and collecting of psalms and prayers. We cannot be sure which psalms belong to the early period of the monarchy, but such a dating cannot be ruled out for several (e.g., 2, 18, 29, 110, 132).

The establishment of rival centers of worship in BETHEL and Dan by JEROBOAM I must have brought about the production and collection of psalms from this source. We may have some of these psalms in the present Psalter (e.g., Ps 68), but no one can be absolutely sure. Some of the psalms must have been written in the postexilic community that was centered in Jerusalem, and that community preserved and arranged the Psalter in the present order. It was once assumed by many biblical critics that a good number of the psalms were as late as the Maccabean period (second–first century BCE), but the view has little support in present scholarship.

The Poetry of the Psalms

Modern translations distinguish by form poetic from prose sections. The reader will see at once that the psalms are poetic. A full understanding of them involves an awareness of the basic formal and stylistic features of Hebrew POETRY. The most important of these features is the use of what is called PARALLELISM. In its simplest form parallelism is the supplementation of one short line (colon) by another that either essentially repeats the meaning of the first line or adds to it: "This is true, and so is this" (e.g., see Pss 2:1; 3:1; 5:1; 24:1). However, there are many variations and expansions of this pattern. There are also rhythmic patterns ("meter") in Hebrew verse. These are rarely without some irregularity and are frequently read in different ways by different readers. The poets seem to have exercised great freedom with rhythmical (metrical) patterns. The poetry of the OT also displays a wide array of sound patterns, stylistic features, structuring devices (such as the CHIASM, INCLUSIO, and theme words), and the literary arrangement of texts to form strophes (see Ps 107) or other sections.

Another form of poetry found in the Psalter is that of the "alphabetic" or "acrostic" type. These poems have successive lines, verses, or stanzas that begin with the letters of the Hebrew alphabet in order. The alphabetic design in Pss 9–10, 25, 34, 37, 111, 112, 119, and 145 cannot be carried over into translation, but it is helpful for the reader to be aware of this poetic formation.

The poetry of the OT is not confined to the Psalter. The Israelites were a people who, like other peoples, loved songs and singing. It is true that the OT does not contain a great deal of what we would call "secular" songs or poems, but there is evidence that the Israelites knew and used such songs on many occasions. Prophets used the forms, and even the words, of various kinds of songs (see Amos 5:1-2 [cf. 6:5]; Isa 5:1-7; 23:15-16; 37:22). And there is the example of the well-known song that greeted David when he returned from his exploits against the Philistines (1 Sam 18:6-7). The presence in the Psalter of an essentially "secular" poem for the wedding of the king (Ps 45) is significant, as are the many references to musical instruments and activities in the psalms (e.g., Ps 150). In terms of what may be called "cultic" poetry (having to do with worship), there are extensive sections elsewhere in the OT (e.g., Gen 48:1-28; Exod 15:1-18, 21; Deut 32:1-43; 33; Judg 5; 1 Sam 2:1-10; 2 Sam 1:19-27; 22:1-51 [=Ps 18]; 23:1-7; Isa 38:9-20; Jonah 2;

Hab 3; Jer 15:13-21). The Book of Lamentations and the Song of Songs also contain collections of poetry.

The Classification of the Psalms

The collections of the Psalter show evidence that one of the factors in their formation is the similarity of psalms according to type. Most of the Davidic psalms are lamentations or prayers closely associated with complaint and lament. The close linking of Ps 93 to 95–99 is related to the fact that they deal with the kingship of Yahweh. Another example is the section formed by Pss 146–150, marked by the use of *Praise the LORD!* The titles give indications of attempts by the early Jewish communities to classify the psalms (see above). The church continued with various classifications of the psalms. The best known of the Christian classifications is that of the seven "Penitential Psalms" (6; 32; 38; 51; 102; 130; 143) and the classification of the Royal Psalms (2, 20, 21, 45, 72, 110, 132) as "Messianic."

In the early stages of the development of modern critical study, the Psalter did not receive the same measure of attention as the Pentateuch, but in time biblical scholars also came to apply the methods of historical-criticism to it. The first stage of this study was concentrated (1) on discovering the most suitable historical context for the composition of each psalm, assuming that each was the result of the literary activity of a single individual poet, (2) and on reducing the present form of the psalms (where necessary) to an authentic nucleus assumed to have been written by a poet out of personal experience.

The historical-critical approach has, however, been mostly superseded by the form-critical approach. Form-critical study does not begin with the assumption that each psalm represents the literary activity of an individual poet writing out of personal experience in a given historical context, although it does not exclude the validity of personal experience. Instead it begins with comparative study of the psalms with one another (and with poetry outside the OT) in order to ascertain common features of structure, style, and content within certain groups of psalms. Beyond the form, form criticism seeks to discover a *Sitz im Leben* ("situation-in-life") that could have elicited the form in question. These situations can be historical, but they normally belong to the basic affairs of life: birth, death, marriage, sickness, disaster, legal proceedings, war, harvests, and so forth. Form criticism also seeks to understand how the literary unit ("form") passed from one generation to another in the course of history, a process that sometimes involved changes of the *Sitz im Leben* from the original, plus expansion or modifications of the original unit.

The legacy of the investigation of psalm types or categories from Hermann Gunkel (1929 and 1933) has had wide acceptance by interpreters of the Psalms in the twentieth century. Gunkel (1929) defined five main types of psalms: hymns, communal laments, royal psalms, individual laments, and individual songs of thanksgiving. He also recognized other categories, and four are of special note: songs of pilgrimage, communal songs of thanksgiving, wisdom poetry, and liturgies.

He made allowance for the difficulty of defining some psalms in any of these cate-gories because of a mixture of types and set forth a type called "mixed poems" (actually, quite a number of psalms).

The changes in method and result have been considerable, but the framework of his analysis has been remarkably durable. The discussion that follows is limited to three broad classifications: psalms of lament, psalms of praise, and other types of psalms. The third, of course, is not a form-critical category, but only an umbrella designation for a variety of psalm types.

Psalms of Lament

These psalms are found in individual forms (the speaker is a first-person "I") and communal forms (the speaker is a plural "we"). The individual lament is the most numerous type in the Psalter (e.g., Pss 3, 4, 5, 6, 7, 13, 17, 143). The laments are prayers addressed to God concerning complaints, lamentations, and frequently enemies. God is addressed directly (typically, "Hear O God" or "My God, my God") with complaint about distressful conditions. Petitions to God for divine action is an expected feature, especially for action relating to enemies (enemies are not normally addressed directly). These psalms may contain appeals to God, which seek a favorable hearing for the prayer, and there is a tendency for them to move toward praise. In most cases the speaker seeks grounds for praising God, and vows of praise, contingent on a favorable response to the prayer, may occur.

Psalms of Praise

This broad category encompasses psalms designated by Gunkel as thanksgiving psalms as well as those known as hymns. A category of such scope includes great diversity. Thanksgiving-praise (Claus Westermann's [1981] "declarative praise") is marked by direct address to Yahweh and a testimony element of proclamatory and exhortative speech directed toward the people who may be listening to the praise (e.g., Pss 18:46-50; 22:22-31; 30:4-5; 34:9-22; 66:15-20; 107:43). The more "descriptive praise" (Westermann's [1981] term for the general hymns) features a summons to praise, or a call to worship, addressed to varied groups (e.g., 33:1, *O you righteous*; 113:1, *O servants of the LORD*; 148:2, *all his angels . . . all his host*—vastly extended to include all creation). The summons may be elaborated, of course, in terms of how, when, and where to praise Yahweh (e.g., Pss 113:1-3; 149:1-3). The praise poetry is replete with reasons for the praise: personal experience of deliverance, works of creation, saving works, and the goodness and glory of the divine nature.

The individual poetry of thanksgiving-praise is focused more closely on personal help and deliverance (e.g., Pss 18, 30, 116, 118), sometimes recalling the prayers of complaint directed to God before the deliverance. The more descriptive praise has a tendency to focus on the qualities of God and the works of creation and establishment of the earth and heavenly bodies (e.g., Pss 33, 93, 113, 136). However, the saving acts of Yahweh in making Israel his people are not neglected (e.g., Pss 98, 114, 135). Alternative expressions of praise, such as praise wishes and blessings, may be found (e.g., Pss 19; 85:6; 103:1-2; 104:34). Despite the fact that commentators have struggled to devise adequate classification systems (including those of Gunkel) for the wide diversity of praise poetry, no consensus has emerged. The poetry has a high degree of mixing (e.g., elements of thanksgiving and descriptive praise are usually blended, and praise elements may be found in laments).

Other Types

A goodly number of psalms do not fit the standard categories very well. Among these is one of Gunkel's categories called "royal psalms," psalms that appear to have content focused on the kingship in ancient Israel, especially dealing with the Davidic kings in Jerusalem. The commonly accepted royal psalms are Pss 2, 18, 20, 21, 45, 72, 89, 101, 110, 132, 144. Some scholars, however, argue that this list should be expanded to include many more psalms. A small group of psalms are usually called "historical psalms" (Pss 78, 105, 106, 135, 136), though by genre these psalms are properly praise poems or hymns. Psalms 15 and 24 are commonly referred to as entrance liturgies to worship. Psalms 1, 19, and 119 (an alphabetic psalm) are centered on the praise of Yahweh's *torah*. While major efforts to establish a category of "wisdom psalms" or "didactive poetry" (Kraus 1988, 58–60) have met with only limited acceptance, there is wide agreement that Pss 37 and 73 may be treated as such.

The Relationship of Psalms to Life Situations

As noted above, one facet of form-critical analysis has been to seek a *Sitz im Leben* or situation-in-life for literary units. In the twentieth century, scholars have devoted much time and effort to this task as related to the Psalms, with mixed results. Sigmund Mowinckel has been the most influential scholar in this regard, arguing for the direct relatedness of psalms to cultic (organized worship) rites and ceremonies. In Mowinckel's approach many psalms are considered to have been designed and produced to accompany liturgical actions, and it has been assumed that these actions can be recovered, in large measure, from the psalms themselves. This cult-functional approach centered on preexilic Israelite worship, especially in the Temple in Jerusalem and in the context of the autumnal festivals (chiefly the Festival of Tabernacles in the OT). Mowinckel (1962) argued for an Enthronement Festival celebrating the victory of Yahweh over chaos and his enthronement as the divine king. Others have emphasized New Year festivals, covenant renewal ceremonies, and Zion-Davidic king celebrations.

The autumn festival has not been the sole concern of scholars. In regard to the laments, it has been argued at length that they arose out of sacral judicial procedures in the sanctuaries, especially the Temple in Jerusalem. A number of the laments (e.g., Pss 3, 4, 5, 6, 17, 26, 27, 54, 55, 57, 59, 63) have been interpreted as prayers for those who would flee to a sanctuary for asylum and deliverance from enemies who were falsely accusing them. In some cases, it has been argued, they were intended to be inscribed (perhaps on the wall or on a SCROLL) or engraved on a stele which was placed in the sanctuary (cf. Exod 22:8-9; Deut 17:8-13; 19:15-21; 1 Kgs 8:31-32). Some laments have been assumed to be prayers of sick persons who would go to the temple for purification and healing (e.g., Pss 6, 38, 39, 62, 69, 88).

Recent interpretations of the Psalms have seen a departure from the cult-functional approach defined exclusively in terms of the major Israelite festivals and the Temple. One of the factors involved has been the emphasis on the literary art of biblical narrative and biblical poetry, with a tendency to read a psalm in terms of its own context and structure, with diminished interest in its situation-in-life or situation-in-worship. The forced reading of some psalms in the cult-functional approach has also been a factor. The reconstruction of worship situations assumed to be directly related to a psalm is a highly subjective endeavor that inspires confidence only in the general features of the liturgies and rituals postulated. The reflection of cultic traditions and practices in psalm texts can hardly be doubted, but this does not necessitate the detailed reconstruction of an actual worship situation and the assumption that a given psalm was composed for that particular situation—either purely cultic or historical.

Increased recognition of the composite nature of psalms and the use of mixed and traditional material in a given psalm is found in recent work on the Psalter. Along with this has come heightened appreciation of scribal psalm writing (e.g., see Mowinckel's discussion of "learned psalmography" [1951, 104–25]) and the long-continued tradition of such in postexilic Israel, including the Qumran community and early Christian communities (e.g., see the poems of praise attributed to MARY and ZECHARIAH in Luke 1–2). The dating of psalms is as slippery as ever, but scholars seem more willing to eschew the early dating of a psalm in its present form because it may contain some material that is quite old.

Continuing sociological analysis of community life in the ancient world and the study of ritual texts from the ancient Near East have led to a broader understanding of the probable nature of the Israelite cult and the relationship of psalms to it. For example, it is unlikely that sick people would normally have been taken to a temple for healing. The Israelite priests were involved to some extent with certain illnesses (e.g., skin diseases, Lev 13–14; Deut 24:8), but were not responsible for the actual treatment of illness. When well again, a sick person would go to a temple for purification and thanksgiving ceremonies. The care and treatment of the sick took place in homes or at special places for healing (e.g., see 1 Kgs 8:37-40; 2 Kgs 1:2-8; 20:1-11; Job 2:7-8; 2 Chr 26:21; Mark 2:1-12; John 5:2-3). Some psalms were probably used as prayers by persons in such home or healing-place contexts, perhaps assisted by a ritual expert, not a priest but someone trained to help people engage in prayers and healing rites (Gerstenberger, 1988). Scholars involved in such sociological analysis stress the importance of individual participation in primary groups (such as families, groups of friends, and communities of common interests) and avoid the tendency to think of prayer and worship as either purely individual or else wholly corporate (as in the great festivals and official worship of the temples).

For Further Study

In the *Mercer Dictionary of the Bible*: CULTS; DEAD SEA SCROLLS; DISEASE AND HEALING; ESCHATOLOGY IN THE OT; FEASTS AND FESTIVALS; HYMNS/CREEDS; MASKIL; MUSIC/MUSICAL INSTRUMENTS; ORACLE; PARALLELISM; POETRY; PRAYER/ THANKSGIVING IN THE OT; PSALMS, BOOK OF; RESURRECTION IN THE OT; RIGHTEOUSNESS IN THE OT; SALVATION IN THE OT; SOUL IN THE OT; TEMPLE/TEMPLES; TESTIMONY; THEOPHANY; UGARIT, RAS; WISDOM IN THE OT; WISDOM LITERATURE; WORSHIP IN THE OT; WRATH OF GOD.

In other sources: A. A. Anderson, *The Book of Psalms*, NCB; L. Allen, *Psalms 101–150*, WBC; B. Anderson, *Out of the Depths*; W. H. Bellinger, Jr., *Psalms: Reading and Studying the Book of Praise*; P. C. Craige, *Psalms 1–50*, WBC; M. Dahood, *Psalms 1–50, Psalms 51–100, Psalms 101–150* AncB; M. Tate, *Psalms 51–100*, WBC; A. Weiser, *The Psalms*, OTL; C. Westermann, *Praise and Lament in the Psalms*.

Commentary

An Outline

I. Book One. Psalms 1–41
II. Book Two. Psalms 42–72
III. Book Three. Psalms 73–89
IV. Book Four. Psalms 90–106
V. Book Five. Psalms 107–150

Book One. Psalms 1–41

Psalm 1

Psalm 1 belongs in a general way to the WISDOM LITERATURE of the OT. It is one of several psalms in the Psalter that show features of poetry like that in the Book of Proverbs. The reward of *the righteous* and the punishment of *the wicked* is a major theme in both the Wisdom and Deuteronomic teachings in the OT.

Verses 1-3 tell of the blessedness of *the righteous* person (v. 6), who is first defined in a negative way (v. 1): as one who does not walk in the counsel of *the wicked*, does not follow the ways of *sinners*, and does not sit with the *scoffers*. The verbs indicate a habitual or regular way of doing things; that is, *the righteous* have a daily course of life separate from *the wicked* (cf. Ps 26:4-5).

The exact identity of *the wicked* is a problem throughout the Psalter. However, it is most probable that the reference here is to those who are recognized as despisers of the TORAH of Yahweh. They are characterized by hostility to godliness and to the righteous behavior of the *torah*-keeping community. The righteous make the correct negative judgments by not doing certain things.

The positive side of the picture presents the *delight* of the righteous person *in the law* [Heb. *torah*] *of the Lord* (v. 2), the good fortune of the one whose *delight* is centered in those teachings that reveal the merciful will and power of Yahweh. In this context, the verb *meditate* denotes the low murmur of reading aloud to one's self. The kind of life that results for the righteous person is compared with a tree that does not fail in leaf or productivity because it is "deeply rooted" and its water supply is constant (v. 3), free from the withering of drought. The comparison occurs elsewhere in the OT (Amos 2:9; Jer 11:19; 17:7-8; Ezek 17:5-6; Pss 52:8; 92:13-15), and appears also in non-Israelite wisdom literature.

The metaphor of a green and productive tree is a common one for strength and well-being. The use of the "tree of life" for Wisdom in Prov 3:18 (cf. Prov 15:4) is especially significant for Ps 1 with its wisdom-*torah* characteristics (cf. Gen 2:9; 3:22). Those comforted in Zion will be called "trees of righteousness, the planting of Yahweh, to display his glory" (Isa 61:3). The "streams of water" (v. 3) is derived from an expression that refers to artificial watercourses through which a controlled supply of water is provided. The result is abundant and perennial fruitfulness. The last statement of v. 3 is a key one: the righteous person is able to carry through to a successful result all he or she endeavors to do (cf. Josh 1:8).

The wicked lack the stability and nourishment of the righteous (vv. 4-5). They are compared to the *chaff* that is blown away from the threshing floor by the wind (cf. Ps 35:5; Job 21:18; Isa 17:13; Hos 13:3). They lack the security of the righteous.

The judgment (v. 5) poses a problem. Most commentators do not believe that the final, eschatological judgment is intended here, although it is the common meaning of later Jewish and Christian interpreters. Some understand the idea as that of divine judgment in general; every act by which Yahweh separates between the righteous and the wicked and shows his ruling power in the world (Sarna 1993, 45). A more probable interpretation seeks the background for *the judgment* here in passages such as Pss 5:4-7; 15:1; 24:3. The questions of 15:1 and 24:3 are answered negatively: the wicked will *not* stand in the holy place of judgment. In the background are actual cultic rituals by which those whose conduct did not conform with the *torah* of the congregation were excluded from worship at the holy places.

The congregation of the righteous (v. 5) is the fellowship of those who are permitted to praise God at the sanctuary (Pss 111:1; 118:19-20), perhaps *the great congregation* at Zion (see Pss 35:18; 40:9-10). However, in the present psalm such an actual cultic situation may not be intended. Indeed, it seems more probable the verse has an eschatological thrust looking beyond the cultic present to the ultimate judgment of God, and to a purified congregation of the righteous in which sinners will be unable to participate.

Verse 6 concludes the psalm by setting forth in summary fashion the ways of the righteous and the wicked. To be known by Yahweh means to be in an intimate relationship with God. Intimacy with God is the real source of the blessedness (or happiness) with which the psalm begins, a word that expresses an exclamation regarding the well-being of an individual: "Oh, how well-off is that person!" (cf. Pss 112:1; 128:2; Matt 5:3-12). The death-way of the wicked lacks the "rightness" that produces such good fortune. Psalm 1 calls for faith in God's ways for the righteous, and confidence that those ways bring pleasure and fruitfulness.

The meaning of the word *torah* (*the law*) in this psalm continues to be a subject of discussion. There is no reference to any body of literature in Ps 1, or in other *torah* psalmic material (Pss 19:7-14; 119:1-176; 37:31; 40:8; 78:1, 5, 10; 89:30; 94:12; 105:45). Therefore it is likely that in the Psalter *torah* should be read as "instruction," "teaching," or "guidance," which is the fundamental meaning of the word (cf. the *torah* in the "heart" or "inward being" in Pss 37:31 and 40:8; see commentary on Ps 119).

In subsequent readings there can be little doubt that *torah* was understood as the Torah, a defined body of law and narratives. In the course of time, the Torah came to be identified especially with its core material in the canonical form of the Pentateuch. However, even when Torah was basically the Pentateuch it was at the same time a composite entity. The Pentateuch itself is not composed of legal formulations alone, but contains extensive narrative and poetic sections (both story and commandments). Further, the prophetic literature was associated with Torah (including Joshua, Judges, Samuel, and Kings), and in time the concept of an oral Torah derived from Moses was authoritative along with the written Torah. Indeed, *torah* has never been a simple, clearly identified entity.

Finally, the arrangement of the Psalter with Ps 1 as introduction to the whole collection must indicate that in some sense the Psalms are also Torah (McCann 1993b). The Psalter is also a *torah* worthy of continual delight and meditation, a "tree of life" that never fails to yield fruit and whose leaves never wither.

Psalm 2

This is a royal psalm, paired with Ps 1 at the beginning of the Psalter as a powerful affirmation of the sovereignty of Yahweh. In the course of the postexilic history of Israel the royal psalms came to be interpreted messianically, as referring to a future Messiah who would come to rule over Israel. Psalm 2 was so considered and is applied to Christ in the NT (Acts 4:25-28; 13:33; Heb 1:5). A proper understanding of the royal psalms, however, must begin with their place in the context of Israelite kingship. In the case of this psalm, most commentators have interpreted it as belonging to the enthronement and coronation of a king of JUDAH in JERUSALEM, possibly DAVID himself. However, rebellion and the threat of attack may be equally as probable as royal coronation. It is possible the psalm was repeated on periodic occasions when the establishment of the Davidic dynasty would have been celebrated or when the Israelites were threatened by enemies.

It is strange that the psalm has no title. The title may have been lost when Ps 1 was prefixed to the whole collection but it is more probable that Ps 2 was left untitled and added as a sort of messianic prelude to the Davidic collection of Pss 3–41.

A tense scene of rebellion by earthly nations and kings *against the LORD and his anointed* is introduced in vv. 1-3 by a question that expresses astonishment that these hostile forces would dare risk an insurrection. The same verb used for vocally expressed meditation (Heb. *hgh*) on *torah* in Ps 1:2 is used for the rebellious mutterings of kings and nations who *conspire* and *plot* [Heb. *hgh*] . . . *against the LORD and his anointed* (Ps 2:1). However, their efforts are *in vain* because a rebellion against the "anointed one"—the king in Jerusalem (1 Sam 2:10; 35; 12:3; 5; Pss 18:51; 20:7; 28:8; 89:39; 52; 132:10; 17; etc.)—is a rebellion against the power of Yahweh himself. Verse 3 expresses the desire of the hostile kings for complete autonomy.

It becomes clear in vv. 4-6 why the poet thinks the insurrection is such a futile venture. Yahweh surveys the scene from heaven and *laughs* . . . *in derision*, unintimidated by the hostile counsels and plots of the kings (cf. Pss 37:13; 59:8). God is not remote and indifferent toward those who challenge his purpose in history; he will speak to them with terrifying fury. Verse 6 contains the divine word: Yahweh, himself, has established his king (*my king*) on Zion, his holy hill (*my holy hill*).

In vv. 7-9 the speaker changes and the king tells of his commission by Yahweh to reign with potential power over the nations of the earth. It was by *decree* of Yahweh that he had obtained his authorized status. The "decree" reflects the practice of using some documentary record or protocol of the king's legitimate right to the throne. In Egypt the protocol seems to have contained the Pharaoh's coronation names and the affirmation of his divine sonship and power. There probably was a similar custom in Israel (cf. 2 Kgs 11:12).

The thrust of the king's testimony in vv. 7-9 is twofold. First, he declares that his reign is legitimate. He is no usurper who has seized the throne by force or fraud, or even merely because he is a king's son. The kingship in Israel was never purely hereditary; there was always some need for a charismatic legitimation. The king had to become a *son* of Yahweh as well as a *son* of David.

However, the "sonship" of the king did not represent an actual divine begetting—as the literal wording of v. 7 would indicate, and as is found in texts referring to kings from Egypt and Mesopotamia. The OT "sonship" (see 2 Sam 7:13; 1 Chr 28:6; Ps 89:27-28) represents adoption (cf. Gen 15:2; 30:3; 50:23) rather than begetting in the literal sense, that is, the king was either physically or mentally begotten, but begotten by a decree that expressed the word of Yahweh (cf. the creative speaking of God in Gen 1). By decree the king becomes the heir and representative of the sovereignty of Yahweh.

Second, the king declares that his divinely granted status has endowed him with tremendous potential power. He has been granted the privilege of prayer which opens up unlimited possibilities (v. 8). Such privilege enhances the status of the king on the one hand, but it shows his dependence on Yahweh on the other. Great dominion is to be obtained as the gift of the heavenly king (*and I will make*). Further, the king is promised the potential of great power in dealing with alien nations (v. 9; read as "You can smash them . . . you can shatter them . . . " [author trans.]).

Verse 9 also reflects an Egyptian practice in relation to kingship. In the Egyptian ritual of coronation, the extensive power of the king was demonstrated by the smashing of earthenware bottles that bore the names of foreign peoples, or by the symbolical destruction of four pillars that represented the four cardinal points of the heavens. Similar language was applied to the conquests of Mesopotamian kings.

In vv. 10-12 an ultimatum is directed to the hostile rulers: serve Yahweh or experience the quick and sure judgment of divine wrath (cf. v. 5). The psalm does not close with this warning but with a blessing (*Happy are all who*) that frames Ps 2 with Ps 1 (cf. 1:1). These verses make it clear that the rebellion of the earthly kings is really against Yahweh, even though the immediate target may be the king in Jerusalem. Thus, the rulers are not directed to serve the honor of the Davidic king.

A great scope of sovereignty is attached to the Davidic kings in the royal psalms (see Pss 2:8; 18:44-48; 71:8-11; 17; 89:27-29; 36-37; 110), which seems to be out of harmony with the historical realities of their modest kingdoms. How could such grandiose concepts have been taken seriously?

First, there is considerable use of "court-language" in these psalms. The Israelites adopted a good deal of the language and ideology of kingship from their neighbors, along with the institution itself.

Second, the Israelite concept of kingship was modeled on the reign of David, who did eventually rule over an extensive empire that for a time held an important role in ancient Near Eastern affairs. In subsequent generations the extent of the kingdom was diminished but the language of the Davidic reign remained fixed and finally was projected into the future as a hope.

Third, it is important to remember that the dominion of the Davidic king is a conferred one, transferred to him by virtue of his election or adoption to the office of king. However, the dominion transferred was not the dominion of David his father; but the dominion of Yahweh. To Yahweh as creator and Lord of the world belong *the nations* (Ps 82:8) and *the ends of the earth* (Pss 24:1-2; 47:3; 9; 89:12; Isa 6:3). This became the *heritage* (Ps 2:8) of the Davidic king. The really determining factor was not the geographic extent of the Davidic kingdom, but the entire redemptive purpose of Yahweh's choice of Israel.

Fourth, it is also significant that the power and dominion of the king are expressed primarily as potentialities. It is nowhere claimed that the conditions described currently prevailed. The channels for their fulfillment were, however, open to the king (and to the people) through the king's special relationship with Yahweh.

Taken together, then, Pss 1 and 2 constitute a prologue to the canonical Psalter. The two psalms are linked by the INCLUSIO formed by the "blessed" (or *happy*) in Ps 1:1 and Ps 2:12. This linkage is strengthened by the use of the verb *hgh* in 1:2 (*meditate*) and in 2:1 (*plot*, lit. "mutter"). In Ps 1 the "murmuring" aloud in meditation on *torah* is positive; in Ps 2 the "murmuring" becomes "muttering" by the nations and their kings in rebellion against Yahweh and his anointed, and such "muttering" is *in vain* ("empty") because it arouses the wrath of God. The wicked in Ps 1 will *perish* (v. 6) and so will those in Ps 2 who conspire against Yahweh in (v. 11). Thus in a fashion like that of the WISDOM LITERATURE (cf. Prov 10-15) there is a contrast between *the righteous* and *the wicked* in these psalms: Psalm 1 is individual and Ps 2 is corporate (McCann 1993b, 41–42). The summation of the message of both psalms is found at the end of Ps 2:12: *Happy are all who take refuge in him* (i.e., in Yahweh)—the fundamental message of the Psalter.

The kingship ideology in Ps 2 has attracted much attention, but in its canonical function as part of the prologue to the Psalter we should concentrate on the sovereignty of God (McCann 1993b, 42), linked of course with the Davidic kingship exercised *on Zion* (v. 6). The ultimate reign belongs to Yahweh, not to the earthly potentialities of the king. The *king on Zion* represents "an extension of Yahweh's reign into the murky world of human politics" (Levenson 1986, 48).

Psalm 89 contains the same high kingship ideology as Ps 2 (although in different words), but emphatically confronts the seeming failure of Yahweh to keep his commitment to the Davidic dynasty (Ps 89:38-51), a failure that was a major part of the theological crises emerging from the EXILE after 587 BCE.

Books four and five function to respond to the unanswered question of Ps 89:46: *How long, O LORD? Will you hide yourself forever?* Part of the answer is found also in Ps 2: Yahweh reigns and is not intimidated by the world powers and he still intends to maintain his commitment to his *king on Zion*.

If faithful Israelites cannot forget Zion (Ps 137:5), surely Yahweh will not do so. The emphasis on Zion is a major one in the Psalms (see commentary on Pss 42–50, and the summary of book five at the end of Ps 150). However, the royal psalms leave the matter of the kingship open and without resolution. Expectantly, not in despair, the reader of the Psalms is led toward saying, "How long, O Yahweh, until you reign through your king on Mt. Zion?" Thus the prologue of the Psalter points toward the future and calls for faith.

Psalm 3

This psalm belongs among the laments, but notes of trust also are strong. The title contributes little directly to interpretation. It does illustrate the practice of assigning psalms (and speeches) to prominent people in especially dangerous or climactic moments.

The suppliant begins with a cry to Yahweh (vv. 1-2) that is characteristic of the laments, and expresses the greatness of the speaker's distress and danger. The mention of *foes* (or "enemies") is not uncommon in the laments and presents a special problem (see commentary on Ps 7). The suppliant is beset by foes who taunt the speaker by saying that *no help* from God can be expected.

The mood changes abruptly in vv. 3-6 from lament to confidence. The *but you* (v. 3) is a strong beginning of a statement of confidence, which is grounded in Yahweh, who is my *shield*, my *glory*, and the lifter of *my head* for the speaker. The last term may reflect the freedom of an accused person to lift up the head after prostration on the floor before charges of guilt hurled in the gate by adversaries. Verse 4 may indicate that the psalm was designed originally for a king (see Ps 18:6). Three statements of confidence follow one another: the certainty of being heard in prayer (v. 4); the security of sleeping and waking in the sustaining providence of God (v. 5); the freedom from fear, even when the situation seems impossible (v. 6).

Petitions for divine help appear with great force in v. 7. *Rise up* echoes the ancient invocation of the ark (Num 10:35). The references to *the cheeks* and *teeth* are in harmony with the language of the individual laments where frequent mention of the mouth, throat, lips, and teeth is made (Pss 5:10; 10:7; 31:19; 52:4; 57:5; 59:8; 140:4). The psalm closes with a positive note of confidence and blessing (v. 8). We could read this verse as relinquishment of the situation to the power of God. It also indicates that the individual laments must not be considered as purely private poetry. Concern for the people of the covenant community is included: *may your blessing be on your people!*

Psalm 4

Psalm 4 is best treated as an individual lament with such a preponderance of confidence that it becomes a song of trust. The situation of the suppliant is not defined in detail, although the general condition is stated. Yahweh has shown the speaker grace and lifted him or her out of the constrictions of distress into a new freedom. Nevertheless, the suppliant is experiencing vicious attacks from foes (v. 2), and finds many who are discouraged and discontented in their faith (v. 6).

Verse 1 appeals to God, based on past reception of help. *Distress* carries the idea of being restricted to narrow limits, pressed in on and deprived of freedom. God's intervention had relieved this terrible pressure.

The suppliant turns immediately to the opponents who are, apparently, men of influence (vv. 2-5). The *you people* suggests outstanding people rather than the ordinary numbers of the community. Thus the psalm reflects the abuse and oppression of the POOR by rich and influential people. One particularly dangerous weapon used by the rich was the false accusation of social or ritual crimes—charges that could result in the loss of property and life unless refuted (e.g., Nabob in 1 Kgs 21). The psalm represents a situation in which such false charges have been repudiated, in part at least, by a trial, but in which the speaker is still abused and slandered by foes. The affirmative judgment already given (vv. 1, 3) is cited, and the adversaries are warned to stop their opposition and bring themselves into right relationship with Yahweh (vv. 4-5). Verse 4 can be rendered in connection with v. 5 as: "Tremble, and do not continue to sin; think about it upon your beds, and be silent" (author trans.).

Verse 5 may point to a worship context, possibly in the sanctuary where charges against the suppliant have been heard. The person involved is admonished to go to the sanctuary and *offer right sacrifices*. The sacrifices must be *right*, not misused for malicious endeavors as they were on occasion. Verse 5 also provides a succinct summary of the basic nature of worship in Israel. The cult was always essential and, therefore, the sacrifices must be "right," that is, they should conform to the regulations stipulated for the covenant people. Sacrifices also must be accompanied by trust in Yahweh. The poles of obedience and reverence were to be held together in worship.

The speaker (vv. 6-8) addresses those in the congregation who are spiritually discouraged. Verse 6 includes a direct quotation from them. The supplicant's testimony of inner peace and strength is the confession that a "glad heart" is greater than rich harvests (v. 7). Despite the slanderous attacks from false accusers, the speaker is able to sleep well (v. 8). The supplicant's sleep (the accused and accusers may be passing a night together in the SANCTUARY [see Ps 17]) is not disturbed by fears of the future (cf. Isa 50:8-9).

Psalm 5

This individual lament is a prayer for deliverance from the charges of enemies. The speaker, despite accusations of wrongdoing, has gained admittance to a temple area in order to plead a personal case before Yahweh and the temple priests. The speaker prays and prepares to receive some revelation of innocence.

In the style of the laments, the supplicant prays that Yahweh will heed a cry for help (v. 1). *My King and my God* (v. 2) is a fixed formula that seems to have been used often (cf. Pss 44:4; 68:24; 74:12; 84:3). The supplicant has a case to be judged by Yahweh and waits for a verdict with the coming of morning, which probably reflects the custom of an accused person passing a night in a SANCTUARY while waiting for vindication (see Ps 17).

There is no word for "sacrifice" in the text (cf. v. 3 RSV), which literally reads, "I prepare for you." The word "prepare" can denote the preparation of a sacrifice (see Gen 22:9; Lev 1:8, 12), explaining the addition of "sacrifice" in some English translations. The verb that follows (*and watch*) indicates a worshiper waiting for a divine response. Such waiting may accompany sacrifice (Num 24:3; cf. Gen 15:7-18), but the verb is most commonly used of the prophets waiting for a revelation (Hab 2:1; Mic 7:7). When "watching" is combined with the word "prepare" the meaning also can refer to the preparation of words and speeches (Job 32:14; 33:5; 37:19; Ps 50:21). Thus it may be that "presenting one's case" (v. 3) and waiting for some indication of the divine verdict is a better reading of the text than "preparing a sacrifice."

The supplicant gains confidence from the privilege of worship in the temple (vv. 4-8), while the boastful evildoers are denied access to Yahweh's presence. *Stand before* (v. 5) is used of the assembly of the covenant people before Yahweh (Josh 24:1; 1 Sam 10:19). *The boastful* are denied participation in the assembly (cf. Ps 15:1-5). The speaker is one of *the righteous* (v. 12) who is permitted access to the divine presence by means of the *steadfast love* of Yahweh (v. 7). The *steadfast love* (*hesed*) of Yahweh refers to the force of will to remain committed to obligations—enduring loyalty and love. The supplicant disavows any arrogance in approaching worship (v. 7) being one who knows the need for protection and instruction (v. 8).

A charge against the enemies and a prayer for their destruction are found in vv. 9-10. A bright and joyful comparison in the mood is found in vv. 11-12 as the speaker urges all who take refuge in Yahweh to rejoice in the providential care they receive, praying that those who love the divine name (vv. 11-12) will rejoice because Yahweh will keep them safe.

Psalm 6

This individual lament includes a plea in the first part (vv. 1-5) with an abrupt change to confidence and answered prayer in the last part (vv. 8-10). Psalm 6 was first among the penitential psalms of the ancient church (others were Pss 32, 38, 51, 102, 130, 143).

The psalm begins with the agonizing prayer of a person under great suffering (vv. 1-5). The exact reason for the prayer is not given although sickness easily is suggested. The suppliant prays for release from the rebuke and wrath of Yahweh (cf. Pss 27:9; 90:7; Jer 10:10; Job 9:5; 17:1). The speaker knows the torment of the chastisement of God, although the reasons for the punishment are not specified. The speaker is *languishing* (v. 2), which indicates that the vitality and strength of life are draining away (cf. Ps 37:2; Job 14:2; 18:16). The speaker's *bones* (which equals "body"; see Pss 35:9-10; 42:10; Jer 20:9) are "troubled" (RSV) or, perhaps (with slight text changes) we should understand them as decayed or weakened.

The continuation of the prayer in vv. 4-5 emphasizes what commentators call "motivations" or reasons God should hear and answer a prayer. Two are given. The first is an appeal to Yahweh's *steadfast love*, the loyal-love (*hesed*) that transcends the weaknesses and failure of Israel. The second appeal (v. 5) is based on the inability of the dead to participate in worship (cf. Ps 88:11; Isa 38:18). If Yahweh expects to receive the praise of his people, he must keep them out of SHEOL.

A further description of the speaker's condition is given in vv. 6-7. Suffering is accompanied by moaning and the flowing of copious tears, and the speaker's situation is aggravated by the presence of foes (vv. 7-8). The change of mood from v. 7 to v. 8 is remarkable. The suppliant declares that the prayer to Yahweh has been heard, and the *workers of evil* (v. 8; see Ps 7) are summarily bidden to leave.

Psalm 7

The context of this individual lament is revealed in vv. 1-2. The suppliant has fled from unidentified pursuers to Yahweh's presence (cf. Ps 11:1), although the *refuge* may be metaphorical rather than cultic. The speaker feels like one being torn apart and dragged away by a lion (v. 2). The opening statements are followed by a protestation of innocence.

After the affirmation of innocence (vv. 3-5), the suppliant appeals to Yahweh to arise in anger against the enemies and "wake up" for judgment (vv. 6-8; on God awakening from sleep, see commentary on Ps 44). The prayer is a bold one—almost a challenge—that brings the suppliant to the brink of irreverence.

The terse, sharp idiom of these verses communicates the speaker's deep feelings and great agitation. *Awake, O my God* (v. 6) is derived from an ancient cry that signaled the movement of the ark of the covenant (see Num 10:35-36; Ps 68:1); it was a battle cry (adapted to liturgical poetry) for Yahweh to arise against enemies. Thus, the prayer is directed to the great leader and judge (i.e., the LORD) of the nations who comes to the throne above the ark in the Temple. The speaker appeals a personal case to the judge of *the peoples* of the earth (v. 8), on the basis of *righteousness* and *integrity*, boldly urging Yahweh to *judge me.*

The end of the wicked and the establishment of the righteous is sought (vv. 9-11) and an appeal is made to God who knows the inner mind and heart of human beings (cf. 17:3; Jer 17:10), and who can establish genuine judgment. The suppliant changes to affirmations of confidence in vv. 10-11. Verse 11 is uncertain, but may refer to God's attitude toward the wicked.

Verses 12-16 are clearly separated from the preceding verses, and from v. 17, which is a vow of thanksgiving and praise. They may have been added later as comment. A problem concerning the subject arises in vv. 12-13. The RSV assumes that God (not mentioned in the MT) is the subject, and the text is corrected and translated accordingly. It may be, however, that the subject is the enemy who is pictured preparing deadly weapons for battle. Thus the translation of vv. 12-13 would be

> If the enemy does not repent, but whets his sword,
>   bends and strings his bow,
> he has prepared weapons of death against himself,
>   making his arrows glowing hot. (author trans.)

The action of the enemies is described with a striking succession of verbs related to childbirth (v. 14), which is an ironic use of the ideas of conception and birth blessing. The entire passage stresses the teaching that the wicked suffer their own wickedness as judgment. Sinfulness judges itself. The *pit* which is dug for others becomes a trap for the digger (v. 15), who suffers the boomerang effect of ungodly conduct. To the person who lacks spiritual sensitivity, the fate of the wicked seems to be but a part of the paradox of life or the irony of existence. Those who have faith perceive the providential judgment of God.

This psalm is a suitable context for discussing two matters that often occur in the interpretation of the laments. The first of these is the protestation of innocence (vv. 3-5). The statements lack contrition and exhibit a deplorable self-righteousness on the part of the suppliant. In the case of Ps 7 the problem is not great because the vigorous declarations are clearly aimed at specific charges made against the accused—who emphatically denies them. Further, the speaker does not claim a general perfection and freedom from all faults. The claims are more sweeping in passages such as Pss 17:1-5; 26:1-6; Job 31, where they sound like declarations of absolute rightness before Yahweh. How should such passages be understood?

An answer begins with the recognition of cultic formulae used by worshipers to declare their fitness to participate in the worshiping fellowship on the basis of having fulfilled its requirements. An example of the use of such formulae is found in Deut 26:13-15, which contains statements to be used by the Israelite at a tithe-offering ceremony. The gate liturgies or formulae found in Pss 15 and 24 are closely related; they stipulate the requirements laid upon a worshiper who seeks to enter the sanctuary and participate in the ceremonies. Persons who declare themselves to have met the requirements are "righteous," that is, they are in a right relation with Yahweh and the people. Thus, the supplicant in v. 8 asks for judgment *according to my righteousness.* Remember that RIGHTEOUSNESS IN THE OT is neither a virtue or work of merit, nor a legalistic concept. Instead it refers to rightness of attitude and relationship.

Nevertheless, this is hardly an adequate explanation for the wide-ranging claims of innocence and virtue that are affirmed in passages like Ps 7. The relatively simple affirmations of cultic righteousness may become generalized statements of moral perfection. There are at least two roots to this development. First, never in Israelite worship was there a middle way between the "righteous" and the "wicked." A person was either one or the other. Israelite theology did not allow for a "fringe" member!

Another angle acknowledges the didactic design of liturgies and formulae. The confessions of innocence were intended to challenge and to instruct the worshipers in facets of life and devotion that made an ideal righteous person. The didactic features must have become stronger when the psalms were no longer used in specific cultic situations and were interpreted as scripture.

The second subject that needs attention is that of "the enemies" referred to in many psalms. Foes are described in manifold ways. If Pss 3–7 alone are surveyed a considerable list will result: *my foes,* and those who *are rising against me* (3:1); *ten thousands of people who have set themselves against me all around* (3:6); *the wicked* (3:7); *the boastful* and *evildoers* (5:5), and so forth. Such a listing could be extended throughout both the individual and communal laments. While such psalms are generalized descriptions that never specifically identify an adversary, the descriptive language is vivid, intense, and carries powerful emotional content.

Scholars have advanced several theories about the identity of the enemies. One interpretation understands the enemy as self-righteous neighbors or former friends who interpret the sufferings of the accused (especially in illness or economic distress) as a retribution for former sin. In other cases the enemies are seen as rich, powerful, arrogant, and oppressive members of society who take advantage of poor and humble folk.

Others emphasize the role of the enemies as false accusers, whose accusations necessitate the flight of the accused to a sanctuary where the charges could be laid before the priests (and before God) in order to secure a judgment that would release the accused (see above). A variation of this situation would occur in cases of sickness. The enemies may have had no direct connection with the illness, but they aggravated the condition of the sick person with charges of guilt, and with whispers and taunts of being forsaken by God. Many psalms probably contain references to such false accusers (e.g., Pss 3, 4, 5, 7, 17, 57, 59, 143).

Another theory is concerned with the *evildoers* or *workers of evil* found in the psalms (e.g., 5:5; 6:8; 14:4; 28:3). The word translated "evil" (*awen*) carries the idea of "power." In this usage, the power would be devoted to destructive and antisocial objectives. The power of the spoken word is particularly significant, thus it is assumed that the *workers of evil* are "sorcerers" or "cursers" who hurled their abusive words and curses at others with traumatic results. It is not necessary, however, to assume that such "sorcerers" were professional MAGICIANS or practitioners of the occult. The "sorcerer" could have been anyone who made use of cursing or condemning words, especially in community gossip. A person suffering from such attacks would use suitable laments and prayers provided by priests or some other liturgists. In addition to the prayers, some type of purificatory ritual, with a sacrifice and offering, was probably used to insure the supplicant's proper relationship to God and to nullify the effects of the *workers of evil*. The sick person, family, friends, and members of the community also would participate in the ceremonies.

Another important theory begins with the fact that some references to enemies identify them as foreigners. This is true in the community laments of the people, and in the royal psalms (e.g., Pss 44:9-16; 54:3-11; 18; 79:1-7; 89:22-23). The enemies of the king and of Israel are also the enemies of Yahweh (e.g., Pss 2; 18:3; 21:8-12; 66:3; 83:2-8; 89:10; 42; 52; 92:9; 110:1; 2; 132:18) although domestic enemies also may be included. Some references in the individual laments point in the same direction (e.g., Pss 9:5; 43:1-2; 54:3 [reading "strangers"]; 56:7; 59:5). Such psalms were originally intended for the use of the king although they were also recited by ordinary Israelites in subsequent usage. There is some logic in the conclusion that since "enemies" refers to foreigners in many places, the same meaning may be given to its use in other places. The analysis, however, must not be taken too far.

Such generalization is not confined to the descriptions of "enemies." It is found also in the descriptions of the condition of the worshipers. Repeated and varied accounts of distressing situations are found in the laments. Specific diagnoses of the speakers' troubles elude the interpreter again and again. This is less the case with the "we" laments, where there are fairly clear indications of attack from external foes (e.g., Pss 44, 74, 79, 80). The situation is far more difficult in the individual laments.

Two psalms (42–43 as a single psalm and 137) show that separation from Zion is the cause of lamentation. Others are characterized by such expressions as *I am weary* (Pss 6:6; 69:3), *my groaning* (Pss 22:1; 32:3); *my bones are out of joint* (Ps 22:14), *my eye wastes away* (Ps 31:9); and *my spirit faints* (Pss 77:3; 143:4). Even relatively precise passages such as Ps 38:3-8 permit no firm conclusions. The prayers of the suppliants do not help either. Such terms as "deliver me," "be gracious unto me," "forsake me not," or "save me" do not add greatly to the diagnosis.

Generalization indicates that psalms were composed for the common use of worshipers in ceremonies of different types. General formulae that could be used on many occasions had to be used. An example is found in the title of Ps 102: "A prayer for one afflicted, whenever one is faint and pours out complaint before Yahweh," a title that means the psalm is suitable for anyone in the condition described.

This judgment is no denial of the authenticity of the experiences described in the psalms. After all, professional poets and writers are among the most sensitive and perceptive of human beings. The mark of great writers is that they are able to transcend their own experiences and become fully "human." The cultic nature of the psalms enhances their power and has contributed immeasurably to their unique place in Jewish and Christian devotion.

Psalm 8

This is a hymn of praise that glorifies God the Creator whose handiwork is visible both in the heavens and in humanity. The major emphasis is not on the acts of creation themselves, but rather on the lordship of Yahweh over creation. It is God's "name" that is *majestic* in all the earth; it is God' *glory* that is "chanted" (RSV) above the heavens; it is the work of God's "hands" (*fingers*) that has been given over to the dominion of human beings.

There are problems in the translation of the invocation (vv. 1-2) that cannot yet be solved with assurance. The "chanted" of the RSV is uncertain, but it is possible that it should be understood in the sense of "recite in antiphonal song," referring to praise being sung by celestial beings (cf. Isa 6:3; 1 Kgs 22:19; Job 1:6; 38:7). A change of vowels (and reading the first two words in the Hebrew text as one) yields the translation: "O let me chant your glory above the heavens, with a mouth of babes and infants." The meaning, then, would be that the worshiper wishes to join in the heavenly chorus of praise even though his or her own voice would be like the babble of an infant in such exalted company. Although such a reading is attractive, however, it is conjecture.

The NRSV (also NIV; cf. NAB) *You have set your glory above the heavens* (v. 1c), is linked to v. 2, which seems awkward. The RSV of v. 2 assumes that the chanting of Yahweh's glory is done "by the mouth of babes and infants" (i.e., by the weakest members of humanity). Commentators have noted that a child has the capacity (often lacking in adults) to surrender to the great and glorious without repressive inhibitions. Childlike language may voice the praise of God in a manner worthy of the celestial chorus.

I prefer to treat v. 2 as a separate sentence with a period at the end of v. 1 (NRSV's two sentences in v. 1 seems less likely to me). The recitation (not *set)* of the heavenly glory is done by celestial beings (v. 1c). The meaning of v. 2 is pointed toward an earthly context. The praise of weak and mortal human beings is used by God to construct a *bulwark* against dangerous *foes* (cf. 1 Cor 1:27; 29; Matt

21:16). The weakness of human beings who trust in Yahweh is used as a fortress of strength against evil foes. *Founded a bulwark* (or "strength") seems strange; the NIV reflects the Greek text (cited in Matt 21:16) that reads "perfected [or prepared] praise." This eases the expression in v. 2: "From the mouth of babes and infants you have ordained praise." However, the Greek text is probably an interpretation of the Hebrew and indicates that the meaning is a "bulwark of praise": that is, foes and avengers cannot break through the praise of God that flows forth both in heaven and on earth.

There may be a thought pattern in the psalm, beginning above the heavens (v. 1) and moving to the earth (v. 2). Again, there is an upward look to the heavens (v. 3) followed by a consideration of humanity (v. 4). The pattern continues in the following verses. The exalted status of humanity is declared in v. 5 while the earthly role of humanity is established in vv. 6–8. The psalm opens in the plural person but a solo voice begins in v. 3. Verse 9 is a repetition of v. 1a.

The solo voice marvels at the wonders of the heavens, which are *the work of [Yahweh's] fingers* (v. 3). A night scene is indicated since there is no mention of the sun. There is no praise of the heavens as such; it is *your heavens, the work of your fingers, the moon and the stars that you have established.* The Creator, not the creation, is glorified. In v. 4, the comparison is not between humanity and the creation, but between humanity and the Creator. What are finite human beings in comparison with the glorious One whose praise is sung in the heavens and on earth and whose handiwork the moon and the stars show forth? Both terms for humanity in v. 4 point to a mortal and earthbound status. Human beings are mundane creatures, afflicted by transience and death. Yet, they have been the object of the concern of God, who is *mindful* of them and visits them both in salvation and in judgment.

Yahweh's care for humanity is grounded in creation itself (v. 5). Humanity has been made by Yahweh to be a *little lower than God,* that is, a "little less" than divine (Heb. *elohim*; "angels" in LXX). This is the place for humans in the universe, their "slot" in the cosmic order. Human beings do not belong among the celestial beings of the heavenly court, but they are given an exalted status and crowned with the *glory and honor* that belongs to God (cf. Pss 29:1; 104:1). The same terms are also used of kings (cf. Ps 21:5), and the role of humanity in creation is expressed in terms of royal ideology (cf. Gen 1).

The verses that follow (vv. 6-8) expound the status of humanity in the arena of human action in the world. Humanity has been given dominion over the works of God's hands, and *all things* have been put *under his feet*—placed under human power. No other animal threatens human dominion (vv. 7-8), because all other classes of animal life are subordinate to humanity.

The psalm closes with a repetition of the doxology of v. 1a, because it is the glory of Yahweh that is praised. Modern readers may miss the point. The exalted status of humanity in vv. 3-8 is often seen as separate from the glory of God. Such is not the case with the psalmist. The glory of Yahweh overshadows all other beings and things. Both the world and humanity are subordinate to the Creator. The real significance of human beings consists in their relationship to God's majesty and to God's *mindfulness* of them. The true glory of humanity is to live as God's creatures whose status is a given one.

Psalms 9–10

These two psalms belong together. They are printed as one psalm in Greek texts, and are linked by the acrostic principle, meaning that successive verses begin with words that begin with successive letters of the Hebrew alphabet (other examples of the acrostic style are Pss 25; 34; 37; 111; 112; 119; 145; Prov 31:10-31; Lam 1–4; Nah 1:2-11). Other evidence that Pss 9–10 should be treated as a single work include (1) Psalm 10 has no title, the only such psalm in Pss 3–41 except for Ps 33 (which may be read with Ps 32); (2) the *selah* occurs at the end of Ps 9, whereas elsewhere it appears in the body of psalms rather than at the end; (3) common language and form also join the two psalms; and (4) the two psalms together form a considerably extended and modified individual lament and thanksgiving.

The psalm begins with a thanksgiving vow (9:1-2), which occurs more normally at the end of a supplication. The speaker vows to praise Yahweh for all his *wonderful deeds* and declares an intention to testify of them to others. The "wonderful deeds" are explained in vv. 3-6: the grateful worshiper has been delivered from enemies by the righteous judgment of Yahweh. The exact nature of the judgment is not explicitly given, although vv. 5-6 indicate that the defeat of foreign foes was involved. If we think of a king (like DAVID) reciting this psalm, the context is probably that of victory in war. If an ordinary Israelite is the speaker, the reference is more probably to the judgment the suppliant has received, possibly at a SANCTUARY.

In 9:7-8 the horizon widens to include the whole world and all times. Yahweh is the king and the judge of the peoples of the world, whom he judges with justice and equity. Possibly a historical event lies behind vv. 5-8, but it is more probable these verses are drawn from festival worship when Yahweh's universal power and kingship were celebrated (cf. Pss 24:1; 8-9; 47:6-7; 96:10-14; 98:9; 1 Sam 2:10; Acts 17:31; Lev 20:11-15). The power of Yahweh, so strongly stated in vv. 5-8, is available for the oppressed and for all who seek a place of security in times of trouble (9:9–10).

In 9:11-12 an invitation to sing the praises of Yahweh is directed to the congregation and correlates with vv. 1-2. Verse 12 reminds the worshipers of an aspect of Yahweh's attitude that often is found repeatedly in the OT, namely God's mindfulness of the oppressed and afflicted, whose cries he never forgets.

In 9:13-14 the psalm swings back to the personal situation of the worshiper. The speaker is confident that Yahweh will lift him or her *up from the gates of death* (cf. 107:18; Matt 16:18), and that he or she may recount the praises of Yahweh in the *gates of daughter Zion* (i.e., the Temple).

The word *daughter* refers to the people of Zion as a unit (cf. the "daughters of Egypt," Jer 46:24; and Isa 22:4; Jer 44:11; Lam 4:10). The translation should be either "the One who will lift me up from the gates of death" or "O One who lifts me up from the gates of death!" The judgment of Yahweh is especially manifest in the ways nations and the wicked fall by their own pits and devices: in nets made for others, that is, *in the work of their own hands* (9:15-16).

Yahweh's praise is set forth in the powerful affirmations of 9:17-18. *The wicked shall depart to Sheol* where they belong (v. 17). Verses 19-20 express both confidence and strong pleading for judgment of the wicked peoples: *Let the nations know that they are only human* (cf. Pss 8:4; 90:3; 103:15-16).

Psalm 10:1-11 begins with an introduction that is typical of the complaints, and expresses the speaker's concern with the apparent remoteness of God. Why does God seem to hide *in times of trouble?* Verses 2-11 give a detailed picture of the situation that results when arrogantly wicked members of society are allowed to have their unrestrained way.

The evildoers care only for themselves and seek their own profit and security. They counsel their own hearts to have assurance in their self-gained prosperity (v. 6). The poor always suffer most from the wickedness of the godless (vv. 9-11).

In the closing section (10:12-18), the worshiper prays to Yahweh and implores him to arise to meet the needs of the afflicted. The bases for the appeal are set forth in v. 14. "Arise, O Yahweh" (v. 12) is a regular cultic formula (Num 10:35-36; Pss 3:5; 7:6; 17:13; 74:22; 132:8). The language of this passage contains a polarity between petition and statements of confidence, ending with the positive assertions of vv. 17-18.

Psalm 11

This psalm is one of trust and confidence, closely associated with the laments. The speaker addresses a demoralizing crisis of faith. The situation of the worshiper is described as one who takes refuge with Yahweh (possibly in a place of worship) from the persecution of enemies. The victim expects to find security and vindication with Yahweh. There are some, however, who counsel the speaker to flee to the mountains. However appropriate such advice may be at some times, the speaker rejects flight and chooses to rely on the power and righteousness of Yahweh (vv. 1-2).

The speaker quotes what appears to be a proverbial saying (v. 1; cf. Ps 55:6). The saying incorporates the message of unidentified counsellors, who add to their admonition a description of the dangerous situation (v. 2) in which the enemies of the speaker have prepared a deadly ambush by night.

Another proverbial saying is found in v. 3: *If the foundations are destroyed, what can the righteous do?* It means that the righteous have no basis for effective action if the very foundations of justice and religion are destroyed.

The real foundation of the worshiper's faith is Yahweh's righteous judgment (vv. 4-7). Yahweh makes no mistakes in his assessment of people (v. 4c); the statement that "his eyelids test" (RSV) refers to the movement of the eyelids when the eyes are focused for close scrutiny. The righteous judgments of Yahweh will bring terrible punishment to the wicked (v. 6). On the other hand, the upright ones will have the privilege of seeing the *face* of Yahweh (v. 7), that is they will experience God's presence, possibly with some reference to a theophanic appearance.

Verse 4ab express a paradoxical tenet of the faith of Israel. Yahweh is both in heaven and in the Temple (cf. the prayer of Solomon at the dedication of the Temple [1 Kgs 8:27-30; 12–13]). In the ancient world there was a strong tendency to identify an earthly temple with its heavenly counterpart because they shared the same qualities. The presence of Yahweh in the Temple on Zion does not indicate God's absence from the heavenly throne. The two merge into one reality and the Temple links heaven and earth.

Psalm 12

This psalm is a lament, but it is not clear whether it is individual or communal. It has some of the characteristics of a liturgy. In any case, its emphasis is on *the promises of the LORD* (v. 6) that are pure and reliable, even in a prevailing context of moral degeneration and spiritual bankruptcy.

A faithless situation is described in vv. 1-4. The godly people have vanished from human society (cf. Mic 7). Lying and *flattering lips* (v. 2; lit. "lips of smooth things") mark the decadence of the time. The flatterers and liars boast of their power (v. 4) because they know the effectiveness of "smooth talk" in deception and fraudulent manipulation. Their deceitful behavior arises from a *double heart* (v. 2), an idiom that designates the opposite of the "one heart" (cf. Jer 32:39; Ezek 11:19; 1 Chr, 12:39; Acts 4:32) that is found in a mature unity of will, thought, and feeling. Such "double-heartedness" tears the fabric of society and destroys the basis for fellowship. No challenge to the godly person exceeds that of a *generation* (v. 7) characterized by double hearts and smooth lips.

The worshiper(s) pray for deliverance from this sorry plight (v. 3). The reply is put in the form of a prophetic ORACLE (v. 5) that quotes Yahweh's response (cf. Ps 91:14-16; Isa 33:10). He will arise *now* to intervene on the part of the poor and needy.

The last part of v. 5 has an uncertain text. A hymnic element in v. 6 stresses the purity of the promises of Yahweh: there is no double-heartedness here! Verse 7 may be translated: "You, O Lord, will keep them [i.e., the promises of v. 6]; You will guard us ever from this evil generation." Translated in this way, it becomes a statement of confidence. In this case, v. 8 should be understood with the force of "even though on every side the wicked prowl." Yahweh's protective care will be adequate even for such a degenerate time.

Psalm 13

This psalm has been described as a model individual lament (Gunkel 1929). It contains, in brief form, the major elements of the laments, and its depth of emotion is rarely exceeded in the Psalter.

A fourfold *How long?* adds great force to the complaint that opens the psalm (vv. 1-2). The problem of the speaker is revealed as a terrible sense of godforsaken-ness that is almost unendurable (cf. Ps 22:1-2). Yahweh's face seems hidden (v. 1);

enemies rise against the speaker (v. 2); and the suppliant dreads the potential cry of victory and rejoicing from the adversaries (v. 4).

From lament the speaker turns to petition in vv. 3-4. The prayer seeks to span the gap that separates the worshiper from Yahweh, and to reestablish the communion that had been broken. The speaker complains of the nearness of death and expresses a desperate need for a response from Yahweh (v. 3) because the light of his eyes is about to go out in death (cf. 1 Sam 14:27; 29; Lam 5:17; Pss 6:7; 38:10). Verses 3c-4 contain what is sometimes called a "motivation"—a prayer statement that gives the rationale for God's granting the requests of a worshiper. Motivations are varied in content, and they add extra force and urgency to the prayers.

The mood of the psalm changes abruptly from lament and prayer to confidence and a vow of praise (vv. 5-6). The speaker anticipates rejoicing in forthcoming deliverance and being able to sing the praises of Yahweh. These verses strengthen the petitions in v. 3 that form the heart of the psalm.

Psalm 14

Psalm 14 is identical with Ps 53 except for some textual changes. However, the messages of the psalms are different and should not be dealt with as merely the product of textual corruption or editorial changes.

Psalm 14 usually has been considered as a mixed type, almost in a class by itself. However, the psalm seems to fit the genre of prophetic-judgment speech, with two of its main features being (1) a lament or complaint by a speaker regarding social conditions and (2) either the citation of or reference to a speech by God. The social complaint is clear in vv. 1-3, and it is possible that v. 4 (or even vv. 4-7) forms a speech by Yahweh, although it seems more probable that these verses are written as from a PROPHET who reproaches evildoers in a taunting style. The psalm is converted into a prayer by the wish expressed in v. 7.

An abrupt statement introduces the situation and interprets its cause: a corrupt society where the fool says, *"There is no God"* (v. 1, lit. "absence of a god") and *no one . . . does good* (lit. "absence of one doing good"). *No God* does not refer to theoretical atheism, but to a practical atheism that may be paraphrased "God is not here." *Fools* have formulated judgment in their *hearts* (or minds). Such persons may not speak of it with their lips, but at the volitional power center of life they act as if God is absent.

The *fool* is designated by one of several terms used in the OT. *Nabal*, used here, represents the condition that is neither the result of inexperience and lack of education (the *pethi*) nor that of a brutish, stupid, and barbarous manner. The *nabal* is not stupid but rather one with a stubborn will and deliberate disregard of spirituality. By conventional standards the *nabal* may have been judged anything but a fool.

Yahweh is portrayed as looking *down from heaven* upon the activities of human beings (v. 2). This seems to refer to his role as the king-judge of the world and of all mankind (cf. Pss 2:4; 7:7; 9:7-8; 11:4; 33:13-14; 102:18-20). The focus of the divine scrutiny falls on the shockingly complete depravity of human beings (v. 3). They have all *gone astray* "together."

Verse 4 returns to the *evildoers* (the *corrupt* of v. 1) and expresses divine amazement at the thoughtless conduct of human beings who do not know the true nature of their way of life, The *no God* people *eat up* their neighbors (*my people*) as casually as people eat bread, unconcerned by thoughts of God's presence.

The judgment of God will not fail "the generation of the righteous" (i.e., those who are true to their relationship with Yahweh [v. 5]). The *there* of v. 5 is strongly emphasized: it may refer to the place where the evildoers try to carry out their foolish deeds against the people of Yahweh—the arena of their actions will be the place they will know the terror of judgment. More probable, however, the reading for *there* is in the sense of "that being so" or "then."

Verse 6 follows with the affirmation that Yahweh is the *refuge* of *the poor* whose *plans* are caused to fail by the evildoers who devour them in arrogant disrespect for the divine will (v. 4).

Verse 7 expresses a prayer in the form of an ardent wish for the deliverance of Israel by Yahweh coming forth from Zion to restore the fortunes of his people (cf. Amos 9:14; Hos 6:11; Joel 4:1; Jer 31:23; 33:7; 11; 26: Job 42:10). Such a deliverance would change the situation in vv. 1-6. Then Jacob-Israel would *rejoice* and *be glad*, and humankind would know that evil efforts to manage the world in defiance of God will finally fail.

Psalm 15

This psalm reflects the form of a "liturgy of entry" into a holy place or temple. Psalm 15 is not necessarily an actual admission liturgy; it may have been used in school and family teaching to express norms and ethical standard of the community.

The questions in v. 1 reflect those asked by approaching worshipers. The use of the word *tent* rather than "temple" is probably an archaism (cf. Ps 61:4; Isa 33:20) that kept alive the old tradition of the tent-SANCTUARY of Yahweh—here shifted to Mount Zion the *holy hill* (cf. Pss 2:6; 3:4; 43:3; 48:2). Possibly, however, there was a tent-shrine or tabernacle in the Temple itself, which would have eased the fusion of the two concepts. The terms "sojourn" and "dwell" (RSV) reflect the old practice of providing camping space in the sanctuary area for pilgrims. The worshipers wished to receive the privilege of being guests of Yahweh and of enjoying the benefits of divine hospitality (cf. Pss 65:4; 84:4).

A general statement of entrance requirements appears in v. 2, while vv. 3-5 explain it. Nothing is said of ritual requirements—such as purity rites and sacrificial correctness—since the essence of OT theology focuses on obedience in ethical relationships rather than ritual correctness. Obedience is better than offering sacrifices (1 Sam 15:22), although sacrifices had great significance (see Ps 4:5).

Verse 2 describes a trustworthy, mature person whose *heart* (mind) is a source of *truth*. Such persons "do righteousness" (*do what is right*) by behaving in a manner that sustains healthy relationships, both in the community and in worship.

Of the statements in vv. 3-5, two should receive special note. The "reprobate" (*the wicked*) is to be *despised* (v. 4a). The "reprobate" is one who is rejected and barred from worship because of behavior.

Verse 5a is startling for modern readers, but it reflects the laws that prohibited changing interest to fellow Israelites (cf. Exod 22:25; Deut 23:19; Lev 25:36). The Israelites attempted to eliminate the very high and destructive interest rates common in ancient times.

Psalm 16

Translators have had difficulty with this psalm, probably because it originated in the northern kingdom and its language contains elements of northern Israelite Hebrew (Rendsburg 1990, 29–30). It belongs to the psalms of confidence, those that affirm trust in God.

The opening petition is brief and changes quickly into testimony (vv. 1-2). In v. 3 the term for *the holy ones* can be understood either as the people of Israel who are especially devoted to Yahweh, or the priests. The more general reference to devout worshipers is better. In v. 4, the speaker refuses to be associated with the practice of IDOLATRY.

There is a THANKSGIVING addressed to God (vv. 5-6), a testimony of the happiness of communion with God, and a declaration of the assurance of victory over death in vv. 5-11. A remarkable use of the terminology of the allocation of the land of Canaan to the Israelite tribes occurs in vv. 5-6 (cf. Josh 13:23; 14:4; 17:5; Num 18:21-24; Deut 4:21), used here of the thanksgiving of an Israelite who has experienced a prerogative like that of the Levitical priests: *The LORD is my chosen portion and my cup* (see Deut 10:8-9; Num 18:20). The *cup* points to an intimate association with Yahweh. The conjecture has been advanced that there was a "festival cup" that was passed among those dining together at a feast. To drink from a common cup bound those participating in peace and fellowship.

Verses 7-8 also express a close relationship with Yahweh. It is Yahweh who *gives . . . counsel* that was received intuitively at night (*my heart* is lit. "my kidneys," a designation of the seat of inner feeling and emotion). The content of the *counsel* is not explicitly stated, but is probably included in v. 11. The speaker has been "caused to know" *the path of life* and has experienced a renewed measure of the *fullness of joy* and *pleasures* found in the presence of Yahweh. Even the thought of death cannot disturb the resulting joy and security (vv. 9-10).

Verses 9-10 contain no doctrine of a resurrection or any development of the idea of life after death. But v. 10 should not be reduced to only confidence that Yahweh would spare the speaker a premature death. The central point is that communion with Yahweh leads one onto a *path of life* that cannot end in death. Yahweh's inexhaustible resources for life will not be surrendered to SHEOL. So far as the speaker is concerned, the future holds nothing but life (cf. Ps 73). The Greek text of vv. 8-10 is used in Acts 2:24-28 to support the resurrection of Jesus.

Psalm 17

Psalm 17 is an individual lament in which the speaker makes a strong claim of innocence (vv. 3-5). Although the setting is vague, the psalm would have been suitable for varied contexts: one falsely accused seeking vindication in the temple; a king confronted by rebels and/or foreign foes; or a prayer of a person of faith oppressed by the wicked.

The opening verses (1-2) contain a prayer for Yahweh to grant judgment and *vindication*. The opening prayer is followed by an assertion of innocence (vv. 3-5). The speaker asserts a purity from guilt under vigorous testing (cf. Ps 7). The mention of *night* (v. 3) may indicate that the psalm reflects the practice an accused person spending a night in the *sanctuary* in order to receive an *oracle* or other indication of Yahweh's decision. The night was considered to be especially favorable for receiving a divine message (e.g., JACOB at BETHEL [Gen 28:10-17], SAMUEL at SHILOH [1 Sam 3:2-14], SOLOMON at GIBEON [1 Kgs 3:4-15], and GIDEON at ophrah [Judg 6:25-27]). Night also heightens the expectation of help and deliverance that comes in the morning (Pss 3:5; 4:8; 5:3; 16:7; 59:16; 143:8).

Assertions of innocence were designed to refute specific charges against the accused, charges that would have excluded them from communion with Yahweh. The declarations of innocence were not intended to be used in a boastful way. The language in declarations of innocence is standardized and reflects an ideal of the righteous person. The confessions of innocence also are testimony to the boldness and forthrightness of Israelite prayer. The very prospect of such prayer was calculated to produce repentance.

After the declaration of innocence, the psalm moves into a prayer (vv. 6-9), and on to a description of the conduct of deadly adversaries (vv. 10-12). The torment felt by the speaker explodes with the powerful petitions found in vv. 13-14. With the ancient battle cry of Israel over the ARK—*Rise up, O Lord . . . !* (cf. Num 10:35-36)—the speaker prays for Yahweh's deliverance from enemies. Verse 14a is a strong expression of the desire for judgment upon the children of the wicked (see Ps 58). Verse 14b refers to a mysterious "food of wrath" that is stored up for the wicked and their posterity (the meaning of this part of the verse is very uncertain).

Verse 15 reflects the confidence of the speaker who is sure of a meeting with Yahweh where the divine face will be seen *in righteousness* (i.e., with vindication and deliverance). Some interpreters think *when I awake* refers to awaking from the sleep of death in a resurrection, but it is more probable the verse reflects an expected deliverance, in a sanctuary, that the speaker anticipates receiving at dawn (cf. v. 3). The worship background may possibly go back to a vigil in the sanctuary with worshipers waiting for a solar THEOPHANY at dawn (when the light of the sun rising over the Mount of Olives shined into the Temple, enhanced by the gold plating of many objects in the interior). In time the actual rite of the theophany faded, while the imagery remained as figurative speech for God's face and presence (cf. Pss 4:8; 89:15; 90:8; 119:135).

Psalm 18

This psalm, which also appears in 2 Sam 22 with some changes of detail, is a royal thanksgiving psalm. The psalm is "royal" because it was intended to be spoken by a Davidic king. Some scholars question the unity of the psalm, but when it is interpreted from a traditio-historical perspective the difficulties largely disappear. The psalm apparently had a long history in the traditions of Israel, through which it was modified, especially the addition of the victory song in vv. 31-45. The powerful theophanic description in vv. 7-15 seems inserted into the main frame of the psalm, found in vv. 1-6, 16-19.

Commentators have dated Ps 18 as early as the tenth-century BCE (some even to the time and authorship of DAVID himself). Others, however, date it to later periods, particularly the period of HEZEKIAH (727–698 BCE) and JOSIAH (640–609 BCE). There can be no certainty about a specific date.

18:1-3. The context. Some scholars have argued that, regardless of later usage in the cult, it was prepared for a king on the occasion of some historical deliverance. Others maintain that it refers to the conflict and suffering experienced by the king in a ritual humiliation, and the deliverance that it is supposed was part of the autumn festival (Tabernacles) in preexilic Israel. The hypothesis of the humiliation of the king in the Israelite cult is plausible, but it is supported by very little evidence. The psalm invites the reader to think of a king, especially of David, as the speaker (note the superscription).

The opening testimony of love for Yahweh (vv. 1-3) is unusual in the OT. These verses contain a treasury of metaphors that describe attributes of Yahweh; strength and action are the qualities most evident. The king has available a great source of energy and power (and when the psalm became "democratized" they were available to ordinary worshipers). Yahweh has *saved* the king from his *enemies* (v. 3).

18:4-24. Thanksgiving. Verses 4-24 is a long THANKSGIVING. The conditions that prevailed when the king was delivered are described in vv. 4-5, 16-19. The "waves of death" (v. 4) had threatened to overwhelm and carry down the speaker to the primeval deep of death. Such language (reminiscent of mythological texts from the ancient Near East) apparently is applied to the threat posed to the king (and the nation) by enemies (vv. 16-19, 37-42). Those who interpret the psalm in a purely cultic context see a cultic drama in which the king has been attacked by his *enemies* (representative of the enemies of Israel) before he cried out to Yahweh and was delivered.

In any case, the king called out to Yahweh, who heard his voice in the heavenly temple (v. 6). Yahweh's response to the prayer of the king is a thunderous, earthshaking theophanic intervention (vv. 7-15). This passage is heavy with the imagery of a thunderstorm used as the instrument of divine action (cf. Pss 29; 97; 114). The description of the theophany is closely related to those that refer to Yahweh's coming to SINAI and those of his going forth to save his people in war (see Exod 19:16-24; Deut 33:2; Judg 5:4-5; 1 Kgs 19:9-18; Pss 50:1-6; 68:7-8; Isa

30:27-28; Hab 3:3-15). The king is delivered from his distress into a new freedom (vv. 16-18), which is not of his own doing. The repeated emphasis on divine action—*he reached, he took me, he drew me out, he delivered me, he brought me out*—is noteworthy.

The testimony of the king continues in vv. 20-24, emphasizing that his deliverance has been a vindication of his *righteousness* (his "right-relatedness" to Yahweh). This passage is very similar to the protestations of innocence in the laments (cf. Ps 7:3-5), except that it is put into the form of a testimony, a common motif for thanksgiving psalms. These verses should not be read as making a claim to a general sinless perfection. They constitute an affirmation of faith and a testimony of the salvation received from Yahweh.

18:25-30. Testimony. The king continues the testimony in hymnic terms (vv. 25-30). He declares that human behavior does matter to God, whose response is appropriate to the attitudes manifest towards him. In v. 27 what is true for an individual is applied to the people: the king knows that he, alone, has not been saved but as one of the company of *humble people* who have taken refuge with Yahweh.

18:31-50. God's strength. The second part of the psalm begins in the third person plural (*our God*), which can be either an opening verse spoken by the congregation, or by the king praising Yahweh before the congregation and identifying himself with them in loyalty to Yahweh. The verses that follow tell of the charismatic equipment and training Yahweh has given to the king (vv. 32-36). A graphic picture of victory in battle follows (vv. 37-42). The victory of the king (either cultic or historical) was complete, and afterwards he was made *head of the nations* (v. 43) and served by foreigners who, cringing before him, cease their opposition to him (vv. 44-45; cf. Ps 2).

Verses 46-50 contain closing sections of praise and thanksgiving. Again, Yahweh is lauded for the triumphs he gave the king over his enemies. Verse 50 establishes the connection of the psalm with *David and his descendants*.

Psalm 19

Two separate and independent units compose this psalm (vv. 1-6 and vv. 7-14). The units differ in subject, language, and poetic meter. The first unit is hymnic praise of Yahweh's glory in creation; the second unit praises the *torah* (cf. Pss 1; 119). The originally separate units have been deliberately bound together; the resulting combination ought to be interpreted as a whole. The link that binds them is theological: Yahweh's will and action.

19:1-6. God in creation. The *glory* and *handiwork* of God in creation is praised in vv. 1-4b. The testimony of creation is a perpetual one, *day to day* and *night to night*. Yet the testimony is given without speech, words, or voice. The "silent eloquence" (Kirkpatrick 1901) of their witness goes out to the ends of the earth. These verses mock the beliefs of many in ancient Egypt and Mesopotamia, where there was a tendency to identify the heavens, as well as the forces of nature, with deities. For the Yahweh worshiper, however, the FIRMAMENT was a witness of the handiwork of God.

Verses 4c-6 refer to the course of the sun across the heavens, and recall numerous examples of ancient Near Eastern praise of the sun-god. However, vv. 4c-6 is not a hymn to the sun, since there is no summons to praise or any direct access. By juxtaposition, these verses praise the God whose handiwork is displayed in the heavens (v. 1). A small change in the text of "in them" (NRSV mg.) of v. 4c results in the reading "in the sea." However, the change is unnecessary and the "in them" provides a connection between vv. 1-4b and 4c-6. The *tent for the sun* is set *in the heavens* (vv. 1, 6). The note of comprehensiveness in vv. 3-4 appears again in v. 6c. Both the glory of God and the heat of the sun pervade the whole world.

19:7-14. The will of Yahweh. The second unit, vv. 7-14, is concerned with the *torah* of Yahweh. With an abruptness similar to v. 1, the psalmist begins the description of the "*torah* of Yahweh" in v. 7. A series of terms for *torah* are used (vv. 7-9), along with repeated praise of its effects. Its comparative value is stated in v. 10; v. 11 is the speaker's own testimony, a joyful affirmation of the goodness and greatness of the *torah*, which is the revealed will of Yahweh (note that LORD is used repeatedly in vv. 7-14 while not at all in vv. 1-6).

The mood of the psalm changes quickly to that of prayer in vv. 12-14. *Meditation* on the *torah* leads to awareness of one's own inner needs. The prayer expresses a consciousness of the liability of all people to sin, for there are those *hidden faults* no one avoids. Verse 13 addresses the rebellious and proud will that so easily rises to usurp the behavior of human beings. This verse may have in view the provision of the *torah* for the atonement for sins of inadvertence (Lev 4–5; Num 15:22-29) while lacking any provision for a sacrifice for sins with a "high hand" (Num 15:30-31).

In the closing verse, acceptance of prayer by Yahweh is sought. The word translated *be acceptable* is used in cultic regulations for proper sacrifices (cf. Lev 1:3-4). Perhaps the prayer is offered here as a substitute for sacrifice (see Pss 40:6-8; 141:2).

It seems that the poet wished to bring together creation and *torah* as the two great works of Yahweh. In its present form, Ps 19 probably originated in those Israelite theological circles associated with WISDOM LITERATURE. Elements of wisdom vocabulary are found in vv. 7-11, and the cosmological view of vv. 1-6 is that of the fixed, stable, and silent universe of wisdom theology. The stability of creation was matched by the certainty and dependability of the *torah*.

From another angle, the poet wanted to bring such "natural theology" as that in vv. 1-6 into subordination to the revealed will of Yahweh. The heavens silently tell the glory of God, but only the *torah* restores life, rejoices the heart, and enlightens the eyes. The will of Yahweh for the people is not in speech or knowledge of the heavens (v. 3); it is in *torah*. A person may contemplate the handiwork of God in the heavens, but a person becomes a *servant* (v. 11) who can speak of God as *my redeemer* (v. 14) only by the *torah*.

Psalm 20

This royal psalm in the form of a prayer for the king has two main parts: a prayer for the king (vv. 1-5, although the king is not mentioned until v. 9), and the assurance that the prayer has been heard (vv. 6-8). Verse 9 is a concluding exclamatory statement that recapitulates the main idea of the psalm. The people pray for the king in vv. 1-5. An individual speaks (v. 6) and affirms that Yahweh will answer the prayers for *his anointed,* the king. The solo voice is not identified, but may be a priest. The group joins in the affirmation in vv. 7-9. Verse 7 sets forth the basic faith of Israel when confronted by the powers of the world. The heart of this faith is the confidence that the ultimate decisions of history do not depend on the might of military armaments (see Ps 33:16-17). Israel's power lies in the privilege of pronouncing (RSV, "boast of") the name of Yahweh (cf. Ps 118:10-12).

The occasion for the recitation of this psalm was probably a day of prayer for the king prior to an engagement in war. The ceremonies would have included prayer and sacrifices (see v. 3; cf. 1 Kgs 8:44-45; 1 Sam 7:9; 13:9-12; 2 Chr 20).

Psalm 21

This royal psalm contains three different types of literary material: vv. 1-7 is a thanksgiving; vv. 8-12 is an affirmation addressed to the king; v. 13 is a short prayer similar to those found in the laments of the people (cf. Pss 44:23; 74:22; 79:9). The mixture of literary types points to a liturgical character of the psalm with change of speakers, probably priests or other liturgists.

The psalm is usually considered to be a thanksgiving after a king's victory in battle, intentionally paired with Ps 20. That conclusion is doubtful since the victory in vv. 8-12 seems to be in the future. It is more likely that the psalm's context is in the festival rituals centering around the Davidic king. The welfare of the nation depended upon the welfare of the king.

The first section (vv. 1-7) opens with praise to Yahweh for answering the king's prayer. The general nature of the prayer and its answer are found in vv. 4-5. The exalted language was used of kingship (cf. 2 Sam 7:13-16; 23:3-5; 1 Chr 18:6; Pss 2; 61:6-7; 72:15-17; 89:19-37).

The king has been given *life* (v. 4) that will endure *forever and ever,* a Hebrew idiom that carries the connotation of "many years" of indefinite duration, plus the blessing of vitality (cf. Pss 2, 110). The phrase is probably an honorary attribution (Neh 2:3; Dan 2:4).

Verses 8-12 is an affirmation (or perhaps an ORACLE) addressed to the king, declaring that he will be victorious over his enemies. The victory will not be that of the king alone, however, because an annihilating fire will go out from Yahweh and engulf his foes (vv. 9-10; cf. Exod 24:17; Deut 4:3; 9:3). Yahweh is Israel's "devouring fire" (v. 9) the one who defends the king and his people. The psalm closes with a brief prayer and vow of praise by the congregation (v. 13).

Psalm 22

By form this psalm is a combination of individual complaint and thanksgiving (v. 22-31). The marked change of mood after v. 21 is a common characteristic of the laments. The shift in mood can be explained either by spiritual and psychological changes in the worshiper, by some ORACLE or cultic act carried out in response to the first part of the psalm, or more easily by assuming that there is a time span between vv. 1-21 (or 1-21a, NRSV) and the thanksgiving ceremony assumed in vv. 22-31. If there is a temporal change, the agonizing prayer in vv. 1-21 is recalled after divine relief of the sufferer's distress; thus the psalm takes its orientation from its second part.

The psalm is deeply embedded in Christian tradition because Jesus quotes the first line of v. 1 from the cross (Matt 27:46; Mark 15:34). The long tradition of Christological exegesis is appropriate, but the psalm in its OT setting is not a prophecy of Jesus, regardless of how significant the Gospel writers' use of v. 1 may be. Psalm 22 is a prayer of complaint, which expresses the agony of great suffering and plumbs the depths of the human experience until it rejoices in the divine deliverance. In the latter part, the psalm celebrates a triumphant faith that has overcome the terrible sense of godforsakenness that dominates the first part of the psalm.

The context of the lament (vv. 1-21) is not certain. The language is to a degree that of the conventional complaint (a lament), but the dimensions of the suffering seem to exceed the distress of an ordinary worshiper. Possibly the psalmist had a king in mind, even if the psalm was later "democratized" and placed in common cultic use. The condition of the suppliant also is not clear. There are striking descriptions of adversaries (vv. 6b, 7, 8, 12, 13, 16, 17b, 18), but illness appears in vv. 14, 15, 17a. There may be no opposition between the two views, however, if we think of the enemies as those who mock the speaker as one godforsaken on the basis of the suffering from physical misfortune.

The sense of being abandoned by God is poured out in the repeated cries of vv. 1-2. The cries of despair are addressed to *my God*, a personal God, and could come from a king. The cries may also recall the worship of families or other small groups. There is no loss of faith, only the incomprehensible remoteness of God. Despite the importunity of the prayer there is no answer (v. 2). *Groaning* (v. 1) is a translation of a word commonly used of the roar of a lion (Isa 5:29), but when applied to human beings it is a wail of pain and anguish.

In vv. 3-5 the mood shifts to the first statement of confidence. Yahweh is addressed as *holy* and *enthroned on the praises of Israel*. This strange phrase is similar to "enthroned on the cherubim" in Pss 80:1 and 99:1, a reference to the ARK of the covenant. The expression reflects the concept, known elsewhere in ancient Near Eastern religions, of a deity whose throne is supported above the earth by the loyalty and praise of his subjects. The faith of the ancestors is recalled in vv. 4-5. The individual finds comfort by identification with the sacred history of the people.

Overwhelmed by suffering, which is aggravated by the taunts of adversaries, the speaker again falls into despondency (vv. 6-8). The speaker is so despised and mocked by the people that there is a loss of a sense of human status. The validity of the speaker's commitment to Yahweh also is scornfully questioned by the adversaries (vv. 7-8; cf. Matt 27:42-43).

Again the attention of the worshiper turns to the acts of God, but this time to God's involvement in personal existence (vv. 9-11). The speaker has been a child of God since birth, and now prays (v. 11) to the God on whom he is totally dependent.

The pilgrimage through suffering and doubt does not end, however, with v. 11. Emotional turbulence arises again in the lengthy complaint found in vv. 12-18, which extends the complaint in vv. 6-8. The descriptions of the suppliant's condition are extreme and show that death is near (v. 15, *you [are about to] lay me in the dust of death*). Indeed, the enemies are so sure of impending death that they have already divided the victim's clothing among themselves (v. 18).

In vv. 19-21, there is a return to prayer and to the sense of God-remoteness that was dominant at the beginning of the psalm. Probably the last word in v. 21 (see RSV mg. and NRSV mg.) represents the sudden turning point in the psalm. The prayer is broken off abruptly with "You have answered me!" (NRSV mg.). If this is correct, a sudden realization of contact with God breaks into the speaker's consciousness.

There is a change of mood and a shift of context in vv. 22-31. The suppliant expresses a determination to bear testimony to *the congregation* (lit. "my brothers") of worshipers at the sanctuary (v. 22). The speaker also invites the assembled worshipers to join in praise (v. 23). Yahweh has been exceedingly gracious to the suppliant, as to all who cry out to him (v. 24). The praise of suppliant will be accompanied by the fulfillment of vows, probably with offerings (v. 25). Some interpreters think v. 26 indicates a communal meal, to be shared by the rejoicing person with the poor.

A remarkably extended view concludes the psalm (vv. 27-31). The suppliant turns attention from the immediate context in Israel to include *all the families of the nations*. In a VISION of the future, a vast panorama of people will prostrate themselves in worship before Yahweh. The central verse (v. 28) asserts that sovereign kingship belongs to Yahweh, for God is the ruler of the nations.

Verse 29 is difficult to translate. The general thrust of vv. 29-31, however, seems clear: not even death will stop the testimony of praise (cf. 6:5; 88:10-12). It is doubtful that v. 29 conveys an idea of resurrection, but the limitations of death are broken. The psalm closes with an abrupt cry of triumph: *he has done it*. The completeness of Yahweh's great deliverance will be proclaimed from generation to generation. The terrible forsakenness of vv. 2 and 11 is replaced by the joyful praise of those who have been delivered.

Psalm 23

This best-known psalm is a declaration of trust, and implies an audience for the speaker, who directly addresses God (v. 5). The speaker testifies to a close relationship with Yahweh (*my shepherd* is possessive). The psalm uses three images: shepherd (v. 1), guide-protector (vv. 3-4), and host (v. 5). The metaphors of the psalm are held together by three elements: (1) they are associated with kingship; (2) they are used elsewhere for Yahweh; and (3) the name Yahweh (LORD) in vv. 1 and 6 forms an INCLUSIO that binds the parts together.

The psalm is very personal, but may have been designed as a confessional prayer for worship, perhaps for a thanksgiving-praise service. The first three verses contain a concentration of verbs and figures of speech that evoke images of security and well-being. *Shepherd* is a universal figure, associated with both the care of sheep and the function of kings.

The shepherd is also the guide-protector who directs the sheep to a secure camp near water (the emphasis is not on the stillness of the water but the security and comfort of the site) and protects those whom he leads with rod and staff—symbols of kingship—even when they pass through "the valley of death." Verse 4 is sometimes read as "the valley of deep darkness" or as *through the darkest valley*, carrying the idea of great danger and the nearness of death.

Thus the speaker can declare that there is no "lack" in Yahweh's providing for his people (v. 1), and no fear as he guides them through the times of terrible distress (v. 4). The divine presence (*you are with me*) guarantees safety. Yahweh leads his people in "paths of righteousness" (v. 3 KJV, RSV, NIV), that is, in those ways that go where they are supposed to go (one does not get lost on such paths) and those that are beneficial. He restores and fortifies the vigor and vitality of his flock (v. 3, *restores my soul*; cf. Ps 19:7; Lam 1:11; 16; 19).

The restoring of the *soul* in v. 3 is matched by the metaphor of the host (v. 5) who prepares a safe and abundant table, and extends hospitality despite the presence of enemies (cf. Ps 78:19). Yahweh as host provides a place of life and comfort for his guests. The background of this image includes the protection that is required for the host to extend to a guest. The guest is well cared for by the host in v. 5: the table is prepared, the guest's head is anointed with oil, and a cup filled to the brim is provided. The *presence of my enemies* (v. 5) indicates that enemies watch impotent to do any harm, while the speaker is blessed by the protective hospitality of Yahweh.

The change of metaphor from shepherd and guide to that of host is not surprising when it is remembered that *shepherd* is kingship language. Kings have great houses and entertain favored guests with lavish hospitality. Further, the shepherd in this case is Yahweh; and it is customary for reigning deities to have "houses" (temples) in which they dwell. The setting of vv. 5-6 is that of the Temple, a place where the worshiper feels safe and well supplied with food and drink (as those who attend the festivals). The idea of defeated enemies looking on while a victorious deity prepares tables for its soldiers is found in the Canaanite accounts of the goddess Anat at Ugarit (cf. Ps 27:6).

Follow me (v. 6) is too weak for the verb that means "to pursue" or "to chase." *Goodness* and "enduring-love" (a better translation than *mercy* or "kindness" [NRSV mg.]) will pursue the speaker *all the days of my life* (cf. the pursuit of the wicked by tempest and hurricane in Ps 83:15). The pursuit by enemies is terminated and replaced by being chased by Yahweh's fidelity and love.

The last part of v. 6 expresses confidence that the longing of pilgrims participating in the festivals at the Temple for permanent residence there will be fulfilled (cf. Pss 15:1; 27:4-6; 36:7-9; 52:8-9; 61:4; 65:4; 84; 92:12-13). The literal "I shall return to the house of Yahweh" probably means "I will be a regular guest in the house of Yahweh," that is, it will always be "home" for me. Verse 6 expresses a close and enduring contact with the divine presence. Indeed, *the house of the LORD* here may include the idea of "the household of Yahweh" in a broader sense—even to the land of Israel and the company of Yahweh's people.

Psalm 24

This hymn of praise opens with a declaration of Yahweh's cosmic ownership of the peopled and fertile earth and of his establishment of it on the *seas* and the *rivers*, which recalls the concept of the bringing forth of an ordered world out of the unruly forces of chaos. The COSMOLOGY is that of an established world founded above the primordial seas and rivers below it (see Gen 1:6; 7:11; Exod 20:4; Deut 33:13; Pss 18:15; 77:16-20; 93:1-4; 95:3-5; 104:5-9; 136:6; Job 38:4-11). Yahweh has given the world its stability but the reader is also reminded that the raging floods flow beneath the surface of earth and are always a potential threat.

The rest of this psalm has a liturgical aspect that recalls processions of worshipers going to Zion (and the Temple) for festivals. Verses 2-6 have been described as an "entrance liturgy" (cf. Ps 15), recalling the instruction and encouragement exchanged by pilgrims as they approach the Temple. The question-answer-promise format sets forth the nature of those who are worthy to come to the holy place of Yahweh and *seek the face of . . . God* (v. 6).

The last part of the psalm (vv. 7-10) also has a liturgical character with the question–answer form. These verses suggest a procession into Jerusalem and the Temple area. The assumption of a cultic ceremony involving the movement of the ARK of the covenant into the inner area of the Temple as a part of the celebration of the kingship of Yahweh is rather widely held. Heralds of the king address the gates and doors as a prelude to the entrance of the victorious monarch.

The cry to the gates to *lift up your heads* (vv. 7, 9) has been the subject of considerable difference of opinion. Is it simply the poetically exaggerated language of worship because even the highest gates and doors would be too low for the King of Glory? Are they the gates of the heavenly abode of Yahweh? (Sarna 1993, 133–34). Does the cry reflect the destruction of the Temple in 587 BCE (see Lam 2:9) and, therefore, represent a call for its rebuilding?

The most likely interpretation is that the *heads* do not refer to the gates but to the people on the towers of the gates who are depicted as expectedly waiting for the return of a king from battle. The gate towers are personified as those who wait, bent over in fear, for the return of the king. The situation envisioned is that of Yahweh, the divine warrior, returning victorious after going forth to battle against the forces of evil and death that threatened the land and the world. Verses 1-2 announce success. Yahweh of Hosts is described in v. 8 as *strong and mighty . . . mighty in battle*." For *the LORD [Yahweh] of Hosts*, see 1 Sam 1:3; 4:3-4; 2 Sam 6:2; Pss 80:4; 7; 14; 19; 84:1; 3; 8; 12; 89:8; and LORD OF HOSTS; cf. 2 Kgs 19:15; Ps 80:1. *Hosts* refers to the heavenly armies that are led by Yahweh, who *is the King of glory*.

Psalm 25

This individual lament is in an alphabetic, or acrostic, form (i.e., each verse begins with a successive letter of the Hebrew alphabet). This form does not lend itself to a smooth logical development of thought, and accounts for a degree of literary "stiffness" in the POETRY of the psalm.

The exact context of the psalm is impossible to determine. There are references to the presence of violent enemies (vv. 2, 19) and statements of innocence (vv. 15, 21), which may indicate that the poet had in mind the situation of a person who seeks vindication from false charges by going to the SANCTUARY in order to plead a case before Yahweh. The most interesting element in the psalm is the prayer for forgiveness of sin (vv. 6-7, 11).

The opening verses (vv. 1-3) express a prayer to Yahweh. Verse 3 may be read as a statement rather than a petition: "Yea, no one of those who put their hope in you will be put to shame / but those who are treacherous without cause will be put to shame" (author trans.). Such conviction provides the basis for the prayer in vv. 1-2.

The prayer continues in vv. 4-7, as the suppliant seeks divine instruction. The terms *ways*, *paths*, and *truth* are all similar to the term *torah* (law), and refer to Yahweh's will for the people. In vv. 6-7 the prayer becomes petition for the forgiveness of personal sin.

A short hymn-like section interrupts the prayer in vv. 8-10. These verses lay a theological foundation for the prayer as they describe the ways of Yahweh with *sinners* and *the humble*. The prayer resumes (vv. 11-22) with a renewed plea for pardon from guilt (v. 11). Verses 12-15 contain statements of confidence about the condition of the person who "fears Yahweh" and express the posture of the speaker toward Yahweh. Verse 22 is a prayer for all Israel attached to the end of the lament.

Psalm 26

The dominant features of this individual lament are confidence and certainty. Imperative petitions for acquittal and vindication dominate vv. 1-2, buttressed by a confidence in personal faith and unwavering loyalty.

The opening of the psalm is followed by a declaration of innocence (vv. 4-7) that also describes the ritual actions of the accused (vv. 6-7). Washing hands was a rite that publicly proclaimed purity (see Deut 21:6; Ps 73:13; Matt 27:24). To *go around your altar* may refer to joining a solemn procession during which the worshipers chanted the great acts of Yahweh. The sanctuary proper was not open to lay persons; only priests and Levites could enter it. The courts were accessible to non-priests, however, and the altar was located in one of them. The speaker's love of the Temple is expressed in v. 8, and petitions are renewed in vv. 9-11. The speaker contrasts hands washed *in innocence* (v. 6) with hands *full of bribes* (v. 10).

Verse 12 is a closing statement of certainty. The metaphor of the foot, in one form or another, is frequently found in the Psalter (see Pss 31:8; 40:2; 56:13; 66:9; 73:2).

Psalm 27

The sharply defined break in mood and language between vv. 6 and 7 has led some commentators to treat this psalm as composed of two independent and unrelated parts. On that analysis, vv. 1-6 is a song of trust that expresses a powerful and steady faith in Yahweh and vv. 7-14 is the lament of one who is in great distress.

The contrast between vv. 1-6 and vv. 7-13 should not be exaggerated because there is considerable correspondence between the two sections. The statements of vv. 1-6 may be read as presupposing a context of danger and distress. Psalm 27 may reflect, but is not necessarily directly related to, the experience of an Israelite pilgrim going for festival worship who is attacked by enemies (probably false accusers) while some distance from the Temple. Verses 1-6 may be read in the context of danger and distress where the speaker is nonetheless sure that security and vindication will be found at the holy place (vv. 4-6, 13).

The prayer of vv. 7-12, then, is that offered by the persecuted pilgrim after arrival at the sanctuary. The speaker prays in the presence of the congregation and, probably, before threatening *false witnesses* (v. 12). At the close of the prayer, a word of encouragement is given to the speaker by a priest (v. 14).

Psalm 28

This psalm belongs to the individual laments, but the situation that lies behind the speaker's prayer is not very clear. There is a reference to *the wicked . . . who are workers of evil* (v. 3), and the prayer is made toward, not in, the inner part of a SANCTUARY, probably the Temple in Jerusalem.

The opening call in vv. 1-2 is directed to Yahweh as the suppliant's hands are lifted *toward your most holy sanctuary* (v. 2; NRSV mg.: "your innermost sanctuary"). The speaker probably should be thought of as a worshiper in an outer court of the Temple. The term *debir* (*sanctuary*) in v. 2 refers to the Holy of Holies (Heb 9:3) where the ark of the covenant was kept (cf. 1 Kgs 6:16-19; 8:6; 24-30). The ark was the locus of Yahweh's appearing to his people (cf. 1 Sam 4:4; 2 Sam 6:2; Exod 25:22).

For *my Rock* (v. 1a), see Pss 19:14; 31:2; 92:16; 94:22; Deut 32:15; 30; 31. A silent response from Yahweh to prayer is equal to a death sentence (v. 1b).

The speaker pleads not to be destroyed in the judgment of *the wicked* (vv. 3-5) whose judgment is prayed for (vv. 4-5). The speaker seeks to disassociate from the wicked who *do not regard the works of* Yahweh, who treat lightly the saving acts of God.

The mood changes to a hymnic testimony of thanksgiving in vv. 6-7. The individual praise of vv. 6-7 broadens to include the whole people of Yahweh in vv. 8-9, with special mention of the king (*his anointed*). The confession of v. 8 becomes an intercessory prayer for the people in v. 9.

Psalm 29

Psalm 29 is a hymn that glorifies Yahweh's power and majesty. There are significant parallels between this psalm and Ugaritic poetry (which incorporates much of Canaanite religious understanding). The hymn probably was modified for Israelite theological purposes from a Ugaritic prototype. For example, it has been observed that BAAL, the name of a major Canaanite deity and one associated with thunderstorms, can be substituted for Yahweh (LORD) in the psalm with an improvement of the poetry, especially in terms of alliteration and rhyme with the sounds *b*, *l*, and *ah* (Holladay 1993, 21–2).

Verses 1-2 are a prelude or overture that is set in the heavenly court of Yahweh. The *heavenly beings* are more accurately the "sons of gods" (cf. Pss 82:1; 89:6; 7; 97:7), members of the celestial court where they worship and serve Yahweh (see commentary on Ps 82). The assembly of the gods, a rather common idea in the world of Israel's day, has become the court of Yahweh. The divine beings are divested of their status as deities and reduced in rank to that of servants of Yahweh.

In holy splendor (v. 2) is a doubtful translation. It can be "bow down before Yahweh in holy attire" (in suitable garments) or "bow down before Yahweh when the Holy One appears." The first translation is better for the poetic parallelism, but the entire context of the psalm can be cited in favor of the idea of the second, which would indicate a THEOPHANY.

Verses 3-9 describe a thunderstorm, understood as a manifestation of Yahweh's POWER and GLORY. It is a poem that links the power of the thunderstorm (one of the most awe-inspiring releases of energy experienced on this planet) with Yahweh. Distant thunder as it rolls in over the waters of the sea and gathering cloud masses (cf. 1 Kgs 18:44) is suggested by vv. 3-4. The "voice of Yahweh" expresses the thunder and power of the storm, which seems to reach a climax in v. 4. If *voice* is translated as "roar," v. 4 may be read as follows: "The roar of Yahweh—powerful! The roar of Yahweh—awesome!"

The full fury of the storm breaks over the land (vv. 5-7). The great trees of *Lebanon* go down, while the mountains themselves shake and quiver until they seem to move like jumping young animals (v. 6). *Sirion* in v. 6 refers to Mount Hermon (cf. Deut 3:9).

Verse 7 is much shorter than the other verses. It possibly belongs with *the God of glory thunders* (v. 3), which seems isolated in its present context. Or the line may be read as a part of v. 8, forming three colons to correlate with the tricolon in v. 3.

On the other hand, the poetic irregularity may be deliberately intended to emphasize the climax of the storm in *flashes . . . of fire* that issue forth from the voice of Yahweh.

The movement of the storm into the wilderness is described in vv. 8-9. The mention of *the wilderness of Kadesh* first marks the general southern border of Palestine as Lebanon (vv. 5-6) marks the north. Second, the wilderness was associated with the great formative events in Israel's religion. There Yahweh had appeared both to deliver and to judge. Third, thunderstorms, while they have destructive aspects, were above all the bringer of the rain that broke long dry seasons and restored fertility to the land. The fertility aspect is taken a step further in v. 9 if *causes the oaks to whirl* is translated "makes the hinds to calve" (RSV mg.; cf. NRSV mg.), referencing the premature calving of deer.

The isolated third colon of v. 9 (*and in his temple all say, "Glory!"*) does not seem to fit into its present context very well because one half of a colon stands alone without a counterpart (also in vv. 3b and 7). However, v. 9c should be read as the conclusion of vv. 3-9, and it picks up the "glory" theme of the praise of Yahweh in the heavenly temple called for in vv. 1-2. In fact, vv. 3-9 may be read as a series of five tricolons (vv. 3abc; 4ab-5a; 5b-6ab; 7-8ab; 9abc).

The *heavenly beings* in vv. 1-2 are summoned to praise Yahweh, but they do not do so expressly until 9c, after they have seen the mighty display of divine power in vv. 3a-9b. Thus vv. 1-9 of this psalm seem to leave out the human community reciting the psalm. However, there may be a double reference in 9c to both the heavenly temple and the earthly temple. The coming of the rain and the breaking of the dry season seems to have been a major feature of the Tabernacles festival (cf. Zech 14:16-19). Thus the statement may have a deliberately double sense. The praise on earth joins with that in heaven, with a kind of synergistic merger of the heavenly and earthly dwelling places of Yahweh as found in some psalm references (see Pss 11:4; 48:2). The Temple in Jerusalem is the earthly form of the heavenly temple.

Verses 10-11 form a postlude and benediction. Above the raging storm, Yahweh *sits enthroned* over the tumultuous scene on earth. He is enthroned above *the flood*, which refers directly to the downpour of rain that follows an initial line of thunderstorms, but which also alludes to the primordial FLOOD that must be overcome for ordered life to exist (see Gen 6:17; 7:6; 7; 10; 17; 9:11). Behind this term is the connotation of the great chaotic flood that had to be controlled in the creative process. Yahweh is master of the chaotic powers that threaten the ordered universe; he can cause them to flood the earth or to subside.

The psalm closes with a prayer to Yahweh in v. 11, indirectly expressed in a wish form. Yahweh is implored to *bless his people with peace*. This is the last word in the psalm and the translation "peace" is only partially suitable, because the word is *shalom*, which refers to a condition of wholeness, health, and prosperity—a positive situation rather than the absence of war and calamity that is conveyed by the modern term "peace." Yahweh's supreme blessing bestowed on people is *shalom* (cf. John 20:19; 21), which is the opposite of the *flood* (*mabbul*) in v. 10.

Psalm 29 is the classic example of what has been called the "Canaanite Connection" in the study of the Psalms (Kugel 1986, 119–21). Actually, the connection might be more broadly expressed as the "Ancient Near East Connection." These terms refer to resemblances, sometimes involving the same words and styles, between the POETRY of the Psalms and compositions from Mesopotamia, Palestine-Syria, and Egypt. The most extensively discussed of these "connections" are those between the poetic material from Ugarit and the Bible. Ugaritic poetic style and language are very close to that found in much biblical poetry. The diction of the Ugaritic texts has been incorporated into texts of the psalms, and in many cases remained unrecognized by later scribal copyists.

Psalm 30

This individual thanksgiving psalm expresses praise to God from an individual who received deliverance. The psalm seems especially appropriate for one who has been healed from illness (vv. 2-3). The illness is described as bringing the person to the brink of death (vv. 3, 9); the recovery is described with joyous language. The psalm probably was written for recitation at a ceremony and festive meal for a circle of family and friends called together to rejoice over an experience of deliverance and healing. The psalm may be very old. The title, which is later than the psalm, associates it with the dedication of the Temple, probably the dedication of the second Temple in the time of EZRA (see Ezra 6:16-18; Neh 12: 27-43). The psalm may also be inclusive of the Hanukkah celebration (see DEDICATION, FEAST OF) of the restoration of the Temple in 165 BCE.

In vv. 1-3, Yahweh is praised because he has *drawn . . . up* the suffering person from SHEOL and prevented the triumphal rejoicing of personal foes. Note the four verbs in vv. 1-3b: "drawn up," "healed," "brought up my life (soul)," "restored to life." Verse 3 does not mean a resurrection from the dead is intended. The reference is to a condition fraught with the qualities of SHEOL, a condition in which the speaker had joined the company of those who were ready to descend to *the Pit* (a synonym for *Sheol*).

In vv. 4-5, the restored person calls on the *faithful ones* of Yahweh to join in the praise and thanksgiving. A general basis for such praise is given in v. 5. It affirms the conviction that the joy that God gives exceeds his wrath (cf. Isa 54:7-8).

In vv. 6-7, the speaker recalls presuffering prosperity and (false) confidence. This comfortable situation was devastated when Yahweh hid his face (vs. 7). Then the speaker recalls how he had cried out to Yahweh from a suddenly desperate situation (vv. 8-10). Among those ready to go down to *the Pit* (v. 3), the speaker pleaded with Yahweh not to be allowed to pass into the profitless and praiseless condition of Sheol (v. 9). The worshiper who is cut away from praise dies (cf. Isa 38:19).

Psalm 31

This psalm is a composite prayer that incorporates elements of trust, thanksgiving, and complaint. The situation reflected in the psalm is that of a person who has suffered for a long time from illness (vv. 9-10), accompanied by the abuse and scorn of enemies (vv. 4, 11, 18, 20), but whose trust in God remains strong (v. 14). The speaker recites the prayer in the presence of a group of people of like faith.

Verses 1-5 reflect the faith of a person who has "taken refuge" with Yahweh (v. 1). The statements of the security that Yahweh provides are blended with petitions (vv. 1b-3c). Verses 3b-4a may be read as statements rather than petitions: "You lead me and guide me as befits your name. You free me from the net laid for me, for You are my stronghold" (NJV). Following that reading, vv. 3-5 form a unit composed of statements of confidence.

The first part of the psalm closes with a testimony of deliverance (vv. 6-8) that differs considerably from vv. 9-13. The latter verses are a complaint, using language that is typical of individual laments. The sufferer's personal distress has been augmented by the attacks and plots of neighbors and adversaries (vv. 11, 13), and total ruin seems imminent (vv. 10, 12).

Statements of confidence return in vv. 14a, b, 15a, corresponding to v. 1a. They are prelude to further petitions in vv. 15-18. *Do not let me (ever) be put to shame* (vv. 1 and 17) links the two sections that express confidence in God. In vv. 19-22, the speaker voices praise and thanksgiving. The supplicant has experienced the abundance of Yahweh's *goodness* and *steadfast love*. Prayers have been heard and the sense of estrangement from Yahweh (v. 22) is no more.

In vv. 23-24, the thanksgiving becomes an exhortation addressed to the *saints* or *faithful*, meaning those who are faithful worshipers of Yahweh. The Hebrew *hasidim* ("saints") is derived from *hesed* ("steadfast love") and refers to the loyalty and devotion directed toward the keeping of a relationship.

Psalm 32

This was the favorite psalm of the early Christian scholar Augustine. It is one of the seven penitential psalms of the ancient church (Pss 6, 32, 38, 51, 102, 130, 143). Modern scholars classify Ps 32 as an individual thanksgiving combined with some elements of wisdom poetry, instead of listing it among the penitential psalms. The psalm assumes an experience of forgiveness and deliverance in the past that has become the subject of grateful testimony to a congregation at the SANCTUARY, or to a similar group.

The happy state of the forgiven person is expressed (vv. 1-2) in language hardly surpassed in the Bible. The "happiness" (cf. Ps 1) of the forgiven person permits a look back on the agony of past experience.

Verses 1-2 contain a concentration of OT terms for SIN. TRANSGRESSION conveys the idea of willful disobedience and rebellion against the divine purpose. It has been called the OT's most profound word for sin.

Sin translates the most common Hebrew word for sin in the OT. The basic idea is of missing the mark of the thing aimed at, failure.

Iniquity indicates an action or omission of action that produces some twisting effect or deviation from the straight. It carries the idea of distortion and warping of character and of relationships.

The word translated *deceit* bears undertones of self-deception and unwillingness to honestly assume responsibility for one's actions.

The terminology of sin is matched by the terminology of forgiveness. To be *forgiven* is to have a burden lifted away so that it no longer interferes with one's freedom of action. When sin is *covered* it is treated in such a way that the offense is no longer seen as the subject of judgment. In this context it is God who has "covered" the sin. If a person has *no iniquity* imputed he is no longer held guilty.

Verses 3-4 express the distress that had developed in the worshiper before confession and forgiveness relieved the condition. The hand of God *was heavy*—as it always is for the unforgiven. Relief came to the speaker when sin was confessed to Yahweh (v. 5). *Then* (i.e., after the confession) the speaker received forgiveness. Honesty before God is an essential prerequisite for a satisfactory relationship.

There seems to be a dual address in vv. 6-7, which are directed both to God (as prayer) and to the congregation (as teaching).

The vocabulary used in vv. 8-11 is either that of the wisdom traditions or very similar to them. The determination of the speaker in v. 8 is uncertain. The verse may be understood as a message from God, or it may be treated as instruction by the speaker in the main part of the psalm. It seems more probable that God is the speaker.

A parable-like saying is found in v. 9, which is a warning against stubborn, mulish behavior. The plural form of the command indicates the speaker wants to admonish the group addressed to be open to the instruction referred to in v. 9. Verse 10 is a general statement that contrasts the ways of *the wicked* with *those who trust in the* LORD. A hymn-like call to praise concludes the psalm (v. 11).

Psalm 33

This communal hymn falls into three main divisions: vv. 1-3, 4-19, and 20-22. The main division (vv. 4-19) also divides into three sections: vv. 4-9 (the creative word of Yahweh), vv. 10-12 (the enduring counsel of Yahweh), and vv. 13-19 (the rule of Yahweh from his heavenly throne). The twenty-two verses correspond to the number of letters in the Hebrew alphabet, but there is no acrostic structure. The psalm probably was designed to be sung in festivals and for worship contexts (including the SYNAGOGUE).

33:1-3. Call to worship. The "righteous ones" of the congregation are urged to praise Yahweh with musical instruments and *a new song*.

What is the meaning of the *new song* in v. 3? The term also appears in Pss 40:3; 98:1; 144:9; 149:1; Isa 42:10; Rev 5:9; 14:3. In its most direct sense, a "new song" would have been a new composition for a new occasion of worship, possibly referring to the psalm itself. Note that "new" things are appropriate for worship (1

Sam 6:7; 2 Sam 6:3). Such a psalm will celebrate the "new" things Yahweh does, such as the "ever-newness" of Yahweh, whose mercies are "new every morning" (Lam 3:23). A *new song* reflects new experience (cf. Ps 40:3) and anticipates a new future.

33:4-19. The word, counsel, and rule of Yahweh. This is the main part of the hymn. The *for* of vv. 4 and 9 is characteristic of the hymns and points to the reasons for praising Yahweh. The first *for* emphasizes the power of Yahweh's *word*, which is linked to creation in vv. 6-9 (cf. Gen 1). In vv. 10-13, the emphasis shifts from *the word* of Yahweh to the *counsel* of Yahweh that guides history. Yahweh created by *the word* but rules history by divine *counsel*. The counsel of Yahweh survives the catastrophes of history that brings even the greatest *nations to nothing*.

The hymn is expanded in vv. 13-19 by stanzas that center around the "eye" of Yahweh. Nothing that happens on earth escapes the scrutiny of Yahweh, who *looks down* upon it. God's eye is on everything that happens, but especially *on those who fear him* and *on those who hope in his steadfast love* (v. 18). A better translation might be "those who wait for his steadfast love" (i.e., those who wait with hope).

33:20-22. A testimony. In vv. 20-22, the trust of the congregation is sung in testimony and supplication as the hymn closes. The last verse looks to the future and prays that Yahweh's response may meet the hope the congregation projects toward him (lit. "as we wait for you"; cf. vv. 1-3, 18; 31:24).

Psalm 34

This is an acrostic psalm (cf. Ps 9) of the individual thanksgiving type. In vv. 1-10, Yahweh is praised in the worship services of the community. The praise lauds Yahweh's past acts of deliverance and the unfailing goodness of God's providential care. Verses 11-22 are written in the style of the instructions given by wisdom teachers to their students. The general theme of these verses is the fear of Yahweh.

In the hymnic section, the speaker has a good message for *the humble* (v. 2); they can rejoice when they hear it, and join with the speaker to magnify Yahweh and *exalt his name* (v. 3). In this context, the "humble" are those who *take refuge* with Yahweh (v. 8), those who *fear Yahweh* (vv. 7, 9), and those who are *his holy ones* (v. 9)—those who have been willing to be set apart by devotion and commitment to God (cf. Ps 16:3), but not necessarily priests.

In vv. 4-10, the speaker recounts personal experience of deliverance and exhorts others to enter into a relationship of trust with Yahweh. Yahweh had responded to a quest for divine help (v. 4). *This poor soul* of v. 6 can refer either to the speaker or to one of those who in like manner had received help from Yahweh. Exhortations are found in vv. 8-10.

The reference in v. 7 to the *angel of the LORD* recalls old traditions (cf. Gen 16:7; 21:17; 32:1; 2; Exod 14:19; Josh 5:14; Zech 9:8; Ps 103:20). Although the verbs *taste and see* in v. 8 are metaphorical for judgment and discernment (cf. Prov 31:18), the verse reminds the reader that spiritual experience also involves the physical senses (cf. Heb 6:5; 1 Pet. 2:3).

Verses 11-22 are in the wisdom style, and *the fear of the LORD* is advocated as the key to the good life (v. 12). *The fear of the LORD* links the first part of the psalm (vv. 7, 9) with the latter part (v. 11). The "fear of God" is an expression that combines meanings of reverence for God's sovereignty over life, obedience of the divine will, and commitment to the divinely ordained ways of life.

The focus shifts in vv. 15-22 to an emphasis on *the righteous*, who are given well-being by Yahweh (vv. 15, 17, 19-20). In this context, *the righteous* are those identified by several expressions: the humble, those who fear Yahweh, Yahweh's holy ones, *the brokenhearted* and those *crushed in spirit* (v. 18; cf. Ps 51:17), those *who take refuge* with Yahweh (vv. 8, 22; see Pss 5:11; 7:1; 11:1; 16:1; 25:20; 31:1, 19; 37:40; 57:1; 64:10; 71:1; 118:9; 141:8; 144:2; Isa 14:32; 30:2; 57:13; Nah 1:7), and the *servants* of Yahweh (v. 22). As in Ps 25:22, v. 22 is added beyond the alphabetical order followed in the previous verses and begins with the word for "redeem" or "deliver"; Yahweh *redeems his servants . . . those who take refuge in him*, which contrasts with the fate of *the wicked* in v. 21.

Psalm 35

This long psalm has a multiplex lament-complaint character. It begins with a series of petitions directed to Yahweh (vv. 1-3). The speaker implores Yahweh for help and deliverance, concluding with a request for a divine declaration: *"I am your salvation"* (v. 3c).

In vv. 4-8, a series of imprecatory wishes relating to the suppliant's enemies are directed to Yahweh. Imprecatory wishes are designed to counter EVIL schemes and actions of foes and strengthen the speaker and the speaker's group against the foes.

The speaker moves to a vow of rejoicing and praise in v. 10. Seven imprecations appear in vv. 4-6, 8, matched by seven petitions in vv. 17-25. *All my bones* (v. 10) is an idiom for the whole human being, thus the whole self will be put into the TESTIMONY.

In vv. 11-16, the complaint returns to evil *witnesses* who seek to falsely accuse the speaker. The speaker had attempted to comfort them in illness (v. 13) and had shared their suffering in true sympathy (vv. 13-14), but his own *stumbling* (illness? economic misfortune? loss of popular favor?) brought no reciprocity on their part. They had gathered about like wild animals eager for the kill (vv. 15-16). Petitions for divine redress, and another vow of praise follow in vv. 17-18.

More petitions follow in vv. 19-25, with an imprecatory wish in v. 26, matched by a wish that those who desire the speaker's vindication would be able to *shout for joy* and praise (v. 27). The psalm closes with a vow of praise (v. 28). On the concept of God waking from sleep (v. 23), see commentary on Ps 44.

Psalm 36

None of the major categories of psalm classification exactly fit this psalm and, therefore, it is frequently identified as a mixed-type psalm. Verses 1-4 are often treated as derived from wisdom teaching, and indeed their descriptive language is similar to that found in WISDOM LITERATURE. Actually, however, vv. 1-4 compose a description of godless people more commonly found in the prophetic literature (e.g., see Isa 59:4-8; Mic 2:1-2; 3:3-4; 7:2-6). Verse 1 begins literally as "an oracle of transgression to the wicked," possibly a parody of an ORACLE form, and means that the message heard by the sinner is that of sin rather than a message from God. Another option is to take the "message" or "oracle" as an independent word serving as the title of the verses that follow. In any case, the description of the wicked serves as a complaint in the psalm.

Verses 5-9 have the qualities of a hymn that praises Yahweh for his great loyal-love and righteousness. Those who participate in Temple worship (vv. 7-8) have access to the great abundance of feasting and drink that Yahweh gives. Yahweh is the *fountain of life* and the giver of light (v. 9). Without the light-giving presence of Yahweh, human beings would be like the earth without the sun (Weiser 1962).

In vv. 10-12 the psalm becomes a prayer. The reference to *the foot* (v. 11) alludes to the custom of conquering kings placing a foot on the neck of defeated opponents. The concluding statement (v. 12) refers to vv. 1-4 and expresses the certainty of vindication.

Psalm 37

If any psalm should be properly classified as a wisdom psalm, Ps 37 should be it. It is acrostic in form and strongly didactic in content. The success of *the wicked* and the seeming triumph of the evil ones are major concerns. The acrostic form causes a certain rigidity in the psalm and it becomes, to a degree, similar to the collections of wise sayings in the Book of Proverbs.

In vv. 1-11, counsels of calm faith are directed to those who *fret* over the well-being of *the wicked*. There is a twofold concern. First, there is no need to allow in-ner attitudes toward evil to dominate one's life. The restraint of anger and emotion can be accomplished by trusting in Yahweh. Second, the well-being of *the wicked* is of short duration (v. 10). The ultimate victory belongs to *those who wait* for Yah-weh (v. 9). *Those who wait for the LORD*, who are *the meek, shall inherit the land* (vv. 9 and 11). *The meek* (cf. Matt 5:5) were originally those who were "overcome with want" (poverty stricken), but in time the word came to represent "the poor in spirit," meaning those who knew and accepted their dependency on God.

Verses 12-22 tell some of the dreadful things *the wicked* can do. They *plot against the righteous* and kill *the poor and needy* (vv. 12, 14). This, however, is not the whole story, for *the wicked* will receive retribution corresponding to their deeds. The weapons of the wicked will be turned back against them (v. 15), so that the *little* of *the righteous* is better than *the abundance* of *the wicked* (v. 16). The godly person errs when begrudging the wicked rich their abundance, for the godly should know that such wealth brings more liabilities than assets. The ultimate judgment of the person who trusts in wealth is found in v. 21: perpetual debt (read v. 21 as in RSV: "cannot pay back").

Verses 23-26 include the personal testimony of the teacher in vv. 25-26 (also in vv. 35-36). The first premise is that the providential care of Yahweh misses no one (v. 23). The wicked as well as the righteous must reckon with God. No person can fall out of his hand (v. 24). Second, the duration of the wicked is short. They may have their day, but their judgment comes quickly (vv. 13, 20). Further, while the teacher generalizes in v. 25, it is testimony out of personal experience and not intended to establish a comprehensive ideal of righteousness and rewards.

The dominant note in vv. 27-40 is the providential power of Yahweh that gives victory to the righteous. Yahweh *loves justice* (v. 28), that is, God is devoted to keeping the relationships of society in the right order so that the righteous can live securely in the land. Yahweh will not abandon to the power of *the wicked* those who are faithful to him (vv. 28, 33, 39-40).

Psalm 38

The traditional seven penitential psalms (Pss 6; 32; 51; 102; 130; 143) included this lament. The lament is marked by the confession of the suppliant's *sin* (vv. 3, 4, 18) and by expressions of anguish. The physical condition of the sufferer is given more specific description than is common in the laments. It is possible the disease described is leprosy (or a leprosy-like disease), and reflects the situation discussed in Lev 13:1-46.

In vv. 1-2, the opening cry for help states the conviction that the condition of the sufferer is the result of Yahweh's *wrath*, assuming that bodily suffering is the discipline of Yahweh. In vv. 3-10, the condition of the suppliant is described and declared to be the result of a merger of divine wrath and personal *sin* (v. 3). The burden of the speaker's iniquities adds to the suffering of the illness (v. 4).

The spiritual and physical suffering is greatly aggravated by the speaker's loneliness (v. 11; cf. Pss 88:8; 18; Job 19:14; 15; Lam 1:2) and by vicious attacks from enemies (v. 12). Nevertheless, the suffering has been accepted without loud and angry protest (vv. 13-14a; cf. the "servant" in Isa 50:4-6; 53). The speaker continues to pray and expects an answer from Yahweh (vv. 15-16), having confessed *sin* (v. 18) and protesting that foes are punishing goodness with evil (v. 20). A concluding prayer for help closes the psalm (vv. 21-22) and emphasizes the urgency of the speaker's distress.

Psalm 39

This psalm has some close relations with the preceding one. It is less of a lament, however, and more of a prayer of reflection on experience. A condition of severe illness may be indicated, a condition that is augmented in its gravity by the scornful charges of those who oppose the suppliant.

In vv. 1-3, the psalm begins in an unusual manner with a TESTIMONY of the suppliant's experience. The speaker had struggled with the agony of a distressful condition, and had resolved to endure the suffering silently rather than lash out at *the wicked* and encourage them (vv. 1-2). The burning distress grew worse, however, and now has forced the suppliant to speak (v. 3).

The brevity of human existence is stated repeatedly in vv. 4-6. Life is as fleeting as a *breath*; human beings pass away from it like the going of a *shadow*.

The evaluation of the status of humankind in this psalm is at an extreme polarity from that in Ps 8:5-8.

In vv. 7-11 the personal condition of the suppliant comes into clearer focus. The speaker commits his entire future to Yahweh (v. 7) and prays for deliverance *from . . . transgressions* (v. 8) and for the removal of a *stroke* (v. 10) from Yahweh. The speaker knows that the divine punishment is for sin, but does not want this to provide an opportunity for the scornful abuse of fools (v. 8).

In v. 9 the speaker again reverts to an attitude of silent submission, helpless before the power of Yahweh. The blows of Yahweh's hand (v. 10) reduce those whom he punishes until all that is human is *a mere breath* (v. 11—see v. 5; also in vv. 5 and 6, *as/for nothing*).

In the closing prayer (vv. 12-13) the speaker prays that Yahweh will not allow death to take him. Verse 12 is a confession of humanity's true relationship to God. Humans live before God as do sojourners on the land. The terms *guest* and *alien* may also convey the position of a worshiper in the sanctuary (Ps 15:1).

The prayer in v. 13 reverses the usual petition for Yahweh's attention (e.g., Pss 13:4; 25:16-18; 59:4; 139:23-24). In this case, however, the suppliant knows he is suffering under the wrath of God and prays for alleviation before death (cf. Job 7:19; 10:20-22; 14:6).

Psalm 39 differs from most laments in the absence of any statement of confidence or of the certainty of answered prayer.

Psalm 40

Two divisions make up this psalm (vv. 1-10 and 11-17) suggesting that two originally independent units have been combined. The appearance of 40:13-17, with a few variations, in Ps 70 supports this suggestion. Verses 1-10 is a thanksgiving psalm that was written for individual use, while vv. 13-16 are composed of petitions and complaints, with a closing verse of confidence (v. 17). Verses 11-12 provide the transition linking the two units. The usual order in the Psalms is for thanksgiving to follow lament, but the reversed order, as here, appears elsewhere (see Pss 27, 44, 89).

In vv. 1-2, the worshiper recalls with forceful metaphors an experience of deliverance by Yahweh. Verse 1a may be read as "I waited intensely for Yahweh," that is, for Yahweh's help. The exact nature of the situation is not given. *The . . . pit* (v. 2) suggests the realm of the dead (SHEOL), and it is possible that the poet recalls a nearly fatal illness.

In v. 3, the delivered one declares that Yahweh has charismatically endowed *a new song* (cf. Pss 33:3; 96:1; 98:1; 144:9; 139:1; Isa 42:10) that is identified as a *song of praise to our God*. Its purpose is evangelistic and didactic (v. 3cd). The *new song* is one that sets forth the new work of God. New songs are required because God is always doing new things (see Lam 3:22-23).

The "beatitude" form (*Happy are those . . .* , v. 4; see Pss 1:1; 2:12; 32:1; 2; 34:8, etc.) is used for statements of general truth or the good fortune of those so described. The speaker gives a testimony that is conscious of the congregation (see *our God* and *us* [vv. 3, 5]). One of the characteristic tendencies of the individual thanksgiving psalm is a shift towards the instruction of others, acknowledging that thanksgiving is communal.

The poet seems to incorporate into the psalm a negative judgment of the sacrificial cult (vv. 6-8) in words similar to other OT passages (cf., e.g., 1 Sam 15:22; Amos 5:21-27; Hos 6:6; 8:11-14; Isa 1:10-17). The intention behind the negative judgments is directed toward "sacrifices of righteousness" or *right sacrifices* (Ps 51:19) those made properly by persons who are devoted to the will of God and whose behavior reflects the divine will. Acceptable sacrifices are those offered with *broken spirit* and *contrite heart* (Ps 51:17).

What is meant by *in the scroll of the book it is written of me* (v. 7)? One view suggests a reference to Yahweh's "record scroll" mentioned in other contexts (see Pss 56:8; 69:28; 87:6; 139:16; Dan 7:10; 10:21; Mal 3:16). If so in this case, what is written on the scroll is found in v. 8. More likely, however, *the scroll* is the *torah* (law), and the prepositional phrase at the end of the line means "for me."

This reading is in keeping with v. 6b (*you have given me an open ear*: lit., "you have dug ears for me"), which means that the speaker has been "gifted to hear and understand the will of the LORD" (Gerstenberger 1988, 171).

This reading also is consistent with v. 8 where the speaker declares that "your *torah* (law) is within my inner being (intestines)." The speaker offers himself as a living sacrifice, with the *torah* of Yahweh assimilated into personal life.

In vv. 9-10, the speaker declares that the obligation of testimony and praise has been carried out: *I have not concealed your steadfast love and your faithfulness from the great congregation* (v. 10c). The confession has been made despite the *evils . . . without number* that *have encompassed* the speaker (v. 12). The speaker identifies with the *poor and needy* (v. 17; cf. 35:10; 37:14) who love the salvation of God (v. 16) and who do not waste the glad news of Yahweh's faithfulness and salvation.

Psalm 41

This psalm is best read as a thanksgiving psalm intended for recitation following an answer to prayer. There is, however, the peculiarity of the presence of a long lament (vv. 4-10) in place of the more commonly seen narration of past troubles and sufferings. The final verse is generally recognized as the closing statement of the first division of the Psalter and, therefore, it was probably not originally included in the psalm.

The introduction is phrased in the "beatitude" formula (*Happy are those . . .*) that expresses congratulations to those who are concerned for the *poor* (LXX, "poor and needy"). The verbal form for *consider* implies careful thought and action rather than mere attention. That these verses are a prayer addressed to Yahweh is clear by the *you* in vv. 2c and 3b.

"Blessed is he who considers the poor!" (v. 1 RSV) is unique among the beatitude-like statements of the Psalter. Normally the beatitudes refer to one's behavior towards God. Concern for the poor was deeply planted both in Israel's worship and wisdom teaching (see Pss 35:13-14; 72:4; 12-14; Prov 14:31; 19:17).

In vv. 4-10, the speaker quotes the prayer of lament that was directed to Yahweh before it was answered. The description of the actions of the enemies is unusually detailed (vv. 4-9). They speak maliciously against a sick person, anticipating the coming of death with no sympathy. Their comfort is devoid of any real significance (*empty words*). They spread disturbing reports abroad in whispering campaigns. The enemies include a close friend of the sick person (v. 9).

A closing confession of gratitude is spoken to God in vv. 11-12. The speaker is grateful for healing and deliverance, which has thwarted a triumph of the enemies and vindicated his integrity (v. 12). The last word of the speaker is an affirmation of having been established in the *presence* of Yahweh *forever*.

In the psalm's present arrangement, v. 13 is intended for a family group or a congregation, and marks the end of book one.

Summary of Book One

By the superscriptions throughout, book one is certainly a Davidic collection. Only Pss 10 and 33 lack a Davidic title, and these are tucked under the Davidic umbrella by close connections with preceding and following psalms. We may assume book one was read as if DAVID, or a person like him, were the speaker. The psalms in this collection were judged to be representative of David's faith and charisma.

The postscript in Ps 2:12 (*Happy are all who take refuge in him*) links Ps 2 both to Ps 1 and to the collection that follows. Also note that Ps 41 begins *Happy are those who consider the poor*, recalling the beatitudes of 1:1 and 2:12. Seybold (1990, 146) says the beatitude in Ps 2:12 refers to all "who are able to find their way to the kind of faith which is demonstrated by the king who speaks in Ps 2:10-12a." The speech in Ps 2 is a confident affirmation of the power of Yahweh to deal with kings and nations.

The prologue in Ps 2 and the general character of book one point to the provenance of this collection, in its present form, in a community or communities facing "the disorienting reality of foreign domination" (McCann 1993a, 104) and the continuing threat of the loss of trust and assurance in God's power and purpose for Israel.

Especially in such a community context, the strong and numerous individual laments easily lead to the conclusion that lament/complaint is the major component of book one (e.g., Pss 3–7, 12, 13, 17, and the extraordinarily powerful lament in 22:1-21, as well as 35, 36, 31, 35, 38). Testimonies of trust, thanksgiving, and praise, however, compose an equal or larger part of Pss 3–41 (Pss 8; 9:1-12; 11; 15; 16:5-11; 18; 19; 20:6-8; 21; 22:22-37; 23; 24; 27; 29; 30; 32; 33; 34; 37; 40; 41). Some psalms are mixed but on the whole they give positive testimony (14, 16, 36, 39). The confidence and praise in the laments is not to be overlooked. Thus, despite strong elements of lament, book one is actually focused on faith and praise.

The thesis that book one focuses on faith and praise is substantiated by the language. For example, the verb *hsh*, "take refuge," is important (that it occurs in Ps 2:12 is significant). The use of the *hsh* in affirmative statements is found in Pss 7:1; 11:1; 16:1; 18:2; 25:30; 31:1 (other forms are found in 5:11; 18:30; 34:22; 37:40; and the noun *mhsh*, "refuge," is used in 14:6). The verb expresses faith in the protective care of Yahweh, despite unfavorable circumstances. Seybold (1990, 145) argues for a "creedal intention" in the usage of *hsh* in the Psalms, meaning that the statements in which the verb appears set forth affirmations of faith directed both to God and to other persons.

The verb *bth*, "trust," is closely related to *hsh*, and is found in varied forms in Pss 4:5; 9:10; 13:5; 21:7; 22:4; 5; 25:2; 26:1; 27:3; 28:7; 31:6; 14; 32:10; 33:21; 37:3; 5; 40:3; 41:9. Seybold (1990, 145) argues that *bth* is less dynamic and active than is *hsh*, indicating a state of feeling secure, and lacking the "creedal tone" of "take refuge." However, I fail to see that this is the case. The verb "trust" seems as "creedally intentional" as the verb "take refuge." Both verbs are used in statements affirming active faith that are intended to promote faith in others.

Thus book one in its present form is primarily intended for the encouragement of those who might waver in their commitment to Yahweh, designed to focus the mind on faith, and crafted to emphasize the life-giving function of divine instruction (Pss 15; 19; 24; 37). In the language of Ps 1, book one is *torah* (cf. Pss 37:31; 40:8).

Book Two. Psalms 42–72

Psalms 42–43

These two psalms should be read as one. The repetition of the refrain in 42:5, 11, and 43:5 points to Ps 43 as the third strophe of one psalm. Further, Ps 43 is one of only two psalms in book two that lacks a superscription (the other is Ps 71). There is also a close connection of thought between the two psalms (see 42:9 and 43:2).

Psalms 42–43 form a lament composed of three stanzas and a refrain (42:5, 11; 43:5). The speaker appears to be a devout worshiper living in the far north of Israel, and is unable (either because of oppression by enemies or illness) to join pilgrims to the festivals at a central place of worship. In the present form of the Psalter the worship center would certainly be Jerusalem, but in the original design of the psalm the place may have been in the northern kingdom of Israel, perhaps the SANCTUARY at Dan. The psalm reflects an experience typical of the Israelite exiles who were cut off from the joy of festivals, for whatever reason and in whatever place.

The opening words of the psalm (42:1-4) express a passion for worship. The image is of a thirsty, timid deer tortured by thirst and vainly seeking water in the dried up wadis of an arid region. The speaker also is terribly thirsty, even though he lives among the cataracts that roar down the slopes of Mount Hermon to form the Jordan river (42:7). The speaker's thirst is *for God* (42:2). The suffering of thirst is augmented by the taunts of people around the poet: *"Where is your God?"* (42:3; see Pss 79:10; 115:2; Joel 2:17).

The suppliant remembers participation in the processions into the Temple and the *shouts and songs of thanksgiving* (42:4) of a great festival. There were no questions then about the reality of God!

The refrain first appears in 42:5, and the suppliant speaks in a kind of personal dialogue. In the inner self (*soul*) the speaker is depressed like a groaning and grieving mourner. In the manner of a priest who delivers an ORACLE of deliverance and encouragement to a lamenting worshiper, the speaker counsels himself: *Hope in God.*

The lament resumes (42:6-11) as the suppliant remembers God in the present situation of remoteness from worship, and feels overwhelmed by the roaring waves of the surging deep—the *t'hom* (42:7). The water seems like the waves of a great flood to the speaker because it represents separation from the worship of Yahweh in the festivals. Psalm 42:8 may be read as a statement of confidence, despite the thunderous *waves and . . . billows* (42:7). On the other hand, it can be read as a supplicatory wish:

> By day may Yahweh grant his steadfast love,
> so that at night his song will be with me,
> a prayer to the God of my life. (author trans.)

The taunting of adversaries is again a concern (42:9-10) and the refrain re-appears (42:11). The taunting of enemies is like "murder in my bones" (i.e., a shocking, bruising trauma).

In the final stanza (43:1-5) the suppliant prays for vindication from the attacks of ungodly and deceitful people, imploring God to send out *light and . . . truth* as agents from the heavenly council to ensure safe passage to the *holy hill* in order to approach the altar and join in the worship. The refrain (43:5) closes the psalm with a note of hope.

My help in 42:5, 11, and 43:5 is too weak. The expression (lit. "the salvation of my face") means something like "my deliverer" or "my personal savior."

(For discussion of the *Korahites* titles and collection, see the end of Ps 49.)

Psalm 44

This psalm is a communal lament designed for the use of Israelite congregations on occasions of disaster, such as war or other calamities (cf. 2 Chr 20:5-19; Joel 1:13-14; 2:15-17). In Ps 44, the armies of Israel appear to have been defeated in battle (v. 10), many being killed and taken as prisoners (v. 11). Israel has received the scorn of her neighbors (vv. 14-16); Yahweh no longer gives his people victory (vv. 4, 9). The people have been *broken* (or crushed) in a *haunt of jackals* (v. 19). A better reading is "crushed us into a place of jackals" (i.e., a place where the jackals live; see Jer 9:11; 10:32; Isa 13:22; 34:13). The proposed reading is supported by the parallel in v. 19b. The nation now dwells desolate in *deep dark-*

ness or in "the shadow of death" (cf. Ps 23:4—the same word is used in 23:4 and 44:19).

A long tradition holds that this psalm was composed during the time of the Maccabean Wars (second century BCE), but that is doubtful. Other dates have been assigned to the psalm, including preexilic ones.

The psalm begins with a hymnic narration (vv. 1-3) by the congregation of the sacred history they had received. They had been told of the victories of Yahweh *in the days of old*, when he won the land of CANAAN for them (cf. Deut 4:37-39; 8:17-18; 9:4-6). The ancestors of Israel had been faithful in passing on the history to new generations (see Exod 12:26; Deut 6:20; Josh 4:6; 21).

The opening statements are supplemented by declarations of trust (vv. 4-8). Note the change of person in these lines: a lone voice speaks. The verses may have been intended for recitation by the king, or a priest, or a precentor who was leading the congregation in lamentation, but in any case the solo speaker personifies the nation and declares that Yahweh is the King who gives triumph over Israel's foes.

A complaint (vv. 9-16) describes the terrible condition of Israel. The situation contrasts sharply with the glories of the sacred history in vv. 1-8. The complaint lays an intolerable present before Yahweh, juxtaposed with the victories of previous times.

Verses 17-22 correspond closely to the protestations of innocence in the individual laments (see Ps 7). The people declare that they have not behaved in a manner that justifies their plight. The theological background of this passage should be sought in the Book of Deuteronomy and the Deuteronomistic History (Joshua–2 Kings; see DEUTERONOMIST/DEUTERONOMISTIC HISTORIAN) where the oppression of Israel is caused by the breaking the COVENANT with Yahweh. The statement here, however, rejects Deuteronomic theology and postulates another cause (v. 22): *because of you* (i.e., God). Yahweh is held responsible for the present calamity of Israel: *You have sold your people for a trifle* (v. 12). They claim that they have neither violated the covenant nor forgotten the name of their God, but suffer because of their faithfulness to the covenant (vv. 17-19). The suffering of innocent people was the great theological problem of Israel after 587 BCE.

The closing petitions (vv. 23-26) are agitated and boldly anthropomorphic. God is addressed with calls to wake up and rise up for the help of his people: "Help us and redeem us for the sake of your loyal-love" (v. 26).

The language of a "wake-up call" for Yahweh (see Pss 7:6; 35:22-24; 59:5; 78:65; 80:2; Isa 51:9-11; Zech 2:13 [17]) seems to be grounded in the notion of a "sleeping deity" found in ancient Near Eastern literature. The concepts of a deity resting in leisure (*otiositas*) and that of a sleeping god are primarily motifs of divine sovereignty and not those of idle, distracted, or tired gods. Sleeping in peace was a prerogative of a sovereign god. If other gods, or human beings, disturbed the rest of such a deity, they were considered to be in rebellion against the divine rule; they challenged a symbol of divine authority. Thus the call for Yahweh to wake up and come to the help of his sorely troubled people symbolized two things. (1) It acknowledged Yahweh's absolute sovereignty as the divine king. (2) The situation is so bad that he can no longer rest and sleep; the disorder that now rages must be put down again if God is to sleep in peace (and for the people to rest with God).

Psalm 45

The speaker in this royal wedding poem identifies himself as a professional writer (*a ready scribe* or "an expert scribe"). The first part of the psalm (vv. 1-9) is addressed to the king. The speaker, probably a court poet or prophet, begins with enthusiasm, "bubbling over" within and with a tongue prepared to pour forth words like the pen of a skilled scribe (cf. Job 32:17-20). The king is praised with exalted language (cf. Pss 2, 72, 89, 110, 132): he is *handsome*, victorious in war, fluent in speech, and *blessed . . . forever* by God (v. 2). He is a superlative warrior, who goes forth in the cause of truth and justice for the poor (assuming that is what v. 4 means). He is dressed in royal robes and exudes a fragrant aroma of *myrrh and aloes and cassia* (vv. 7-8). He dwells in pleasant and luxurious surroundings (v. 8).

Verses 6-7 assign an extremely elevated status to the king. It seems best to stay close to the Hebrew text and read *Your throne, O god, endures forever and ever* (v. 6). In this way the king is addressed as an *elohim* or a god. However, it is most probable that something less than the full status of deity is intended here (any theory of kingly apotheosis would be alien to the OT context).

In vv. 10-12a, the poet addresses the bride. He advises her to forget her people and her father's house and to give herself wholly to the king she is to marry. She is addressed as a "daughter of Tyre" in v. 12 (NRSV requests a different interpretation). The wedding procession of the princess into the palace is described in vv. 12b-15, and the king is addressed with promises for the future in vv. 16-17.

Why is a psalm about the marriage of a king in the canon (Kraus 1988, 457)? Jewish interpretations solve the problem by reading the psalm as about David, or his messianic son and eschatological Israel. Christian tradition follows by reading the psalm in terms of the marriage of Christ and the church (cf. Heb 1:8-9). These views merit respect and contain valid content.

A historical-critical analysis of the psalm, however, works with a different approach. First, we should try to read the psalm in terms of a history of interpretation in ancient Israel. Perhaps it was composed for a royal wedding in the northern kingdom (traditionally supposed to be that of AHAB and JEZEBEL), and later adapted for the monarchy in Judah (possibly for HEZEKIAH). In post-monarchial contexts the psalm would be read with the sense of the union of Zion–Israel as the bride of Yahweh, a union that will cause the King's name (i.e., Yahweh's name) *to be celebrated "in all generations* and praised forever by the peoples (v. 17). Thus the Christian extension to the marriage of Christ and the church was in line with the psalm's tradition history. The psalm is implicitly messianic, but not explicitly so.

The speaker in this psalm praises a king who loves *righteousness* and hates *wickedness* (v. 7) and defends the cause of truth and justice (v. 4). In this regard, the psalm may be compared with Pss 72 and 101. These psalms express the high ideals of Israelite kingship and have a message for public servants in every age. The royal throne, which represents the divine kingship of God on earth, is intended to promote and establish stability and justice in society.

Psalm 46

This psalm is famous in its own right and has been made more so by Martin Luther's great hymn "A Mighty Fortress Is Our God," which is based upon it. The general classification of the psalm is as a hymn of confidence, of the song-of-Zion type (see Pss 48, 76, 84, 87, 122). The psalm has been connected in much interpretation with the deliverance of Jerusalem from the invasion of SENNACHERIB in 701 BCE (2 Kgs 18:13-19; 37), although there is no proof to support the tradition. It may have been a hymn prepared for recitation during the great religious festivals of preexilic Israel, but the specific festival context is uncertain. Since the autumn festival (Tabernacles) was the most important one in preexilic Israel, it is probable Ps 46 represents some of its major themes (e.g., the supply of water). The general tenor of the psalm seems to fit better in exilic and postexilic Israel, when the people felt threatened by the uproar of the nations and by the foreboding return of chaos.

The psalm consists of three stanzas (vv. 1-3, 4-7, 8-11) with a refrain (vv. 7, 11). There is no refrain after the first stanza in the present text, but one may originally have been there. Some translators, therefore, insert a duplicate of vv. 7, 11 into the text after v. 3.

Verses 1-3 contain a powerful affirmation of trust. The community (note the communal *we* and *us* throughout) shows an awareness of God's help in the past (v. 1b). Confidence in God's care allows for the renunciation of fear (vv. 2-3), even in the face of changes that threaten the dissolution of the created order. The expressions of vv. 2, 3 represent those forces that lie beyond the control of human beings. They do not shatter, however, the refuge that God provides.

The mood and scene change from the shaking, roaring turbulence of vv. 2-3 to a peaceful picture of Zion, *the city of God*, secure in the midst of the raging nations of history, and rejoicing because of her streams of a river (vv. 4-7). Jerusalem is not built on a river; this picture probably arises out of the application to Zion of ideas of the Garden of Eden (see Gen 2:10-14; Isa 33:20-22; Ezek 47:1-2; Joel 3:18; Zech 14:8; Rev 22:1-2). The raging waters of the primordial flood in v. 3 are transformed in v. 4 into a river that gives joy to the city. The archetypal river becomes streams which make *the city of God* a place of gladness.

The real security of Zion is God's presence (v. 5). His power will manifest itself at the darkest hour, which is just before the dawn (v. 5). The onslaught of the nations, which surges against the city of God (Zion) like the waves of the cosmic sea (v. 6), will be broken by the thundering voice of God from *the holy habitation of the Most High* (v. 4, God's heavenly dwelling place). God is identified in v. 7 and 11 as *the God of Jacob* and "Yahweh of Hosts" (see Ps 24).

The invitation to the congregation in v. 8 has led some interpreters to think that some ritual-dramatic presentation of the pictures described in vv. 1-7 was given in the cult.

The sight that greets those who respond to the invitation in v. 8 is, at first, a dreadful one of the desolation of a battlefield (vv. 8, 9) with broken bows, spears cut to pieces, and burning vehicles (*shields* follows LXX and some Ugaritic evidence for the use of the word that normally means "cart" or "wagon" [see Dahood 1966, 280]; if *shields* is correct it refers to wooden frames covered with oiled leather). Yahweh passes through the nations and leaves desolate battlefields behind. The objective of the destruction of armaments by Yahweh is world peace (Mic 4:3), which is what the community needs so badly. The nations are summoned to desist (*be still*) from their militant ventures and acknowledge the power of Yahweh (v. 10). The psalm is framed by statements of confidence in the refuge and help offered by Yahweh (vv. 1-2 and 11; "God" is equal to Yahweh in this psalm).

Psalm 47

This is a hymn that praises the kingship of Yahweh (see Pss 93; 95–99). Such psalms are frequently referred to as "Enthronement Psalms." Yahweh is the one "enthroned" as the Divine King, not the Davidic king in Jerusalem.

The term "Enthronement Psalms" originated out of the hypothesis that there was a periodic celebration and re-enactment on Mount Zion of Yahweh's coming to the throne. It is assumed that this was ritually dramatized by the carrying of the ARK (above which was considered to be the place where Yahweh was revealed) in a procession into the city and up to the Temple (see 2 Sam 6; 1 Kgs 8:1-11).

Some scholars associate an enthronement ritual with the autumn festival (Tabernacles), but "enthronement" should not be read as excluding the kingship of Yahweh that always exists. He *is* King (v. 8) but he also *becomes* king in ritual reenactment and in a new realization of divine sovereignty over the powers of evil and disorder that are continually active in history and nature. The celebration of the divine kingship also had a future thrust toward a fuller coming of Yahweh's sovereignty (see Zech 14:9).

An exhortative summons to "all the peoples" (vv. 1-4) to join in hand clapping and shouting out exclamations of joy to God opens the hymn (cf. v. 6). The celebration of Yahweh's kingship in enthronement psalms shows many parallels with kingship in Israel. Shouting and trumpet blowing (v. 5) were parts of the demonstrations that greeted a newly anointed king in Israel (see 1 Sam 10:24; 2 Sam 15:10; 1 Kgs 1:34; 39; 40; 2 Kgs 9:13; 11:12). The *peoples* of v. 1 may have originally referred to the pilgrims who had gathered from various places for the festival (cf. v. 9).

Yahweh is the *great king* who has given Israel wide dominion over *subdued peoples* (vv. 2-4). He is identified as *the Most High* (v. 2, Heb. *Elyon*), overlord of heaven and earth, a title that appears to have been used in Jerusalem before David's conquest and only subsequently applied to Yahweh (Gen 14:17-24). Verses 2-5 have the character of a victory song and make this psalm a communal hymn.

Verse 5 almost certainly refers to the carrying up of the ARK of the covenant to the Temple in a procession, rather than a return of Yahweh to his heavenly abode, although the actions are not mutually exclusive. The going up of Yahweh's ark was accompanied by enthusiastic songs and praises by the people. He is praised as *the king of all the earth* (vv. 6-7).

Some interpreters read vv. 8-9 to refer to the future (i.e., eschatological) consummation of Yahweh's kingship. The first part of v. 9 is understood by others (as in NRSV): *The princes of the peoples gather as the people of the God of Abraham.* Thus, "the gathering" is interpreted as fulfillment of the promise made to Abraham (Gen 12:3) and a realization of statements by the prophets that anticipated the joining of the gentiles with the people of God (Isa 19:23-25; 49:6; 56:6-7; Zech 8:20-23; cf. Matt 8:11). The gentiles become part of the people of the God of Abraham.

An interpretation that includes gentiles as part of *the people of the God of Abraham* is doubtful. It would be unique indeed for the title "the people of the God of Abraham" to apply to gentiles (although Egyptians are called "my people" in Isa 19:25 and gentiles are included among God's people in Rom 9:24). It seems more plausible to conjecture that a "with" has fallen out of the text of v. 9. In this case, the princes of the nations gather *with* the Israelites; not *as* Israelites.

The reader is invited to ponder a manifestation of God that is not yet. The historical background (as in vv. 2-4) probably lies in the actuality of the kingdom of DAVID and SOLOMON. The conquests of David were extended over a number of non-Israelite peoples (vv. 3-4). It was according to the customs of the ancient world that captive people should gather with their conquerors to pay homage to the god (in this case, Yahweh) who had subdued them. In the course of Israel's history, the historical actuality in the psalm faded and an eschatological reinterpretation emerged.

We should note that the enthronement psalms lack the royal ideology of the Davidic monarchy. The community in Pss 46, 47, and 48 has no earthly king to rule and defend it: *God is in the midst of the city; it shall not be moved* (Ps 46:5). Thus, in these psalms we probably are dealing with postexilic liturgies that "jubilantly recall the history of Israel's election by Yahweh . . . and glory in his supreme, as yet unrealized, power over all the earth" (Gerstenberger 1988, 198).

Psalm 48

This psalm is a hymn that praises the glories of Zion, the City of Yahweh (see Pss 46, 76, 84, 87, 122). As in the case of Pss 46 and 47, some interpreters argue that the psalm can be traced to the deliverance of Jerusalem from the Assyrians in 701 BCE. If so, Ps 48 is a testimony of the peril from which the city was saved. Some details, however, seem inappropriate for a deliverance context (e.g., *the ships of Tarshish* in v. 7 and *the kings* of v. 4). The origin of the psalm in the northern sanctuary of Dan has also been proposed. The psalm probably originated in cultic use, rather than from a specific historical situation. In its present form the psalm describes a worship experience on Mount Zion, such as would have been experienced by pilgrims to an Israelite festival. This does not exclude all historical and eschatological significance, but it does point to the main angle of interpretation.

The beauty and significance of Mount Zion is praised in vv. 1-3. The psalm opens with a shout of praise declaring the greatness of Yahweh (v. 1). Supremely *the city of the great King* and *the city of our God*, Zion belongs to Yahweh and is *his holy mountain*. The passage borrows heavily from Canaanite descriptions of Mount Zaphon (or "North"), which is the mountain of BAAL in the Ras Shamra texts. These descriptions developed from Jebel al-Agra (called *Mons Casius* by the Romans) near Ugarit, a mountain whose height dominates northern Syria, that served as a Canaanite version of Mount Olympus.

The idea of Zion *in the far north* is impossible geographically, and Zaphon should not be read as an actual place name in the psalm. Mount Zion is declared to be the real mountain of the gods (Zaphon was the place of the assembly of the gods; see Isa 14:13-14; Ezek 28:14; 16). A reading of the last part of v. 1 as "Mount Zion, the summit of Zaphon, city of the Great King" fuses the concept of Zion with that of Zaphon, the home of the creator god El. The only god who really matters, however, has his city on Mount Zion: Yahweh, *the great King* (the only use of this title for God in the Hebrew Bible).

The significance of Yahweh's presence in Jerusalem has been manifest in the way that attacks against the city have broken up (vv. 4-8). Assembled kings fled in panic at the mere sight of *it* (v. 5)—apparently Zion, where Yahweh had made himself known as *a sure defense* (v. 3). The confusion and fear of the kings is like the anguish of women in travail (v. 6). The strange reference to *the ships of Tarshish* (v. 7) seems originally to have been the deep-sea vessels used in the Mediterranean trade from Phoenician seaports to the port of Tartessas in Spain, or Sardinia (and may further indicate a northern origin for the psalm). In the present usage they become a metaphor for pride, destroyed by an *east wind* (see 1 Kgs 10:22; Isa 2:16; Ezek 27:25; 27:26; Isa 27:8; also Jonah 1:3).

There is an eyewitness quality about these verses that is very striking. Something has been *seen* and *heard* in Jerusalem (v. 8). It was *there* (v. 6) that the attack of the kings was thwarted. Verse 9 indicates the scene of action is the Temple area. A ritual portrayal of Yahweh's defense of Zion may have been acted out during festival times.

In vv. 9-11, the worshipers tell how they comprehended Yahweh's praise and power through worship in the Temple. The right hand of Yahweh is *filled with victory* (v. 10; cf. 118:15-16). Verse 10 makes it clear that Yahweh's power and presence are not confined to Zion; his name and powerful right hand reach out to *the ends of the earth*.

In vv. 13-14, the congregation is exhorted to begin a procession (or perhaps, a tour) about Mount Zion, and to note carefully the outstanding features of the city. Such a procession would have had at least a twofold objective. First, the pilgrims (many of whom had come from *the ends of the earth*, v. 10) could be reassured that the city was safe under the protective care of Yahweh. Second, the procession would recall the salvation-history that had centered in Jerusalem, and equip the pilgrims to pass it on *to the next generation* (v. 13).

The RSV and NRSV translation of the last statement of v. 14 hides some of its force: "He will lead us against (or over) Death." However, the translations may be correct if the two words "over death" are read as one word "eternally" or *forever* (cf. v. 8). Regardless of the translation, these words speak of confidence that the power of death will not prevail over Zion.

Psalm 49

This psalm is frequently classified as a meditative wisdom psalm, and it has some affinities with Pss 37 and 73. The speaker struggles with the problem of the well-being of the wicked versus the suffering of the righteous. The distribution of wealth in the world follows a seemingly unfair pattern. The wicked gain more than their share and persecute the righteous who have less than their due. The main concern of the speaker is not an analysis of the problem, however, but the one solution of death that levels out all inequalities. The rich person and the poor person approach death on level ground. Life should be lived on the basis of this fact.

The speaker begins (vv. 1-4) in the manner of the prophets, but with a vocabulary more like the WISDOM LITERATURE. Unlike the prophets, he brings no word from God, but he speaks of *wisdom* (v. 3) and the *meditation of my heart* (cf. Ps 1:2) that will be recited to the accompaniment of music (v. 4).

Next, the speaker meditates on the features of the *riddle* referred to in v. 4. Death is a universal experience from which no person finds a *ransom* (v. 7). There is no exit by which a person can evade "the pit" (v. 9, NRSV mg.). *The wise* and the *fool* alike perish and leave their wealth behind (v. 10).

The recapitulation of the analysis of vv. 5-12 in vv. 13-14 adds a comment on the futile confidence of human beings in their wealth and achievements. In reality they live like a flock of sheep, shepherded by *Death* and bound for SHEOL (v. 14, although this verse is uncertain in part)—a striking contrast to Yahweh as shepherd of his people (cf. Ps 23).

An abrupt contrast is interjected at v. 15. The speaker of vv. 1-2 declares that *God will ransom my soul* (i.e., "me") out of *the power of Sheol*, an act that lies beyond the capacity of any human wealth and wisdom (vv. 7-12).

The basic meaning of this "boldly confessional statement" (Brueggemann 1984, 109) is probably that of assurance of God's power to take the person out of "the hand of Sheol" (i.e., protection from the conditions that endanger life), but we should not narrow the meaning too strictly.

Verses 16-20 have the didactic form of instruction, as the speaker exhorts and teaches a group of people who seem to be both cowered and tempted by the wealthy who surround them—especially tempted as poor people to adopt the values and way of life of the rich: *Do not be afraid when some become rich, when the wealth of their houses increases* (v. 16).

Verse 20 closes the psalm and functions as a refrain with v. 12. The NRSV reads the two verses as the same, but the Hebrew text (and other ancient versions) read *cannot abide* (or "will not last long") in v. 12 and "do not understand" in v. 20: "Mortals in pomp do not understand."

The "Korahite" collection. Psalm 49 is the last of a collection of Korahite psalms in book two (Pss 42–49; but Korahite psalms are also in 84–85, 87–88). The

Korahites appear to have been temple singers and functionaries (e.g., Exod 6:21-24; Num 16:31-35; 26:28; 1 Chr 6:22; 2 Chr 20:19), who were probably active in both preexilic and postexilic times, eventually, at least, related to Jerusalem and the Temple.

Psalm 50

This psalm is a "liturgical sermon" (Gerstenberger 1988, 210), which is closely related to Pss 81 and 95. These three psalms have a sermonic style of admonition and instruction, plus content similar to oracles in the prophetic literature (vv. 7-23) without, however, the use of the messenger formula ("Thus says Yahweh") common in prophetic literature.

The first part of the psalm (vv. 1-6) is a report of a THEOPHANY in which God comes out of silence to give a great summons that resounds in the heavens above and on the earth: *"Gather to me my faithful ones, who made a covenant with me by sacrifice"* (v. 5). The *sacrifice* alludes to Exod 24:5-8 (note also Gen 15:8-20; Jer 34:18; for another theophanic summons to judgment, see Mic 1:2-7 and cf. Joel 2:16-17; Isa 48:14-16). The speaker describes the coming of Yahweh to a meeting with his "covenanters," in which he will be *the judge* (v. 6) who deals with *his people* (v. 4), against whom he has charges that are spelled out in vv. 7-23. The heavens and the earth are summoned as the covenant witnesses of the behavior of the people.

The theophany with its stress on the "coming" of God to his people is an important element of Israelite religion (see Pss 18:7-19; 68:7-8; 50:1-6). The God of Israel was not permanently fixed on some far-off SINAI or other sacred mountain, nor in heaven, nor only present in a past history of events. A renewed experience of the divine "coming" was one of the major aspects of Israelite worship.

In vv. 7-23, divine discourse (God is present as the speaker) is used for instruction and impeachment of the people for religious practices without proper ethical prerequisites. They are not reproved for any failure to provide suitable sacrifices (vv. 7-8), but for their thinking that God has need of their sacrifices. If God were hungry, he could help himself to the cattle and goats of the world without dependence on human resources: *for the world and all that is in it is mine* (v. 12). This psalm should not be read as a rejection of sacrifices as such. True sacrifices of thanksgiving—which involved the sacrifice of an animal, a fellowship meal, and a renewal of covenant (v. 5)—are proper and honor God (vv. 14, 23). Those who make these sacrifices "fix" or "set" their ways so that the salvation of God may be experienced.

The style of preaching found in Pss 50, 81, 95 finds its closest counterpart in Levitical preaching in Deuteronomy and Chronicles (see Kraus 1988, 490; Gerstenberger 1988, 207; Tate 1990, 321). The Levitical preachers were probably priests who exercised a prophetic-type function in the postexilic festivals, especially the Festival of Booths (Tabernacles). These psalms were possibly part of covenant-renewal liturgies, but may have been used in other contexts as well.

The title of Ps 50 is worthy of note, as well as its placement in book two of the Psalter. In book two this is the only psalm ascribed to ASAPH (a traditional singer and liturgical expert whose descendants were among the personnel of the postexilic temple; see Ezra 2:41; 3:10; 2 Chr 35:15; a collection of eleven consecutive Asaph psalms is found in Pss 73–83). Psalm 50 seems to have been detached from the Asaph collection in Pss 73–83 and placed before Ps 51 because of its emphasis on Zion (see v. 2). It concludes a run of Korahite psalms (42–49) that have the divine presence on Zion as their central focus. For further discussion of the psalms of Asaph, see the commentary on Ps 83.

Psalm 51

This is the best known of the traditional seven penitential psalms of the ancient church (also Pss 6, 32, 38, 102, 130, 143). It is an individual lament that probes deeply into sin and forgiveness. The psalm assumes a worshiper who bears a crushing sense of guilt, and whose culpability has already been made clear. There is some indication of illness (v. 8), but the main concern is with spiritual restoration. Although not all of the historical notes in the psalms superscriptions are appropriate, the note here, referring to DAVID and NATHAN, is apt.

In vv. 1-2, the suppliant prays to God for mercy and cleansing from sin. As in Ps 32:1-2, the vocabulary of sin and forgiveness is prominent in these verses. The terms *blot out my transgressions* (cf. Num 5:23; Isa 43:25; Ps 109:14) and *wash me thoroughly* are very strong, and both are related to cultic acts of purification.

The confession of sin in vv. 3-6 is strongly personal and direct: *For I know my transgressions. . . . Against you, you alone, have I sinned.* The speaker is continually aware of sin and realizes that acts of sin against other people are actually sins against God.

The suppliant confesses that the judgment of God is deserved (v. 4) because of involvement in a sinful nature from conception onwards (v. 5). Verse 5 does not refer to a concept of sinfulness attached to sexual intercourse, but to the human condition in which every person is conceived and born. Sins are inherent in character, they are not freak events (Kidner 1975a, 190) that merit no response from God. The language is hyperbolic and should not be taken literally. The interpretation of v. 6 remains obscure, but the most common interpretation is: *You desire truth in the inward being; / therefore teach me wisdom in my secret heart.* This interpretation links v. 6 with vv. 7-12 (Tate 1990, 3, 6, 20 offers an alternative reading).

In vv. 7-12 the prayer that follows the lament uses language borrowed from ritual procedures. The suppliant prays for a word of *joy and gladness* (v. 8), which may refer to a hoped for ORACLE of forgiveness and promise of salvation from God (to be delivered by the priest). The consciousness of the true nature of human sinfulness is evident in vv. 10-12. Forgiveness really involves a new creation, a radical change of inner being that makes a new relationship possible (v. 10). It also includes a regenerative process. The suppliant, having confessed lifelong sinfulness (vv. 3-5), now prays for a new beginning. Such a new status can be achieved only by the *holy spirit* of God (v. 11), for *the joy of . . . salvation* is only God's to bestow (v. 12).

In vv. 13-17 the prayer of vv. 7-12 is followed by a vow by the suppliant to teach sinners the *ways* of God (v. 13), and to praise him for his salvation (v. 14). The nature of the deliverance sought in v. 14a is uncertain. Perhaps the reference to *bloodshed* is to the death of uninstructed sinners (v. 14; cf. Ezek 3:18-21; 33:7-9). Many scholars interpret the word as a reference to the suppliant's own death, and as a prayer for continued life in order to praise God. They may be correct. The numerous references to "bloodguiltiness" on the part of David (see 1 Sam 25:26; 31; 33; 2 Sam 1:16; 3:28) suggests that either the original writer, or a later reviser, wrote the phrase with David in mind (as the title suggests). It is also possible that the expression is simply hyperbole for "deadly guilt."

The attitude toward sacrifice in vv. 16-17 is similar to that in Ps 40:6. The sacrifice that God wants most is a living sacrifice of a life with pride and rebelliousness broken before the divine will; God is not willing to accept any other kind. Verses 18-19 seem to look forward to the rebuilding of Jerusalem and were probably added in the exilic or postexilic periods. The reviser seems to have interpreted the "I" of the psalm as the nation, most probably reflecting the experience of the Babylonian exile. The denial of the validity of sacrifice in v. 16 was considered to be a temporal one that applied to the limited period shortly before and during the EXILE. The highly personal and individualistic expression in the psalm does not negate the significance of corporate religious experience. The context for the most personal and private religious experience is in the worshiping community. Further, the lament and prayer of vv. 1-17 prepare the worshiper in mind and spirit for sacrificial rituals. It was not, therefore, an act of theological violence to adapt the psalm for recitation in the postexilic rituals of the Temple.

One of the interesting features of this psalm is the threefold work of the spirit of God in vv. 10-12. The "steadfast spirit" (NRSV mg.) in v. 10 provides enduring strength; the *holy spirit* in v. 11 marks and activates the empowering presence of God; the *willing Spirit* in v. 12 gives sustaining energy to a person freed from the bondage of guilt which makes possible steadfast and willing commitment to God.

Psalm 52

Commentators disagree about the classification of this psalm, but it seems best to read it as a prophetic judgment speech, or if not actually a speech of judgment then like one (for such speeches, see Isa 22:15-19; Jer 20:3-6; 28:12-16). The prophetic judgment speeches have varied features, but two common ones are an accusation, and an announcement of judgment. An accusation of a rich, haughty, deceitful person is found in vv. 1-4. The essential charge is in v. 3: *You love evil more than good.* The announcement of judgment in vv. 5-7 is expressed in strong language. The contrast between the righteous and the wicked is a motif commonly found in the WISDOM LITERATURE.

A contrast to the judgment on the boastful person of vv. 1-7 is found in vv. 8-9. The style is that of the thanksgiving psalms: testimony by one who has experienced the help of God and now voices a thanksgiving in the presence of the "godly", that is, *the faithful* in the congregation. The person who has been expelled from the Temple (if that is the correct interpretation) lacks the blessing of participation in worship. The reader will easily relate the *green olive tree* (v. 8) that grows in the Temple—a figure of the blessing of worship—and the tree *by streams of water* in Ps 1:3 that is a symbol for the blessing of the person who is devoted to *torah*. The purpose of this psalm is to encourage the faithful in a community under stress to be faithful to God.

The title of this psalm is the first of a run of four with the expression *a Maskil of David*. The Heb. *maskil* is found in a total of thirteen psalm inscriptions (32, 42, 44, 45, 52, 53, 54, 55, 74, 78, 88, 89, and 142) plus in Ps 47:7 (translated *psalm*). *Maskil* probably indicates a psalm judged to be artistically devised and productive of thought and meditation (note the title of Ps 32 and the use of the verb from *maskil* in 32:8: *I will instruct you and teach you the way you should go*). These psalms invite reflection. Second Chronicles 30:22 refers to a group of Levites spoken to by King Hezekiah as *Maskilim*, who have "good understanding as to Yahweh." This may indicate that the *maskil* psalms were the work of a group of liturgical specialists in the Temple. It is interesting that the four *maskil* psalms in 52–55 are followed by five *miktam* psalms in 56–60.

Psalm 53

This psalm is usually treated as a slightly different version of Ps 14, perhaps the result of textual corruption. Each is a discrete entity, however, even though they are versions of the same psalm. Both psalms belong to the genre of prophetic speech, at least in a general sense. Therefore Ps 53 is closely related to Ps 52 and Ps 14. Verses 4-5, however, seem to indicate a prophetic-like taunt or mocking speech (e.g., Num 21:27-30; Isa 14:4-20; Ezek 28:2-10; 12-19).

In Ps 53 the *fools* are understood as foreigners, not Israelites as in Ps 14. The *fools* are foreigners who think they can attack Zion and destroy the people of Yahweh (retaining the Hebrew text "for God scattered the bones of your besieger[s]" in v. 5). The people have been put to shame because they have failed to trust God to deliver them. The psalm seems to appeal for faithfulness on the basis of God's past performance. Future deliverance and restoration is anticipated in v. 6. For vv. 1-3, see the commentary on Ps 14.

Psalm 54

This psalm follows the general style of a lament. There is a cry for help (vv. 1-2), followed by a complaint (v. 3). As usual in the laments, the references to the *enemies* (v. 5) lack preciseness, but v. 3c may indicate that they were Israelites. In any case, the suppliant expresses a sense of deadly danger.

The NRSV reads vv. 4-5 as statements of confidence based on faith in God. This may be correct, but it is better to read these verses as petitions:

Surely, O God, my helper,
O Lord, the sustainer of my life,

let evil turn back onto my slanderers;
in your faithfulness put an end to them! (author trans.)

A vow and anticipated testimony of victory follows easily in vv. 6-7. The name of God is emphasized in this psalm (see vv. 1 and 6), which represents his presence and availability to those who know and use that name in prayer and praise.

Psalm 55

This psalm is a lament or complaint of the individual type, but it also has mixed elements. Textual uncertainties and changes from the singular to plural in references to *adversaries* (vv. 12-13, 15, 20-21, 23) add difficulty to interpretation. The adversary is described in vv. 12-14 and vv. 20-21 as a friend and companion who has turned against the supplicant. The foe is described in the language of hostile enemies (vv. 9-11 and vv. 15, 16-19). The theme of trouble because of the treacherous actions of a friend holds the psalm together, and is a type of attacks by enemies in general (see esp. v. 15).

The psalm is a mixture of prayer, complaint, and declarations of confidence, found in a natural sequence: prayer (vv. 1-2a), complaint (vv. 2b-8), prayer and complaint (vv. 9-11), complaint (vv. 12-15), declarations of confidence (vv. 16-19), complaint (vv. 202-1), and declarations of confidence (vv. 22-23). The title is identical with Ps 54 (except the historical note added in Ps 54), which probably indicates that later scribal interpreters read them together. If Pss 54–55 are read together, the historical note in the title of Ps 54 applies to both psalms. The psalms have some parallels in content and the declarations of confidence in 55:22-23 follow well the ending of Ps 54.

Psalm 56

This individual lament is a prayer for deliverance from personal enemies. Problems in the text and the uncertainty of the speaker's situation make interpretation difficult. Lament because of the oppression of enemies is found in vv. 1-2, 5-6ab. Verses 3-4, 8-11, are statements of trust in God; vv. 6c–7 express prayer for the judgment of God. A vow to render thank-offerings to God for the deliverance experienced appears in vv. 12-13.

The use of language that applies to military enemies (vv. 1-2) may suggest a general or king as the supplicant, but the statements in vv. 5-6ab and v. 9 seem to preclude it. The enemies are in the community; it therefore is better to think of an ordinary supplicant to whom the language of king and military leader is applied.

The lament closes with thanksgiving for deliverance from death and for continued life. The speaker has no doubt of God's attention during times of distress (v. 8). Regardless of the circumstances, the speaker has a basic certainty: *This I know, that God is for me* (v. 9). The repeated use of the *word* of God (vv. 3-4, 10-11) constitutes two foci around which the psalm is constructed. The *word* of God the speaker is determined to praise probably refers to the promises of God, but could also indicate an expected word from God.

The "Miktam" collection. The title of this psalm contains the term *Miktam*, which is found in the titles of five other psalms: 16, 57, 58, 59, 60. The meaning of the word is not certain, but its form suggests it means "written" or "inscribed." The psalms designated as *miktam* may have been "letter-prayers," written to God and placed in the Temple (cf. Hezekiah's prayer in Isa 38:9; possibly the word in Jer 2:22 usually translated as "stain" should be read as "inscribed": "your guilt is inscribed before me" [Craigie 1983, 154]). The six *miktam* psalms all seem to reflect a time of crisis, which is in keeping with the prayer of Hezekiah in Isa 38. The use of "letter-prayers" seems to have been a feature of ancient Near Eastern religions. Psalms 56–60 form a core near the center of book two of the Psalter.

Psalm 57

This psalm is a lament-prayer of the individual type, with two distinct parts. Verses 1-4, 6 have the content of lament, and vv. 7-10 is thanksgiving (substantially the same as Ps 108:1-4, and v. 10 is similar to Ps 36:5). The psalm is held together by a refrain in vv. 5 and 11 (= Ps 108:5).

A cry for help, directed to God (v. 1) is followed by statements of confidence (vv. 2-3). The speaker has taken refuge under the protective *wings* of God (v. 1)—possibly in the Temple, although this does not rule out the figurative, spiritual significance of the term. The expression *I will take refuge* is equal to "I place my trust in," so the line can be rendered: "In the shadow of your wings I place my trust." *In the shadow of your wings* suggests the wings of the cherubim over the ARK in the Temple, and the wings that bear the throne of God.

God will send forth *his steadfast love and his faithfulness* (v. 3) as agents from heaven (cf. Ps 43:4). The situation of the speaker is described in v. 4 as like that of Daniel in a den of lions (Dan 6:16-24), but these lions are human beings who wait to attack with their sword-sharp tongues.

Verse 5 is a hymnic refrain that is repeated in v. 11. The transition to thanksgiving is made in v. 6, where it is declared that the suppliant's adversaries have fallen into their own ditch (cf. Pss 7:15; 9:15).

A joyful song of thanksgiving and praise forms the last part of the psalm (vv. 7-11), verses also found in Ps 108:1-5 with minor changes. The speaker experiences an inner "steadfastness" of heart. HEART in biblical language usually refers to the mind and the will of a person. Verse 10, along with the refrain in vv. 5 and 11, reflects the ancient Near Eastern idea of the huge stature of deities, whose *steadfast love* and *faithfulness* ("reliability" or "truth") extends into the clouds and the heavens.

Psalm 58

This psalm has characteristics of the laments, but it is most similar in form to prophetic judgment speech as found in Pss 14, 52, 53, and 55. The psalm's primary purpose is to strengthen *the righteous* (vv. 10-11) against *the wicked* (vv. 3-5).

The psalm opens with a prophetic type of condemnation of "mighty ones" (usually read as "mighty lords" [NRSV mg.] or as *gods*) because of their failure to conduct human affairs correctly (vv. 1-2). If *gods* are rebuked in vv. 1-2, the psalm may be read as an attack on pagan deities who have responsibility for the conduct of human affairs (see Deut 32:8-9; Ps 82).

An earlier version of the psalm may have been a judgment speech against divine beings who had failed to establish justice and order in human affairs, but in the present version of the psalm it seems more likely that the "mighty ones" (reflecting a slight change in the Hebrew text) refers to the leaders of society.

The terrible consequences of the failure of the "mighty ones" is described in vv. 3-5—the sinful condition of society (cf. Gen 6:1-8) and the class to which the "mighty ones" belong. The sinful propensity of *the wicked* (cf. Pss 36:1-4; 10:3-11) goes back to *the womb* (cf. Ps 51:3-5). They are so completely evil that they are like deaf cobras that cannot be charmed for the removal of their venom (vv. 4-5).

The prayer in vv. 6-11 is not exceeded in its violence by any other prayer in the Psalter. The NRSV sufficiently conveys its fury. Psalm 58, therefore, provides a good example of the type of material in the Psalms that raises ethical problems for the modern reader. Should such psalms be allowed to remain in the canon of the church? Do they not foster attitudes of vengeance and violence that violate all the standards of proper attitude and behavior? What shall we say to these questions?

First, we should not attempt to evade the issue by resorting to spiritualizing or allegorical interpretations, although such approaches are valuable in the larger picture of biblical interpretation. Further, any reductionist approach—a method that simply eliminates from the canon and liturgy those portions of the Bible that are found to be offensive—should be resisted. Selective reading of scripture has its place (see Holladay 1993, 304–15), but it suffers from the constant danger of excessive subjectivity and the tendency of theologians to import foreign elements into basic biblical understanding.

The Israelite commitment to Yahweh resulted in a remarkable freedom of worship. In the sanctuaries of Israel, men and women were free to speak, to pray, to confess, to sing, to shout, to dance, even to curse their enemies—and, above all, to praise God. They were also liable to receive oracles of judgment that laid on them unavoidable demands. In such honest worship there was no need to disguise one's true feelings. Israel's worship as it appears in the Book of Psalms has a childlike adulthood about it. God is real and present, and his people know it.

Further, the nature of the "enemies" must be considered when evaluating the imprecations in the psalms (on the "enemies," see also the commentary on Ps 7). The "enemies" were both the foes and adversaries of the suppliants and the enemies of Yahweh. Only rarely does the suppliant pray for the power for personal vindication through personal acts of vengeance against enemies (see, e.g., Ps 41:10; 52:6-7; 62:3). The speakers in the Psalms usually pray that Yahweh will judge and punish. The imprecations may be vengeful at times, but they are not prayers *for* vengeance.

The character of the "enemies" as presented in Psalms reveals a profound awareness of the actuality and depth of human wickedness. Indeed, the "enemies" are more than human (as in Ps 58) because they are allied with cosmic beings and forces that threaten the very order of creation and lie beyond the power of humans. The imprecatory fury of sections like Ps 58:6-11 is not aimed primarily at wicked, weak mortals who stand on the same ground with the suppliants, but at foes and forces that threaten the created natural, historical, and moral orders of Yahweh and his people.

Psalm 59

This psalm is an individual lament with the usual themes expressed forcefully, although there seem to be communal elements in vv. 5, 6-8, and 11-15.

The psalm opens with a prayer for deliverance from enemies who threaten the life of the suppliant, but for no reason on the speaker's part (vv. 1-4a). The enemies are described in vv. 6-7 and 14-15 as *dogs . . . prowling* who howl and snarl as they roam about for food. The prayers in vv. 4b-5; 11-13 are almost as furious as those in Ps 58:6-11.

For the idea of God waking from sleep, see comment on Ps 44. Statements of trust are found in vv. 8-10 and a vow of praise appears in vv. 16-17.

The psalm may have been designed for a king as the speaker, possibly DAVID himself, although the speaker could also be a priest or other leader. In time, any individual could use the psalm as a prayer for deliverance from a dire situation. The title indicates that later circles in Israelite history read the psalm as being a prayer of David (which is true of many psalms). The scribal historical note sets the psalm in a crisis context in the life of David and is probably derived from an exegesis of the accounts of David in 1 Sam 19 and 24.

Psalm 60

All interpretations of this psalm are problematic, but it appears to be a prayer of communal complaint. There is a mood of humiliating defeat as the people bring their laments and prayers to God. Attempts have been made to fit this psalm into a historical context; the superscription assigns it to a situation in the career of David (see 2 Sam 8; 1 Chr 18). Other suggestions have ranged from David's time to the time of the MACCABEES. Verse 9 may indicate that some campaign against Edom was the occasion, but provides no definite clue as to date. The psalm probably had a long history in the traditions of Israel. The psalm's concern with Edom points to the exilic and postexilic periods as the psalm's basic provenance.

The complaint is marked by the fact that it emphasizes the suffering of the people as the direct result of divine action (cf. Ps 44). The action of God is ascribed cosmic features (v. 2) usually associated with theophanies (see Pss 18:6-15). In this case it is a THEOPHANY of judgment. Interpretation of v. 4 is uncertain. It may mean *a banner* has been set up to warn farmers and others in outlying areas to flee to a fortified city before it is too late. However, in this case the refuge has failed and the people have suffered *hard things* (v. 3).

The prayer of the people, with its emphasis on an answer, is given in v. 5. The answer is received in the sanctuary in the form of an ORACLE, that would have been spoken by a priest or prophet (the oracle in v. 6-8 is also found in Ps 108:7-9). The oracle itself is probably not original to the psalm, but was one already used in worship and inserted here. Its main point is Yahweh's ownership of the land of Canaan, which he gave to the Israelites. The geography of the psalm reflects the Davidic empire.

A solo voice prays with questions that express concern over a campaign against Edom, and suggest that the speaker is a king or leader of the army (v. 9). It is possible, however, that Yahweh is the speaker (Gerstenberger 1988, 241), summoning Israel to take part in his triumph. The congregation responds in vv. 10-12, moving from a lament in v. 10, to a petition in v. 11, to a statement of potential victory. Verse 12 could read "With God we could do valiantly, he could tread down our foes" or, "With God we can do valiantly. . . . " Despite defeat, the people know that God's power to save is intact and essential. All human help is vain. The prayer represents a struggle for faith.

Psalm 61

This psalm is an individual lament that is concerned with the security found by those who take refuge in the protective care of God. It is possible the lament is that of a king whose testimony (v. 5) is followed by a congregational prayer for him (vv. 6-7). It seems more probable, however, that the psalm is a pilgrim's prayer spoken far away from the Temple (*from the ends of the earth* [v. 2]).

The speaker knows *the heritage of those who fear your name* (v. 5), and expresses a wish in v. 4 to continue forever to dwell *in your tent* and *find refuge under the shelter of your wings* (on the *tent*, see Ps 15:1; 27:4-5; Isa 33:20). Goulder (1990, 152) calls attention to the concentration of leitmotifs and other features in this psalm that also are found in Pss 51–71: *refuge, rock, fortress* (NEB, REB, "strong tower") in 59:9, 16, 17; 62:2, 6, 7, 8; 71:3, 7; shelter under the divine *wings* in 57:1 and 63:7; (the Temple on) *Zion* in 52:8; 53:6; 63:2; 65:1; 68:24, 29; *vows* of *praise* in 52:9; 56:12; 65:1; 66:13; 69:30-31; 71:8, 14-15, 17-18, 24; reference to the king in 64:11 and possibly in 65:4; the divine agents *steadfast love* and truth (*faithfulness*) sent to protect the speaker in 57:3, 10 (*steadfast love* and *strength* in 59:9-10, 16-17). Clearly these are basic concepts in this set of psalms.

The prayer for the king would not have been out of order for preexilic Israelites visiting Jerusalem for one of the festivals or because of some urgent personal reason. In the later periods when there was no king, it is probable that the prayer for the king became a messianic prayer for a future king. Note the divine agents who are to guard the king in v. 7: *steadfast love and faithfulness*, the same as found in Ps 57:3. Verses 2c-3 is an excellent example of prayer. The vows in vv. 5 and 8 are not defined, but we may surmise that they are a response of the speaker to a divine deliverance from a threatening situation (see Ps 56:12-13).

Psalm 62

This psalm is usually treated as a song of trust, and an affirmation of faith in God. It may be more properly classified as testimony and instruction. The prayer element is minimal, lacking any direct address to God until the last verse, and the speaker assumes a human audience. Verses 1-2 express a basic affirmation of trust in God. The assurance expressed has come about through a struggle (cf. Pss 73, 131). The opening word (*alone* or "surely") expresses assurance despite outward circumstances to the contrary. The Hebrew particle for "surely" or "even so" occurs six times in this psalm (vv. 1, 2, 4, 5, 6, and 9) and gives it a "nevertheless" quality—*power belongs to God* (v. 11) regardless of commonly perceived appearances. The speaker has seen through the veil of human riches and power.

In v. 3 the speaker addresses enemies directly, which does not happen often in the Psalms (see note on Ps 58). Ordinarily speakers talk to God *about* their enemies. In v. 4, however, the speaker talks about the enemies to an audience. The enemies are described as hypocrites: blessing with their mouths while cursing inwardly. A testimony of confidence in God follows (vv. 5-7).

In vv. 8-12, the speaker turns to the audience and instructs them as a wise teacher. On the basis of personal experience the speaker exhorts all who listen to trust God (v. 8), because their own achievements can provide no dependable and enduring base for confidence (vv. 9-10; cf. Jer 17:5-8). In the ultimate balance of things human glory is ephemeral. It is foolish to set one's heart on riches, even when they increase (v. 10). The speaker has firsthand knowledge, for God has "spoken" once, even twice (vv. 11-12). The *once . . . twice* formula is found in the WISDOM LITERATURE (see Prov 6:16; 30:15, 21; Amos 1:3; etc.). In this case, however, the *once . . . twice* may refer to *power* (or strength) and the *steadfast love* that belongs to God (v. 11c-12a).

Psalm 63

This psalm is usually considered to be a song of trust and praise recited by a worshiper who has participated in a worship experience in the sanctuary (v. 2). The speaker is now assured that those who seek to destroy him (vv. 9-10) will suffer the wrath of divine judgment. The mention of *the king* in v. 11 seems unrelated to the preceding verses (cf. Ps 61:6-7), but it is probable that affirmation of, and prayer for, the king was a regular part of Israelite worship. The life of the nation and well-being of individuals were inseparably linked to the kings.

In vv. 1-4, the desire of the suppliant for an experience of the nearness of God is strongly expressed (v. 1; cf. Ps 42–43). A burning thirst for the divine presence characterizes the speaker's life; it is a thirst that has been satisfied in the sanctuary (v. 2). A lifelong vow of praise is made in v. 4.

In vv. 5-8, the speaker continues to praise God for the richness and power of the communion experience. Verses 6-7 possibly allude to the practice of spending a night in the area of the sanctuary in order to await a word from God at dawn. *In the shadow of your wings* refers to the protective presence of God, and may allude to the ARK in the Temple and to the cherubim whose wings were extended over it (1 Kgs 6:23-29; 8:6-7). This psalm is unusual in its degree of emphasis on the intimate relationship between the speaker and God: *My soul is satisfied. . . . My soul clings to you* (vv. 5, 8).

Verses 9-11 include a prophecy of the coming judgment of the adversaries followed by an affirmation of the well-being of the king and *all who swear by him*. *Him* can refer to either the king or God; it is difficult to decide which is intended because there is support for both interpretations (see Deut 6:13; 10:20; Isa 65:16; 1 Sam 17:55; 25:26; 2 Sam 11:11; 15:21).

The historical note attached to the Davidic title is the last of eight such notes in book two (Pss 51, 52, 54, 56, 57, 59, 60, 63). The historical notes are probably scribal additions that assign the reading of certain psalms to life situations in the career of David. These notes seem to be artfully constructed on the basis of word-plays and general associations of content with the Davidic accounts in the books of Samuel and Chronicles. They have little or no value for the actual history of David, but they are helpful in understanding later interpretation of the psalms. Since there are only thirteen psalms with historical notes in the Psalter, the appearance of eight of them in sequence is striking and may be a clue to the intention and use of book two (see the summary that follows the commentary on Ps 72). The effect of the Davidic notes provides a context for them as prayers of David. Individuals could identify with David and the stories about him, and thus make the prayers their own.

Psalm 64

This psalm belongs to the individual laments; perhaps more specifically it is a prayer for protection. The first part (vv. 1-6) is composed of a prayer to God for deliverance from the plots and schemes of evildoers who threaten the life of the speaker. Because the text is difficult to read, the exegesis is tentative at several points. The adversaries seem to make special use of their tongues and words (v. 3). Perhaps curses and deadly accusations are indicated. The speaker complains of the threat of ambush (v. 4).

In vv. 7-9, there is a "certainty of hearing" passage. The verbs should be trans-lated as future tense, or as characteristic present tense (as in REB): "God will shoot an arrow at them unexpectedly and suddenly they will be wounded." The punish-ment of the wicked will result directly from their own behavior (v. 8). Verse 11 is a closing statement of encouragement of the righteous and the upright.

The key statement in this psalm is the passing comment in v. 6: *For the human heart and mind are deep*. The devious and corrupt nature of the human heart (mind) defies logical explanation, being both sinister and deadly as well as hidden from normal scrutiny.

Psalm 65

This is a psalm of praise with a variety of stylistic features, such as the beatitude form (*Happy are those*) and the extended length of v. 4. Opinions of commentators about the situation behind the psalm vary. The most common position is that the psalm was designed for a harvest festival, when God was praised for the bounty that he had bestowed on crops and people (esp. appropriate for a praise service after the end of a drought). It has also been read as a prayer for rain, by reminding God of past blessings of rain and fertility (vv. 9-13).

Verses 1-4 praise the God who is present on Mount Zion and who "hears prayer." Further, God forgives sins (vv. 2-3), which is a need of *all flesh*. Verse 4 adds a note on the happiness of those who have access to the nearness of God in Temple worship. The worshipers are permitted to share in the "goodness" of God's house, (i.e., in the joyful fellowship and all the blessings that flow from Zion). This means more than sharing in the sacrificial banquets; a share in the "goodness" of God in a broader sense is intended.

Verse 4 uses the language of priests who are "chosen" and "brought near" to God (see Num 16:5; cf. Jer 30:21; Zech 3:7). The language here should be understood to include all worshipers who "come near" to God at the Temple; they share the priestly privilege. Although v. 4ab uses the singular ("Happy is the one . . . he will dwell in your courts"), the meaning is collective (as v. 4de indicate).

In the pivotal verses 5-8, the great acts of God are praised. With awe-inspiring deeds of deliverance, God has made himself known to the ends of the earth. The God who hears prayer in Zion is the master of the world, who sets the mountains in place, and who controls the chaotic forces of the universe and of history (v. 7). The inhabitants of the whole earth are awed by God's *signs* (v. 8).

In vv. 9-13 the praise of God continues with an emphasis on the giving of rain and fertility. The "land" (v. 9; better than *earth*) receives water from the *river of God* (really an irrigation canal as in Ps 1:3) that *is full of water* and is the source of rain cascading in a downpour for the grain and the pastures (see Ps 46:4; Isa 33:21; Joel 4:18; Ezek 47; Zech 14:8). The hills and valleys become verdant and all of nature is awakened to abundant life to shout and sing the praise of God (vv. 11-13). Because this description seems to fit the Palestinian spring better than the autumn, some interpreters assume the psalm was intended for a spring festival (either Passover or Weeks).

Psalm 66

The three sections of this psalm (vv. 1-7, 8-12, 13-20) all have praise-thanksgiving content. The original speaker may have been a king, but that is not required for the use of the psalm in the present collection. The psalm has a liturgical character and was probably designed for use in thanksgiving ceremonies led by the king in preexilic Israel. In later usage the speaker could be anyone speaking for the congregation.

The psalm begins with a typical call to praise God, directed to *all the earth* (vv. 1, 4). A song suitable for such praise is given in vv. 3-4. The awesome power of the divine deeds will send the people of the earth to their knees, singing praises to the name of God.

A second summons is found in v. 5; a summons to *come and see* the awesome deeds of God. The deeds recall the deliverance of the Israelites from the Egyptians at *the sea* (v. 6; Exod 14:21; 15:19), and perhaps the crossing of the Jordan (Josh 3) as well (*the river*, although never elsewhere used of the Jordan). The summons in v. 5 and *there* in v. 6 is similar to the language of Pss 46:8 and 48:4-8, leading some commentators to conclude that some the of worshipers were being urged to see a cultic ritual that reenacted the ancient events. This may be, but *there* is subject to different interpretations (see Tate 1990, 146, 149), and may simply refer to the place where those summoned in v. 5 would assemble: "Come and see . . . there let us rejoice in him!" The place of assembly would almost certainly have been primarily the Temple. In more general usage, the *come and see* of v. 5 may mean basically to become acquainted with and to understand the works of God.

Two probable merisms in vv. 6 and 12 (a merism cites extreme or contrasting examples in order to be comprehensive, such as "from A to Z"). The *river* in v. 6a may be another term for *the sea* and the two words stress the great dimensions of the divine deeds. The same thing is probably true of *through fire and through water* (v. 12), meaning all manner of testings and trials. Verses 6 and 12 join vv. 1–7 and 8–12. The deliverance of God described in vv. 10-12 has not been easy for the Israelites, but he has kept them *among the living* (v. 9) and brought them out to abundance (v. 12).

Verses 13-20 constitute an individual thanksgiving section setting forth the fulfillment of vows (vv. 13-15) and the testimony of a speaker (vv. 16-20). The speaker summons all those *who fear God* (v. 16), that is, all true and serious worshipers. The speaker refers to vows made in a time of great trouble (cf. Pss 22:25; 61:8; 116:18; Jonah 2:10). Verse 20 is a closure for the entire psalm, picking up the *bless our God* of v. 8.

"*Songs (of David).*" Pss 66 and 67 do not refer to David in their titles. Pss 51-71—except 66, 67, and 71—refer to David. Ps 71 should be read with Ps 70, which leaves 66 and 67. The scribal interpreters who supplied the titles probably intended for Pss 66 and 67 to be covered by the Davidic references in the titles of Pss 65 and 68, forming a small collection (or run) of psalms in Pss 65–68.

Psalm 67

Usually classified as a thanksgiving psalm, especially designed for a good harvest, Ps 67 is more nearly a prayer for continued blessing. It may have been used during the festival of Tabernacles as a prayer of thanksgiving for the harvest (v. 6). If so, it shows considerable connection to Ps 65. This psalm functions well as the closing prayer of a festival or worship service. The Jewish use of the psalm at the end of SABBATH is appropriate as well.

Verse 1 adapts the priestly blessing of Num 6:24-26 into a prayer for God's blessing and presence. The motivation for such blessing is so the *way* and *saving power* of God may be known *among all nations* (v. 2).

The prayer becomes praise in v. 3—5—actually a short hymn with a refrain at the beginning and end. What God does in Israel becomes a testimony to the whole world because the lordship of God over history is not confined to Israel. God judges and guides all nations (v. 4). This is a prayer for the inclusion of the nations in praising God's blessings.

The thanksgiving of vv. 6-7 refers to the blessing that is prayed for in v. 1. The nations can see how God has blessed Israel.

The *increase* of *the earth* (v. 6) is a word that refers to the harvest that God gives in fulfillment of his promise (Lev 26:4; Deut 11:17; 32:22; Judg 6:4; Ps 85:12). It need not, however, refer to the final harvest of the year but to growing grain and other crops (cf. Ps 78:46). Verse 7 is a prayer for the continuation of the process of blessing that begins in v. 6. For a survey of the comprehensive range of divine blessing, see Deut 28:1-6.

Psalm 68

This psalm is exceedingly complex. The difficult text is matched by a style that oscillates from one form of speech to another, and by historical and geographical allusions that elude positive identification. These problems have led some commentators to consider the psalm as a collection of poetic pieces, perhaps incipits (beginnings of independent poems) rather loosely joined together in an anthology with little or no inner relationship. Others are more constructive and, despite the psalm's "disconnectedness," consider it as a liturgical collection designed for use in the communal worship of the festivals. Identifying the psalm as a liturgical collection seems the better option.

The context of the psalm seems to be that of a procession entering the Temple (vv. 24-27). The exact nature of the festival intended is a matter of considerable debate among scholars, although it is highly probable this psalm was used during the autumn festival of Tabernacles.

Apart from a liturgical unity, the psalm has a fair degree of internal consistency and literary structure. In terms of genre, the psalm is a supplicatory, hymnic prayer designed to exalt the victories of Yahweh and seek further victories and blessings from him. The concentration on God and praiseworthy divine deeds transforms the disconnectedness of the psalm into a poetic, theological display of the saving works of God.

The prelude (vv. 1-2) is an adaptation of the ancient cultic cry that signaled the movement of the ARK of the covenant (Num 10:35-36). The verses are appropriate as an invocation to begin a procession, and may have been so used when the people and the ark started toward the SANCTUARY. The petitions in vv. 2c-3 express the familiar contrast between *the wicked* and *the righteous* (cf. Ps 1).

In vv. 4-6 a hymnic section praises God who blesses the needy while he leaves those who rebel against him to perish in the desert (v. 6). *Who rides upon the clouds* (v. 4) represents a small textual change from the "who rides through the deserts" (NRSV etc. mg.) of the Hebrew text. The validity of this widely accepted correction is debatable. It does bring the expression into harmony with v. 33, but the context of the desert in vv. 4-6 and vv. 7-10 may point to God's presence with his people during the wilderness wanderings and the settlement of Canaan. However, the giving of rain (vv. 8-9) is more easily linked with the idea of the "Cloud Rider" (cf. NJB).

The hymn continues (vv. 7-10) with allusions to major events in the early history of Israel: the EXODUS from Egypt and the passage through the wilderness. There is a close relationship between these verses and the Song of Deborah in Judg

5:4-5. The motifs of the THEOPHANY (see Ps 18:6-15) and the giving of rain are blended. The literal expression "this Sinai" in v. 8 is uncertain; the interpretation represented in the NRSV *(the God of Sinai)* may be correct. Another interpretation reads the phrase with the force of a divine name: "Him of Sinai" or "The Sinai One." In any case, this section recapitulates in hymnic form the providential care by which God (now understood as Yahweh) brought his people to dwell in the land of Canaan and provided the rain that made life possible. In Canaanite worship, BAAL was the great rain giver, but for Israel Yahweh poured out the rain and restored his languishing *heritage* (v. 9)—the land of Canaan where the Israelites lived.

An abrupt transition into a new section (vv. 11-14) recalls the victory of the Israelites over Sisera (Judg 5:16, 28-30). The interpretation of these verses is plagued by several uncertain details. *Wings of a dove covered with silver* may refer to booty captured in war, but perhaps more probably it refers to the release of colorful messenger doves to signal a victory in war. The location of *Zalmon* (v. 14) is uncertain. It may have been a mountain in the area of Shechem (see Judg 9:48). The mention of *snow* (v. 14) has been explained in varied ways; perhaps it recalls a meteorological phenomenon that occurred in connection with a victory over enemies of the Israelite tribes. However, it is probable that the imagery in this section is more poetic than historical.

Verses 15-18 glorify the "high mountain" that Yahweh has chosen as a dwelling place. In the present context it is clear Zion is intended. The mighty mountains *of Bashan* (vv. 15-16) are taunted for their envy of Yahweh's choice of Zion. Some scholars, however, suspect that the original reference of these verses was not to Zion, but to a sacred place of worship in northern Israel (possibly Mount Tabor). The ascent to the high holy place was made by Yahweh as a mighty warrior, returning with his armies from a great victory (vv. 17-18). It seems more probable that *Sinai* (v. 17) should be read as a divine name ("the Lord is among them, Sinai in holiness" or "among the holy ones"; cf. v. 8), but the emendation followed by the NRSV is popular. In any case, the main point of these verses in that of a "change of mountains" in Israel from Sinai to Zion (Deut 33:2). Yahweh, long associated with Sinai, has now made Zion his abode.

In vv. 19-23, the congregation sings the praises of Yahweh, who continually sustains the people and gives them victory over their enemies. There is no escape from divine power (v. 22; cf. Amos 9:3). *Bathe your feet in blood* (v. 23) perhaps should be read "shake the blood off your feet," meaning to stamp the blood of battle from the feet.

Verses 24-27 give a description of a procession into the sanctuary. A solo voice, perhaps one of the singers, excitedly points to various groups in the procession. The "fountain of Israel" can refer to the starting place of the procession (perhaps the spring Gihon at Jerusalem), or the text may be modified to read "assembly" or "convocation" of Israel, which agrees better with the *congregation* of the preceding line.

Four tribes are mentioned in v. 27. There is no clear reason these four are named. Among the more probable reasons are: (1) the tribes named are representative of all the tribes; (2) dependence on the song of Deborah (see Judg 5:18) led to the mention of *Zebulon* and *Naphtali*, while *Judah* and *Benjamin* are added because they are so closely associated with the monarchy and Jerusalem; and (3) the psalm was originally used in a northern cult center especially associated with *Zebulon*, *Naphatali* and *Benjamin*, to which *Judah* was added after the psalm was adapted for use in Jerusalem.

In vv. 28-31, a prayer is directed to God for continued manifestation of his strength and power in defeating the hostile forces of Israel's enemies. If there is a historical referent in v. 30, it is probably Egypt. In any case, these are types of powerful forces subdued by Yahweh.

A hymn in vv. 32-35 summons all the *kingdoms of the earth* to praise Yahweh, who is described as the one "who rides in the heavens" with a voice of thunder (cf. Ps 29). This powerful, majestic God of the heavens gives power to the people from the (heavenly) sanctuary.

The closing statement, *Blessed be God!* (v. 35), serves both as the end of Ps 68 and as the end of the run of pss 65–68 (see commentary on Ps 66). It summarizes a major thrust of all these psalms, since all four focus attention on the powerful deeds of God, the *God of our salvation* (Pss 65:5; cf. 68:19, 20).

Two broad movements seem to characterize Ps 68: (1) a theophanic emphasis on God's rising up and coming forth to defeat enemies and provide for his people; and (2) an emphasis on Yahweh's role as the divine warrior who *gives power and strength to his people* (v. 35). He is *awesome in . . . his sanctuary* because he is the victorious divine warrior. Two aspects of the psalm are held together by two uses of the name "Yahweh" in vv. 16 (LORD) and 20 (GOD). The coming God and the abiding God are the same; both give power and strength to the people.

Psalm 69

This is an individual lament in which the speaker complains bitterly about the attacks of enemies and prays for their punishment. The speaker claims to be a servant of God (v. 17) whose zeal for the house of God (v. 9) has provoked humiliating and deadly opposition. This psalm is noted for its graphic language and its frequent use in the NT (e.g., Matt 27:34; Mark 15:26; Luke 23:36; John 2:17; 15:25; 19:28-29; Acts 1:20; Rom 11:9-10; Rev 16:1). The speaker's *zeal for your house* in v. 9 leads many interpreters to find a context for the psalm in the time of HAGGAI and ZECHARIAH and the rebuilding of the Temple in Jerusalem (see also vv. 35-36; Ezra 4:1-5, 23-24; 5:2-3; Neh 4:1-5). The zeal of a devoted servant of Yahweh for the Temple could have been true, however, throughout a long span of Israel's history.

Some parts of the psalm suggest a context of sickness, intensified by callous treatment by members of the speaker's community (vv. 19-21). In fact, the language of the psalm is general enough to cover almost any situation of severe distress on the part of a devoted servant of God (cf. Ps 102). The psalm probably emerged in the exilic or postexilic periods and likely was used in ceremonies of fasting and penitence. In such usage the speaker would have been a priest or other representative of the community.

Psalm 69 contains three major sections: vv. 1-13b; a parallel section (vv. 13c-29); and a vow to praise God and a hymn of praise conclude the psalm (vv. 30-36). The heart of the psalm is in vv. 16-18. Yahweh is implored to answer the speaker's prayer on the basis of *steadfast love* and not to *hide your face from your servant*. The hidden face of God is an expression of divine wrath, the negative counterpart of God turning his face toward those in distress in order to help them (cf. Pss 13:1; 3 22:24). The hidden face of God means separation from his attention and care (cf. Ps 51:9 where the hidden face is positive because God's face is hidden from the speaker's guilt). The prayer of the speaker in this psalm is bold and forthright, in which folly and wrongdoing are freely admitted (v. 5), and there is no false modesty about the basic character of the speaker (vv. 6-9). The heinous actions of the enemies are put forward in stark detail (vv. 19-29).

Psalm 70

The psalm is a lament, a prayer for deliverance. It is nearly identical with Ps 40:13-17. Psalm 40 probably depends on Ps 70, but this is uncertain since (1) Ps 70 could be a detached section of Ps 40 or (2) both could be versions of common poetic content.

Psalm 71

Psalm 71 should be read with Ps 70 as a single unit. The two psalms were probably juxtaposed to form a unit because of liturgical use. Perhaps the two psalms were read together to form two units of about the same length.

The two units of Pss 69 and 70–71 form a frame with Pss 61–64 around the "victory songs" in Pss 65–68 (incidentally composing a run of ten psalms, 61 to 70–71, that matches the ten-psalms run of 51–60).

The speaker in Ps 71, and by extension in Ps 70, speaks from the perspective of maturity looking ahead to old age (vv. 9, 17-18). The speaker manifests a serenity often lacking in the young, the product of a long memory of God's faithfulness.

The structure of Pss 70–71 can be analyzed as follows: 70:1-6 is an urgent appeal for help against those who seek to hurt the speaker (the language is dominated by entreaty for God to hasten to help); 71:1-4 begins with an affirmation of trust and moves to petitions for protection and deliverance; 71:5-11 sets forth the main complaint of the speaker, juxtaposed against a life of trust and dependence on God from birth (vv. 5-6); 71:13-18 includes petition and a vow of praise (vv. 14-16); 71:19-24 contains another vow of praise (multiple).

Verse 12 may be read with either the preceding or following section; it is the key verse that functions as the center of the compound psalm formed by Pss 70 and 71.

The speaker could not keep the vow unless God heeds the prayers—it would be physically impossible; the dead cannot praise Yahweh (see Ps 115:17). The vows are explicitly conditional, but implicitly they are expressions of faith because they represent the speaker's dependence on God. The petitioners in such prayers and vows expect to be answered and they are prepared to deliver on their vows.

Psalm 72

This is a royal psalm that expresses prayer for God's blessing on the king. The superscription ascribes the psalm to SOLOMON (cf. Ps 127). A postscript refers to the prayers of David, suggesting that later scribal interpreters read it as a prayer of David for Solomon.

The petition in v. 1. is followed by prayer for a favorable reign of the king (vv. 2-7), in two stanzas (vv. 2-4, 5-7). The reference to the *king's son* (v. 1) may indicate that the poet has the coronation of a new king in mind. The phrase may mean no more, however, than that the king is the scion of the royal family. The petitions for the king give helpful insight into the Israelite conception of the role and significance of kingship. The king sustains the right order of life in the nation. The emphasis is on the words for *justice* and *righteousness*. Special attention is given to the king's defense of the *poor* and *needy* (v. 4). The total welfare of the nation is bound up with the monarch's reign. Thus the king needs the charismatic endowment of divine qualities for his task (v. 1). The king is dependent on Yahweh and responsible to God for the conduct of his reign. The people are Yahweh's people (v. 2); the king is Yahweh's agent.

The prayer continues in vv. 8-12 with wishes for a wide and victorious dominion (cf. Ps 2). God is asked to give the king a universal hegemony that will sway the kings of far-distant places, who will bring him tribute and fall down before him in homage so that he draws together the world. *The River* (v. 8) is not the Euphrates but the cosmic stream that waters Zion and flows out to bring fruitfulness to the land (Ps 46:4; Ezek 47; Zech 9:10). The dimensions of the reign that are envisaged become, therefore, almost cosmic.

Verses 12-14 return to the theme of vv. 2 and 4, stressing the king's role as the helper of the weak and the poor. Of course, this also is the role of Yahweh (Pss 116:15; 146:6-10). The prayer resumes in vv. 15-17 with a plea for long life for the king and for the prosperity of his reign that he, like Abraham (Gen 12:1-3), may become a source of blessing and model for all nations (v. 17). The prosperity of the king's reign will be a fulfillment of the promises of God to the ancestors of Israel.

Verses 18-19 constitute a doxology that has been added to the closing psalm of Book Two of the Psalter. Verse 20 is an editorial note, now attached to this psalm, that probably marked the end of an earlier collection of Davidic psalms.

Summary of Book Two

Two major sections make up book two of the Psalter. The first section (Pss 42–50) centers around the role of Zion in the life of the people of Yahweh. The second section (Pss 51–72) may be called the Prayers of David (see Goulder 1990). The combination of the Korahite psalms, plus one Asaph psalm (Ps 50), with the Prayers of David may seem odd at first. Psalms 42–43 and 44, however, establish an exilic context for both the Korahite psalms (in their present setting) and for the rest of book two (McCann 1993a, 102–103).

The perspective of the speakers in book two is set by Ps 44:11: *You have made us like sheep for slaughter, and have scattered us among the nations.* The individual speaker in Pss 42–43 becomes an example for the community (42:5, 11; 43:5). Psalms 42–43 and 44 form the prologue to Pss 45–50 that sets forward the continued place of Zion in the life of Israel and indirectly keeps the royal hope alive in Ps 45.

Thus in book two Yahweh's abiding presence on Zion is a fundamental focus: *Out of Zion, the perfection of beauty, God shines forth* (Ps 50:2). Zion remained as a fundamental element of Israelite theology in the exilic and postexilic period. The monarch was gone and EXILE had become a permanent way of life, but Zion remained, the Temple was rebuilt, and from there Yahweh comes and calls out: *"Gather to me my faithful ones, who made a covenant with me by sacrifice!"* (Ps 50:5). Yahweh refuses ordinary sacrifices (Ps 50:8-13), but seeks sacrifices of genuine thanksgiving and the faithful keeping of vows (50:14; 23). Indeed, *The sacrifice acceptable to God is a broken spirit; a broken and contrite heart, O God, you will not despise* (Ps 51:17).

The *broken and contrite heart* mingled with praise and thanksgiving is set forth in the powerful Prayers of David in Pss 51–71. These are prayers for a people whose history has imposed on them great hurt, but who rise up out of their guilt, and agony to present their case to God and to vow commitment and praise if he will answer. They have found their mentor in David and the stories of the crises in his life (see the historical notes in the titles of Pss 51–64). In him they found a mixture of iron and clay that reflected their own spiritual condition.

The ancient promises given to David (see Ps 89) are not dealt with explicitly in book two, but two psalms implicitly point to the possible future reality of the promises. Ps 45 revels in the glory of a king who is blessed by God and who fights victoriously for the cause of truth and justice. Such a king will have his name *celebrated in all generations* and be praised by the peoples forever (v. 17). Psalm 72 closes book two with a prayer for Solomon, who represents David's future. David left behind much unfinished business (see 1 Kgs 1–2 and Chronicles 1–2), including the building of the Temple on Zion.

Book two ends with a benediction (Ps 72:18-19) that focuses all eyes on the *blessed* and *glorious name* of Yahweh, the God of Israel, *who alone does wondrous things. . . . may his glory fill the whole earth.*

Book Three. Psalms 73–89

Psalm 73

Form critics have had a difficult time deciding on the proper classification of this psalm. It seems sufficient to say that it is a testimony of the thanksgiving type that also has the form of a reflection. Its content, therefore, is similar to the WISDOM

LITERATURE, which has led to its common designation as a wisdom psalm. The psalm assumes the speaker is addressing a group of listeners, who could be almost any group in worship, community, or family contexts.

The literary structure of the psalm divides rather nicely into eight parts, with two major parallel sections: vv. 2-16 (2-3, 4-12, 13-16) and vv. 18-28 (18-20, 21-26, 27-28); v. 17 serves as a pivot between the parallel sections and v. 1 is a prologue. The reading of v. 1 as "Truly God is good to Israel / to those who are pure in heart" (RSV mg.) is better than *Truly God is good to the upright* (RSV and NRSV). The short colon in v. 1b is the result of ellipsis in which *truly God is good* in the first colon are double-duty words and are understood in the second colon but without direct expression. Ellipsis is common in the poetry of the Psalms (Dahood, 1970, 429–39).

The speaker has a message for the Israelite community and his own experience embodies the life of Israel. The parallel colon makes it clear, however, that the primary audience in Israel is *those who are pure in heart* (i.e., those whose devotion to God is pure and makes them fit for worship [cf. Isa 1:15-16]). Verse 1 also sets forth a thesis that will be tested in this psalm (and indeed throughout book three of the Psalter): God may be good to those who are pure in heart, but is he really good to Israel?

This psalm is marked by the forceful use of the Hebrew particle *'ak* (vv. 1, 13, and 18), which has the force of indicating a condition that is contrary to what is normally expected: a "yes, but" construction (the particle can also mean "surely" or "truly"; note its sixfold usage in Ps 62). This construction has led commentators to label Ps 73 as "The Great Nevertheless." This is especially evident in vv. 18-19, where *the wicked* whose prosperous and arrogant ways had produced such envy in the speaker that he reached the brink of spiritual disaster (vv. 2-3, 4-12, 13-16) are perceived to be themselves standing on slippery ground with no enduring security.

The outward demeanor of the wicked seems strong and vibrant with successful life, but appearances are deceptive: "The LORD does not see as mortals see; they look on the outward appearance, but the LORD looks on the heart" (1 Sam 16:7). The real power of the wicked is their ability to evoke jealous envy in the righteous. Incidentally, *heart* (the volitional center of being, the mind) is used six times in this psalm (vv. 1, 7, 13, 21, 26 twice) and is a major emphasis.

The speaker in Ps 73 testifies to a liberating reorientation of understanding, a breakthrough that occurred in the SANCTUARY (v. 17). We are not told how the new way of thinking happened, but the results are dramatic.

First, as already observed above, there is a reorientation of understanding toward the wicked (vv. 18-20). The veil of invincibility is taken away from them and their true future is perceived.

Second, there is a reorientation of the speaker's own self (vv. 21-22): acceptance of the stupid bitterness of a heart ruled by envy (v. 3).

Third, there is a new orientation toward the presence of God, in which the speaker now realizes that God's presence and guidance is continuous, even when human flesh and heart are spent (vv. 23-26).

Fourth, the speaker has a new orientation towards the future, which will not be ruled by the wealthy and arrogant who are so much envied. The speaker's "strength" and *portion* ("heritage," as in land that belongs to a family) is secure and a glorious reception by God awaits (vv. 24-26). On the basis of the new orientation, the speaker affirms traditional faith in Yahweh in vv. 27-28.

The title of this psalm attributes it to ASAPH. It is the first in a run of Asaph psalms that extends through Ps 83 (see comments on Ps 50 and on the Asaph psalms at the end of commentary on Ps 83).

Psalm 74

This is a communal complaint that describes the grief and dismay following a destruction of the Temple on Mount Zion (vv. 3, 4-8). The date is uncertain. Some commentators read the psalm in the context of the profanation of the Temple by Antiochus Epiphanes IV (175–163 BCE). Others relate it to the destruction of 587 BCE. The psalm may have originated in preexilic times in a northern context (Rendsburg 1990, 69–71), and later transferred to Jerusalem. In its present form the psalm clearly applies to *Mount Zion* (v. 2) and Jerusalem.

The opening cry for help (vv. 1-3) pleads for God to remember Zion, and to bring to an end the terrible godforsakenness of his people. There is a sense of an unbearably long duration of calamity, which may indicate that the psalm was written some time after the attack on the sanctuary to which it refers (v. 3). Verse 2 recalls the sacred history of Zion and the worshiping *congregation* of Israel. The place where Yahweh dwelt is now in ruins.

In vv. 4-11, the enemies of Israel have invaded the *holy place* (lit. "meeting place"), where they have carried out brutal devastation. The exact meaning of the *emblems* or "signs" in v. 4b is uncertain. The reference can be either to religious or military symbols (cf. Num 2:2) or to both. Verses 5-6 are uncertain, but the NRSV translation conveys the general sense. Verse 8 indicates the destruction was not con-fined to the Temple but included all the sacred sites in the land. In this distressing situation, there are no "signs" (v. 9) that Yahweh is about to intervene and redeem his people. There is no PROPHET (see Lam 2:9; Ezek 7:2-6; 1 Macc. 4:46; 9:27; 14:4) who knows the duration of the ruined condition. Yahweh's hand is "held back" from smiting the foe and comforting his people (v. 11).

A hymnic passage probably intended for a solo voice (vv. 12-17; see esp. v. 12) follows the complaints and petitions of the previous verses. God is addressed as *my King* and as the salvation-worker. The great acts of God in the past are recalled: his triumph over the monster of chaos, his control of the waters, and the order that he fixed in the natural world. If he broke the power of chaotic forces then, why not now? *The heads of Leviathan* (v. 14; see LEVIATHAN) is an allusion to the seven-headed monster Lotan that was crushed by the god BAAL. The poet has borrowed some of the imagery of the Canaanites to describe the power of Yahweh.

The petition of the people is resumed in vv. 18-23. Repeated supplications for divine intervention and deliverance are made. *Your dove* of v. 19 refers to Israel's defenselessness before the violence that spreads throughout the land. *The dark places of the land* (v. 20) may refer to places where Israelites fled to protect themselves from the invaders. Yahweh is implored to keep his covenant commitments (vv. 20-23).

Psalm 75

Frequently designated as a communal thanksgiving, this psalm has more of a prophetic-didactic nature, and is a prophetic exhortation. The speaker could be a king, but more likely we should think of a PROPHET or other leader. The communal nature of the thanksgiving-praise in v. 1 indicates that the psalm is set in a public worship context.

The presence of Yahweh is invoked by the use of his name in recalling his wondrous deeds of the past, which would include his judgments on *the wicked* (vv. 3-4). Perhaps we should read at the end of v. 1: "Your name is brought near as they [the people] tell of your wondrous deeds" (cf. REB).

In vv. 2-5, an ORACLE received from God is related—probably by a prophet or priest. God is coming for judgment. He is identified in v. 3 as the one who maintains the stability of the earth. This is followed by a warning to the foes of Israel who might dare to attack, the meaning of *lift up your horn* (vv. 4-5).

A commentary on the oracle follows (vv. 6-8), spoken by an unidentified speaker, but probably by a prophet or other leader. Those who boast and *lift up [their] horn* against Yahweh will have to drink from a cup of judgment (v. 8; cf. Ps 60:3; Jer 25:15-16; Isa 51:17, 22; Ezek 23:31-34; Hab 2:16; Zech 12:2; etc.). The concept of the cup of judgment may have been borrowed from the custom of an ordeal involving drinking from a cup (see Num 5:11-28).

The cup may also reflect the festival cup passed around by members of the fellowship who participated in communal meals during the festivals (see Pss 16:5; 116:13; Jer 16:7; 1 Cor 10:16). Ironically, this is a cup of fellowship for *the wicked*, and they will drink it *down to the dregs*.

The certainty of divine intervention is the basis for the joy and praise which closes the psalm (vv. 9-10). *The horns of the wicked [will be] cut off* while *the horns of the righteous shall be exalted.* Verse 10 is a short oracle, corresponding to the oracle in vv. 2-5.

Psalm 76

Traditionally understood as one of the Songs of Zion, this psalm is a hymn of praise. It has some of the characteristics of Pss 46, 47, and 48 (see also Pss 84, 87, and 122). The psalm may have been written for, or in commemoration of, a historical event. The defeat of SENNACHERIB in 701 BCE (2 Kgs 19 and Isa 37) and David's defeat of the Philistines (2 Sam 17-25) are two possible events behind the psalm. The psalm has the generalized language of cultic poetry and it celebrates the kingship of Yahweh (although it is not specifically mentioned). The reality of

Yahweh's power for those who wait and trust is the main point developed in the psalm.

The first part of the psalm (vv. 1-6) recalls the revelation of Yahweh to Judah that focuses on the history of Judah and Zion, specifically the Davidic tradition of the conquest of Jerusalem and the establishment of Yahweh's sanctuary there. *Salem* (v. 2) is an old designation for Jerusalem (Gen 14:18), which also is reminiscent of the term *shalom* (peace, salvation, well-being). The dwelling-place of Yahweh is intended to be a city of peace and salvation (cf. Ps 46:9; Hos 2:18; Isa 2:4; 11:9), thus the implements of war are smashed by dazzling displays of sovereign power. The language of Yahweh's breaking *the weapons of war* (v. 3) is similar to Ps 46 (see also Hos 1:4; 2:18; Jer 49:35; Mic 5:9-13; Zech 9:10). Yahweh destroys both the weapons of the enemies of Israel and the weapons of Israel. Yahweh is Israel's sole warrior, defender, and the peacemaker among the nations. Compare the emphatic *there* in v. 3 with Pss 46:8-9; 48:4-8; 66:5-7.

Verses 7-12 exalt the role of Yahweh as judge of the earth. Human powers are immobilized before the irresistible force of God's wrath. Let the mighty ones of this world prepare their gifts and homage for Yahweh! Let *the oppressed of the earth* (v. 9) rejoice and praise God for the liberating judgment of the Terrible One (*the one who is awesome*, v. 11)! The redeeming purpose of God will not be thwarted by the wrath of the wicked; *human wrath* will praise him (v. 10).

Psalm 77

This psalm begins with a lament that conveys the acute distress of a speaker (vv. 1-3) who is suffering from a severe sense of godforsakenness (vv. 7-10) that causes soul-torment day and night (vv. 2-4). The present situation is contrasted with that in the past (v. 5). There is a vagueness about the nature of the trouble that has beset the speaker, but it seems best to assume it is not a personal calamity so much as it is the condition of the people of Israel.

The general historical context is most probably that of the exilic or postexilic period of Israel's history (at least for the psalm in its present setting; it may have been a northern psalm originally) when doubt of Yahweh's *steadfast love* (*hesed*) and *promises* (v. 8) was prevalent. The personal crisis of faith has arisen out of the national crisis of Israel.

Verse 10 has been given different renderings and interpretations, but it seems best to interpret it in the sense of the preceding verses—God's providential power no longer seems to be effective.

In the second part of the psalm (vv. 11-20) the speaker recalls the wonderful deeds of Yahweh. These verses, however, do not represent a shift of mood from lament and complaint to praise. The words are full of praise, but the mood is that of the perplexed and painful reflection in vv. 1-11.

The point is that a God of such great power and wondrous deeds should be able to duplicate such power and deeds in the present. The speaker meditates on the inscrutable ways of God that were so great in the past, but seemingly are so impotent in the present. Yahweh's powerful *right hand . . . has changed* (v. 10) and no longer effects the deliverance and defense of his people (cf. v. 15).

This psalm is "a prayer of unanswered lament" (Tate 1990, 275). The speaker's hand is stretched out in unwearying prayer, but God's hand no longer has its power—and there is no *hand of Moses and Aaron* (v. 20) to lead the people. In vv. 16-19 the EXODUS event is portrayed in terms of the ancient idea of the deity battle against the chaos-force represented by the sea (cf. Pss 66:6-7; 74:13-14; 89:9-10; 93:3-4; 114:3, 5).

Perhaps the last clause of v. 19 contains a veiled hope: *Your way was through the sea . . . yet your footprints were unseen* (or, "your trail was not recognized"). The rule of God leaves no visible trace in normal human events, although it was manifest in crashing thunder, flashing lightnings, swirling winds, and the wild turbulence of the raging sea.

Psalm 78

Psalm 78 is ordinarily grouped with Pss 105, 106, 135, and 136; together they are designated "historical psalms." They use a poetic form of narrative storytelling in order to recite Yahweh's deeds in Israel's history. Psalm 78 has, by form, elements of the thanksgiving psalms and the hymns. In addition, the influence of wisdom poetry appears in vv. 1-3.

The place of this type of psalm in the worship of the Israelites is not certain. It may have been used, however, in ceremonies for the renewal of the COVENANT between Yahweh and Israel. Such a usage is supported by the liturgy of the feast of the renewal of the covenant of the sect of Qumran. In this liturgy, a recapitulation of the great saving deeds of God was given by the priests and followed by an account of the "sins of Israel" given by the Levites. The congregation then confessed its own sins and those of its ancestors and affirmed its commitment to God (cf. Josh 24:1-28; Deut 29:1-31:13; 2 Kgs 23:1-3; Neh 8:13-9:38).

In its present form Ps 78 reflects the preaching style of the Levites in 1-2 Chronicles, and may come from the period after the Babylonian EXILE. However, the historical retrospect of the psalm reaches a climax with the reign of DAVID, leading some interpreters to date it as early as the tenth century BCE. An early date seems unlikely, although use may have been made of very ancient traditions that extend back into the early history of Israel. Despite the lack of reference in the psalm to the destruction of the Temple in Jerusalem, a postexilic date should not be ruled out, although any dating is speculative. If a preexilic date is preferred, the time of the reform of HEZEKIAH (late 700s BCE) would be a good guess.

Psalm 78 was not intended as a mere recital of a series of events in Israel's history. Rather, it aims to show how God has worked in that history, and to probe the mystery both of the divine providence and of the persistent APOSTASY of Israel. The opening verses indicate that the sacred history is a "parable"—the translation of the Hebrew word *mashal* (more commonly PROVERB). This word has a wide range of meaning, but in its most fundamental form it is used for the expression of relationships between things, or between persons, that are difficult to grasp or are obscure.

The user of a *mashal* aims at pungent, sometimes ironic, statements of what has been called "capsulated wisdom" that need to be taught and interpreted. The *dark saying* (v. 2) or RIDDLE has a similar function. In brief, it may be said that both the *mashal* and the "dark saying" seek to express the deeper aspects of that which may appear to be simple and superficial. Thus, the history of Israel is known (v. 3), but without interpretation its meaning may remain hidden from new generations. The didactic nature intended for the psalm is made clear in vv. 1-8 by the repeated emphasis on causing the children to know about *the glorious deeds of [Yahweh]* (v. 4, 5, 6) so they will *not forget the works of God* (v. 7) and follow the *rebellious* ways of *their ancestors* (v. 8).

The historical allusion of vv. 9-11 is uncertain. It could refer to the failure of the Ephraimites to drive out the Canaanites (Num 14:1-10; Judg 1:22-36), or even to the defeat of Saul on Mount Gilboa, or to the fall of Samaria in 722 BCE, or to some otherwise unrecorded tradition. In any case, the Israelites "forgot" the wonderful acts of God and did not keep the *torah* of the covenant.

Verses 12-32 contain a recitation of God's wonderful acts in caring for his people in the EXODUS from Egypt and the wilderness wanderings. This recitation includes the "riddle" of Israel's response: the rebellious sinfulness that matched the mighty acts step by step and aroused the wrath of God. Despite the doubt and lack of faith, God continued to bless the Israelites with food.

The enigma of Israel's history is continued in a sequel (vv. 33-39). Under the wrathful judgment of God, the Israelites sought for God and repented, but their repentance was *not steadfast*. Even though God was compassionate and patient, Israel was "not faithful to his covenant" (vv. 37-39). Neither miracles nor mercy was sufficient for the sinful heart of Israel.

The historical summary continues in a second recital in vv. 40-64 with a recitation of the *signs* in Egypt (i.e., the PLAGUES). The account of the plagues differs from that in Exod 7-12 both in number and in details. There seems to have been varied forms of the accounts until later, and the tradition varied from place to place. The plagues were followed by the leading forth of the Israelites from Egypt (v. 54). The story of the conquest and settlement is greatly abbreviated in vv. 54-55 and linked with Mount Zion (*the mountain* of v. 54).

The sad summary of Israel's sinful response to God's gracious acts continues in vv. 56-64. Rebellion and IDOLATRY again aroused the full wrath of God (v. 59; cf. v. 38) and he abandoned Shiloh to the sword and to captivity (vv. 60-64). The destruction of the temple at Shiloh (1 Sam 1:9) is mentioned elsewhere in the OT only in Jer 7:12-14; 26:6; the defeat of the Israelites by the Philistines (which probably included the destruction of Shiloh) is found in 1 Sam 4:1–7:2. *Power* and *glory* in v. 61 refer to the ARK of the covenant that was captured by the Philistines (cf. Ps 132:8). The sequel to the recital of history in vv. 40-64 is found in vv. 65-72, which corresponds to the sequel in vv. 33-39. The severe judgment of God seemed to mean the end of Israel. But God *awoke as from sleep* like a strong man arousing from intoxication (a very bold portrayal of God; cf. 2 Kgs 18:27), and he put his adversaries to rout (vv. 65-66). Afterwards, he rejected the tribes of northern Israel (v. 67) and chose the tribe of Judah, David, and Mount Zion.

Psalm 79

This communal lament has as its context an invasion and destruction of Jerusalem and the sacking of the Temple (but the particular situation is, like that of Ps 74, difficult to establish). Psalm 79 has been dated to the Maccabean period, but this seems improbable (cf. 1 Macc 7:17). The disaster of 587 BCE provides a better context, although it is possible that some unknown catastrophe after 500 BCE, or even some disaster prior to 587 BCE, lies behind it.

A complaint (vv. 1-4) describes the disaster of an invasion of Jerusalem and its ruin. The enemy is not identified, but if the date of the calamity is 587 BCE, the Babylonian army was responsible.

The prayer of the people (vv. 5-12) reveals their deeper concern about the wrath of Yahweh, which they understand to be at work in the terrible events described in vv. 1-4. They confess the sinfulness of their past (v. 8), but pray that the compassion of God will meet them with speedy salvation. The force of the prayer conveys the agony the people experience. The congregation prays for God to help them for the glory of his name. God's servants have had their blood poured out, God's name has been mocked and derided by Israel's neighbors, and God's Temple has been ravished (v. 1). The reputation of God is at stake; let him listen to *the groans of the prisoners* who are doomed to die unless he acts (v. 11).

The closing verse expresses the congregation's hope and vow of praise for the future. Despite the appalling disaster that has come upon them, they are still the flock of the great shepherd and prepared to pay their vows of thanksgiving.

Psalm 80

This is a communal lament that verbalizes the prayer of the people in the midst of a disastrous historical situation. Good arguments have been advanced for dating Ps 80 in one of two periods: (1) the period preceding the fall of the Northern Kingdom, 732–722 BCE and (2) the reign of JOSIAH, 640–609 BCE The former is supported by the superscription of the psalm in the LXX, which contains a reference to the Assyrians. Of these two, probability leans toward the period of Josiah and JEREMIAH, at least for parts of the psalm. The present psalm also may be a scribal composition from the postexilic period that utilizes older preexilic Ephraimite traditions and content.

The opening prayer (vv. 1-3) is directed to the *Shepherd of Israel* (see Pss 23:1; 78:52; Gen 48:15; 49:24; also Exod 15:13) who leads and cares for the people. The reference to *Joseph* suggests the northern tribes of Israel. The *Shepherd of Israel* is further identified as the one who is *enthroned upon the cherubim* (or the Cherubim-enthroned-One), which relates to the ARK of the covenant and goes back at least to SHILOH (see 1 Sam 4:4; 2 Sam 6:2; Ps 99:1). God is asked to *shine forth* (Exod 24:10; Deut 33:2; Num 6:24-26; Ps 50:2; 67:1; 94:1) in salvation to EPHRAIM, BENJAMIN, and MANASSEH—tribes that belonged to the Northern Kingdom, although

Benjamin is sometimes grouped with Judah. The mention of the three tribes possibly points to the period when the district of Galilee was under Assyrian domination, but before 721 BCE when Samaria fell. Verse 3 is a refrain that is repeated in vv. 7 and 19. It uses the ancient term for Yahweh: "Yahweh of Hosts" (*O LORD God of hosts*, v. 19, here with the addition of *elohim*) associated with the ark (see Ps 24 and LORD OF HOSTS).

The prayer of complaint (vv. 4-13) indicates the situation that has come to pass for the people: the language suggests prolonged suffering. The general picture would fit well the period after 722 BCE, but, as previously noted, an actual historical referent is secondary. Israel is compared to a *vine* (vv. 8-13) that Yahweh brought out of Egypt and planted (cf. Exod 15:17) in ground prepared for it (i.e., in Palestine). Growing in this ground, it grew large, but now Yahweh has broken down the walls that protected it from exploitation by those who passed by and from the ravages of wild animals (cf. Isa 5:1-7; Hos 10:1; Jer 2:21; Matt 21:33-43; John 15:1-11). Yahweh has allowed a terrible catastrophe to come to the people; the great vine and its vineyard has been ravaged by wild boars (originally, perhaps, the Assyrians).

The prayer continues (vv. 14-19) with the plea that Yahweh will again be the vine dresser who cares for the vine (Israel) that he planted. God is reminded that Israel's enemies have burned the vineyard and cut down his vine. There is some uncertainty about the meaning of v. 17. The reference to *the one at your right hand* may be a play on the name Benjamin (which means "son of the right hand") and be a special prayer for that tribe, or it may be a reference to the king (cf. 110:1). It refers more probably to the *stock* and "son" (Israel) in v. 15 (obscured by the NRSV; see Tate 1990, 304, 307, 315).

Verses 14-19 continue with a vow of fidelity and loyalty to God: "We will never be backsliders again!" (v. 18). Verse 19 repeats v. 3, and closes the psalm (v. 14 is a variant of vv. 3 and 19). The prayer assumes the ravagers of the vineyard would perish (v. 16) if Yahweh turned his face toward the vineyard and beheld its destruction.

Psalm 81

This psalm falls into two distinct parts: vv. 1-5b and 5c-16. The first part begins in a hymnic fashion, while the second part is a prophetic ORACLE. Treating the two parts separately, however, is not necessary. The psalms often contain bits and pieces that are shaped into whole compositions.

Psalm 81 is clearly associated with one of the festivals of Israel. Both OT evidence and Jewish tradition agree that the Feast of Tabernacles is most likely, although its use at the PASSOVER in postexilic Israel cannot be ruled out entirely. It has also been argued that the autumn festival (Tabernacles) was a feast of COVENANT renewal and that this psalm was associated with the ceremonies; the suggestion is possible, but not certain. The date of the psalm cannot be fixed any better than many other psalms, but it is possible that its origin was in the period of Israel's history before the monarchy when the tribal groups gathered annually at a cultic center for festivals (SHECHEM, SHILOH, BETHEL—since Jerusalem was not an

Israelite city before the days of David). The close association of Ps 81 with Pss 50 and 95 is widely accepted—all of them seem to be festal psalms. Also, all three are marked by the presence of ORACLE material in which God speaks directly.

The hymnic opening (vv. 1-5a) is a call to praise God with "shouts of joy" and with songs and music. It reminds us that the festivals, while solemn, were also occasions of great joy—and exceedingly noisy! The large assemblies of the people echoed with the festival shouts, while trumpets sounded their commanding blasts and other musical instruments added to the volume of sound. The interpretation of v. 3 raises considerable debate. The blowing of the trumpet at the *new moon*, the first of the month, is provided for in Num 10:10. The reference here, however, is more probably to the special occasion at the beginning of the seventh month referred to in Lev 23:24 and Num 29:1.

The words for trumpet vary. The primitive *shofar*— the horn of a ram, goat, or cow, and primarily an instrument for giving signals—is used here. This word is found in the Pentateuch only once (Lev 25:9) where it is associated with the tenth day of the seventh month, the Day of Atonement. The word used in Num 10:10 seems to refer to a metal, therefore a more sophisticated instrument, while the word in Lev 23:24 and Num 29:1 is a general term for giving a signal without specific indication of the instrument (but the *shofar* was probably used as in Lev 25:9). The *shofar* along with the trumpet is indicated in Ps 98:6.

A further problem arises in connection with *the full moon, on our festal day*. Since Tabernacles begins with the "full moon" (fifteenth day of the seventh month, Tishri) it is assumed the reference is to the beginning day of that festival (Lev 23:33-36; Num 29:12), but some interpreters argue that all of the references in v. 3 refer to the same day, a New Year's day. An alternative interpretation may be best (Kraus 1989, 149): the *shofar* was blown twice, at the beginning of the festival period (*new moon*) and at the beginning of Booths (*full moon*), that is, on the first day of the seventh month (Lev 23:24) and on the first day of Tabernacles (the fifteenth day), a period that includes the Day of Atonement.

Verses 4-5b stress that the festival celebration was established in Israel by divine decree and associated with the experience of the Israelites in the EXODUS from Egypt (see also, v. 10). *Joseph* may be a synonym for all of Israel, but it has special reference to the Israelites who were in Egypt. The purpose of the festival is to serve as a "testimony" (better than *decree* in v. 5a) to Israel of Yahweh's great saving acts in bringing her out of Egypt (see Lev 23:42-43; cf. Deut 16:3).

A solo voice delivers a prophetic oracle to the people in vv. 5c-16. Verse 5c is difficult (lit. "a lip I know not I hear"), but is best understood as referring to the reception of an oracle by a prophet or priest. The message has been received from God; it is not one *known* to the speaker in terms of personal experience. Verse 10 (*Open your mouth wide, and I will fill it*) seems to follow v. 5c, and the colons have been separated in a kind of "envelope" construction for the insertion of vv. 6-9, which contains the message of the oracle.

The oracle itself recalls Yahweh's redemptive act of deliverance from slavery in Egypt and the situation at the sacred mountain in the wilderness when Yahweh made his covenant *torah* known. The *secret place of thunder* (v. 7) recalls the THE-OPHANY of Yahweh in the thunderstorm (Exod 19:16-19; Pss 18:7-15; 77:18; 104:7; Isa 29:6). The testing at *the waters of Meribah* (v. 7) alludes to Exod 17:1-7; Num 20:1-13 (cf. 95:7-11)—but the situation is reversed here: the people do not "test" God, but he "tests" them!

The understanding of vv. 6-7 depends upon close attention to the changes in tense and person in the Hebrew text (obscured in the NRSV). Verse 6 should read: *I relieved [his] shoulder of the burden; [his] hands were freed from the basket.* The "his" refers to Joseph in the preceding verse, and to the generation that had undergone slavery in Egypt. However, in v. 7 the pronoun changes to a collective *you*, that is, to the festival congregation now being addressed as the people of the exodus generation had been addressed in the wilderness (for a striking illustration of a similar change of person, see Deut 26:5-11). The interval of history is removed, as it were, and theologically the people are once more before Yahweh in the wilderness.

In vv. 13-16, it is interesting to note that God vows to defeat the enemies of his people and care for them with abundance (v. 16; cf. Deut 32:13-14) if they will listen to him and walk in his ways (v. 13). Vows of individuals or groups (e.g., Pss 79:13; 80:18) to praise and serve God on the condition that he will do what is asked of him are more common. In this case, God vows to respond to Israel's affirmative acts.

Psalm 82

This important psalm has sparked considerable controversy among interpreters. One controversial point has been the identity of *the gods* (vv. 1 and 6). One interpretation assumes they are human judges who have failed in their responsibilities. This view follows the Targum and cites such passages as Exod 21:6; 22:7-8; 28; 1 Sam 2:25. Another interpretation considers them to be kings of earthly nations who are judged because of their corrupt ways. There may be truth in both interpretations, since the function of the judge and king (often the same) was to mediate the divine will and to act as an agent of God (cf. Deut 1:17). The references cited for the interpretation of *gods* as judges, however, can be more properly understood as referring to deity. If kings or judges were intended, v. 7 seems strange indeed.

It is much more probable that *gods* refers to divine beings, and, thus the psalm must be interpreted against the background of a heavenly assembly over which Yahweh presides (see Pss 29:1; 58:1; 89:5-7; 103:20-21; 148:2; 1 Kgs 22:19-22; Job 1:6-12; 2:1-6; Dan. 7:9-10). This is in line with ancient Jewish interpretation that "gods" refers to angels who failed to carry out their authorized functions properly. Behind this interpretation is the concept that the nations were allotted to individual gods, who were responsible for their proper administration (see Deut 32:8; 29:25-26; Isa 24:21; Dan. 10:13, 20-21; Eccl 17:17). This concept makes use of the ideas pertaining to the assembly of the gods prevalent in the thought of the ancient world.

Psalm 82 is related to the Canaanite poetry from Ugarit. Therefore, it is best to deal with Ps 82 as an effect, a brief dramatic scene "in the affairs of the assembly of the gods" (Miller 1986, 121).

The charge against *the gods* is found in vv. 2-5; they have failed to defend the rights of *the weak* and poor within their territories, while showing partiality to *the wicked*. They stumble about so much in their ignorance and darkness that the very *foundations of the earth are shaken* (v. 5). Their failure threatens a return to the chaos from which the world has been delivered. This must be read against the arbitrary and often capricious activity of the gods in the pagan myths. Such gods provided no stable order of life for either divine or human life, and no consistent standard for human behavior. In Ps 82, the divine world is rendered impotent and the gods are sentenced to die as mortals do.

The judgment of Yahweh relegates the gods to the status of ordinary human mortality (vv. 6-7). They had been given a higher status (v. 6; the *I say* should be read as "I said" indicating divine appointment), but by their failure they have forfeited it. Yahweh, who alone is the giver of life, is left alone in his sovereignty. He is the only one who is able to rule the earth, thus the prayer in v. 8. *All the nations* belong to God, and the congregation prays that he will take possession. The assembly of the gods has become an assize; Yahweh alone is vindicated. But the earth is bereft of divine administration unless Yahweh himself rises to judge.

This psalm reflects part of the theological process of the Israelites confronting the worship of various deities in the cultures among which they lived. The gods were overcome by their reduction to a rank subordinate to Yahweh and deprived of their prerogatives and powers. They became no-gods. The psalm also attempts to explain the presence of EVIL in human existence. Evil conditions continue because the divine beings responsible for the administration of the nations tolerate it. A cosmic aspect is given to the presence of evil in the world. The failure of justice in the world is rooted in the necessity of a judgment of the gods by Yahweh. The psalm should not be read, however, as relieving human beings of their responsibilities.

Psalm 83

The historical situation that produced this lament of the people cannot be determined exactly despite the several references to particular nations, places, and events. Attempts have been made to relate the psalm to the Assyrian threat of the eighth century BCE, but we do not know of any coalition of nations against Israel such as the one given (and Syria is not mentioned). A specific historical situation, therefore, may not have been in the poet's mind, and the psalm is worked out on the broad flow of Israelite traditions. The list of nations may be a more or less standard recitation of the enemies of Israel. The speaker is not identified, but we can think of an Israelite leader praying for the nation.

After the urgent petitions to God (v. 1) their basis is laid out (vv. 2-8). The nations are in commotion as they conspire together to obliterate Israel. ASSYRIA is the great power that lies behind the hostile actions of Israel's immediate neighbors. The Assyrians are described as *the strong arm of the children of Lot. Children of*

Lot refers to the Moabites and Ammonites (Gen 19:36-38; Deut 2:9, 19) who are supported by the Assyrians in their endeavors against Israel.

Verses 9-18 contain extended petitions for deliverance from enemies. The conspiracy against Israel is actually against Yahweh (cf. vv. 4-5). Therefore, this prayer is for swift and certain judgment aimed at bringing the enemies to seek the name of Yahweh. The events referred to in vv. 9-12 reflect the destruction of the Canaanites by DEBORAH and BARAK (Judg 4-5) and the rout of the Midianites by GIDEON (Judg 7-8). Yahweh is implored to mightily act again as he did in the history of Israel, so that he alone may be exalted *over all the earth* (v. 18).

"Psalms of Asaph." Psalm 83 is the last of eleven consecutive psalms (73–83) associated by their titles with ASAPH. (Psalm 50 is also an Asaph psalm.) Some features of these psalms show a fair degree of commonality (helpfully summarized by Day, *Psalms*, 118): concern with divine judgment; appeals to Yahweh's mighty deeds in the past; more allusions to Israel as a flock and Yahweh as its shepherd than in all the rest of the Psalter (Pss 74:1; 77:20; 78:52; 70-72; 79:13; 80:1); relatively high number of references to the northern tribes, especially to Joseph (Pss 77:15; 78:9; 67; 80:1; 81:5) who is mentioned elsewhere in the Psalter only in Ps 105:17; and (added to Day's list) attention to the condition and significance of Zion-Jerusalem (Pss 50:2; 74:2; 76:2; 78:68; 79:1; 3). The arguments for an original northern Israelite provenance for these psalms has been revived and extended by Rendsburg (1990, 73–81) and it seems plausible to accept his conclusion. In their present forms and setting, however, the psalms are clearly centered on Jerusalem and Zion.

"Elohistic Collection." Psalm 83 also marks the end of the section of the Psalter frequently called the Elohistic Collection (Pss 42–83) because of the frequency of the use of *elohim* as a name for Yahweh. (*Yahweh* [LORD] occurs 272 times in Pss 1–41 and *elohim* (*God*) fifteen times; in Pss 42–83 *elohim* occurs 200 times versus forty-three times for *Yahweh*.) The change of Yahweh to Elohim seems to have been deliberate in many cases (e.g., cf. Pss 14 and 53; 40:13-17 and 70), but no one knows for sure why Pss 42–83 were so treated. These psalms probably functioned as a separate Psalter at some time in the history of Israel. The use of *elohim*, as in the case of the widespread use of *adonai* (*Lord*), was probably to avoid the divine name Yahweh except in very important contexts, and may indicate that Pss 42–83 were intended for the teaching of the laity in postexilic Israelite communities.

Psalm 84

This hymn (with mixed elements) praises Zion and the temple of Yahweh with its joys of worship. It would have been appropriate for pilgrims making their way to Jerusalem for participation in the festivals, especially Tabernacles, which was associated with the coming of the rains in the autumn (see v. 6). The psalm has features similar to other Songs of Zion (e.g., Ps 48), the Songs of Ascents (120–134), and Pss 42–43. The viewpoint of the speaker in the psalm is that of a pilgrim on the way to Zion (v. 7). Perhaps, the *dwelling place* of Yahweh has come into view (v. 1), and the pilgrim describes the longing of mind and heart for the joy of worship in the Temple (v. 2).

The pilgrim recalls the blessedness of those (priests and others) who have the privilege of abiding in the Temple (vv. 3-4), like the birds that nest in the Temple courts. Also blessed are pilgrims who make their way through difficult journeys to Zion (vv. 5-7) and those who have their heart set on *the highways to Zion* (although this involves correction of the text in v. 5).

The *valley of Baca* (v. 6) is unknown. *Baca* refers to a species of tree (2 Sam 5:23) that grows in dry soil and the word is also related to weeping. *Valley of baca* has been translated "valley of weeping." It is better to think of an arid territory, perhaps even a place name, that becomes a valley of springs as the pilgrims pass through it. The strength of the pilgrims is constantly renewed until they appear before God in Zion (v. 7).

A prayer is interjected in vv. 8-9. The pilgrim prays for *our shield* and *your anointed*, perhaps terms for the king. If so, these terms point to a preexilic date for this part of the psalm at least, and to the significance of the king in the festival. In postexilic times, however, when there was no monarchy, these terms would have referred to the HIGH PRIEST in Jerusalem.

In the last section of the psalm (vv. 10-12), the pilgrim returns to the theme of the blessings of worship at Zion. There is no *elsewhere* (v. 10) in the Hebrew text, but it seems required. It may be that the psalmist meant "at home." *Doorkeeper* may refer to a temple servant charged with menial duties, but more probably refers to a pilgrim suppliant who waits at the doors of the Temple to be admitted to the holy precincts (see Ps 15). The pilgrim would rather be an entrance-seeking worshiper, a humble pilgrim who has given up much to beg permission to enter the sanctuary of Yahweh, than to dwell among those whose attitude and conduct cut them off from access to the holy place.

The speaker is confident Yahweh will respond favorably to the upright (v. 11). *No good thing* is withheld from the righteous person; true blessing is not found among the wicked. The truly blessed person (cf. Ps 1) is the one who trusts Yahweh (v. 12) and longs for his courts.

Psalm 85

Usually classified as a national lament, this psalm is assumed to reflect harvest festivals. An argument can be made for dating the psalm to the period after 538 BCE when some of the Israelites returned to Palestine from the Babylonian EXILE. The economic and spiritual depression of this period, as reflected in the Books of Haggai, Zechariah, and Malachi, contrast strongly with the exalted hopes of Isa 40–55. In this interpretation, the great restoring acts of Yahweh in vv. 1-3 refer to the restoration from the Babylonian exile, and the speaker in the psalm seeks an extension of these saving acts in the future.

Verses 1-3 look back to Yahweh's acts when he restored the fortunes of Israel and forgave their sins. Deliverance from exile probably is meant (see also Ps 126) in an immediate sense, but Exod 32–34 may be in the background. These verses form the basis for the petitions in vv. 4-7, which contain the passionate prayer of the people for a restoration. The gracious acts of vv. 1-3 have not continued in full effectiveness and the people again feel themselves to be under the burden of divine wrath. Further revival of life is needed (cf. Isa 59:9-15; Hag 1:5-6; Zech 1:12). Their great need is for Yahweh to *show* (i.e., demonstrate in action) his *steadfast love* and grant his deliverance or *salvation* (v. 7).

In vv. 8-13 it is frequently assumed that the voice of a PROPHET or priest follows the prayer of the congregation with an ORACLE of comfort and assurance. It is not necessary, however, to conclude that there is a change of speakers. The speaker of vv. 1-7 may continue with a reflective message of assurance and encouragement.

Note the personification in vv. 10-11 of the great characteristics of Yahweh as divine agents: *steadfast love . . . faithfulness . . . righteousness and peace (shalom)* —as well as *glory* in v. 9 (representing the powerful presence of Yahweh). The description of physical and spiritual well-being culminates in bountiful supplies for human needs through the coordinated endeavors of these agents (vv. 10-12). In v. 13, *righteousness will go before* Yahweh as a herald before the visit of a king to his land (cf. Isa 40:3-5; 46:13; 58:8; 62:11).

Psalm 86

Little of the suppliant's personal situation can be gathered from this individual lament. Adding to the difficulty of establishing the precise situations, a prevalent problem in most laments, is the fact that this one is heavily dependent on other passages from the Psalter and the OT. Its date cannot be fixed exactly, but it probably belongs to the postexilic period of Israel's history (at least in its present setting).

In vv. 1-7 the speaker prays for a hearing by Yahweh. A series of statements beginning with *for*, and interspersed with the petitions, indicate motivation for the hearing desired. The speaker claims to be *poor and needy*, but one who trusts in Yahweh as a person and as a servant. The *devoted* ("godly") servant places a claim on Yahweh's goodness and *steadfast love*. The *for* statements change from being statements about the suppliant to statements about God as the prayer moves to a basis of firm trust in God.

In vv. 8-13, the prayer and lament become a hymn-like expression of praise and thanksgiving. The incomparable God will receive the homage of all nations (cf. Pss 22:27-28; 65:2; 66:4; 8; 67:1-7; Isa 45:22-23; 66:23). He is the worker of *wondrous things*, and no works like his are found among the nations and their gods. The certainty and confidence of the speaker lead to a prayer for instruction as a disciple (v. 11) and to a vow of praise and testimony of deliverance in vv. 12-13.

The lament and prayers of vv. 1-7 are renewed in vv. 14-17. Enemies oppress the speaker (vv. 14), but their presence does not destroy his confidence in Yahweh. The *sign* requested in v. 17 refers to some sort of favorable indication of divine action, perhaps an ORACLE or a token of healing from illness.

Psalm 87

This is a hymn of the "Songs of Zion" type, praising Zion as the city founded and loved by Yahweh, whose citizens are especially recorded in God's census records of the world (v. 6; cf. Pss 56:8; 69:28; 139:16; Isa 4:3).

The meaning of vv. 4-6 is not entirely clear, but it is best to interpret these verses as meaning that all those who "know Yahweh" belong to Zion in a spiritual sense. For Zion is the mother city (*this one was born there*) of all God's children regardless of where they live (cf. Phil. 3:20; Gal 4:26; Rev 21). God is depicted as keeping a birth register, and Zion becomes the birthplace of the nations (v. 6). The background of this action is found in the practice of kings declaring that conquered foreign peoples now belong to the royal realm of the conquering country (Tate 1990, 385–93). In the case of Ps 87, Yahweh has decided to make Zion the universal birthplace of the world (translate v. 5b "Everyone was born in her [Zion]", and read v. 6b read as a performative statement of Yahweh that establishes the Zion birthright of the peoples). Even hostile peoples nearby and those far away are included (v. 4). "It is a bold picture—Yahweh taking inventory of the peoples of the world, all of them his . . . and giving everyone a birth certificate marked 'Zion'" (Durham 1971, 350).

The psalm reflects the exuberant mood of Jerusalem when pilgrims gathered for festivals from many "dwelling places" (v. 2) both in Judah and in other lands to praise Yahweh and to renew their devotion to him. This is evident in v. 7, where the psalmist's attention falls on the *singers and dancers* who participate in the festival celebrations, perhaps including the foreigners in vv. 4-6. *All my springs* (or fountains) in v. 7 is a metaphor for the source of life and blessing (Ps 36:9; Isa 12:3; Joel 3:18).

Psalm 88

This individual lament has been called "the saddest psalm in the Psalter" (Kirkpatrick 1901) and described as without "a single ray of comfort or hope" (Weiser 1962, 586). The shift of mood from lamentation and petition to that of confident testimony, which is found in some laments, is missing. Some interpreters postulate that a sequel of certainty and assurance has been lost from the psalm, but there is no proof to support the conjecture. As it stands, the speaker clings to God in passionate lament and petition, despite the fact of having been swept near death by a flood of divine wrath.

The psalm begins with direct address to God and moves quickly to complaint focused on unanswered prayer, prayer directed day and night to God (vv. 1-2). The condition of the speaker is graphically presented as one near death (v. 3). The suppliant is already reckoned with the dead, who are remembered no more and cut off from the powerful aid of God's hand (vv. 4-6). *Forsaken among the dead* (v. 5), is read better as the "free among the dead" KJV, in the ironic sense of being "set free" (i.e., already judged by family and community as dead and thus relieved of the normal obligations of life).

The wrath of God *lies heavy* upon the speaker (v. 7), although there is no confession of sin in the psalm. Like JOB (Job 19:13-19), the speaker charges God with causing companions to turn away as from a *thing of horror* (v. 8). The praiseless quality of death is emphasized in vv. 10-12 where the rhetorical questions call for negative answers. *Abaddon* (v. 11) is a synonym for SHEOL (see v. 3), the realm of the dead.

The complaint resumes (vv. 13-18) after being interrupted by the rhetorical questions of vv. 10-12. The condition described is that of a person shunned by God (the speaker assumes this, vv. 13-14) and friends: "afflicted and near to death from youth" (v. 15) and attacked by *terrors* (v. 15) and *dread assaults* (v.16)—agents of divine destruction let loose by the wrath of God. Thus, although different words are used, the theme of divine wrath is renewed (cf. v. 7). The last word of this terrible psalm is *darkness*; the dreadful darkness of the Pit of death from which there is no exit.

Psalm 88 is a bold prayer of protest that creates a verbal lifeline between ebbing human life and God who gives and saves life. Anger and protest are forms of energy for resistance and modes of connectedness to God. The psalm assumes God can still speak and act and thus seeks to forge a solidarity with God in suffering. The psalm also assumes the deadly silence of God will not last forever, even if it seems so.

A conflation of collections. The title of Ps 88 is strangely compounded: "a song, a psalm of the Korahites, to the leader according to *mahalath leannoth* [probably a tune or chanting pattern], a *maskil* [possibly a well-written and strongly expressed psalm] of Heman the Ezrahite." The solution may lie in scribal conflation of an original postscript for Ps 87 with the superscription of Ps 88. The postscript of Ps 87 may have read: "A song, a psalm of the Korahites. For the leader: according to *mahalath leannoth*," leaving "A *maskil* of Heman the Ezrahite" as the title of Ps 88. Possibly the postscript to Ps 87 marked the end of a small collection of Korahite psalms (Pss 84, 85, 87) and called the reader's attention to the addition of two Ezrahite psalms (Pss 88 and 89). The Ezrahite psalms are attributed to two different scribes, Heman and Ethan, who appear in lists of scribal singers associated with KORAH and ASAPH (see 1 Chr 6:33-48; 15:17; 19); The postexilic scribal interpreters would have had no difficulty in linking Asaph, Korahite, and Ezrahite psalms, and this may account for the conflation. The Asaph collection in Pss 73–83 is supplemented by the Korahite and Ezrahite psalms, all likely to have originated in scribal circles.

Note that Ps 86 is the only Davidic psalm in book three of the Psalter. It may be where it is simply because it is suitable for the context, but it also serves to provide Davidic authority for book three. Taken with Ps 89 (which deals with the Davidic covenant), Ps 86 makes a frame around Pss 87 and 88, thereby forming a closing to book three.

Psalm 89

This long psalm is usually classified as a royal lament. Verses 1-18 are identified properly as a hymn (in two parts: 1-4, 5-18), and vv. 19-37 (along with vv. 3-4) compose a divine ORACLE that recounts the divine election of and the promises made to David. The last part of the psalm (vv. 38-51) is a lament over the disaster that has come to the king and to the nation and the failure of Yahweh to keep the promises he made. The key to the interpretation of the psalm in its present form is the prayer in vv. 38-51.

The psalm addresses the problem of unfulfilled promises and expectations relating to the monarchy of David "Where is your former steadfast love, O Lord?—(Those promises) you promised on oath to David?" (v. 49, author trans.). The psalm also asks why the *enemies* of Yahweh (v. 51) have been allowed to overcome and mock his *anointed* with impunity.

Interpreters have sought a specific historical context for Ps 89, but there is no consensus. Major suggestions include the time of REHOBOAM, the crisis during the reign of ahaz of Judah (735–34 BCE), and the time of JEHOIACHIN after the Babylonian attack on Jerusalem in 597 BCE A postexilic date seems more likely (see Tate 1990, 416–17). The speaker in vv. 39-51 may be one of the faithful servants of Yahweh (v. 51), pious folk who sought to maintain their faith during the bleak period after 515 BCE.

In vv. 1-4, a solo voice (priest or prophet), begins the hymn with an announcement of intention to proclaim the *steadfast love* and *faithfulness* of Yahweh. The faithfulness of Yahweh is especially manifest in the COVENANT with David, a covenant that embodies the promise of a perpetual dynasty (vv. 3-4; cf. 2 Sam 7). The Davidic covenant should be as lasting as the *steadfast love* of Yahweh himself (cf. Isa 55:3).

The hymn proper (vv. 5-18) opens with a call to the members of the divine *assembly* to praise the wonders of Yahweh (on the heavenly *assembly*, see Ps 82 and COUNCIL, HEAVENLY). Yahweh is presented as the incomparable God who rules the raging sea and brings the chaotic forces of the universe into created order.

Rahab (v. 10) is a name for the primeval chaos monster, also known as LEVIATHAN (cf. Ps 74:12-17; Isa 27:1). *Tabor and Hermon* (v. 12) are mountains in northern Israel, which could indicate that this part of the psalm originated in north Israel—but this is not certain. Both mountains were sites of Canaanite worship in pre-Israelite times, but it is now declared that they praise the name of Yahweh.

The people who know the festal shout (v. 15; cf. 1 Sam 4:5; 6; 2 Chr 15:14; Pss 27:6; 33:3; 47:5) of praise to Yahweh, and who have experienced his glory and strength in their behalf are blessed people. The significance of the king in the life of the people is indicated by the language of v. 18.

In vv. 19-37, a prophetic revelation or oracle recalls the covenant Yahweh made with David and the promises that were included (already set forth briefly in vv. 3-4). The key concept in this passage is that of the enduring faithfulness with which the throne of David was established (see vv. 24, 28, 29, 36-37). The scope of

David's dominion is given cosmic dimensions (see v. 25 where the *sea* and *rivers* refer to the primeval waters). David is designated as the son of Yahweh (by adoption) who cries *my Father* (vv. 26-27), and who is the most exalted of the kings of the earth (on the scope of the reign of the Davidic king, see Ps 2). Nevertheless, the Davidic king is subject to the covenant *torah* of Israel (vv. 30-34), although the word of promise will not be broken (vv. 34-35). Yahweh will punish the descendants of David who do not keep his commandments, but God affirms his intention to maintain the dynasty.

The change of mood and style that begins with v. 38 is drastic. The language is emphatic and strong as the charge is made that despite the solemn promises of the past, Yahweh has *renounced the covenant with your servant* (v. 39). The king has suffered a humiliating defeat while his foes have been exalted. The strongholds of the nation have been invaded and ruined (v. 40). His reign has been discredited and brought to shame. The lament changes to prayer in vv. 46-51, with the speaker crying out *How long, O [Yahweh]? Will you hide yourself forever?* (v. 46). Pleas for God to remember the finite nature of human life are found in vv. 47-48; these verses seem to intensify the complaint that Israelites cannot be separated from the frailty and finitude of all humanity, and that Yahweh's actions relating to David call into question his purpose for all human beings.

Yahweh is reminded again (v. 49) of his oath of faithfulness made to David, which is not now in evidence (vv. 50-51). The hurt and anger are not resolved. The speaker "can only lift his hands to God in prayer . . . and lay before him the problems which his own thinking and reasoning are unable to master."

Summary of Book Three

The blessing of Yahweh (Ps 89:52) marks the end of book three. The placement of Ps 89 in the canonical arrangement of the psalms seems significant. The emphasis in Ps 89 on the failed covenant with David is an appropriate finale for book three, which is marked by communal laments and complaints. The collection is rather clearly from the postexilic period, reflecting on the sad development of events after 597 BCE.

As noted in the commentary on Ps 73, book three begins with the thesis: "Truly God is good to Israel, to those who are pure in heart" (Ps 73:1, author trans.). The psalms that follow test the thesis. Is Yahweh really good to Israel and to those who are pure in heart? The answer seems to be affirmative for individuals who are "pure in heart" (i.e., fully devoted to Yahweh). Psalm 73:21-28 contains forceful affirmations of the presence and care of God: *But for me it is good to be near God; I have made the LORD God my refuge* (73:28).

This personal faith and satisfaction in the presence of Yahweh is expressed elsewhere in book three (see Pss 75:69; 84:1-12; 86:5-7; 8-13, 15, 17). The personal faith expressed in these psalms constitutes an example both for individual Israelites and for the community as a whole. J. Clinton McCann (1993a, 96) argues that Ps 73 sets the tone for all of book three with a reorientation of insight into the actual nature of things in the world, and the closing expression of hope (1993a, 96). Individuals are given grounds for confidence that reorientation and a sense of powerful solidarity with God are possible.

Book three surfaces a major problem of faith that may be put in the form of a question: Is individual faith and experience of the divine presence enough when the whole enterprise of saving history seems to have failed? Thus Ps 78 is at the heart of book three, with its explanation of the "riddle" of Israel's history with Yahweh (see commentary on Ps 78). What about the *glorious deeds of the* LORD . . . *and the wonders that he has done* (78:4)? Clearly, the communal aspects of Yahweh's saving work are endangered, as the repeated use of communal laments indicates (Pss 74, 79, 80, 83, 85). Psalm 89 culminates in the charge that Yahweh has defaulted on his commitment to the Davidic dynasty. As a result, individual faith is brought to the brink of failure by the collapse of the communal framework of salvation, and the individual is plunged from the victory of faith in Ps 73 to the nadir of depression and darkness in Ps 88.

Book three, therefore, presents a struggle for a viable faith and asks if it is possible for faith to live while wild boars ravage the vineyard of Yahweh (Ps 80:13) and there is no evidence that God intends to keep his solemn commitment to David (Ps 89). Is personal faith sufficient when the nation and all its institutions are gone? The high triumph of Ps 73 descends to the deep depression of Pss 88–89. Between these psalms the depths of faith's struggle are plumbed.

Psalm 81 is an anomaly in book three, with significantly different content in two instances. First, it begins with a summons to praise, which is characteristic of the hymns: *Sing aloud to God our strength, shout for joy.* . . . Second, it contains a lament on the part of God, who mourns over the people and longs for them to listen to him so he can bless them again (vv. 6-16). God also identifies himself as *I, [Yahweh], am . . . your God who brought you up out of the land of Egypt* (v. 10; cf. Exod 20:1). Lament and complaint do not belong to Israel alone; Yahweh also has disappointment, grief, and frustration. Psalm 81 seems to set a boundary for the protest of book three and provides a counterpoint for the rest of the collection. As Israel grieves and struggles for faith, it is wise to remember how the people have wounded the heart of God, and how God suffers with the people.

Book Four. Psalms 90–106

Psalm 90

Psalm 90 is the first psalm of book four and the only psalm attributed to Moses. For discussion of these matters, see the summary following the commentary on Ps 106.

Most commentators treat this psalm as having two major divisions: vv. 1-12 and 13-17. The structure seems somewhat more complicated, however, since v. 4 seems to follow v. 2 more closely than it does v. 3, and thus forms an envelope around v. 3, which in turn relates closely with vv. 5-10. Within vv. 5-10, v. 8 is in an envelope formed by vv. 7 and 9, followed by an envelope containing v. 11 formed by vv. 10 and 12, while vv. 9 and 12 frame both v. 10 and v. 11. The *anger* and *wrath* of God in v. 11 is paralleled by the *wrath* in vv. 7 and 9. Verse 11 also relates to vv. 13-15, and vv. 13 and 16-17 frame vv. 14-15.

The content of the psalm seems a character as intricate as its form. Verses 1-2 express affirmations of God, while vv. 3-11 deal with the conditions of human finitude under divine wrath, ending with the petition in v. 12. The petitions in vv. 13-17 are direct and in the common language of laments. The psalm as a whole is a communal prayer composed of reflection, complaint, and petitions. The content of the psalm points to long-lasting communal distress: *Make us glad as many days as you have afflicted us, and as many years as we have seen evil* (v. 15). The conditions of immediate distress that seems to characterize the communal laments in Pss 44, 74, and 79 are missing in Ps 90, which suggests it is a literary composition belonging to scribal psalmography in postexilic Israel.

Psalm 90 is well known for its treatment of the transitory condition of human life (vv. 1-6) in which Israel fully participates (vv. 7-12). The *servants* of Yahweh (vv. 13, 16) have experienced the full measure of human finitude. They know the fragile nature of human endeavors, thus they pray to experience the favor of God, to have an awareness of what he is doing in the world, and for the establishment of the work of their hands (v. 17). They pray that their work may have a place of significance and importance and for deliverance from meaninglessness.

Psalm 91

This psalm should be read with Ps 90. The scribal placement of the psalm is probably not incidental: the lament and petition of Ps 90 finds its counterpart of bold faith, confidence, and safety in Ps 91. The two psalms together and with Ps 95 seem to form an INCLUSIO around Pss 92–94. Psalm 91 has the character of instruction and exhortation, and it has been described as a sermonette of encouragement (Stuhlmueller 1983, 73).

Verse 1 should be read as a thematic statement: "Whoever dwells under the protection of the Most High will abide in the shelter (shadow) of the Almighty" (author trans.). Verses 3-13 are in the form of direct address to an unidentified person, and spoken by an individual person of faith who offers testimony and encouragement. The person addressed could be anyone willing and privileged to dwell under the shelter of Yahweh. The speaker does not argue the case for the security of those under the protection of Yahweh but declares it.

The references in vv. 5-6 are probably to the fear of unseen powers that exercised such a tenacious grip on so many in the ancient world. *The arrow that flies by day* is the missile of dreaded demonic power, whether exercised by divine or human beings. Further, the poet may have in mind sickness and sunstroke (vv. 5b and 6b), which were often thought to be the result of supernatural forces. In the hot sunlight of the Middle East, sunstroke can strike with fearful suddenness like arrows shot from ambush (cf. 2 Kgs 4:8-37; Exod 11:4-7; 12:29-30; Isa 37:37; Pss 121:6; God himself is the archer in Ps 38:2; Lam 3:13; Job 6:4). Lightning also strikes suddenly and *the arrows* could be a synonym for "flashes of lightning" (Pss 18:14; 77:18).

The fourfold danger in vv. 5-6 that alternates between darkness and light is probably a merism (see commentary on Ps 66:6, 12). The ministering *angels* of Yahweh (vv. 11-13) are set over against the destructive demons of the night and day (cf. Ps 34:7; Exod 23:20; Tob 5–12; Bar 6:6). The wings of the Almighty are over all (v. 4). Verses 7-8 depict a battle-like scene, but the addressee is assured of personal safety. The plagues of vv. 5-6 may be understood as causing the carnage.

The psalm concludes with an ORACLE (vv. 14-16). Note the change of person from *you* in vv. 1-13 to *he* and the *I* of Yahweh in vv. 14-16. The oracle is a message of assurance and a promise of long life and well-being to those who cling to Yahweh and who *know* his name. (cf. the oracle in Ps 95:7d-11).

Psalm 92

This psalm combines the characteristics of a hymn with the form of an individual thanksgiving. Such psalms were designed for recitation in the company of other worshipers, and are marked by testimonial elements intended for both speaker and audience.

The singer declares the goodness of praising Yahweh throughout each day. The reason for such comprehensive praise is stated in v. 4: *You, O LORD, have made me glad by your work.* Verses 5-9 praise the mystery and power of Yahweh, attributes that a *dullard cannot* properly appreciate. Among Yahweh's thoughts that *the stupid cannot understand* is the doomed condition of the wicked who temporarily seem so prosperous (cf. Pss 73:21-22; 94:8).

The worshiper praises Yahweh for deliverance from the power of enemies (vv. 10-11). The speaker has been given the horn of an ox (a symbol of strength) and supplied with fresh oil, which may refer to a priestly anointing for healing (Lev 14:10-20), or to another ritual act. The meaning of the verb is not clear, but it may refer to horns rubbed with oil and, thus, gleaming with strength and virility (Tate 1990, 467). After the personal testimony of vv. 10-11, general statements about the blessedness of the righteous are given in vv. 12-15 (cf. Ps 1).

The righteous are compared to healthy, growing trees planted in the Temple courts. Whether the poet had in mind trees that actually grew in the Temple courts is secondary to the emphasis on the life-giving power of Yahweh (cf. references that link the source of water and life to the Temple area, e.g., Ps 46:4; Ezek 47:1-12; Isa 33:20-21; Zech 14:8; Rev 22:1-2).

The title prescribes this psalm as "for the sabbath day," the only psalm with this rubric, and it is so used in Jewish tradition. The psalm contains nothing that is specifically sabbatical, but it is reasonable to think that there were reasons for its selection. Themes in the psalm that relate to sabbath observance include creation (v. 4; cf. Gen 2:1-3; Exod 20:11; 31:17), thanksgiving for Yahweh's *steadfast love* (v. 2) and great works (the name Yahweh is repeated seven times in this psalm), and the thriving of the righteous (vv. 12-15)—the Sabbath was an expression of social morality and concern for the whole community (see Deut 5:14-15; Isa 56:1-2; Ezek 22:6-8).

Psalm 93

This short hymn belongs to the so-called Enthronement Psalms of Yahweh (Pss 47, 93, 96–99) that praise the kingship of Yahweh. They are marked by the use of the phrase "Yahweh (the LORD) reigns" and other references to the divine kingship. Enthronement Psalms were appropriate for any occasion when the worshiping congregation desired to praise the reign of Yahweh, but the autumn festival (Feast of Tabernacles) was their most specific context.

However the expression "the LORD reigns" is translated (see Ps 47:8), the emphasis is on Yahweh and his reign. The description of divine kingship borrows from the language used of earthly kings, but the scope of praise surpasses that of human kings. Yahweh's reign is based on cosmic victories over great forces, such as the surging floods and roaring seas, that constantly threaten creation. The *floods* may also be historicized references to hostile human powers. The verbs should be read as past tense in vv. 3-4, but the cosmologic victory of Yahweh is not purely a past event. In the last verse of the psalm attention passes from the thought of Yahweh as the conquering creator to the exceeding dependability of the decrees of the divine King and to the holiness that belongs to Yahweh's "house" (or temple).

Psalm 94

This psalm is difficult to classify according to literary types. Verses 1-7 have the form of a communal lament that reflects a disaster that has come to the nation. *Evildoers* crush and afflict the people with arrogant boasting, and disregard the prospect of any effective intervention by Yahweh (v. 7; cf. Pss 10:11; 14:1; 59:7). The *evildoers* are not specifically identified, but they seem to be Israelites of influence rather than foreigners (v. 20). An address in the style of the wisdom teachers is found in vv. 8-15. The speakers in v. 7 are the *dullest of the people* and *fools* (v. 8; cf. Ps 92:6). By the use of rhetorical questions they are called to common sense about the ways of Yahweh (vv. 9-11). In the language of the wise ones, the truly *happy* or "blessed" person (v. 12; cf. Ps 1) is defined as the one who is disciplined and instructed from the *torah* of Yahweh. Verse 14 refers to the situation described in v. 5, and makes a division of the psalm into two independent parts—vv. 1-11 and vv. 12-23—improbable. The people are assured that Yahweh will not forsake his heritage.

The last part of the psalm (vv. 16-23) expresses the thankful testimony of one who has received the help of Yahweh. The speaker is one who had been very near to *the land of silence* (v. 17; a designation for SHEOL), but who had been saved by the *steadfast love* of Yahweh (v. 18). The *consolations* of Yahweh revive the speaker's inner being when trouble becomes a burden (v. 19). The worshiper has found relief from the oppressive reality of corrupt and wicked rulers who constantly threaten the life of the righteousness (vv. 20-23). *Wicked rulers* (v. 20) is literally "throne," so v. 20a should read "Can a throne of destruction be allied with you?" (cf. Ps 122:5). The saving and vindicating might of Yahweh is greater than the iniquity of the wicked (vv. 22-23).

The basic nature of this psalm appears to lie in vv. 8-15 and 22-23, which have the nature of communal instruction. The genre of Ps 94 seems, therefore, to be liturgical instruction for those whose faith is sorely tried (cf. Pss 91:112). The psalm's placement between Pss 93 and 95–99 "creates a counterpoint to the surrounding enthronement hymns by asking in effect that Yahweh exercise his rule of judging the wicked" (Kselman and Barré 1990, 542). The opening petitions (vv. 1-3) address Yahweh in language that denotes kingship (e.g., *O Judge of the Earth*; see Tate 1990, 489–90). Theophanic language (*shine forth*, v. 1; *rise up*, v. 2) is used in the appeals for imminent divine action. The basic message of this psalm is that there is accountability for wicked oppressors (vv. 20-21, 23); the righteous will win (vv. 12-15).

Vengeance/Vindication. The translation of the word *neqamot* (root *nqm*; used of God twice in v. 1) as *vengeance* is unfortunate. In contemporary English, "vengeance" conveys the idea of "revenge" or "getting even." The Hebrew root *nqm* is generally used in a positive sense in the OT and takes its basic meaning from judicial practice. The action involved is commonly that which rectifies wrongdoing or a lack of justice, and is especially concerned for those in need. In Ps 94, Yahweh is not implored to act in "vengeance" in the sense of getting revenge on his enemies; he is asked to judge the earth, rendering to the arrogant wicked what they deserve because they disregard the rights of vulnerable people (v. 6) and *crush your people* (v. 5). "Vindication" is better here than "vengeance" (Holladay 1993, 321). The plea is addressed to the sovereign God to put things right on earth by vindicating those crushed by their oppressors, and by establishing justice (vv. 14-15).

Psalm 95

This psalm is similar in form to Pss 50 and 81. It falls into two parts: vv. 1-7c compose a hymn that celebrates the kingship of Yahweh and vv. 7d-11 form a prophetic ORACLE that warns the people against stubborn disobedience. Commentators commonly speak of the liturgical nature of this psalm, and it is probable that it was shaped by liturgical practice. Perhaps a procession of worshipers entering the Temple area for worship at one of the Jerusalem festivals is the original setting of Ps 95.

The worshipers encourage one another to go into the Temple courts and into the presence of Yahweh in vv. 1-2. The poet may have had in mind the movement of the worshipers into the sanctuary in vv. 3-5. In v. 6 the people have arrived in the holy area and are summoned to assume the postures of worship. Verse 7a-c is an affirmation of Yahweh by the worshipers; it parallels the statements in v. 3 and forms a frame around vv. 4-6. The *great king above all gods* (v. 3) is declared by the speakers in v. 7 to be *our God*, the shepherd of the people.

The voice of a prophet or other speaker, such as a levitical priest, is then heard bringing an oracle of Yahweh to the people. This is, however, no *shalom* (peace) oracle such as that in Ps 85:8-13 or Ps 91:14-16. This oracle warns the people about disobedience. It lays the claims of Yahweh on the people—as do the oracles in Pss 50 and 81, and the historical Pss 78 and 105–16. The Israelites of *today* (note the emphasis in v. 7d) are reminded of the obdurate disobedience of their fathers at *Meribah* ("testing") and at *Massah* ("strife") in the wilderness (cf. Exod 17:107; Num 20:1-13; Ps 81:7) and of the consequent refusal of permission to enter into the *rest* of the promised land (Deut 12:9). The prophet seeks a different response from the present generation (cf. Heb 3:7-4:13).

Psalm 96

This is another of the hymns that praise the kingship of Yahweh. The LORD is praised as the mighty creator, who is *to be revered above all gods"* (v. 4). All people of the earth are summoned to praise Yahweh (vv. 7-9); the physical universe also is called upon to exult and rejoice because "The LORD reigns!" (vv. 10-12). By contrast with Yahweh, *the gods of [other] peoples are idols* or "things of nought" (v. 5; cf. Ps 97:7; Isa 40:18-26; 41:23-24; 44:6-8; 46:5-8). Unlike the impotent gods of other peoples, *honor, majesty, strength*, and *beauty* attend the ways and worship of Yahweh (v. 6). The psalm closes with an affirmation of the coming of Yahweh for worldwide judgeship (vv. 10-13).

All of creation is summoned to greet the manifestation of Yahweh's kingship with gladness and praise, including *the trees of the forest* (v. 12; cf. Isa 55:12). The psalm is set in the worship of the Temple (vv. 8-9; on *in holy splendor*, see Ps 29:2). Verse 6 refers to *his sanctuary* while *strength and beauty* may have reference to the ARK of the covenant (see Ps 78:60-61; 1 Chr 16:27). *Honor and majesty* are descriptive of the attributes of divine royalty (cf. Pss 8:2; 104:1; 11:3; 148:13; 1 Chr 29:11, 25; Jer 48;18; Dan 11:21; Hab 3:3; Zech 6:13). Verses 7-9 use the same language as Ps 29:1-2 (*Ascribe to the LORD*), except that the summons to praise is directed to the peoples of the earth rather than to divine beings.

Two things are worthy of special note in regard to this psalm. First, it has a "missionary" character (Kselman and Barré 1990, 542), calling on the people of Yahweh to declare his glory and marvelous works to all the peoples (v.3). The nations are called to worship Yahweh (vv. 7-9), and the summons is expanded to all creation (vv. 10-13).

Second, the call to sing a *new song* to Yahweh (v. 1) is an expression found elsewhere (see Pss 33:3; 40:3; 98:1; 144:9; 149:1; Isa 42:10). In the most direct sense a "new song" probably refers to a song that is new for each festival occasion. In this regard, a "new song" is analogous to new objects used in some rituals (see 1 Sam 6:7; 2 Sam 6:3). A "new song" would celebrate the new acts of Yahweh, anticipating new works of deliverance and redemption (see Isa 42:10; 43:18-19; 48:6-7; Lam 3:22-23).

Psalm 97

Like Pss 96, 98, and 99, this hymn praises the kingship of Yahweh. After the initial summons to worship (v. 1), a description of a theophanic manifestation of Yahweh is given (vv. 2-5), accompanied by a mixture of thunderstorm and earthquake imagery. Lightning flashes illumine the world, the earth writhes before the coming presence, and *the mountains melt like wax* before the fiery coming of

Yahweh (characteristic elements of theophanic descriptions; see Exod 19:16-20; 24:10, 16-17; Deut 5:4; 9:10, 15; Pss 18:8-16; 50:3; Hab 3:3-12). Theophanic language is highly metaphorical and it should not be read as literally descriptive or as history. The throne of Yahweh, surrounded by clouds and thick darkness, rests on a foundation of *righteousness and justice* (v. 2).

The theophanic manifestation of Yahweh described in vv. 1-5 differs from other theophanic descriptions in that this is an appearance to the whole world (note the framing of vv. 1-5 by the word *earth* in v. 1 and *all the earth* in v. 5), while elsewhere such appearances are primarily for the covenant people of Israel (cf. Exod 19:16-25; Judg 5:4-5; Pss 18:7-15; 50:1-3). All the peoples will see his glory (v. 6; cf. Isa 40:5; 52:10), not just Zion and "the daughters of Judah" (see Ps 48:11). His glorious appearing will bring shame to all the worshipers of images and idols (v. 7; cf. Isa 42:17; 45:16; Jer 10:14).

A question arises about the time of the action presented in vv. 1-9. The action in v. 6 can be read as completed: "The heavens have proclaimed his righteousness and all the peoples have seen his glory." The text probably has a future expectation in mind (though not necessarily the distant future) viewed as already complete. The position is the same as that in Isa 40:5, that is, anticipation in the near future of a great new revelation of Yahweh's "glory"—his power and might in delivering his people and in judgment over all peoples. The anticipated coming may have been celebrated as completed in the cultic ceremonials of the festivals (cf. "for he has come" of 96:13 [NRSV, *for he is coming*]). Psalms such as these were possibly recited in connection with the movement of the ARK into the Temple, a kind of enthronement ceremony for Yahweh. The cry "Yahweh reigns" greeted those coming to the throne of a king. This would not mean, however, that there was any time when Yahweh did not reign, but the ritual acclamation of his newly begun reign should not be ruled out. The rituals were designed to link the worshiper with both the past and the future.

Verses 6-8 describe the response to the THEOPHANY (vv. 2-5), which centered on the "putting to shame" (i.e., a humiliating loss of face for all those who worship images of "mere idols" [v. 7]). This is followed in vv. 10-12 with a description of the kind of righteous and just rule exercised by Yahweh. The righteous can rejoice, because Yahweh guards the faithful.

Psalm 98

The psalm belongs to the hymns that celebrate the kingship of Yahweh (esp. Pss 47; 95; 96–99). It has much in common with Ps 96. Like the other "enthronement hymns" of Yahweh, Ps 98 was probably used in the worship of the festivals, particularly, the Festival of Booths (Tabernacles) in the autumn. The congregation is exhorted to sing *a new song* (cf. Ps 96:1) to Yahweh (v. 1) that corresponds to the "newness" of the *marvelous things* that Yahweh has done, and to the triumph that he has made known *in the sight of the nations* (vv. 2-3). Yahweh's great act of "salvation" (a key idea in vv. 1-3) is defined in terms of his having *remembered his steadfast love . . . [for] Israel* (v. 3; cf. Isa 40:5; 52:10).

A question of the time of the action arises because the verbs seem to represent completed action. It would be a mistake to push the time factor too far, however, because the verbs can be read as referring to the future (completed action in future time); in the language of the cult, time becomes secondary to theological conviction and testimony. The future actuality is even now laid hold of by the worshiping community. The psalm looks back to the past (v. 3) and recalls the salvation-history of Israel, which it then projects toward its ultimate consummation (v. 9). In keeping with the grand vision, *all the earth* (v. 4) and the forces of nature (vv. 7-8) are summoned to praise Yahweh *the King* along with the cultic community whose presence is indicated in vv. 5-6. Yahweh in coming to judge the earth with *righteousness and . . . equity* (v. 9).

Psalm 99

This psalm, like Pss 47, 93, 95–98, belongs to the hymns that celebrate the kingship of Yahweh and are marked by the phrase "the LORD reigns" (v. 1), but it is different from Pss 96, 97, and 98. A refrain (probably designed to be sung by a choir or the congregation) is especially noticeable in this psalm (vv. 3, 5, 9). The refrain emphasizes the holiness of Yahweh: *Holy is he!* The psalm also differs from 96–98 in that it does not have the same degree of parallelism to Deutero-Isaiah, and it is less universal in scope.

Yahweh is identified as: (1) the one who *sits enthroned upon the cherubim* (the reference is to the ARK, which was conceived of as the throne of Yahweh; see 1 Sam 4:4; 2 Sam 6:2; 2 Kgs 19:15; 1 Chr 13:6; Pss 80:2; Isa 57:16; "between the cherubs" was the place of Yahweh's meeting with Israel: Exod 25:10-22; 37:7-9); (2) as the one who is *great in Zion* and *exalted over all the peoples* (v. 2); (3) as the *Mighty King* (v. 4) who loves justice. The peoples of the earth are exhorted to *worship at his footstool* (v. 5). The *footstool* can refer to Zion (Isa 60:13; Ezek 43:7) or to the whole earth (Isa 66:1; Matt 5:35), but more probably here to the ark, above which Yahweh is invisibly enthroned (Ps 132:7; 1 Chr 28:2).

In vv. 6-8, the poet turns to the salvation-history of Israel and recalls the names of MOSES, AARON, and SAMUEL who had served in important ways as intercessors between Israel and Yahweh, and as mediators of the COVENANT, as well as priest-prophets. The reference to the *pillar of cloud* (v. 7) goes back to the revelation of Yahweh to Moses in association with the travels in the wilderness (Exod 33:9; Num 12:5). The ark and the tent traditions were originally separate, but combined in later traditions (see 1 Kgs 8:6, 10-11).

The mention of Samuel in relation to *the pillar of cloud* is strange since there is no specific mention in the extant traditions of such experiences for him. The reference may be simply parenthetical in v. 6 ("Moses and Aaron among his priests—and yes, Samuel too—were among those who called on his name").

The psalm closes in vv. 8-9 with a strong emphasis on Yahweh as *a forgiving God*, although one who punishes wrongdoing: "Yet you called them to account for their misdeeds" (REB). The KJV's "though thou tookest vengeance of their inventions" hardly has meaning any longer and also uses the word "vengeance" for the Hebrew verb *nqm*. This word when used of Yahweh usually refers to "vindication" or the establishment of justice rather than the "vengeance" in relation to personal enemies (see above, Ps 94). In the case of v. 8, it means Yahweh deals appropriately with wrongdoing, even that of people like Moses, Aaron, and Samuel.

Psalm 100

This short hymn that praises Yahweh concludes the series of kingship psalms in 93, 95–99. It has some similarities to Ps 95: a call for shouts of joy and thanksgiving (the noun for *thanksgiving* in v. 4 appears elsewhere in book four only in Ps 95:2a) and the liturgical *come* and *enter* (vv. 2, 4; cf. 95:6). Both psalms also emphasize the close relationship of Yahweh with the people. Psalm 100 suggests a worship setting, probably in festival contexts when people came to sanctuaries to worship (v. 4).

The psalm contains a sevenfold summons to give praise and homage to Yahweh and thus forms a suitable sequel to the psalms that exalt the kingship of Yahweh (Pss 96–99; see Tate 1990, 535–36). Its universal scope (*all the earth* in v. 1) also relates well to the exaltation psalms.

The repeated calls to praise and homage are supplemented by two important statements in vv. 3 and 5. The NRSV adopts a reading that yields *and we are his* in v. 3 (giving the alternate "and not we ourselves" in mg.). A preferred reading is: "He (Yahweh) made us and we are indeed his people and the flock he shepherds (or the flock of his pasture)." Compare the entire statement to Pss 79:13 and 95:5a, 6-7. The second statement (v. 5) declares that "Yahweh is good" and that *his steadfast love* and *faithfulness* never fail.

Verse 5 is a formulaic saying found repeatedly in contexts praising Yahweh (e.g., Pss 106:1; 107:1; 118:1; 129; 136:1; 1 Chr 16:34; 2 Chr 5:13; 7:3; Jer 33:11). Verse 5 seems to be the fullest form of this saying in the OT, including aspects of goodness, steadfast love, and faithfulness.

Psalm 101

This psalm is commonly considered to belong to the royal psalms (Pss 2, 20, 21, 45, 72, 89, 110, 132) and classified as a "loyalty–affirmation" or vow of intention for an Israelite king. It was intended, perhaps, for recitation at a coronation by the new king, who declares his intention to rule properly in the COVENANT made by Yahweh with DAVID (cf. 2 Sam 23:1-7; Pss 89:19-37; 132:11-12). Another view, but improbable, considers the psalm as a kind of royal "protestation of innocence" (cf. Ps 7) recited by the king as a part of a ritual of humiliation carried out as a component of the autumnal festival in preexilic Israel.

Commentators may have been too quick to assume that this is a royal psalm, and that the speaker throughout the psalm is intended to be a king. First, it is not necessary to assume that the speaker in vv. 1-5 must be a king. The speaker could be any devoted Israelite leader or citizen concerned about the spiritual condition and the welfare of the community. The NRSV *When shall I attain it?* obscures the question of complaint in v. 2 that reads "O when will you come to me?"—when will my faithful behavior be rewarded and those who act as in vv. 3b-5 be corrected? (Translate NRSV's *I will destroy* in v. 5 as "I will reduce to silence.") Second, the speaker in vv. 6-8 may be God, with the verses forming a divine ORACLE (cf. Ps 32:3-5, 8-9; 1 Kgs 9:3-7; Kselman and Barré 1990, 543). In this case, *my house* (v. 7) refers to the Temple. This reading seems better in the present context in book four of the Psalter.

Reading the psalm this way does not nullify its centuries-old interpretation as "The Prince's Psalm" or "The Mirror for Magistrates." It still sets forth high ethical standards for rulers and ordinary citizens alike. Even if vv. 6-8 are read as the words of Yahweh, they call leaders toward actions compatible with divine ways. In the ideology of ancient kingship, the king was God's representative on earth and charged with manifesting qualities pleasing to God.

Psalm 102

This is one of the seven penitential psalms of the church (Pss 6, 32, 38, 51, 102, 130, 143), although it has little direct expression of penitence. Modern scholars classify it with the lament-complaints, but note additional elements. Similarities of style and content suggest it belongs to a common context with a group of other psalms: Pss 22, 35, 38, 40, 69, 70, 71 (see Tate 1990, 204–05). Verses 12-22 are hymn-like.

According to the title, the speaker in this psalm can be anyone who is *afflicted . . . faint and pleading before the LORD*, which seems to be appropriate. Interpreters frequently read the psalm as the prayer of an acutely ill person, but it could also be the prayer of anyone in severe distress. The similes and metaphors of the psalm should not be read as directly descriptive of physical conditions (e.g., the speaker would hardly actually *eat ashes like bread*, v. 9).

In vv. 1-11, the speaker appeals to Yahweh to hear a complaint and to respond to an affliction that has grown desperate. As usual in the laments, the situation is graphically described but no precise diagnosis is possible. In any case, the speaker is taunted by *enemies* because of an overly distressed condition (v. 8). The complaints of the speaker resemble those of JOB: *lonely* (vv. 6-7), tormented by the realization of the extreme finitude of human existence (vv. 3, 11), and contending that suffering is the result of God's anger and punishment (v. 10), although the speaker gives no reason for the divine wrath (Allen 1983, 14).

In vv. 12-22, the suppliant turns with an emphatic *But you, O LORD* from personal calamity to consider Yahweh and the condition of Zion. Appeal is made to Yahweh in the traditional cult language of the hymns that praise him as *enthroned forever* (v. 12) and as the one who built *Zion* (v. 16). Zion is the place where Yahweh has appeared *in his glory* and where he has heard the prayers of the people (v. 17). In vv. 18-22, the lament becomes assurance that Yahweh will favor Zion again (cf. v. 13), for the ruins of the Temple remain precious to the servants of Yahweh (cf. v. 14). The suppliant's concern is with the future (v. 18), recalling the history of Zion as a basis for the expectation of future acts of Yahweh (vv. 21-22).

The lament returns in vv. 23-24, followed by a fragment of a hymn that praises the enduring sureness of Yahweh as creator (vv. 25-28). Verse 28 looks to the future that is secure for the people of Yahweh despite the present distressing circumstances. In a manner similar to Ps 90, the psalm contrasts human finitude and brevity of life with the eternity of God.

Psalm 103

As great personal testimony of thankful praise, Ps 103 has contributed significantly to the devotion of the people of faith. It is a personal thanksgiving psalm that becomes a hymn of praise, framed by a personal note: *Bless the* LORD, *O my soul!* (vv. 1, 35). The change from the singular form of the thanksgiving (vv. 1-5) to the plural form of the hymn (vv. 6-14) may reflect the use of the psalm in congregational worship; if so, vv. 6-14 would be recited by the congregation in response to the individual thanksgiving.

In vv. 1-5, the speaker engages in a intrapersonal dialogue, calling upon *my soul* (i.e., myself) to *bless* Yahweh. *Bless* in this context means to praise. Participial forms are used in vv. 3-5 to recall the *benefits* of Yahweh. The successive use of the verbs encompasses the whole of a person's life experience (Westermann 1989, 239). The reference to *the eagle* (v. 5) is similar to its use in Isa 40:31. The long-lived eagle—it molts and renews its feathers annually—is used as an example of the vigor and renewal of life.

Verses 6-14 recall the acts of Yahweh in Israel's salvation-history. The emphasis in these verses is on the merciful and gracious ways that Yahweh deals with his people, not in terms of proportionate measure for their sin, but as God remembers their finitude and acts toward them as a father acts toward the children he loves (cf. Hos 11:1; Exod 4:22; Isa 1:2; Mal 1:6).

Verses 8-10 (cf. Exod 34:6) are key verses. Yahweh's love is greater than his wrath—a doctrine that is verified in the history of the people and in the speaker's personal experience. The GRACE of God abounds more than human sin. Grace is the biblical message of salvation; it is the thrust upward to life and joy. The ephemeral frame of humanity could never endure without the constant sustaining power of Yahweh's providential care. Humanity's finitude is described in vv. 15-16 in a manner similar to Isa 40:6-8 (see also Ps 90:5-6; Job 14:1-2; Isa 51:12). Human transitoriness and vulnerability are contrasted with the *everlasting* value of Yahweh's *steadfast love* and *righteousness* (v. 17), which is for *those who keep his covenant and remember to do his commandments* (v. 18). Human achievements (*place*, v. 16) are soon forgotten, but the *steadfast love* of Yahweh endures.

The conclusion (vv. 19-22) is a song of praise in which the heavenly beings and all creation are urged to praise Yahweh. His is the universal kingdom (cf. Ps 148), over which he reigns on his *established . . . throne*. The psalm closes (vv. 20-22) with nearly the same language as in vv. 1-2, except the self-summons to praise God at the beginning of the psalm now "broadens out to embrace the whole creation" (Westermann 1989, 243): "Bless the LORD, all created things" (v. 22a REB).

Psalm 104

This hymn was written to be sung by an individual (note the first-person singular in vv. 1, 33, 35) who praises God as creator of the heavens and the earth. The psalm reflects the influence of Near East literature contemporary with the history of Israel. Parallels with the "Hymn to the Sun" of the Egyptian Pharaoh Amenhotep IV (AKHENATON, 1377–1360 BCE) are especially close. Any direct literary dependence, however, is unlikely. The same observations are true with regard to Gen 1, to which the psalm has considerable parallel (see Allen 1983, 29-31). The poet drew from a large body of traditional sources and the broad genre of creation accounts in the history of Israel's worship. There is nothing to indicate exactly the psalm's cultic context, but the themes of creation and the lordship of Yahweh must have been prominent in the Festival of Tabernacles (Booths) that included concern with the harvest, the coming new year, and the indispensable rains. Booths would have been an appropriate time to sing about God's creative works. Israelites may also have used the psalm on other occasions.

The psalm opens (vv. 1-4) with the same statement that closed Ps 103. *Bless the LORD, O my soul* may have been added to link the two psalms. In any case they may be read together in the context of book four. Yahweh is praised in exalted language (vv. 1-4): he covers himself with a *garment* of light, which is the source of life and joy (cf. Exod 3:2; Isa 60:1; John 1:5; 1 John 1:5; 1 Tim. 6:16; Rev 21:23). The language is similar to that used to describe theophanic appearances of God (see 18:7-15; 97:1-5; Exod 19:16-19; Hab 3:3-6). The idea of Yahweh riding on the clouds (v, 3) may have a Ugaritic background (see Ps 68:4, 33). The forces of nature are the messengers and ministers of Yahweh (v. 4).

The establishment of *the earth* is presented in vv. 5-13. Yahweh put the earth on its foundations (cf. Job 38:69; Ps 24:1-2). In its primeval condition it was covered with the waters of the great deep (the *t'hom*; cf. Gen 1:2)—waters that covered the mountains (v. 6; cf. Gen 7:19-20). The ordered world resulted when God gave a thunderous shout and the water dispersed to be held within immutable bounds (vv. 7-9).

The description of the creative process continues in vv. 10-13 with provision for springs and streams of water. Animal life (including the birds) appears (vv. 11-12), and Yahweh enriches the earth with *the fruit of [his] work* (v. 13). From his heavenly chambers (*lofty abode* of v. 13 is the same as *chambers* of v. 3) God sends the rain (a major feature in the worship of the Feast of Tabernacles; see Zech 14:16-19). The role of God as creator merges into the role of sustainer of the world. As sustainer, God uses the primordial enemy of terrestrial life (the flood) as life-giving sustenance for the creatures that live on earth (Allen 1983, 33). Waters come from two sources: springs that flow up from below and rain that pours down from the heavenly abode.

Verses 14-23 form the third strophe of the psalm, and continues the description of the divine provisions for life on earth. Verses 14-15 present a compact version of the agricultural year (Kselman and Barré 1990, 544); provisions for the trees, birds, and other wild creatures are described in vv. 16-18. The seasons and the days are marked off and the rhythm of life is maintained (vv. 19-23). The whole ecological organism of the cosmos lives in the ordered patterns created and sustained by God (vv. 21-23, 27-30).

In the fourth strophe (vv. 24-30), v. 24 breaks the context with an exclamation of wonder at the *manifold . . . works* of God and the wisdom with which he has made them (cf. Prov 3:19; 8:22-31), with special attention given to *the sea* and its inhabitants (vv. 25-26). They, too, are under the absolute control of Yahweh. That the poet is concerned with more than the creative works of God once accomplished is clear in vv. 27-30 where the text affirms the continuation of creation. Without the divine breath of life all would be death and dust (vv. 29-30). Yahweh is the great provider and renewer as well as the great creator.

The common distinction between God as creator and God as sustainer/provider/renewer is not theologically valid unless creation is restricted to origination in an absolute beginning. The creative work of God is never "finished" and is manifest in the sustaining and renewing of life as well as in its beginning.

The psalm concludes (vv. 31-35) with a prayer for the continuation of the glory of Yahweh and for the elimination from the earth of two sources of discord and destruction: *sinners* and *the wicked* (v. 35). The ideal is for all of creation and all creatures to praise Yahweh so Yahweh's rejoicing in his creation may be responded to by the creation rejoicing in his works.

In the prayer *May my meditation be pleasing to him* (v. 34), *meditation* may be understood as "poem" or "poetry" and the verse indicates that the individual worshiper is aware of reciting—if not composing—a psalm of praise as an act of worship.

Psalm 105

The psalm is another of the historical hymns (closely related to Pss 78 and 106) that recapitulate the salvation-history of Israel. Commonly it is assumed that Ps 105 was composed for use at one of the major festivals, perhaps in connection with ceremonies of covenant renewal (see vv. 7-11). Verses 1-15 are quoted in 1 Chr 16 (together with Pss 96:1-13; 106:1; 47-48) in connection with the narration of David's moving the ARK to Zion.

With repeated imperatives, the fellowship is urged in vv. 1-6 to remember and to praise the wonderful works of Yahweh. Those who *seek the LORD* are encouraged. The term "seekers of Yahweh" suggests pilgrims who attend a festival or other ceremonies at a SANCTUARY, but should not be restricted to such people. They are exhorted to seek his presence continually, not only in periodic journeys to the sanctuary. The congregation is addressed as descendants of ABRAHAM and JACOB, who were the recipients of the COVENANT and its promises (v. 6).

In vv. 7-25, the historical survey begins with the period of Israel's ancestors and the Abrahamic covenant with its promise of CANAAN as an inheritance. The life of the ancestors as seminomadic wanderers is described in vv. 12-15 and includes an account of JOSEPH and the migration to Egypt (vv. 16-25). The details vary from the accounts in Genesis, but the general pattern is the same. The result of Jacob's sojourn as a resident alien in Egypt was that God made his people to be exceedingly fruitful and "too numerous for their oppressors" (v. 24, Dahood 1968, 59).

MOSES and the EXODUS from Egypt is the subject of vv. 26-42. Moses and AARON were the leaders sent by Yahweh as the agents of the PLAGUES on the Egyptians (vv. 26-36; cf. the plagues in Ps 78:43-51 and Exod 7-12). In a very emphatic way, the actions of deliverance are said to be the direct deeds of Yahweh (see the repeated *he*, referring to Yahweh, in vv. 28-42). Moses and Aaron disappear from the picture (and there is no account of the Sinai covenant). All these great deeds of deliverance were done because *Yahweh remembered his holy promise [to] Abraham* (v. 42, reading the *and* in RSV and NRSV as "to"). Verse 42 forms an INCLUSIO with vv. 8-10 and frames all verses in between.

The closing section (vv. 43-45) refers to the triumphant exodus of the people from Egypt (v. 43) and to the gift of the LAND (cf. v. 11). The final verse states the covenantal obligation of obedience that all of this places upon the covenant people: salvation-history should lead to obedience and faithfulness.

Psalm 106

This psalm is a combination hymn and communal lament. Its content places it among the historical psalms (Pss 78, 105, 106, 135, 136). The sober mood emphasizes Israel's continual guilt, and is contrasted against the much more positive mood of Ps 105. In this respect, Ps 106 is more closely related to Ps 78 than to Ps 105; in the present arrangement of the Psalter, however, Ps 106 is clearly intended to be read with 105. The "Hallelujahs" (*Praise the LORD*) at the end of Ps 104 (which really belongs with the beginning of 105), at the end of Ps 105, and at the beginning and end of Ps 106 further support the intended relationship between Pss 105 and 106. These are the first appearances of the HALLELUJAH formula in the Psalter.

Verses 27 and 47 indicate that this psalm in its present form originated after the Babylonian EXILE in 587 BCE. Some interpreters link it (and Ps 105) with a covenant renewal ceremony assumed to have been a regular feature of preexilic worship. That may be correct, but the covenant renewal liturgies were more probably used in worship at the second Temple after 515 BCE. Verses 47-48 are also found in 1 Chr 16:35-36, and the provenance of the psalm is almost certainly exilic or postexilic.

After an opening call to praise Yahweh (vv. 1-3), a lamenting confession begins. A solo speaker voices a personal prayer (vv. 4-5) and the sin-history of the people (vv. 6-46). The speaker is not identified, but we may think of a priest or devoted Israelite leader speaking for the community. The speaker implores Yahweh for the privilege of personal participation in the joy of a renewed well-being of the people.

The sins of the ancestors began *in Egypt* (v. 7). Even in the Exodus itself there was rebellion and the characteristic *they did not remember*. God continued to perform redemptive acts, despite the rebelliousness of the people, until they believed his words and sang his praises (vv. 8-12).

The people soon forgot the wonders of the Exodus and the chain of rebellion and disbelief extends with the recall of six episodes of sin: (1) their *wanton craving in the wilderness* (v. 14; see Num 11:1-35; Exod 15:22–17:7); (2) their jealousy of Moses and the rebellion of *Dathan and . . . Abiram* (v. 17; see Num 16; Deut 11:6); (3) the making of the golden calf (v. 19; see Exod 32:1-35; Deut 9:8-21); (4) the unbelief in response to the report of the spies (vv. 24-27; see Num 13–14); (5) the participation in Moabite worship (vv. 28-31; see Num 25:1-18; Exod 34:15); and (6) the rebellion at *Meribah* (vv. 32-33; see Exod 17:1-7; Num 20:1-13; Pss 81:7; 95:8). After the wilderness experience, the people failed to exterminate the Canaanites and their practices (vv. 34-39; see Deut 7:2; 16; 20:16-18; Judg 1:21–2:5), and continued their disobedience during the time of the judges (vv. 40-46).

The recall in vv. 40-46 goes beyond the period of the judges and actually summarizes the whole history of Israel. Despite the long extension of Israel's rebelliousness, Yahweh continued to hear their prayers and respond in mercy and deliverance to their distress (vv. 41-46). *He remembered his covenant* and acted toward them on the basis *of his steadfast love*, causing those *who held them captive* to treat them with kindness (vv. 45-46; cf. 1 Kgs 8:50).

In v. 47, the people pray that Yahweh will gather them from among the nations where they are scattered, in order that they may more properly give thanks to him (cf. v. 1).

Ps 106 has been called a "judgment doxology" (von Rad, 1962, 357–58), that seeks to "bring to an end a chapter of history, and to set one's sights on a new beginning" (Seybald 1990, 159). Verse 48 is the doxology that closes book four of the Psalter, and probably did not belong to the original psalms (it is found, however, in 1 Chr 16:35).

Summary of Book Four

Ps 106 ends book four of the Psalter. If book three is especially concerned with the tension between personal faith and the seeming failure of the historical salvation-enterprise, it is appropriate to ask how book four responds to the unresolved dilemma. At least three answers emerge.

First, the extraordinary emphasis on the universal kingship of Yahweh responds to the loss of the Davidic kingship for Israel. The Davidic dynasty is gone, but the *great God . . . great King above all gods* (Ps 95:3) reigns. The Israelites are called to sing *a new song* (Pss 96:1; 98:1) praising the great King because he is not finished with doing new things. He will yet *judge the world with righteousness, and the peoples with equity* (Ps 98:9).

Second, book four seems to be a Moses book, suggesting a shift of authority from DAVID to MOSES (see Tate 1990, xxvi-xxvii, 418). The first psalm in book four (Ps 90) is ascribed to Moses in its title, and Moses is referred to by name in Pss 105:26; 106:16, 23, 32. Also, the wilderness accounts are prominent in Pss 95 and 106. In the case of Ps 106, the speaker is clearly identified in v. 47 as one who is experiencing the "wilderness" again in the form of EXILE. The psalms of book four suggest that the faith of Israelites should be grounded in premonarchical, Mosaic traditions; Moses himself proclaimed the divine kingship of Yahweh (Exod 15:18). The new generation of the postexilic communities should not harden their hearts and test Yahweh as the Israelites did in the wilderness (Ps 95:8-11).

Third, individual faith can rest on the assurance Yahweh has not abandoned his salvation-enterprise with Israel. If I am correct about Ps 101, this seems to be the message in vv. 6-8: Yahweh will purify his elect faithful and rid the land of the wicked, so that the divine name may be declared with praise in Zion/Jerusalem when the peoples and kingdoms gather to worship Yahweh (cf. Ps 102:21-22). The servants of Yahweh may also live secure in the powerful presence of their God (Ps 102:25-28).

Psalms 105–106 are designed to revive faith in Yahweh's enterprise with Israel. The end of the Davidic monarchy is not the end of salvation-history. Faith must be grounded in both the individual and the communal work of God.

Book Five. Psalms 107–150

Psalm 107

Psalm 107 falls into two main divisions, each of which belongs in a different literary classification. The first part (vv. 1-32) is a communal thanksgiving; the second (vv. 33-43) is part of a hymn that has been added to the first section. A popular interpretation of the psalm places it against the background of a festival that attracted groups of pilgrims (they may even have been captives returning from the EXILE). Various segments of the festival participants are called upon to offer their thanksgiving sacrifices, and to give their testimony of the benefits which they have received from Yahweh (vv. 22, 32). The psalm in its present form probably dates from the postexilic period (see v. 3), but it may have an earlier history, with vv. 2-3 and vv. 33-43 added to an individual thanksgiving psalm to make it appropriate for a postexilic communal thanksgiving (Allen 1983, 62-5).

The first division (vv. 1-32) opens with a call to give thanks to Yahweh (v. 1). The *redeemed from trouble*—those who have received special benefits and are prepared to sacrifice (cf. Lev 7:11-15)—are addressed and called to testify. The groups reported in vv. 4-32 are introduced with a threefold form: a description of the trouble the group experienced; a report of their petition to God (*then they cried to the LORD*) and his deliverance from their afflictions; and a summons to thanksgiving which forms a refrain and may indicate some sort of antiphonal recitation of the psalm (vv. 8-9, 15-16, 21-22, 31-32). The groups are (1) desert wanderers who had suffered hunger and thirst, until Yahweh relieved their distress and led them to a city (vv. 4-7); (2) prisoners who rebelled against God and suffered punishment for it until Yahweh gave them their freedom (vv. 10-14); (3) those who were sick until the word of Yahweh went forth and healed them (vv. 17-20); and (4) seafarers who were in danger of losing their lives in a storm until Yahweh quieted the sea and brought them to their port (vv. 23-30). All of these must be considered as poetic expressions of various types of situations in which God's help is powerfully experienced.

The hymnic section (vv. 33-43) praises Yahweh both for his compassionate care for those who are in need and for the thoroughness with which he punishes the wicked. His power over the natural world (both the cultivated land and the wilderness) is complete as he responds to the behavior of human beings (vv. 33-35). The hymn constitutes a suitable response by the congregation to the sacrifices and testimonies of those who have been benefitted, especially Jews who had made their way back to their homeland by what they considered to be the goodness and power of Yahweh. The psalm is not limited to Jews, however—the refrain in vv. 8, 15, and 21 continually acknowledge *his wonderful works to humankind.*

Psalm 108

This is a composite psalm formed from Pss 57:7-11 (vv. 1-5) and 60:5-12 (vv. 6-13). For the exposition of the verses see the commentary on Pss 57 and 60.

The reasons for the combination of Pss 57:7-11 and 60:5-12 into a new psalm are not certain. It may be, however, that the postexilic Israelite communities continued to have their hope framed by the boundaries of the promised land with *Shechem* and *Succoth* (v. 7), representing God's claim to the whole land (Allen 1983, 69). Edom became the archetypical enemy of Israel in the exilic and post-exilic periods (see Obad; Isa 63). The "grim beginning" (Allen 1983, 69) of Ps 60 is replaced with the positive assurance of Ps 57:7-11. In this manner Ps 108 becomes a "believing prayer" for postexilic communities for the God of old—who is still their God—to manifest a theophanic demonstration of his love and power. The key verses are 5-6: *Be exalted, O God . . . let your glory be over all the earth . . . so that those whom you love may be rescued.*

This psalm is a good example of the use of older material in a new context, a method of composition probably used in many psalms, although we often lack earlier contexts to demonstrate it. New demands and pastoral needs brought about the creative reuse of older content (Stuhlmueller 1983, 125).

Psalm 109

This individual complaint is best known for the severity of the imprecations in vv. 6-19. It seems best to interpret these verses, however, not as the words of the speaker in vv. 1-5 and 20-31, but as curses directed toward the speaker by accusers (as in NRSV, cf. RSV). The enemies of the speaker are referred to in the plural in vv. 1-5, the singular is used in vv. 6-19, and the plural returns in vv. 20-31. Thus it is probable that the suppliant quotes the charges that have been made against him (see v. 28 that refers to the cursing on the part of enemies). The situation seems to be that the speaker, under furious attack from enemies (an attack declared to be without cause and, ironically, in response to love, vv. 3-5), brings the charges made before Yahweh (cf. HEZEKIAH and the Assyrian letter in 2 Kgs 19:14-19). The accuser (lit., a *satan* [see SATAN IN THE OT]) stands at the speaker's right hand (v. 6); but the speaker is sure that Yahweh stands *at the right hand of the needy* in order to save

(v. 31), and the speaker places himself among the *needy* (vv. 22-25). Having presented the charges of the accusers, the speaker turns to Yahweh and implores him for deliverance (vv. 21, 26-29).

The charges made by the enemies of the speaker (vv. 6-19) are violent and designed to crush the defendant's answer with their overwhelming force. The translations are mostly self-explanatory and require little comment. Verse 8b possibly should read "take his office" rather than "seize his goods" (RSV) and may indicate that the accused is a person of some *position* (NRSV) and responsibility (cf. Acts 1:20). The person attacked is accused of being himself one who loves to curse others; the accusers pray that the curses will cling to the attacked like a garment with terrible effects (vv. 12-19). If the interpretation indicated above is correct, v. 20 should read: "This is the work (i.e., the curses quoted in the preceding verses) of my accusers (*satans*)"; or, if the verse is read as it stands in the NRSV, it means the suppliant prays that the curses of the accusers be returned upon them by Yahweh. Verse 20 recalls vv. 2-3.

Psalm 110

This royal psalm has been the focus of much attention and dispute. In traditional Christian interpretation it has been interpreted as messianic and Christological (see Matt 22:41-45; 26:64; Acts 2:34; Col 3:1; 1 Pet 3:22; Heb 1:3, 13; 5:6; 7:1; 8:1; 10:12-13). But there can be little doubt that the original reference of the psalm was to the Davidic king in preexilic Israel. It was later given a messianic interpretation, which is the background of Jesus' use of the psalm (Mark 12:35-37 and par.; see Pss 2 and 132). For a full treatment of the psalm in the NT, see Hay (1973). The occasion for the recitation of the psalm could have been the enthronement of a king, or possibly an autumnal festival when the COVENANT with the Davidic dynasty was renewed. The first is more probable. Indeed, it is possible the psalm was composed for the enthronement of DAVID himself.

The psalm begins with an ORACLE from Yahweh with reference to the king (*my lord*). The language is that of the prophets (lit. "oracle [utterance] of Yahweh to my lord"), and the speaker should be thought of as a court PROPHET. The message of the oracle is that of a command of Yahweh granting the king authority and honor at Yahweh's right hand (cf. Ps 45:9; 1 Kgs 2:19; Matt 20:21). The king shares the throne with Yahweh, but his authority remains delegated and not absolute. The second part of the message is a promise to the king of victory over his enemies: *until I make your enemies your footstool* (v. 1b; cf. Josh 10:24; 1 Kgs 5:3; 1 Cor 15:25).

The prophetic address continues in v. 2, but the words are those of the prophet, not of Yahweh. The prophet expands the oracle with a statement that may be interpreted either as a prediction ("Your mighty rod—Yahweh is going to send it forth from Zion") or a wish ("Let Yahweh send forth your mighty rod from Zion"). The first seems preferable. The prophet concludes v. 2 with an exhortation for the king to exercise the power granted him over his enemies.

Verse 3 is the most uncertain verse in the psalm. One approach is to consider it a reference to the willingness of the people to serve the king in times of war (cf. Judg 5:23). We may therefore read the verse as an assurance to the king that his strength and resources will remain fresh and adequate. The *dew*, especially significant in the dry climate of Palestine, marks the invigorated life of a new day. Some ritual in which the people offered themselves as willing servants of the king as part of the enthronement ceremony may be in mind.

In v. 4, a second oracle is addressed to the king: Yahweh has sworn a divine oath which will not be broken, affirming that the king has a perpetual priesthood *according to the order of Melchizedek*. Identifying the king with the priesthood is unusual, although there is evidence kings functioned in priestly roles (see 1 Sam 13:9; 2 Sam 6:12-19; 8:18; 15:12; 1 Kgs 1:9; 8:14; 55-56; 62-63; 9:25; 10:19; 12:32; 16:12-15).

The reference to MELCHIZEDEK is to be understood in terms of Gen 14:18-20, where Melchizedek, who is identified as the "king of Salem" (i.e., Jerusalem; cf. Ps 76:2), blesses Abram (Abraham) and in turn Abram gives him a tithe. It may be that v. 4 refers historically to David and his successors acquiring the priest-king status of former Jebusite kings of Jerusalem, which in time became an accepted role for Israelite kings. The assignment of the king to a priesthood of *the order of Melchizedek* avoided giving the king an Aaronite or Levitical priesthood, and thus distinguished him from ordinary priests. Of course, the transfer of an ancient tradition of authority as king-priest to the Davidic kings enhanced their status.

The style changes again in vv. 5-7 to that of prophetic explanation that interprets and expands the oracle. The king is assured of the protecting power of Yahweh (called *Lord, adonai*—i.e., not LORD—in v. 5, the same term as used for the king in v. 1), who is at the king's right hand (cf. v. 1; Ps 109:31). *The day of his wrath* (v. 5) and the great victories and judgment of Yahweh relate well to passages that deal with the "Day of Yahweh" (see Amos 5:18-20; Zeph 1:14-18; 2:3). The language is violent, but not unexpected in divine warrior passages. The concept is marked by expectation of Yahweh's victories in battle and the judgment of the nations.

Like v. 3, v. 7 is the subject of varied interpretations. If it is assumed that Yahweh is the subject (as in vv. 5-6), then (1) he may be thought of as the divine warrior who executes judgment among the nations, and refreshes his strength from streams as he pursues his enemies or (2) it possibly means that Yahweh "on the way" drinks from the stream (of blood) that flows from his conquered foes and lifts his head in victory. If the king is the subject, the verse refers (1) to the renewing of his strength as he pursues his enemies or (2) to a ritual act in which he drinks from the sacred river (probably the Gihon Spring at Jerusalem; see 1 Kgs 1:9; 38-40; 45) as a part of an enthronement ceremony. If the latter is correct, he symbolically partakes of the stream of life (which literally was so when Jerusalem had to depend upon the spring for its water supply). See Ps 46 and Ezek 47.

Psalm 111

Each succeeding line of this psalm begins with a successive letter of the Hebrew alphabet (other acrostic formations are found in Pss 9–10, 25, 34, 37, 112, 119, 145). This style of writing may seem stiff, but it is a form of literary artistry that merits our appreciation even if it does appear disjointed. The psalm has characteristics both of a hymn (vv. 1a, 2-9), and of a thanksgiving psalm (v. 1), and it concludes with a wisdom saying (v. 10). The basic theme is that of the "works of Yahweh" (vv. 2, 3, 4, 6, 7). These *works* demonstrate both the majesty and power of Yahweh (v. 3) and the gracious and merciful ways in which he has cared for his people (vv. 4-9). The closing verse has the didactic quality of the WISDOM LITERATURE (cf. Prov 1:7; 9:10; Job 28:28), and sets forth the "fear of Yahweh" as the sound basis for wisdom and successful living. Reverence for God is the foundation for abundant living.

The psalm may have come from the postexilic period, aimed perhaps at the kind of tepid religion that is reflected in the books of Haggai and Malachi—religion that had settled into ritual with lethargic commitment. As such it may be a meditation on Exod 34:5-7 (Allen 1983, 90).

Psalm 112

This psalm is commonly designated a wisdom psalm. The points it develops include fear of Yahweh, delight in divine commandment, contrast of the righteous with the wicked, and the act-consequence sequence (or reward and retribution). It also begins with the congratulatory formula *Happy are those who fear the LORD* (cf. Pss 1; 32; 84; 119:1-2). Like Ps 111, it is an acrostic poem; the two psalms share common themes and key words and should be read together (see Allen 1983, 95). Psalms 111, 112, and 113 are also joined together by the use of the HALLELUJAH (*Praise the LORD*) in Pss 111:1; 112:1; 113:1, 9 (although Ps 113 is traditionally related to the Talmudic "Egyptian Hallel" formed by Pss 113–118; see commentary on Ps 114). Psalm 111 praises the works of Yahweh and Ps 112 praises the blessed condition of those who fear Yahweh, continuing a subject begun in 111:10: "The opening beatitude creates the perspective of the whole psalm" (Allen 1983, 97).

The psalm requires little comment beyond its translation. We are reminded in v. 1 that *fear* and *delight* are not antithetical in religious experience. The Bible claims that reverence for God is the real source of joy. Further, this verse equates the one who fears Yahweh with the one who delights in God's commandments. Those who fear God take him seriously and devote themselves to his will. The RSV translates v. 4 with "light" as the subject and adds "LORD" to the text: "Light rises in the darkness for the upright; the LORD is gracious. . . . " The NRSV reads "those who fear Yahweh" (v. 1) as the subject: *They* [those who fear Yahweh] *rise in the darkness as a light for the upright.* Either reading is acceptable, but the NRSV seems better.

In v. 7-8, the *firm* and *steady* heart of the God-fearer is stressed. *Heart* refers to the inner being—the mind and will of a person. The words for *firm* and *steady* are both passive and represent qualities which are given and received (i.e., the heart is made to be firm and steady). The firm, steady heart is the inner power from Yahweh that relieves one of fear and offers calmness in the face of adversaries. In v. 10 the condition of *the wicked* is contrasted with that of the one who fears Yahweh. The angry gnashing of the teeth of the wicked as they see the success of the righteous (vv. 6-9) contrasts with the righteous looking in triumph over their foes (cf. Ps 54:9).

Psalm 113

This hymn is the first in the collection known in the Jewish liturgical tradition as the "Hallel" or the "Egyptian Hallel" (to distinguish it from Ps 136, which was called the "Great Hallel"). Hallel means praise and is derived from the *hall'lu-yah* ("Praise the LORD"; see HALLELUJAH) that is dominant in these psalms. The collection is used in Jewish festivals (except New Year and the Day of Atonement), and in the family celebration of PASSOVER. Pss 113–114 are sung before the Passover Seder meal and 115–118 afterwards (cf. Matt 26:30; Mark 14:26). Psalm 113 was designed for congregational worship, and it contains good examples of the basic elements of the hymn form.

In vv. 1-4, after the initial *Hallelujah*, the congregation (addressed as "servants of Yahweh") is urged to praise the "name of Yahweh." The "name of Yahweh" (three times in vv. 1-3; Yahweh occurs in each of the first five verses) is a concept that denotes divine presence. The summons to praise encompasses all of time and the whole earth (vv. 2-3; cf. 8:1). Yahweh is exalted above all else (v. 4).

In v. 5-9 a rhetorical question is used to introduce six causative participle constructions that affirm the incomparability of Yahweh. He is incomparable both in his exalted status and in his compassion for the *poor* and *needy*. The biblical idiom is so well known in our culture that it is easy to forget that in the ancient myths human beings were considered to be the menial servants of the gods—and on occasion the beneficiaries of their favors—but not the great subject of the actions of the deity. Perhaps, nothing in OT theology is more significant than the constant reiteration of God's preferential option for the lowly, the sick, the captive, the oppressed, and the poor and needy. The almighty king is the savior of the helpless. There may be no finer passage anywhere in the OT than vv. 5-9. Cf. Ps 113 with the "Song of Hannah" in 1 Sam 2:2-8, and with the MAGNIFICAT in Luke 1:46-55.

Psalm 114

The liturgical tradition of JUDAISM associates this psalm with the PASSOVER. It is a short thanksgiving hymn that recounts Israel's history from the EXODUS to the crossing of the Jordan. The psalm seems incomplete, as if it were a section from a longer hymn. Clearly, it should be read with Ps 113, and also may be read with Ps 115 as well. Psalms 114 and 115 are framed by the *hallelujahs* at the end of Ps 113 and the end of Ps 115.

The psalm begins with the exodus from Egypt and the establishment of *Judah* and *Israel*. Judah and Israel in v. 2 could be interpreted to refer to the divided kingdoms, but it is better to read the two names as synonymous. The verse presupposes the fall of the Northern Kingdom and assumes that Judah is the heir of all that was "Israel."

In vv. 3-8, the poet recalls both the crossing of the sea following the exodus from Egypt and the crossing of the Jordan. The language in vv. 4, 6 is that of storm and THEOPHANY (cf. Exod 19:16-19; Pss 18; 29:6; Hab 3:6). The reactions of the natural order are in response to the theophanic appearances of Yahweh (v. 7). The sea flees away, the Jordan turns back, the mountains and hills shake and skip before the divine coming (vv. 5-6). Verse 8 recalls Yahweh's provision of water during the wilderness wanderings (Exod 17:6-7; Num 20:8-13; Deut 8:15; Pss 78:15-16; 20; 107:35). Note the move to present time in vv. 5-8. The events of Israel's salvation-history are entered, as it were, and participated in by subsequent generations of worshipers (cf. Deut 26:5-11).

Psalm 115

The SEPTUAGINT joins Pss 114 and 115 as one psalm; they may be read together even though they have different content. As noted above, Pss 113–118 form the traditional Jewish "Hallel," and when recited at PASSOVER Pss 113–114 are chanted before the meal and Pss 115–118 afterwards. Psalm 115 is probably a prayer of Jews living among foreigners in EXILE (after 587 BCE) and tempted to abandon their faith in Yahweh. Its liturgical nature is widely recognized, although one cannot be certain about the exact assignment of parts to different groups. One possibility suggests the people (vv. 1-2); Levitical priests (vv. 3-8); solo worship leader (vv. 9-11); people (vv. 12-13); Levitical priests (vv. 14-15); and people vv. (16-18).

The psalm affirms that Yahweh reigns in the heavenly realm (vv. 3, 16) and that human endeavors are possible because God allows them. Yahweh has the power to confer blessing, without which life is impossible (vv. 15-16). The Israelites, therefore, are urged to *trust* Yahweh (note the threefold use of the verb in vv. 9-11). The gentiles worship many gods represented as idols, but those idols are only human constructions and are as impotent as the gods they represent (vv. 4-8).

The gentiles taunt the "fearers of Yahweh" (v. 11) with the question *"Where is their god?"* (v. 2). The answer is: *Our God is in the heavens; he does whatever he pleases* (v. 3).

We are given an idea of the composition of the congregation in vv. 9-11: lay Israelites, priests, and "fearers of Yahweh." The last designation may possibly refer to non-Israelites who worship Yahweh, but it more probably seems to be an inclusive term for the whole group, *both small and great* (v. 13).

The worshiping group concludes the psalm with a hymn of praise (vv. 16-18). The heavens belong to Yahweh, not to a pantheon of gods and goddesses. So does the earth. The dead do not praise Yahweh (cf. Pss 6:5; 30:9; 88:4-5; 10-12; Isa 38:18), but the people of Yahweh vow to praise him without limit (vv. 17-18).

Psalm 116

In this thanksgiving psalm, which a worshiper recites in the presence of the congregation (vv. 18-19) as testimony, the speaker tells how Yahweh heard his prayers and delivered him from a situation of "death" (vv. 3-11). The condition from which the speaker has been released is not clearly defined. The speaker testifies that Yahweh saves *the simple* (v. 6), meaning those who cannot help themselves but who are open to trust and instruction.

Apparently, vv. 10-11 recall a time when the worshiper was depressed and despaired of finding any good in life (the LXX divides this psalm into two psalms: vv. 1-9 and vv. 10-19). But faith in God had brought the speaker through that difficult period, he now considers what kind of grateful response should be made to Yahweh (v. 12). *The cup of salvation* (v. 13) must refer to some ritual act, which may have had its ultimate origin in the ordeal of drinking "holy water" to determine innocence or guilt ("trial by ordeal"; cf. Num 5:11-28). In the present reference we should think instead of something like a "festival cup" that was passed among the participants at the communal meals that accompanied thanksgiving sacrifices (see Lev 7:11-18; Deut 32:38; cf. Pss 11:6; 16:5; 23:5). The lifting up of the cup to Yahweh may have been a special ritual gesture of thanksgiving, shared with others. The vows are paid and the sacrifices are offered in the presence of the assembled people in the Temple (vv. 17-19. The gratitude of the worshiper finds expression both in cultic ritual and in the joyful affirmation of personal relationship to God (v. 16). Verse 15 declares that the death of his devoted ones is *precious* in Yahweh's sight (i.e., not something that he allows to happen without concern and grief). The Hallelujah rings out at the end of the psalm.

Psalm 117

This is the shortest of all the psalms, a brief hymn that is probably not even a complete composition. It may be read either with Ps 116 or Ps 118, and also forms a pivot between Pss 115–116 and Ps 118. It is suitable as a brief opening call to worship and was doubtless so used in Israelite practice. The basic elements of a major type of the hymn form are found in it. The form can be analyzed by asking questions: Who is to be praised? Yahweh. Who is to praise Yahweh? *All . . . nations* (i.e., all peoples). Why is Yahweh to be praised? *For* is the characteristic word that introduces the answer to this question, which here focuses on *his steadfast love . . . and the faithfulness* God shows toward the people Israel. Other questions that apply to the hymn (Where is Yahweh to be praised? How is Yahweh to be praised?) are not answered in this brief poem. The psalm emphasizes the universal dominion of Yahweh and the enduring faithfulness that he demonstrates in his relationship with his people. The formula for opening a hymn may be repeated at the end, as is true here.

Psalm 118

This is the last psalm of the "Hallel" collection (Pss 113–118) used at
PASSOVER meals (see commentary on Pss 113, 115). According to other Jewish traditions it belonged to the festival of Tabernacles, and it has features that point
toward that context (*tents* in v. 15; a *festal procession*, possibly carrying *branches*
in v. 27; *this is the day* in v. 24 [cf. Ps 81:4]; also *light* in v. 27). Beyond this it
may have had other liturgical usage, including use in victory celebrations.

The setting of the psalm and the identity of the speakers in it have fostered considerable debate. The psalm is a thanksgiving composition that begins with a
communal summons to praise in vv. 1-4, is followed by an individual thanksgiving
in vv. 5-21, returns to communal speech in vv. 22-27, and then reverts to individual
speech in vv. 28-29.

At least one commentator has argued that three groups are represented by
different speakers in vv. 5-19: the falsely accused (vv. 5-7), travelers (vv. 10-14),
and the sick (vv. 17-19). It seems more probable that one speaker is assumed for
all of vv. 5-21 and that the voice is that of a king (or other leader), who, beset by
enemies, has won a victory by the power of Yahweh (vv. 10-18). In the present
Psalter this psalm has been "democratized" (perhaps it always was) and any individual can identify with the speakers and situation in the text.

If this represents the correct history of the psalm, the democratization was aided
by two factors: (1) the king embodied the life of the nation and spoke for every
Israelite and (2) there is some indication the central section (vv. 5-21) reflects the
"Song at the Sea" attributed to MOSES in Exod 15 (Hammer 1991, 491–92; cf. v.
14 with Exod 15:2 and vv. 15-16 with Exod 15:6). This may indicate that Moses,
represented by a worship leader, was thought of as the speaker addressing the
people in a new situation. Israel may again be in mortal peril, but it need not fear
because *[Yahweh's] steadfast love endures forever* (vv. 1, 29).

The psalm may have been used in actual thanksgiving rites of the Temple
(Allen 1983, 124–25). On the other hand, it may be a purely literary composition
that invites the reader-hearer to participate by imagination in a communal thanksgiving service centered around the victory of a leader.

The opening call to thanksgiving (vv. 1-4) has an antiphonal quality. Three
groups of festival participants are called upon to respond with the liturgical formula
"His steadfast love endures forever" (cf. Pss 106:1; 107:1; 136:1-26; Jer 33:11).
The three are the same as those in Ps 115:9-11. They represent the people, the
priesthood, and the "fearers of Yahweh," possibly non-Israelites who worship
Yahweh (cf. 135:19-21) but more probably "fearers of Yahweh" is a comprehensive
term for the whole community of faith.

The *I* of vv. 5-21 was probably intended to represent a king or other worship
leader. The speaker recalls the lament brought before Yahweh before he heard the
prayer and delivered the speaker from *distress* (vv. 5-9). The speaker continues in
a recital of the situation that prevailed before Yahweh helped (vv. 10-14). Fighting
in the name of Yahweh and by divine help the speaker gained victory, and recalls

the cheers and rejoicing of those *in the tents of the righteous* at the victory of Yahweh's *right hand* (v. 15; cf. Ps 110:1, 5). The speaker resumes the recital (vv. 17-18) with a testimony of continued survival, despite rigorous discipline by the LORD. The speaker is now a living testimony of the saving deeds of Yahweh.

In vv. 19-20, the poet visualizes the king leading a procession of worshipers as he approaches the gates of the Temple courts and asks for admittance (v. 19), speaking for the people. Verse 20 represents the response of a priest or gatekeeper (cf. Pss 15 and 24). The speaker affirms an intention to offer thanksgiving (v. 21); the people, or a choir, then sing of the marvelous nature of the divine deliverance (vv. 22-25).

The stone that the builders rejected (v. 22) has now been made the most important one—either an end-stone which links two walls at right angles or the top-stone which completes a structure (cf. Zech 4:7). (This verse is given Christological significance in the NT: see Mark 12:10 and par.; Acts 4:11; Eph 2:20; 1 Pet 2:7].) The reference to *the day* (v. 24) points to the festival occasion when Yahweh's work is revealed in fullness, the day of victory and thankful praise.

The prayer in v. 25 is well known because of its use in the Festival of Tabernacles and in the NT (Matt 21:9). The NT "Hosanna" is derived from the *Save us* [Heb. *hoshianna*], *we beseech you*. This call upon Yahweh for deliverance should be understood as a call for continued deliverance in the future (Hammer, 494).

In v. 26, a blessing is pronounced on the procession of worshipers as they enters the Temple. *Light* (v. 27) reflects the priestly benediction of Num 6:24-26, and possibly the ceremony of "lights" in the later Jewish celebration of Tabernacles. The Festival of Tabernacles also had a ceremony in which worshipers encircled the altar while carrying palm, myrtle, and willow branches. Such a ceremony probably is indicated here by the liturgical instruction given in v. 27b (see Lev 23:40) although the exact nature of the ritual is not clear.

A solo voice closes the psalm with a vow of praise in v. 28 and a call to the congregation in v. 29 that repeats v. 1.

Psalm 119

This enormous composition is in the form of an alphabetic acrostic (cf. Pss 9-10; 25; 34; 37; 11; 112; 145). Each of its twenty-two sections (each eight verses long) corresponds to a successive letter of the Hebrew alphabet, and each line within a section begins with the letter that marks that section. The acrostic form is useful for extended and repeated treatment of a single subject; in this case it is the TORAH.

In this psalm, the wonders of the life-giving *torah* and the glory of Yahweh—the giver of glory—is the constant focus of the speaker's attention. At least eight different *torah* words are used (*torah* is generally translated "law", but has a broader meaning, not exclusively related to the written *Torah*; see commentary on Ps 19): *law* (v. 1, etc.), *decrees* (v. 2, etc.), *precepts* (v. 4, etc.), *commandments* (v. 6, etc.), *ordinances* (v. 7, etc.), *statutes* (v. 5, etc.), *word* (v. 9, etc.), and *promise* (v. 38, etc.); if *way(s)* (v. 3, etc.) and *faithfulness* (v. 90) are counted, there are ten such synonyms. Eight or more words for *torah* are used in each stanza, and one of the ten words is used in each verse except four (vv. 122, 132, 149, 156). Each of these words has its own shade of meaning, but in this psalm they all refer to the revealed will of Yahweh in *torah*.

The attitude of the speaker towards the *torah* is one of grateful praise. It is a source of *wondrous things* (v. 18), something in which those who fear Yahweh may *delight* continually (e.g., vv. 16, 77, 174). The *torah is sweeter than honey* (v. 103) and loved *more than gold* (v. 127). Unchanging in its dependability (v. 142), it is a source of *light* (v. 105) and those who love it have a great *shalom* (*peace*, v. 165). Yahweh is the source of the *torah* (note the repeated *your law*, etc.; v. 72 refers to *the law of your mouth*).

Psalm 119 manifests a mixture of literary types. In addition to the hymnic and wisdom elements, some sections have a distinctly lament character (vv. 81-88; 105-128; 145-176). The speaker seems to reflect a context in which there is considerable affliction and persecution, while clinging to *torah* in defiance and hope (v. 23). The speaker is confident that Yahweh is near and that the divine commandments are reliable (v. 151). The briefness of this commentary and the repetitive length of the psalm exclude any detailed treatment. Fortunately, the translations are clear and self-explanatory in most cases. Attention should be given especially to vv. 10-11, 17, 19, 34-40, 73, 75-77, 89-96, 97, 103, 105, 125, 127, 135, 160, 165, 171-172.

The speaker in Ps 119 is not specifically identified, but the language of the prayers and petitions points toward a deeply pious person of faith and commitment, who is designated repeatedly as a *servant* of God (*your servant*, vv. 17, 23, 38, 49, 65, 76, 84, 123, 124, 125, 135, 140, 176) and as *a companion of all who fear you* (i.e., God; v. 63). An extensive argument has been advanced to identify the speaker as a king, or alternatively that the content was written from the perspective of a king, perhaps King JEHOIACHIM of Judah during the EXILE (Soll 1991). However, even if this is the case, faithful Israelites could identify with the language and experience of a king (as with DAVID) so that the king's prayer could become that of any devoted Israelite. From another perspective, while the psalm lacks explicit language to identify the speaker as a sage or teacher, nevertheless the closest exemplar may well be Ben Sira (Sirach) in the Book of Ecclesiasticus, who was also devoted to *torah* (see, e.g., Sir 1:26; 2:15-18; 6:37; 15:1-8; 24:23-29). The psalm is an awesome expression of comprehensive faith and devotion.

Psalm 120

This psalm is often interpreted as a lament, a view adopted by the RSV and NRSV. It may be better to treat it as an individual thanksgiving psalm, translating v. 1: "In my distress I cried to the LORD, and he answered me" (cf. REB, NAB, and esp. NJB; see Kraus 1989). Verse 2 would then recall the petition the speaker prayed before the prayer was answered. This view is the more natural one (cf. Ps 30:8-10).

The answer of the suppliant's prayer is not stated explicitly, but the context of the *Songs of Ascents* (see below) gives an implicit answer in the ability of the suppliant to go on pilgrimage and leave behind the condition described in vv. 5-7.

Verses 3-4 are not entirely clear, but it seems best to understand them as a curse directed toward enemies who had attacked the speaker with *lying lips* and a *deceitful tongue* (v. 2). The formula of oath or curse lies behind the language of v. 3: "May God do so to you, and more also, if . . . " (see 1 Sam 3:17; 14:44; 20:13). The punishment that the persecuted one thought appropriate for the enemies is found in v. 4. The wood of *the broom tree* was noted for its intense and long-lasting heat when burned. Since the tongue is compared with an arrow (cf. Pss 7:13-14; 11:2; 57:4; 64:3), it is likely the poet had in mind the destruction of the enemies with their own weapons (i.e., that they receive what they proposed to give to others).

Verses 5-7 indicate that the speaker lives (or better, did live) among a hostile and contentious people, who make peaceful desires difficult to sustain. The geographical references in v. 5 are probably figurative and perhaps descriptive of the hostile character of the people among whom the suppliant lived. The locations of the nomadic tribes of *Meshech* and *Kedar* are separated by too much distance for anyone to live among both groups at the same time (see Gen 10:2; Ezek 27:13; 32:26-27; 38:3; 39:1). Meshech is located to the north of Palestine, perhaps in the area of the Black Sea. Genesis 25:13, Isa 42:11, etc. locate the Bedouin tribe of Kedar in the desert south of Damascus and east of Israel.

This is the first of a series of psalms known as the Songs of Ascents or Pilgrim Songs (120–134). These psalms have traditionally been understood as a collection of psalms sung by pilgrims on their way to festivals in Jerusalem. Thus Ps 120 has been interpreted as the thanksgiving of an Israelite living in a foreign land, possibly in exile, who is now on pilgrimage to Zion. The misery of exile is left behind as the pilgrim moves toward Zion (for further comment on the Songs of Ascent, see Ps 134).

Psalm 121

The change of speaker in v. 3 of this short psalm is an interesting point in its interpretation. There is some sort of dialogue in the psalm, but the identity of the speakers is not clear. Perhaps the speaker is communing with himself on a journey toward Jerusalem and the hills of Zion in a manner similar to the monologues in Ps 42–43. However, it may be best to postulate two speakers, possibly a priest (vv. 3-8) and a pilgrim (vv. 1-2)—or possibly two pilgrims. If this is the case, the setting may belong to the departure of a pilgrim from a home community for a pilgrimage to Zion, or a departure from Jerusalem for home at the end of a festival. It has been suggested that the dialogue is between a father and his son, which is quite possible and cannot be entirely ruled out.

The hills of v. 1 can refer either to the hills of Jerusalem or hills on the pilgrim's journey. Yahweh is the source of help and strength in any case. The KJV prejudices the case for the hills or mountains as the source of help by following the LXX and translating: "I will lift up mine eyes unto the hills, from whence cometh my help." However, it is better to read as (1) "I lift up my eyes . . . [to see] where my help is to come from" (Allen 1983, 150) which leaves the matter open—my help may come from the mountains of heaven where Yahweh dwells (Ps 123:1) or from his dwelling on Zion (cf. Ps 20:2-3); or (2) "I lift up my eyes . . . from where will my help come?" (author trans.)—in this case the hills are hostile and full of danger, and the question is answered by v. 2. However we read, the source of help is not the hills, but Yahweh.

Verses 3-8 responds to the pilgrims' affirmation of faith in v. 2. The message of vv. 3-8 can be summarized around these statements: (1) the creator is able to protect and is available for the pilgrim. (2) Yahweh is the nonslumbering keeper of Israel. Unlike the gods found in a HIGH PLACE (see 1 Kgs 18:27), Yahweh is never absent or sleeping when his people are in trouble. The pilgrim can entrust the keeping of his *going out and . . . coming in* (v. 8) to him.

For discussion of divine sleeping, see commentary on Ps 44. In the case of v. 4 the converse of the sovereign sleep of deity is presupposed, that is, in some circumstances the ability to conquer sleep (considered to be a form of death) was a mark of divine power. In the Gilgamesh Epic from Mesopotamia, Gilgamesh is unable to attain immortality by remaining awake for six days and seven nights, a confirmation of his mortal and human status.

Psalm 122

This "Song of Zion" (see Pss 46–48, 76, 84, 87, 137) is written for a pilgrim who, having come to Jerusalem for a festival (probably Tabernacles), has arrived in the city, or is ready to depart from it for home. Arrival rather than departure seems to be the better choice. Verses 1-2 recall the pleasure of an invitation to go to Zion for a festival. *Jerusalem* is praised in vv. 3-5 as the pilgrimage city of the tribes who go up to worship as decreed (vv. 3-4; cf. Exod 23:17; Deut 16:16). It is the city of *judgment* and the place where the throne of the Davidic king is situated (v. 5). Verses 6-9 is a prayer for the city of Jerusalem. A priest or other leader may speak in vv. 6-7; the festival goer responds in vv. 8-9.

Psalm 123

This is a lament, possibly offered by an individual, a king, or worship leader, but more probably by a pilgrim who is on the way to Jerusalem and festival time, and who speaks for the community. The situation in vv. 3-4 fits the postexilic period when Israelites were under the pressure of living in hostile environments, although such evidence can never be definite. The people have suffered for a long time from the contempt and scorn of those who oppress them. The prayer is directed to the heavenly King (vv. 1-2), whose servants intently watch his hand for a gesture of favor. The individual in v. 1 and the people in v. 2 look up to Yahweh in complete dependence.

Psalm 124

This is a short, but forceful, communal thanksgiving of a group of people for deliverance from a situation that had threatened their life. The poet may have had some particular historical event in mind, or the psalm may reflect Yahweh's manifold acts of deliverance in the salvation-history of Israel.

The translation of the psalm is reasonably clear and requires little comment. It is sufficient here to call attention to the fact that the one who gives *help* (v. 8) is the same as in Ps 121:2: the maker of *heaven and earth*.

The graphic descriptive language of the psalm used to describe the situation from which the group has been delivered is characteristic of the laments and presents the full force of the distress. The group commends their testimony to all Israel: *let Israel now say* (v. 1). Perhaps we should think of a group of pilgrims on their way to Jerusalem who consider their experience representative of that of the nation (cf. Ps 107).

Psalm 125

This is a communal psalm of confidence that affirms the nation's trust in Yahweh and prays for his continued favor. Verse 3 indicates that Israel is under the domination of a foreign power, or possibly of apostate Israelites (v. 5; cf. Isa 56:9–57:13). The context seems to be that of the postexilic period when the circles of *the righteous* (v. 3) were under the pressure of a pagan environment and the threat of alien culture, and when many defected. The righteous ones are being assured that they will inherit the land even though they are temporarily dispossessed (cf. Isa 57:13; 60:21; 65:9). They are called upon to trust that Yahweh controls the future and to reject the ways of those who yield to the pressures of their cultural environment.

The security of those who trust in Yahweh is declared to be like that of Mount Zion, immutably chosen and protected by the divine presence (vv. 1-2; cf. Ps 34:7; Zech 2:5). The actual geographical situation of Jerusalem is reflected in v. 2, since the city is lower than the surrounding hills (cf. Ps 48:1-2). The prayer in vv. 4-5 contains a warning to those who apostatize from the ways of goodness and uprightness, ways that mark those who are loyal to Yahweh.

Psalm 126

It seems best to interpret this psalm in relation to Ps 85 (see commentary there). The tense of the verbs is a problem. Verses 1-3 can be interpreted as referring to the future, looking forward to the completed fulfillment of the prayer in v. 4, but it is better to treat them as looking back to a wonderful restoration of the fortunes of Zion. It seems probable that the great changing event that is recalled is the restoration of Israel after the surrender of Babylon to CYRUS in 539 BCE. An objection may be raised with regard to v. 4. If the fortunes of Zion have already been restored, why does the congregation continue to pray that they will be restored? The answer is found in the condition that prevailed after the first stages of the restoration. A great event had occurred (Babylon had fallen, CYRUS had come to power, and some Israelites had returned), but the full measure of the prophetic promises was lacking. The prayer in v. 4 looks forward to the full manifestation of the glory of Yahweh (cf. Isa 59:9-15).

The *watercourses in the Negeb* of v. 4 recalls the fullness and transformed nature of the wadis when the usually dry NEGEB receives rain. They literally become streams of life in an arid semidesert. Verse 5 may be read as a continuation of the prayer, as in the NRSV, but it is better to read it with v. 6 as positive statements of comfort and assurance in response to the prayer in v. 4. The sowing with tears (v. 5) could allude to customs of weeping for the dead fertility god in Canaanite religion in order to insure the germination of the seed and the growth of corps. The origin of this custom is found in belief that the god of fertility died in the dry season when no vegetation was growing, and that he must be brought back to life through rituals that included weeping because of his death. But here it is most likely a proverbial saying that incorporates a maxim of life: the disappointed sorrow of the people will be changed to joy (cf. Ps 30:5; Job 16:20). Verse 6 expands on the proverb in v. 5.

Psalm 127

The theme that ties the separate parts of this psalm together is that of the dependence of every human endeavor on the purpose and favor of God. The psalm has the characteristics of the wisdom sayings (such as those found in the Book of Proverbs) and this may account, in part at least, for the ascription of it to SOLOMON. Commentators typically read the psalm as composed of two parts (vv. 1-2 and vv. 3-5) that are different and only loosely related. Actually, however, the psalm deals with four activities: house building, protection of a town, daily work, and the blessing of offspring.

House in v. 1 has the double connotation of a dwelling place and of a household or family. The latter relates well to vv. 3-5, and frames the activity of dwellers in a town in vv. 1b-2. "The house that Yahweh builds includes the sons who are the subject of vv. 3-5" (Kselman and Barré 1990, 548).

The futility of godless toil is expounded in vv. 1-2. No amount of rising early and going to bed late and working in *anxious toil* (v. 2) will compensate for the absence of the protection of God (*anxious toil* is better read as "hard work"). The effort to build is *in vain* unless God's blessing rests upon it. The *for he gives sleep to his beloved* of v. 2 has produced different interpretations. Some (e.g., Kraus 1989, 452) suppose that an "in" or "during" should be understood, with the resulting idea that while others may wear themselves out in hard and incessant work, Yahweh "provides for his beloved *during* sleep" (NRSV mg.). However, the blessing of sleep itself is not insignificant, particularly for toilers who know little except exhaustion, and so it is probably better to retain "he gives sleep" and read the "beloved" as plural "his loved ones." The laborer, the watcher, the toiler of long hours—they are all dependent on the favor of Yahweh.

The domestic blessings of the family is the subject of vv. 3-5. The land is not the only *heritage* of Yahweh. Children are a heritage too. They are like the arrows of a warrior, and offer security *in the gate* (v. 5). The gate was the place where legal hearings were held and local administrative matters were decided. One's reputation and so one's situation depended to a large degree on one's status in the gate (cf. Job 29:7-10). Children as the gift of Yahweh secured the existence of the family as well as its prestige.

Psalm 128

Like Ps 127, this is a wisdom psalm in the form of a blessing on the Yahweh-fearer. It probably developed out of the priestly benediction pronounced during the worship of a festival (see. vv. 5-6). The person who fears Yahweh will be one who enjoys *the fruit of [personal] labor* (i.e., endeavors will not result in loss or frustration [v. 2]). This is a blessing of the first-rank importance for happy living. Such a person will know the domestic happiness of a wife who *like a fruitful vine* produces children, who in turn sit about the table *like olive shoots* (v. 3).

The benediction in vv. 5-6 is only loosely attached to vv. 1-4 by the association of the idea of the blessing of children in v. 6. Zion is the earthly source of Yahweh's blessing. Ps 128 is closely related to Ps 127 (note *happy* in 127:5 and v. 1, and the blessing of children in both psalms). The formal blessing in vv. 5-6 is appropriate for a pilgrim at the festivals in Jerusalem, with families actually in attendance at times (see Deut 14:26 and 1 Sam 1).

Psalm 129

This psalm is difficult to classify. The best explanation may be that it is an adaptation of an earlier individual lament of one who had suffered for a prolonged time (vv. 1a, 2-4) and who had asked for judgment (vv. 6-8) on those who attacked "and scored my back with scourges " (v. 3 REB). The revision of the psalm to fit a context like that of the Songs of Ascent (Pss 120–134) is seen in the addition of *let Israel now say* (v. 1) and the identity of the enemies as those *who hate Zion* (v. 5), plus a closing greeting at the end of v. 8. Now the individual experience has been transferred to the whole nation—personal experience has merged with that of Israel.

Like the long furrows left by plowman on the land, the back of Israel bears the indelible stripes of those whose lashes have left their marks. But the congregation also recalls that Yahweh has been faithful and has cut loose the cords by which wicked oppressors bound them. In this freedom the pilgrim goes to Jerusalem to worship. A prayer for the destruction of the enemies of Zion is found in vv. 5-8—petitions that they may be shamed, repulsed (v. 5), and become like the grass that grows accidentally on housetops and withers quickly from lack of rootage and water (vv. 6-7). Such vegetation will never produce a harvest worthy of the blessing of passersby (v. 8). The last line of v. 8 may be a closing blessing by the priests on the congregation.

Psalm 130

This psalm is usually read as a lament of an individual in which a suppliant cries out to Yahweh for deliverance from a present predicament. This may very well be the case, and Ps 130 is one of the traditional seven penitential psalms in Christian tradition (Pss 6, 32, 38, 51, 102, 130, and 143). However, it is quite possible to read this psalm as a thanksgiving, an especially appropriate reading in the context of the festival participation of speakers in the Songs of Ascent (Pss

120–134). In this case read the verbs in vv. 1 and 5 (v. 6 has no verb in Hebrew and takes its tense from v. 5) in past tense: "Out of the depths I cried to you, O LORD! . . . I waited for the LORD . . . and in his word I hoped. My soul waited for the LORD." If this is correct, the psalm recalls blessings already received. The prayer that the worshiper prayed before deliverance is in vv. 2-4. The exhortation to Israel (the congregation) in v. 7 fits poorly in a lament, but it is appropriate for a thanksgiving. Read as thanksgiving, the psalm becomes a testimony of one delivered from *the depths* (v. 1), although the deliverance is not explicitly stated.

However, the traditional reading of this psalm as a penitential lament has a long and moving history among people of faith (e.g., McCann 1993b, 87). The message of the psalm is not significantly changed if it is read as lament, which vv. 2-4 are in any case. If the traditional reading is retained, vv. 5-6 become statements of confidence in the present, expressing assurance that waiting in hope and anticipation for divine action will not be disappointed.

The depths (v. 1) is a metaphor for mental and physical anguish and disaster, reflecting the waters of the cosmic deep (cf. Ps 69:2; 14-15; Isa 51:10; Ezek 27:34), but it is a metaphor suitable for any great distress, such as that in Ps 69 or of an exile living amid contempt and scorn as in Ps 123. From *the depths* the suppliant cried out to Yahweh. The expected answer to the rhetorical question in v. 3 is "No one"; no one has any standing before God on the basis of a sinless life. A relationship may exist, but it is based on God's forgiveness (v. 4). The *that you may be revered* indicates the reverence and willingness to obey that results from the experience of God's forgiveness. Such fear is the fruit of love; it is the "right fear" of John Bunyan's *The Pilgrim's Progress* that reminds us that forgiveness opens up new involvement and obligations in terms of God's will and removes our ability to calculate the cost of our own involvement.

Such a prayer leads to the kind of relinquishment and expectant waiting that is expressed in vv. 5-6. The worshiper's whole being was (or is) "toward God" (*for the LORD*, v. 6a). Like a watchman who expectantly anticipates the dawn, the worshiper waits for the word of Yahweh. We are not told that a word is received and there is a measure of unresolved tension in the psalm. As in Ps 120, we may have an implicit deliverance manifest in the context of a pilgrim able to go to Zion for festivals. In any case, the worshiper is able to exhort the congregation in vv. 7-8 to join in the "hope directed toward the LORD." It is Yahweh who will redeem Israel from iniquity (v. 8). The hope of the speaker is pointed toward a fellowship of the forgiven, for *with the LORD there is steadfast love, and . . . great power to redeem* (v. 7).

Psalm 131

This brief psalm of trust (cf. Pss 16, 23, 62) is one of the finest expressions of humble faith in the Bible. The words require little comment, but meditation upon them may impart something of the full confidence and honest self-appraisal before God that makes for healthy and abundant living. The psalm speaks of a maturity and balance that permits the relinquishment of proud ambitions for the satisfaction of communion with God. Further, the psalm avers that "submissive reliance leaves one free of anxiety," the anxiety that results from the futile attempts to be self-sufficient or of trying to be equal with God (Brueggemann 1984, 49). Verse 3 (a liturgical addition) closes the psalm and binds it to Ps 130 (note *O Israel, hope in the LORD!* in 130:7). Verses 1-2 may have been written by (or for) a woman (cf. NRSV translation; Holladay 1993, 40).

Psalm 132

This is a royal psalm (see Pss 2, 20, 21, 72, 89, 110) insofar as it has to do with Israelite kingship. It commemorates David's bringing the ARK of the covenant to Jerusalem, the Davidic covenant, and Yahweh's choice of Zion as his *resting place forever* (v. 14). There are liturgical features in the psalm, and it may have been designed originally for use in connection with the cultic re-enactment of the bringing of the ark to Jerusalem (see 2 Sam 6) and the founding of the Davidic dynasty (cf. 2 Sam 7). A reenactment probably took place during the autumnal festival (see 1 Kgs 8:2). Note the use of some verses from this psalm in 2 Chr 6:41-42, although in slightly altered form.

The first part of the psalm (vv. 1-10) is a prayer beseeching Yahweh to remember DAVID and his zeal for finding a dwelling place for Yahweh (cf. 1 Kgs 8:13; 2 Sam 7:1-3). The finding of the ark by David and his entourage is recalled in v. 6, which names the places where they went to look for the ark. *Ephrathah* may refer to BETHLEHEM, the hometown of David, or to SHILOH in EPHRAIM, where the ark was once kept. *The fields of Jaar* is a poetic designation of KIRIATH-JEARIM where the ark had been kept until David moved it. Having discovered the ark, the traditional processional summons is given in v. 7 (cf. 122:1). The *footstool* (v. 7) can be either the Temple or the ark, but probably the ark. The procession with the ark is begun with vv. 8-10. *Rise up, O LORD* is the ancient cry pronounced wherever the ark was moved (see Num 10:35; cf. Pss 7:6; 9:19; 10:12; 17:13). Verse 10 indicates this psalm was used as a prayer for a Davidic king, and not by David himself.

The second part of the psalm (vv. 11-19) sets forth the Davidic COVENANT and Yahweh's choice of Zion. The oath of Yahweh regarding the continuation of his dynasty is recalled (see 2 Sam 7; 23:5; Ps 89). Verse 12 qualifies the commitment of Yahweh by making the obedience of David's sons prerequisite for the promise in v. 11. To what do *my covenant and my decrees* in v. 12 refer? They are probably references to the SINAI covenant and the covenant-law of the Yahweh-Israel relationship. It is possible, of course, that they refer to the covenant of Yahweh with David and the stipulations regarding kingship (see Ps 89:3-4; 28; 1 Sam 10:25). (For *my decrees* see the commentary on Ps 2, although it is doubtful the term in 132:12 is the same as the *decree* in 2:7; a relationship to 1 Sam 10:25 is much more likely.)

Yahweh's choice of Zion and his promises to it is the subject of vv. 13-16. The last two verses (vv. 17-18) emphasize that Zion is also the place of the Davidic dynasty, where Yahweh will cause *a horn* to grow and *a lamp* to burn for the Davidic king. The *horn* is a symbol of power and victory and the *lamp* is a symbol of the king's presence before God (note Exod 27:20-21; 1 Kgs 11:36; 2 Sam 21:17).

Verse 18 contrasts the *disgrace* that clothes the kings' enemies with his splendid, gleaming crown.

Psalm 132 may be a psalm from preexilic times, possibly quite early in the monarchy but probably no earlier than the period of JOSIAH (Allen 1983, 208–09). One suspects v. 12 is a later addition (after the failure of the monarchy) to give a conditional nature to the Davidic covenant. The conditional promises to the Davidic dynasty, however, may have been understood as such from the beginning of the monarchy, even when the language was explicitly unconditional (cf. Isa 7:1-9; 28:14-22; 1 Kgs 2:3-4; 9:4-5; for Zion, 1 Kgs 6:11-13). In any case, Ps 132 in its present context was almost certainly read differently than in preexilic Israel. Verse 12 now serves to give a reason for the fall of the monarchy and vv. 17-18 are directed toward a future, messianic hope; the *horn to sprout up for David* will emerge from a now-dead dynasty.

The position of this psalm in the Songs of Ascent is probably due to its emphasis on Zion; David's role is secondary except in terms of messianic promise (Allen 1983, 211; cf. Acts 2:30; 7:46). The monarchy was gone, but pilgrims still made their way to Zion for the festivals and the renewal of their faith. The ark itself does not seem to have been physically present in the Temple after 515 BCE (see Jer 3:16), but the traditions regarding it were doubtless still important.

Psalm 133

The RSV and NRSV follow some text traditions and omit the "to David" (or "Davidic") from the title of this psalm. If the "Davidic" is retained, the psalm is linked to Ps 131 by title. Also note that both psalms are short, both end with the same expression (*forevermore*), and both utilize the language of domestic tranquility; in addition Pss 131 and 133 frame Ps 132.

The opening verse of Ps 133 praises the harmony and well-being of an extended family (cf. Deut 25:5), but in its present context it probably refers to the celebration of the festivals at Zion (see the *for there* in v. 3b). The celebrants were all *kindred* during the times they spent together on Mount Zion, a fellowship described as *good and pleasant* (v. 1). The crowds in the holy city epitomized the nation, bound together as it were not only by race but by covenant relationship with God (Allen 1983, 215).

Two word pictures describe the goodness of the unity experienced at Zion. The first is that of the fragrant oil used in the consecration of AARON as high priest (cf. Exod 29:7; 21; Lev 8:12), which was poured on his head and ran down over the collar of his robes. The oil signified peace, health, joy, and the grace of God (Pss 23:5; 45:7-8; Exod 30:22-33).

The second word picture is that of the *dew of Hermon* (v. 3) that falls on the "mountains of Zion" (Mount Zion). The *dew of Hermon* is a heavy dew like that which falls on Mount Hermon, a mountain in the north of Palestine, more than 9,000 feet high, and known as an abundant source of water (one of its modern names means "the snow mountain"; cf. Ps 42:6-7). In the dry climate of Palestine, a heavy dew was both a pleasant experience in the early morning of a hot day and important for growing dry-season crops. "Dew" was proverbial for refreshment and life (Gen 27:28; Deut 33:28; Hos 14:5; Mic 5:7; Isa 26:19; Zech 8:12; Job 29:19; cf. Ps 110:3).

Mount Zion is the place of divine blessing, the source of life *forevermore* (v. 3). *Hermon* is a larger mountain than Zion and renowned for being the dwelling place of gods and the location of ritual centers (cf. Josh 11:17; 1 Chr 5:23), but Zion is the source of everlasting life—a greater blessing than any offered by Mount Hermon. The emphasis on Zion in this psalm ties it closely with Ps 132:13-16 and focuses attention on the experience of the divine presence attached to that place. Allen (1983, 215) notes that this emphasis prepares the way for the conception of a heavenly counterpart in NT traditions (Heb 12:22-24; 13:14-16; cf. Gal 4:26; Rev 14:1)."

Psalm 134

This very short hymn and priestly blessing closes the series of psalms known as the Songs of Ascent. A night ceremony was an important part of the festival of Tabernacles in later times, and very probably earlier as well (cf. Isa 30:29). A night ceremony marking the end of the festival is probably assumed by this psalm. The picture is that of a festival congregation (*servants of the LORD* [v. 1] is not restricted to the priests and the Levites; see Pss 34:22; 79:2; 86:1-4, 16; etc.) standing before Yahweh in the Temple (cf. Deut 10:8; 18:7; 1 Chr 23:30; 2 Chr 29:11). Those who stand before Yahweh are especially the priests, but ordinary people are referred to in Deut 19:17; Jer 7:10; Ps 135:2, 14. They are exhorted by the priests to praise Yahweh and to lift up their hands toward the holy place; probably the area of the Temple where the ark was kept (cf. Ps 28:2).

Verse 3 is the blessing of the priests pronounced at the end of the ceremony introduced by vv. 1-2. The blessing is appropriate for pilgrim celebrants preparing to leave for home. One suspects this psalm is only part of a liturgy for a major service of farewell.

"Songs of Ascent" (Pss 120–134). One salient feature of the Songs of Ascent is their concentration on Zion (explicitly in Pss 125, 126, 128, 129, 132–134; Ps 122 mentions Jerusalem). Zion remained, indeed probably became more so, the center of the religious world for Israelites in the postexilic period. Even living far from Jerusalem as permanent exiles, Israelites always longed for Zion; in far off Babylonia they sang

If I forget you, O Jerusalem,
   let my right hand wither!
Let my tongue cling to the roof of my mouth,
   if I do not remember you,
   if I do not set Jerusalem above my highest joy. (Ps 137:5-6)

From Pss 120–134 we can gain something of the joys and hopes of devoted Israelites whenever they were able to go to Zion at festival time. Memories and traditions nurtured their faith wherever they lived. Zion was the home for which they longed, hoped, and prayed.

Psalm 135

This is a HALLELUJAH hymn with a rather standard, though expanded, literary form: summons to praise God (vv. 1-3); grounds for the praise (vv. 4-5); explication of the action and greatness of Yahweh (vv. 4-5) set forth in a recital of divine deeds in creation and history (vv. 6-12); a hymnic element that resumes vv. 1-3 (vv. 13-14); a treatment of idols (almost the same as Ps 115:3-8) that magnifies the power of Yahweh by contrast (vv. 15-18); repeated summons to praise God and a closing Hallelujah, verses (19-20) that with vv. 1-3 form a frame for the psalm.

This psalm seems very formulaic and dependent on traditional elements in its composition. The recitation of history in vv. 8-12 is selective, focusing on three deeds: the PLAGUES on Egypt (vv. 8-9), victory over kings and foreign nations (vv. 10-11), and the gift of a LAND for Israel (v. 12). Other great deeds are missing: the deliverance from the Egyptians at the sea, Sinai (Horeb) and the events there, and the wanderings in the wilderness. The purpose of the psalm is not that of a complete recital of God's saving history, but the setting forth of his power vis-à-vis other gods and their idols. The implied community in this psalm (almost certainly actual Israelite communities of the postexilic era) is tempted to doubt the power of Yahweh and turn to other divine sources of power. The psalm also sets forth a classic example of the triangular relationship between Yahweh, Israel, and the land (Allen 1983, 228). The *servants of the LORD* (v. 1; see Ps 134:1) might be prone to doubt the divine intention while living under the domination of world powers who "know not Yahweh." Verse 14 is the answer of Ps 135.

Psalm 136

The twenty-six occurrences of the refrain *for his steadfast love endures forever* is the most distinctive feature of this psalm. It is a communal thanksgiving (beginning and ending with the verb *hodu*, "give thanks") in which Yahweh is praised for his deeds in creation and in Israel's salvation-history. The refrain was an intended congregational response to each verse of the psalm prayer. After the opening summons to thanksgiving (vv. 1-3), the main part of the psalm recalls Yahweh's acts of creation (vv. 4-9); the EXODUS from Egypt (vv. 10-15); Yahweh's providential care of the Israelites in the wilderness (vv. 16-20); and the gift of the LAND as Israel's heritage (vv. 21-22). In vv. 23-25, Yahweh is praised as the great deliverer and sustainer, who remembered and rescued, and who is the one continuously providing nourishment for all creatures (Pss 104:27-30; 145:15; 147:9).

The cultic context of the psalm seems likely to have been the autumnal Feast of Tabernacles, as is the case of Ps 135, but there are those who advocate the PASSOVER, which may have been true in postexilic Israel. The exact festival cannot be determined. Note the psalm begins (vv. 1-9) with the universal work of God and shifts to Israel (vv. 10-24; Israel is mentioned specifically in vv. 11, 14, and 22; *his people* in v. 16), then returns to the universal scope of God's work (vv. 25-26). In

vv. 23-24, the community identifies with the history given in third person and past tense in vv. 11-22: *who remembered us in our low estate* (v. 23). The enduring love of Yahweh is manifest in all his works in creation and in history.

In Jewish tradition, Ps 136 is often known as "The Great Hallel" (see Ps 113 for the "Hallel" or "The Egyptian Hallel"). Some modern interpreters (see Allen 1983, 219) treat Pss 135–136 as a supplement to the Songs of Ascent (Pss 120–134). Psalm 135, as well as Ps 136, is a SABBATH psalm (except for the sabbath before New Year) in Jewish usage, and Ps 136 was attached to "The Egyptian Hallel" (Pss 113–118) on the eighth day of PASSOVER.

Psalm 137

This is an unusual psalm in the sense of its specificity of location: *By the rivers of Babylon* (v. 1). In vv. 1-4, the psalm looks back to the fall of Jerusalem in 587 BCE and recalls the EXILE of Israelites to Babylonia. Jerusalem is addressed in the present in vv. 5-6. The speaker may well be one who has survived the burden of the years in Babylon, and who has returned to Jerusalem where conditions are still bad and arouse the memories expressed in the psalm. The poem expresses the unforgettable devotion of the exiles to Jerusalem and recalls their great reluctance to sing the Temple songs in a pagan land. It was not considered proper to sing the *songs of Zion* (v. 3) in a foreign and unholy context (cf. Amos 7:17; Ezek 4:13).

The Israelites were captives who wept for Zion "by the waters of Babylon." The "waters" or "streams" refer to the irrigation canals that were common in Mesopotamia (cf. Ezek 1:1; 3:15). The psalm itself looks back on the experiences of the exiles, although Babylon seems still to be in existence (v. 8); the description could, however, refer to the situation after 539 BCE when Babylon surrendered to CYRUS without being destroyed. In any case, the psalm probably emerged from the context of ceremonies of lamentation and fasting that were conducted in Palestine during and after the exile (see Jer 41:5; Zech 7:1-7). It also is possible the psalm recalls similar ceremonies of lamentation in Babylon on the part of the exiles (see 1 Kgs 8:46-53).

Verse 3 recalls the tormenting request of their Babylonian captors. *The songs of Zion* probably refer to those psalms that celebrate Yahweh's choice of Zion and his promise concerning the city's future (e.g., Pss 46, 76, 84, 87), promises that seemed irreparably broken to the exiles. They rejected the taunting request of their captors (v. 4), but at the same time they could never forget Jerusalem, still their *highest joy* (vv. 5-6).

Two imprecations are found in vv. 7-9. The day of Jerusalem's destruction is recalled along with the unrestrained hatred and glee with which *the Edomites* encouraged the devastation by the Babylonians (cf. Obad 11-15; Ezek 25:12-14; 35:1-15). The violence of the imprecation against Babylon is severe (cf. Ps 79:10-13; Lam 1:20-22; 3:64-66). Isaiah 13:16 uses similar language for judgment of the Babylonians, and indicates that Babylon had become archetypical of a world power and that the violent language of judgment had become somewhat conventional (see also Jer 50-51).

Psalm 137 represents one pole of the Israelite attitude toward the exile. Jeremiah and Ezekiel express considerably different attitudes. It was in Babylonia, at possibly the same place alluded to in Ps 137:1, that Ezekiel encountered the glory of Yahweh and received his commission to prophecy (see Ezek 1:3-48; 3:22-27). Psalm 137 expresses the grief of exiles, whose "bittersweet memories" of Zion are a daily torment (Allen 1983, 241–42). Theirs is the passion of a people who have been overwhelmed by the injustice of events beyond their control. They live by remembering, which can be traumatic but also healing. Forgetting is a way of death; God's remembering is essential (v. 7).

Psalm 138

This individual thanksgiving psalm has a Davidic title and is the first of eight Davidic psalms (138–145), a collection that seems to be the actual ending of book five, since Pss 146–150 form a separate collection. The LXX of Ps 138 adds "of Haggai and Zechariah" to the title, indicating that an earlier psalm was edited (or reread) for use in the postexilic period. The speaker appears to be either some distance away from the Temple (v. 2; see Dan. 6:10), or in the actual Temple courts (cf. Ps 5:7).

The psalm expresses the praise of a person who has been delivered from great distress (v. 3), and is now confident of ongoing life and protection even *in the midst of trouble* (v. 7).

One point of interpretation concerns the clause *before the gods I sing your praise* (v. 1). The psalmist seems to be thinking of the gods of pagan peoples and rulers, which the worshiper does not hesitate to defy by singing Yahweh's praise. The expression also can be read as a reference to the heavenly assembly of divine beings around the throne of Yahweh (see Ps 82). The LXX reads as "before the angels" which supports the second understanding (cf. 1 Cor 4:9; 11:10; Eph 3:10; Rev 3:5; 14:10). A third reading of the phrase understands the term *elohim* in the sense of "strong (god-like) persons" (cf. the Syriac translation "kings" and the Aramaic Targum "judges"). It seems best to understand *the gods* as in either the first or second sense, probably the first, rather than the third (see v. 4). In the postexilic context of the psalm, at least in its present position in the Psalter, the first interpretation fits well. Yahweh alone has power, despite the claims of worldly powers—an important point for a devout person far from the Temple in Jerusalem.

There is a change in the thought pattern in vv. 4-6 from individual worship to a future, universal worship of Yahweh (cf. 22:27-31). Then *the kings of the earth* will praise Yahweh, who is the Lord of the whole world and of all history.

The singer's own experience is cited (vv. 7-8) as an example of Yahweh's regard for the lowly. The one to whom all the kings of the earth should pay homage has saved the speaker. The confidence in vv. 7-8 is similar to that in Ps 23. The colon at the end of v. 8 (*Do not forsake the work of your hands*) is a brief closing prayer for Israel and the divine purposes for Yahweh's people.

Psalm 139

This psalm is well known in the Christian tradition where it has been quoted especially by theologians developing the concepts of the omnipresence and omniscience of God. The literary form of the psalm is somewhat difficult to determine, but it seems best to consider it a lament in the form of a prayer of deliverance from enemies. The situation of the worshiper is revealed in vv. 19-24, where the suppliant speaks of *wicked* and *bloodthirsty* enemies of God. The psalm assumes the suppliant is pleading a case before Yahweh, having been falsely accused by theses enemies, and is praying for vindication by Yahweh on the basis of divine knowledge of the speaker's personal life. The speaker maintains that the creator knows him completely, and that there are no grounds for identity with the enemies (v. 22, "I hate them without stopping / they are my enemies" [author trans.]).

Verses 1-18 have much the same force as the protestations of innocence found in some laments (see Pss 7:3-5; 8-11; 17:3-5; 26:1-3; 44:20-22; Jer 12:3; Job 31). This psalm is the prayer of a person who bases a case on the omniscience and omnipresence of God in relation to the true and faithful quality of personal inner life.

The suppliant confesses in vv. 1-6 that God has omniscient knowledge of his life; no part of it is hidden from the divine scrutiny (vv. 2-4). Such knowledge lies beyond human capacity (v. 6). The attitude of the suppliant is reciting these verses in different from that of JOB (Job 7:11-21). Job complains that he is receiving too much attention from God and asks for a respite, but the suppliant in this psalm finds confidence in the affirmation that God has such complete and pervasive personal knowledge of his life (cf. 1 Kgs 8:39; 1 Sam 2:3). This speaker does not want to flee from the inescapable presence of God.

The omnipresence of God is described in vv. 7-12. A series of hypothetical statements are used to express the ever-present reality of God. The farthest extremities of the universe provide no refuge from the divine presence and power. There is no darkness black enough to hide one from the creator of both darkness and light.

The suppliant declares praise of God's wonderful work in the creation of the speaker himself (vv. 13-18). This is the basis of God's intimate knowledge of the speaker's life and existence (cf. Pss 33:13-17; 94:8-11).

Verse 15 is rather strange. It can be a poetic reference to the human womb, or it can be a reference to the idea of Mother Earth and the concept of a human being's derivation from the ground (cf. Gen 2:7). In any case, even the fetal stage of human life does not lie beyond the sight and control of God (v. 16). The meaning of v. 16bcd is uncertain; I prefer to read it with the Hebrew marginal text as "and on your scroll all of them (the days of the fetus) were written, (all) the days were formed, and one among them for it (to be born)." However, the most common reading given is that the days of the speaker's life were "fashioned" (or "planned") even before birth and written on the divine scroll (cf. Isa 49:1; Jer 1:5; Pss 56:8; 69:28; Exod 32:32). In any case, no rigid, theoretical predestination is intended. The emphasis is on the absolute and comprehensive nature of God's knowledge and purpose (cf. Jer 1:5; Isa 42:9; Job 14:5). Again, there is an expression of reverent astonishment at the extent of the divine knowledge (vv. 17-18; cf. vv. 1-6).

Verses 23-24 with vv. 1-3 form a frame for the psalm: God's past searching out of the speaker is supplemented by petition for God to continue the process.

This psalm may be classified in the broad category of lament, but it is also an affirmation of faith in Yahweh despite the widespread APOSTASY surrounding the speaker. The psalm was a reminder to exiles of Yahweh's omniscience and omnipresence, welcomed by the speaker but of no comfort for those who hated Yahweh (v. 21). The speaker affirms a way of life devoted to Yahweh in v. 24. Idolatry was a major issue in exilic and postexilic communities.

Psalm 140

This is an individual lament with unusually sharp descriptions of the actions of the suppliant's enemies. The speaker has been seriously threatened by violent, crafty, and arrogantly effective foes (vv. 1-5), and turns to Yahweh with a prayer for deliverance and vindication (vv. 6-11). The depiction of the social situation in this psalm fits' with other descriptions of the early postexilic period (see Isa 56:9–57:13; 59:1–15), even if the psalm itself originated at a much earlier date. (Rendsburg [1990, 95-102] argues for a northern origin for Pss 140 and 141, on the basis of linguistic evidence.)

The petitions for judgment, in the form of imprecations against the enemies (vv. 9–11), are severe (see the commentary on Ps 58). The closing two verses are a fine expression of confidence in Yahweh. In the laments, the suppliants often associate themselves with the *needy* (RSV "afflicted") and *poor* as well as with *the righteous* (v. 12). The imprecations against the evildoers who plague the speaker and the community rest on the faith that Yahweh sustains the cause of the poor and needy. Verse 13 begins with the Hebrew particle *'ak*, which indicates that the following statements are true despite overt circumstances to the contrary (see Pss 62, 73). Thus, v. 13 continues and strengthens the affirmations of v. 12.

Psalm 141

The text of this individual lament presents some problems (see RSV and NRSV mg.), but the attitude of the suppliant is much less imprecatory than in Ps 140. Here the speaker is more concerned with inner conditions and preservation from temptation and evil. The speaker prays that his prayer may be acceptable to Yahweh (vv. 1-2). Verse 2 may recall the use of prayer with the evening sacrifice at the Temple (cf. Exod 29:39-41; Num 28:4-8b; Isa 1:13; Jer 41:5; Neh 13:5, 9), but here there is a spiritualization of the sacrifices in which the prayer itself becomes a sacrifice (cf. Pss 40, 50).

In vv. 3-4, the suppliant prays to be guarded and restrained so as not accept compromises of principle and yield to the temptation of keeping company with *the wicked*. The lure of the wicked is similar to that in Ps 73, namely, the well-being of the wicked versus the distress of the righteous.

Verses 5-6 pose some difficulties and their meaning must be considered tentative (see Allen 1983, 269–71), but the speaker seems to be affirming that it is better to be smitten by the righteous one (Yahweh) and be disciplined by his steadfast love, than to live in style with the wicked (cf. Prov 27:6). The NRSV follows LXX in v. 5, *the oil of the wicked.* The LXX is possibly a better text, but "head" or "choice" is supported by 11QPsᵃ, as is "fine oil." Accepting the Qumran text it is possible to read vs. 5:

> Let the Righteous One Yahweh strike me,
>   the One who is Steadfast Love,
>   let him discipline me;
> my head will not refuse such fine oil!
> My prayer will continue to be
>   against their [the wicked in v. 4] evil deeds.

Verse 6 expresses confidence that when "their judges" (not in NRSV) are condemned (or destroyed) they will hear with understanding the words of the speaker—words they now refuse to heed. Verse 7 seems to be a complaint about the present terrible condition of the speaker's community (read with the MT: "Our bones are scattered at the mouth of Sheol").

Verses 8-10 express the concentration of the speaker on Yahweh and supplication for safekeeping. Verse 10 is a prayer that the wicked experience the consequences of their actions designed to harm others, and is an example of the act-consequence sequence found in a number of places (e.g., Prov 1:18; 26:27; 28:10; 29:6, 23; Pss 7:14-17; 9:16; 38:8; 57:7). The idea behind these statements seems to be that God's faithfulness provides that the built-in consequences of actions are maintained.

Psalm 142

In this individual lament the suppliant cries out to Yahweh for help in dealing with persecution. The NRSV translation needs little comment. The appeal to Yahweh is found in vv. 1-3b. The condition of the suppliant is described in vv. 3c-4. Petitions for deliverance form the last part of the psalm (vv. 5-7). The solitary and forsaken condition of the suppliant (v. 4) is similar to that of JOB (19:13-22; Pss 22:11; 38:11). There is no advocate or helping friend at his *right hand* (v. 4) in the present situation (cf. Pss 16:8; 109:31; 110:5; 121:5)—"No one cares about me!" Such loneliness is one of the most distressing of all human emotions. *Prison* (v. 7) is probably figurative (cf. Ps 88:8; Lam 3:7); however, a literal meaning cannot be ruled out because the poet may have had in mind the condition of a persecuted prisoner, who is near death. Dahood (1970, 316) describes this psalm as "the lament of an Israelite on his deathbed."

Psalm 143

The suppliant in this individual lament has been persecuted by *enemies* (vv. 3, 9, 12). Now in peril of death (vv. 3, 7, 11), the speaker turns to Yahweh and prays for the preservation of an endangered life. In the opening plea (vv. 1-2), the speaker appeals to the *faithfulness* and *righteousness* of Yahweh, but does not follow this appeal with a protestation of innocence (cf. Pss 7:3-5, 8; Job 27:6), but with a further plea that God will *not enter into judgment with your servant*. The basis for the second plea is the universal condition of humanity: *for no one living is righteous before you* (cf. Ps 130:3; Job 4:17; 9:2; 15:14; 25:4; Gal 2:16). None can gain vindication before God on the basis of their own strength and merit. Verse 2 is not intended as an excuse, but as a confession that no one can lay a claim on God that will gain salvation.

The suppliant's condition is described in vv. 3-6. As in most laments, it is impossible to define the exact circumstances. This person, however, is in a condition that already approximates death, languishing in darkness and perishing *like a parched land*. Nevertheless, the speaker can meditate on the great acts of Yahweh in the past (v. 5) and pray with urgent trust (vv. 6-8). *In the morning* (v. 8) may point to the cultic situation in which a suppliant hopes for divine guidance at dawn (see Pss 5, 17). The suppliant prays for instruction in the will of God (v. 8) and to be taught and led to perform it (v. 10). The speaker prays as a servant of Yahweh whose life and well-being depend on God's *righteousness* (delivering power) and *steadfast love*.

The seven penitential psalms of the church (Pss 6, 32, 38, 51, 102, 130, 143) concluded with this lament. The closing statement of the speaker, *for I am your servant*, is the basis for the prayer that precedes.

Psalm 144

A Davidic psalm, indicated both by its title and by an explicit reference to *David* (v. 10). The psalm has a recognizably canto literary character, making use of material found in other psalms and combining different types of psalm elements in vv. 1-11 and vv. 12-15. The relationship to Ps 18 seems especially close (cf. Ps 18:2; 9; 14; 16; 47 and Ps 144:1-2; 5; 6; 7). The content of vv. 12-15 expresses family-community ideas of well-being and prosperity, content that seems to have no formal relation to vv. 1-11 and that constitutes the speech of one who either prays for the nation or expresses the results of a fulfillment of the prayer in v. 11. The disparity of the parts of the psalm probably reflects the reuse of Davidic-kingship prayer by the postexilic Israelite community. The Davidic tradition is recalled and reused for a community which needs to identify with David and Yahweh's great intervention for him. The monarchy is a thing of the distant past, but the traditions of David live on.

The language of v. 2c seems a bit out of place: *subdues the peoples under me* (NRSV "peoples" is probably to be preferred to the Hebrew "my people" and is supported by some ms. evidence and Ps 18:48). The repeated references to requests to be delivered from the power (*hand*) of foreigners (vv. 7 and 11) points to Israel under the domination of foreign powers after 587 BCE. A king as the speaker is not required; rather the Israelite community is praying a king's prayer for Yahweh to "subdue peoples" again (as he had done for David) and break the grip of foreign powers.

The prayer in vv. 1-11 is especially pertinent because of vv. 3-4, which express the finitude and weakness of mortal human beings (cf. Pss 8:4; 90:5-6; 146:3-4), a condition felt acutely by the communities of the exilic and postexilic eras. The community longs for a theophanic intervention by Yahweh to set it free from the *mighty waters* of oppressive domination and the *hand of aliens* (vv. 5-7). The community would delight to take up the vow of the king to praise God for such deliverance (vv. 9-10; translate v. 10b with past tense, "the one who rescued David, his servant"). The Davidic king from the past speaks for the community in v. 11 (the "right hand of falsehood" in vv. 8 and 11 indicates those who swear oaths false or break them, or both—people who cannot be trusted because they break their commitments).

Verses 12-15 may be read as prayer, but this is not certain. It is easier to read these verses as statements descriptive of the people, and the conditions that would result from the deliverance prayed for in v. 11 (v. 12 begins with a relative pronoun, probably added to the text to relate what follows to v. 11, and it can be read as "in order that" or "so that our sons . . . "). The superb description of a healthy and strong community in vv. 12-14 is applicable to every age (disregard the *no exile* in v. 14 and read, "no cry of distress in our public places"). Verse 15 refers to the good conditions of vv. 12-14: "How well-off are the people for whom this would be so!" (for the *happy* or "blessed" of v. 15 see, e.g., Pss 1:1; 34:8; 84:4; 5; 15; 112:1; 127:5; 128:1).

Psalm 145

The skilled use of the alphabetic-acrostic form of poetry marks this hymn. Each verse begins with a successive letter of the Hebrew alphabet (the letter *nun*, missing from MT, is supplied by 11QPs[a], LXX, and Syriac, and appears as v. 13cd in RSV and NRSV). The psalm has some similarities with Ps 111. Psalm 145 weaves together declarations of praise in first person (vv. 1-2, 5-6, 21) with praise in third person (vv. 3, 7-9, 12, 14, 17-20) and praise directed to Yahweh in second person, *your works*, etc. (vv. 4, 7, 10-11, 13, 15-16), providing an intricate poetic structure. The individual speaker seems to be meditating on the praise found in the third person sections (v. 5) and addressing God with praise in the second person verses. Calls to praise alternate with grounds for praise.

In general, the psalm divides into two major sections: vv. 1-9, praise of the might and power of Yahweh (v. 3), and vv. 10-20 praise the kingship of Yahweh (vv. 10-13), including the faithfulness and integrity with which God works. Yahweh's loyal-love provides for the whole creation: *You open your hand, satisfying the desire of every living thing* (v. 16). Yahweh's faithfulness and justice holds together the creation, which depends on his open hand (cf. Ps 104:27-30). The just and reliable ways of Yahweh are especially evident to those who love him, fear him, and call upon him (vv. 17-26). The royal power of Yahweh is used to care for the needy. On the other hand, *the wicked* can expect destruction (v. 20b). Verse 21 closes the psalm with a vow of praise on the part of the speaker and a summons to *all flesh* to *bless his holy name forever and ever* ("all" also is found in the Hebrew text of vv. 2, 9, 10, 13, 14, 15, 16, 17, 18, 20, and 21).

"*Of David.*" Psalm 145 is the last psalm attributed to DAVID in a series of eight psalms (138–145), and in the Book of Psalms. The LXX has Ps 151, which is said to be a genuine but supernumerary Davidic psalm. Psalm 151 is found also (with some different content) in the Qumran scroll 11QPsᵃ. Psalm 151 is a poetic account of how the young shepherd David came to be the ruler of Israel, and is a midrash on 1 Sam 16:1-13 (the David and Goliath narrative). It attempts to describe what Yahweh saw in David's heart (1 Sam 16:7) that led to the anointing by Samuel and David's rise to power. (See "Psalm 151" in MCB, below.)

Psalm 145 has had extensive usage in both Jewish and Christian liturgies. In Jewish settings the psalm may be recited daily in the synagogues for morning, noon, and evening prayers. In one liturgical tradition it is called *Ashrei* ("Blessed") because its recitation is preceded by Pss 84:5(4) and 144:15. In Christian usage v. 2 is included in the "Te Deum," a hymn of praise. Verses 10, 15-16 are used in grace before meals.

Book five terminus? Psalm 145 may be considered as the last psalm of book five of the Hebrew Psalter, since Pss 146–150 form a final set for the Psalter as a whole (Holladay 1993, 80). If this is true the Psalter begins and ends with psalms attributed to David (Pss 3–41 and 138–145). In book five, the Davidic Pss 108–110 and Pss 138–145 bracket Pss 111–137. Psalm 107 constitutes a bridge between books four and five, picking up the gathering of the exiles in Ps 106:4 (MT 107:2-3). Psalm 118 begins and ends with the *O give thanks to the LORD, for he is good* (also used in Pss 104:1; 105:1 and 107:1) and with Ps 107 brackets Pss 108–117. Psalms 108–119 consist of the Davidic Pss 108–110, plus two Hallelujah psalms (111 and 112), and introduce the "Egyptian Hallel" collection in Pss 113–118.

The centerpiece of book five is the massive work of Ps 119, which precedes the "Songs of Ascent" (Pss 120–134). Psalm 119 is a gigantic affirmation of the well-being of those "who walk in the *torah* of Yahweh" (119:1-3). Psalms 135–136 form a supplement to the Songs of Ascent in Pss 120–134 and also bracket back to Pss 111–118 with their "Hallelujah" (*Praise the LORD*) and *O give thanks* beginnings. Psalm 137 stands alone to remind the reader that the setting of book five is the experience of EXILE, with powerful remembrance of Zion-Jerusalem and the dreadful oppression of foreign captors. As noted above, book five moves to its proper conclusion with the Davidic collection in Pss 138–145. This collection is a "little Psalter" in itself, containing the "great notes" of the Psalms: lament and complaint addressed to Yahweh about evildoers and other enemies and praise-thanksgiving-confidence directed toward Yahweh:

> *My mouth will speak the praise of the LORD,*
> *and all flesh will bless his holy name*
> *forever and ever.* (Ps 145:21; cf. 138:1)

Psalm 146

An individual speaker voices praise of Yahweh in this hymn, with a somewhat unusual warning against putting trust in human beings (vv. 3-4). This element is more germane to a thanksgiving psalm, as is the *Happy are those* statement in v. 5, but thanksgiving is a form of praise and the elements are frequently mixed (cf. *Happy is* declaration in Ps 33:12). This psalm brings together praise of God as creator (vv. 1-6) with praise of God as redeemer who delivers the oppressed and cares for the needy (vv. 7-9). Verse 10 declares the everlasting reign of Yahweh, the God of Zion.

The psalm opens with a singer vowing to praise Yahweh *all my life long*. Turning from personal commitment to the listeners in vv. 3-4, the speaker warns them of the futility of trusting in human power and position (read *princes* in v. 3 as "those of influence and power"). On the other hand, the helper of human beings is God; the person who puts hope in the plans and purpose of the creator is in a condition of true happiness (vv. 5-7). The security of those who do trust God is not founded upon mortals, but upon Yahweh who has and continues to demonstrate his power to save (vv. 7-9). The hymn calls for full confidence in God and full dependence upon him.

There are few, if any statements in the OT that exceed vv. 6-9 in describing the basic nature of Yahweh (cf. Ps 113:4-9). He is not described with static concepts or attributes, but with participial constructions that are characteristic of the hymns and of Israelite theology. Yahweh is a God who acts, and is, therefore, known through actions. It has been noted (Weiser 1962) that each case where Yahweh demonstrates his efficacy involves situations where human power falls short. Human beings for whom God is dead are without hope. However, those who put their trust in Yahweh are to be congratulated (v. 5); their confidence and hope will not be disappointed.

Psalm 146 is the first of a series of five HALLELUJAH psalms that form a collection that closes the Psalter. Each of these psalms is formed by "Hallelujah" (*Praise the LORD*) at the beginning and end; a tenfold use can hardly be accidental. In addition, the verb *halel* ("praise") is used in its plural imperative form (*praise you . . .*) ten times in Ps 150 and eight times in Ps 148, plus two imperfect forms that serve the same purpose for a total of ten. These five psalms (Pss 146–150) form a final doxology of praise, a jubilate that climaxes in Ps 150:6: *Let everything that breathes praise the LORD!*

Psalm 147

The second of the Hallelujah hymns stresses one main theme: the creation power and providential care of Yahweh for those who *fear him* and *hope in his steadfast love* (v. 11). His power and sustaining care are demonstrated in the natural order (vv. 4-5, 7-9, 15-18) and in the salvation-history of Israel (vv. 2, 12-13, 19-20). The date of the psalm's origin is rather clearly postexilic (v. 2). Perhaps it originated with the rebuilding of the Temple in the time of HAGGAI and ZECHARIAH or with the work of NEHEMIAH (445 BCE) in rebuilding the walls of Jerusalem (vv. 12-13). The LXX divides it into two psalms (vv. 1-11 and vv. 12-20) and gives to both titles that refer to Haggai and Zechariah. Indeed, the psalm seems to be "stitched together" (Stuhlmueller 1988, 493).

The connection of Yahweh's tremendous power in creation with his tender providential care of Israel is the dominant feature of vv. 1-6. Both RSV and NRSV obscure the PARALLELISM of v. 1, which is retained in NIV: "How good it is to sing praises to our God, / how pleasant and fitting to praise him!" (cf. REB). Verse 2 seems to refer to the rebuilding of Jerusalem and the return of exiles after 538 BCE. A striking contrast is found in v. 6: Yahweh is the one who restores the humble (or, meek), but he is also the one who *casts the wicked to the ground*. This is the God who *builds up Jerusalem* and *gathers the outcasts of Israel* (v. 2; cf. Ps 102:16).

A new section begins with v. 7 and Yahweh is praised for the way in which he sustains the natural order of the world (cf. Ps 104:14-23; 27-30). This section concludes with the declaration that Yahweh takes pleasure only in *those who fear him* and who depend upon *his steadfast love* (vv. 10-11).

Yahweh's blessing of Israel is praised in vv. 12-20. Israel's status as the people of Yahweh results in many blessings, but the one above all is the gift of the *word* (vv. 15-20). Yahweh's *word* of *command* (vv. 15 and 18) sets in motion the natural processes of the land (vv. 16-18) that sustain life on the earth. *The waters flow before his word and wind* (spirit). Yahweh's creating and controlling *word* (vv. 15-18, cf. Ps 33:6-7; Isa 55:10-11) has also been given to Israel in the *statutes and ordinances* of Yahweh (vv. 19-20). This is Israel's peculiar privilege, which is shared with no other nation (cf. Deut 4:7-8; Acts 14:16). The *statutes and ordinances* (synonyms for *torah* or "law") are the expressions of the divine will, which have been given for Israel's guidance as the covenant people.

Psalm 148

This is a superb hymn of praise. Its style shows the influence of the type of writing that enumerated lists of the various features of the heavens and the earth, a style found in the teaching of the Egyptian wise man Amenemope (fl. ca. 11th c. BCE) and reflected in Job 38 (cf. Pss 33, 104). The psalm itself divides into two main parts. Verses 1-6 summon the heavenly host to praise Yahweh for his work of creation (v. 5). As in Ps 19, the heavenly bodies are treated as parts of Yahweh's creation. The view of the universe is common to the ancient Near east and reflected in several OT passages (see Gen 1; Ps 104). Yahweh not only created the heavens and the heavenly bodies, but he fixed their relative positions and functions (v. 6). He is both creator and sustainer of his creation (see Gen 8:22; Hos 2:21-22; Jer 31:35-36; 33:25; Job 28:23-26; 38:8-38; Ps 135:7; etc.).

In vv. 7-14, the praise of Yahweh is summoned *from the earth*. Again, God's absolute command of the forces of nature is affirmed. The summons to the natural world (vv. 7-10) becomes a summons to *all peoples . . . of the earth* (vv. 11-12). The reason for Yahweh's praise is the exalted status of his *name* and *glory* (v. 13).

A final testimony (v. 14) points to a festival congregation of devoted and loyal people. Yahweh has *raised up a horn* for them (i.e., given them strength and victory). He has provided them with a *praise*, or a hymn, that recounts his marvelous acts of creation and salvation history.

The praise of God called for by this psalm is marked by its comprehensive scope. Leslie Allen (1983, 316) notes how the word "all" (it appears ten times) in this psalm "rings out in a striving for totality of praise." Praising God sets off a chain reaction that continues without end, generating its own energy as it spreads.

Psalm 149

The fourth of the five HALLELUJAH Psalms (146, 147, 148, 149, 150) that close the Psalter is a hymn that is marked by a strong warlike character. A long tradition of interpretation links the psalm to a victory of the Israelites in the postexilic period, most commonly related to the events of Maccabean times. The general language of the psalm, however, provides little evidence for such an interpretation. Another interpretation reads the psalm as an eschatological depiction of the triumph of God's cause and future victory over his foes. This approach also seems forced onto the more natural interpretation of the psalm. It is easier to understand the basic orientation of the psalm in terms of a cultic situation, and the most reasonable hypothesis is to assume that it reflects the festival context of Tabernacles, and participation in the celebration by the assembled worshipers in its ceremonies.

The people are urged to praise Yahweh in vv. 1-4. They are to *sing . . . a new song* (cf. Pss 33:3; 96:1; 98:1; 144:9) *in the assembly of the [covenant] faithful* (v. 1). A *new song* is one appropriate for the occasion, one that expresses the new reality of the worship experience as it also revives the spirit of the people. The singing is to be accompanied with music and dancing, for Yahweh has been gracious to his people and has given them salvation (*victory*, v. 4). *The humble* (v. 4) refers to the assembled worshipers. The songs of joy and *high praises of God* are already in their mouths and throats, ready for use.

The *assembly of the faithful* are urged to execute judgment on the enemies of God in v. 5-9 (the translation of *nqm* as *vengeance* [v. 7] should be dropped; see commentary on Ps 94:1). The background here is probably that of a ritual battle drama in which the enemies of Yahweh and of Zion, led by their kings, are routed, defeated, and judged (see Ps 2, 46, 48). Verse 5 refers to the reclining of the worshipers during the festival, probably, during a night that preceded the ritual combat in the morning of the following day. In the Jewish traditions of the Festival of Tabernacles as found in the Mishnah, there is a record of a night ceremony with torches carried by the people while they sang songs and praises and the Levites played various musical instruments. These celebrations continued until the cockcrow of dawn. This later ceremony probably preserved elements of earlier ones.

There is a history of unfortunate Christian interpretation of this psalm. It has been used more than once to justify participation in war and the taking of revenge on enemies, who were conveniently classified as the "enemies of God." Verse 9 declares that it is *glory for all his faithful ones* to carry out the *judgment of*

Yahweh. The *judgment* of God is not executed by Christians by means of a sword, but with a cross.

Walter Brueggemann (1984, 27) says that psalms of praise like Pss 146–148 can be used as a form of social control by entrenched people of power. Thus it is important that in the midst of the exalted praise of Pss 146–150 there is in Ps 149 a statement of "sobering realism" (Brueggemann 1984, 166). Praise keeps at least one foot firmly planted in the messy reality of this world. Yahweh is praised in this psalm because: (1) he *takes pleasure* in the welfare of his people and exalts *the humble with victory* (v. 4) and (2) he executes judgment on the nations, which rebounds to the glory of his faithful people (vv. 7-9). As noted above, *vengeance* in v. 7 should be disregarded and understood as the vindication of the faithful and the imposition of order on the nations in accord with the divine will (regarding *nqm*, mistranslated "vengeance," see commentary on Ps 94).

Psalm 150

The last psalm of the Hebrew Psalter, and the last of the five Hallelujah psalms, is marked by the repeated use of the imperative form of "praise" (see above on Ps 146). The tenfold use of the imperative form of the verb *halel* is augmented by the use of the imperfect form in v. 6, plus the HALLELUJAH at the beginning and end of the psalm, for a total of thirteen times. Jewish tradition was aware, of course, of the symbolism of the number ten (e.g., the Decalogue or "ten words"; Exod 34:38; Deut 4:13) as well as of thirteen (the thirteen times God speaks in Gen 1 and the thirteen divine attributes in Exod 34:6-7 [Stuhlmueller 1988, 494]).

The psalm emphasizes the place of music and musical instruments in Israelite worship, but the details and exact use of the various instruments is difficult to fix. The *trumpet* mentioned is the *shofar*, the ram's horn used for signals as well as for praise (cf. Josh 6:4-5; Judg 3:27; 1 Kgs 1:34; 39; Isa 18:3; Pss 47:5; 81:3; 98:6). Stringed, wind, and percussion instruments are also listed. The enumeration of the instruments includes those more closely associated with priests (*trumpet . . . lute and harp*) and those of more secular relationship. All of them are called into the service of the divine praise. Priest and laity, indeed *everything that breathes*, is exhorted to praise Yahweh. Praising God is the goal of all life, of every living thing. Psalms 146–150 tell us that "the proper mode of existence for humankind and all creation is relatedness to God" (McCann 1993b, 56), and praise is indispensable for that mode. Praise of God is the breath of life. A closing Hallelujah ends the psalm, the Hallelujah collection that began with Ps 146, book five, and the canonical Psalter.

Summary of Book Five.

To focus on the basic message of book five is a daunting task. Book five is the largest of the five books of the Psalter and highly varied. Any attempt to systematize the content of so diverse a collection should be approached cautiously.

First, a setting in postexilic Israelite communities seems rather clear. In this regard, Book five belongs to the same general context as book four: note that Ps

106:47 closes with a plea for divine salvation and for the people to be "gathered" from among the nations. The same verb for "gathered" is used in Ps 107:3a:

> gathered in from the lands,
> from the east and from the west,
> from the north and from the south.

This same idea of "gathering" exiles (although with a different verb) is found in Ps 147:2.

A number of passages indicate exilic contexts (e.g., see Pss 118:12-14; 120:5-6; 126:1-6; 129:1-2; 130:5-8). A powerful and direct testimony of postexilic ethos in provided by the placement of Ps 137 ("How could we sing Yahweh's song on foreign soil?") between the Songs of Ascent (Pss 120–134 plus a supplement in Pss 135–136) and the Davidic collection in Pss 138–145.

In some cases the psalms and psalm content may be quite old, but the collection itself is quite late and older psalms have been reread in new contexts. Thus it is not surprising that these psalms declare that Yahweh will provide and protect his people, and that they sometimes contain appeals for the continuation of such divine help. The expressions of "help" are too numerous and varied to cite here. It is sufficient to note that Yahweh is the great "Helper" of his people: *He is their help and their shield* (Ps 115:9, 10, 11); "Our help is in the name of Yahweh, Maker of heaven and earth" (Ps 124:8; see also Ps 146:5-6). The affirmation of Yahweh's faithful, upholding work also is set forth in an excellent way in Ps 145:13-20.

Second, no reader can miss the emphasis on praise in book five that begins with Ps 107. Lament, complaint, and pain are not absent, of course, but praise overcomes lament, and the collection moves toward the crescendo of the five "Hallelujah psalms" in Pss 146–150. Praise is the lifeblood of faith and worship. Israelites far from their homeland, sometimes oppressed, and always in danger of being intimidated by the power and wealth of the nations, found strength to persevere and overcome in the praise of Yahweh's mighty works.

> Praise the LORD. . . .
> Put not trust in princes or in any mortal,
>   for they have no power to save. . . .
> The LORD your God, O Zion, will reign forever. (Ps 146:1, 3, 10, author trans.)

The speaker in Ps 145 (which actually closes book five) vows:

> *My mouth will speak the praise of the LORD,*
>   *and all flesh will bless his holy name*
>   *forever and ever.* (145:21)

Third, the basic theme of book five seems to be set in Ps 107:1:

> *O give thanks to the LORD, for he is good;*
>   *for his steadfast love endures forever.*

Book five tests whether or not these declarations are true and affirms how they are true.

The affirmation that *he is good* is repeated in Ps 118:1, 29 (the beginning and end of the psalm), 135:3, and 136:1. Yahweh is addressed directly in Ps 119:68—*You are good and do good*—and he is asked to *let your good spirit lead* the speaker in 143:10. The judgments of Yahweh are said to be *good* in Ps 119:39 (cf. 119:66). The *abundant goodness* of Yahweh is declared in Ps 145:7 and Yahweh is said to be *good to all* with his compassion extended to *all that he has made* in v. 9 of the same psalm.

Likewise, the references to the *steadfast love* of Yahweh are especially numerous and striking in book five, appearing sixty times (twenty-six times in Ps 136 alone). Yahweh's *steadfast love* is described as *higher than the heavens* while his *faithfulness reaches to the clouds* (Ps 108:4); thirty-three times his *steadfast love* is said to *endure forever* (Ps 107:1; five times in Ps 118; twenty-six times in Ps 136; 138:8; elsewhere in the OT in Ps 106:1; 1 Chr 16:34; 41; 2 Chr 5:13; 7:3; 6; 20:21; Ezra 3:11). Rather clearly book five was intended to assure postexilic Israelite communities that the *steadfast love* of Yahweh, so powerfully demonstrated in the past (e.g., Pss 106:7-8; 107:8, 15, 21, 136), was still extended to them.

Fourth, the book emphasizes the continuing significance of Zion (Jerusalem) for all who worship Yahweh. Israelites dispersed to the far corners of the known world could still anticipate the actual experience of pilgrimage to the joyous festivals at Zion (cf. Songs of Ascent in Pss 120–34). For those who could not go and had to remain at home, the reports and testimonies of those who did would have been good news (cf. Ps 48). Zion was still the chosen place of Yahweh's habitation (Ps 132:13-14), still the center of the world, theologically speaking, and a place of paradise on earth. Zion was still a place fundamentally different from the rest of the world, *perfection of beauty*, whence God shined forth into the world (Ps 50:2), and where pilgrims drank from *the river of your delights* and from the *fountain of life* (Ps 36:7-9; cf. Pss 122; 132:15-17). From Zion the blessing of Yahweh, *maker of heaven and earth*, went forth (Ps 134:3), and in time Zion would dominate the world (Isa 2:2-4; Mic 4:1-5).

Finally, what of Ps 119? This huge psalm, a psalter in itself, is enigmatic and is indeed a challenge. As noted in the commentary on Pss 1 and 2, it has been suggested that Ps 119 closed an earlier collection of the Psalms, forming a Torah-Psalter. The last appearance of *torah* in the present Psalter is in Ps 119:174, an observation that may or may not be significant. I suggest that Ps 119 is placed in its present position in order to link book five with an earlier Torah-Psalter. It is also possible that Ps 119 was placed after Ps 105 in an earlier collection, as a prelude to Ps 106 and as the end of book four (Ps 105 ends with the expected outcome of the saving history of Yahweh as *that they might keep his statutes and observe his [torah]*, v. 45; Ps 106 laments the failure of the Israelites to do so).

In any case, the present position of Ps 119 may be suggestive. It follows the Hallelujah-thanksgiving-praise series in Pss 111–118, which centers around the deliverance of Israel from Egypt in Pss 113–115 and is placed immediately before the Songs of Ascent in Pss 120–134 (plus Pss 135–136 that appears to be a supplement) with their strong emphasis on Zion. although *torah* does not appear in connection with Zion anywhere in book five, the juxtaposition of the great Torah-psalm (Ps 119) is suggestive of the declarations that Yahweh's *torah* will go forth from Zion (Isa 3:2; Mic 4:2).

Regardless of validity of these matters of shaping and arrangement in the Psalter, *torah* and praise belong together (as in Ps 19). Those who are blessed "to walk in the *torah* of Yahweh" (119:1) are those for whom the praise of God is natural. They are ready for the summons of the Hallelujahs of book five and convert the whole of the Psalter into *t'hillim* ("praises"), its Hebrew title, and a primal expression of faith.

Works Cited

Allen, Leslie. 1983. *Psalms 101–150*. WBC.

Bos, Johanna W. H. 1993. "Psalm 87," *Inter* 47:285.

Brueggemann, Walter. 1984. *The Message of the Psalms.*

Craigie, Peter C. 1983. *Psalms 1–50*. WBC.

Dahood, Mitchell. 1966. *Psalms 1–50*. AncB. 1968. *Psalms 51–100* AncB. 1970. *Psalms 101–150*. AncB.

Durham, John I. 1971. "Psalms" in BBC.

Gerstenberger, Erhard S. 1988. *Psalms*. Part 1. FOTL.

Goulder, Michael. 1982. *The Psalms of the Sons of Korah*. JSOTSup. 1990. *The Prayers of David*. JSOTSup.

Gunkel, Hermann. 1929/1968. *Die Psalmen*. 1933/1966. *Einleitung in die Psalmen.*

Hammer, Reuven. 1991. "Two Liturgical Psalms: Salvation and Thanksgiving," *Judaism* 40:491–92.

Hay, D. M. 1973. *Glory at the Right Hand: Psalm 110 in Early Christianity*. SBLMS.

Holladay, William L. 1993. *The Psalms through Three Thousand Years.*

Kidner, Derek. 1975a. *Psalms 1–7*. 1975b. *Psalms 73–150.*

Kirkpatrick, A. F. 1891–1901. *The Book of Psalms*. The Cambridge Bible for Schools and Colleges.

Kraus, Hans-Joachim. 1988. *Psalms 1–59*. 1989. *Psalms 60–150.*

Kselman, John S., and Michael L. Barré. 1990. "Psalms" in *NJBC.*

Kugel, James L. 1986. "Topics in the History of the Spirituality of the Psalms" in *Jewish Spirituality*, 113–44.

Leslie, Elmer A. 1949. *The Psalms: Translated and Interpreted in the Light of Hebrew Life and Worship.*

Levenson, Jon. 1986. "The Jerusalem Temple in Devotional and Visionary Experience," in *Jewish Spirituality*, 32–61.

McCann, J. Clinton, ed. 1993a. *The Shape and Shaping of the Psalter*. JSOTSupp. 1993b. *A Theological Introduction to the Book of Psalms.*

Miller, Patrick D., Jr. 1986. *Interpreting the Psalms.*

Mowinckel, Sigmund. 1951. *The Psalms in Israel's Worship.*

Pietersma, Albert. 1980. "David in the Greek Psalms." VT 30:213–26.

Rad, Gerhard von. 1962. *O.T. Theology*. Vol. 1.

Rendsburg, Gary A. 1990. *Linguistic Evidence for the Northern Origin of Selected Psalms.* SBLMS 43.

Sarna, Nahum M. 1993. *Songs of the Heart. An Introduction to the Book of the Psalms.*
Seybold, Klaus. 1990. *Introducing the Psalms.*
Soll, Will. 1991. *Psalm 119: Matrix, Form, and Setting.* CBQMS.
Spurgeon, C. H. 1874–1892/1966. *The Treasury of David.*
Stuhlmueller, Carroll. 1983. *Psalms 1* and *Psalms 2.* O.T. Message 21, 22. 1988. "Psalms" in *HBC.*
Tate, Marvin E. 1990. *Psalms 51–100.* WBC.
Westermann, Claus. 1989. *The Living Psalms.*
Weiser, Artur. 1959/1962. *The Psalms.* OTL.

Proverbs

David Penchansky

Introduction

Modern Western society divides into political parties, religions, and even competing factions within religions. In this same manner, ancient Israel breaks into distinct and often competing social groupings. These groupings were both political and religious, although the Israelite would not have understood the distinction. Scholars today call the educated class the sages, or the wise ones. These sages wrote Proverbs, as well as other biblical books. In the same way the voice of one conservative radio commentator does not represent the thinking of an entire country, so the sages must be understood as one voice among many in their culture.

Sages argued with each other. They took positions on controversial issues both among themselves and in opposition to other parties of power within Israel. The Book of Proverbs contains some of these controversies. Although the culture of the sage was often at odds with that of other groups in Israel, among themselves they usually reached a consensus, a standard of wisdom acceptable to the community of the Wise. This consensus is most clearly exemplified by faith in the fundamental orderliness and reasonableness of the universe, a complete confidence that "God smiled on the just and sent transgressors straight to hell" (Hassler 1990, 16), and that following the elders' advice brings life and blessing.

A few questioned the eternal verities. In scripture, readers see imprints of discussion between the dominant group of sages and these questioners. Traces of their doubt or skepticism remain in the text. Thus, although the writings maintain the dominant position, doubt became canonized as it played a role in the discussions that eventually produced Proverbs.

Scholars characterize the book as part of the corpus known as WISDOM LITERATURE. Wisdom literature features two chief concerns: first, an attempt to draw insight from careful observation of the world; second, an effort carefully to assemble and preserve the accumulated insights of previous generations of sages and elders. Proverbs offers instruction in some of the more practical aspects of wisdom. It tells how to get along in life. Much of the book instructs the young student on how one should conduct oneself as an official of the royal court.

The disagreements among the sages derive from the two sources of wisdom mentioned above. The scientific-like observations made by the individual sage often conflict with the appeal to the traditions, the accumulated insights of society. The two differing stances typify the chief concerns of wisdom. First, and most common in Proverbs, is a supreme confidence, a certitude about the ways of the world and about the correct means of advancement in the world. Second, one finds sacred doubt, the questioning of society's truths. Proverbs is the actual arena for this conflict, containing both positions.

Authorship

The ancient collectors of this material ascribed most of it to the fabled King SOLOMON. In Proverbs, the significance of authorship lies not in the question of the origin of the material, but in its authority. When one attributes words to a figure who looms as large in Israel's history as Solomon, who has such a reputation for wisdom in the tradition of Israel, one enables the literature ascribed to him to seem much more persuasive.

Names arise in the book to which no significant tradition is connected, names such as *Lemuel* (31:1, 4) and *Agur* (30:1). Perhaps they were famous at some point in the past, but such information is no longer available to a contemporary reader. The various "authors" cited do suggest a boundary between the particular collections. Most collections begin with the ascription by name to a particular figure or group. Such ascriptions contribute little to our understanding of individual proverbs or individual collections of proverbs, but they do give an air of authority to the statements that follow. These statements claim to be written by men who have a reputation in Israel for wisdom and for access to the upper reaches of power.

Tribal Wisdom. Historical evidence exists for the identification of three distinct purveyors of Wisdom. The earliest form of Wisdom was transmitted orally—presumably never written down—and passed on from parents to children. This early form of Wisdom is commonly called Tribal Wisdom because it reflects an agricultural and pastoral world, offering advice to farmers and the keepers of livestock. These texts provide a raw, common-sense approach to daily life. There is much in Proverbs that brings to the forefront the economic reality of this world of commerce, a world of false weights and measures, of failed crops and livestock.

This accumulated wisdom likely formed into collections, and was enshrined in writing, localized either by clan, family, tribe or even region. These collections of tribal wisdom no longer exist in any "pure" form, but are incorporated into larger collections that originate in a different cultural setting.

Royal Wisdom. Scholars of wisdom literature locate a second type of wisdom found in schools and the royal courts of Israel and Judah. The schools were probably coextensive with the royal court. They functioned to train the children of the bureaucratic functionaries (the "Princes") to take their roles of middle-management leadership in Israel.

In Israel a distinctive class of individuals known as "sages" emerged; they were the teachers and leaders of the "schools." The sages were a cultural elite who defined the intellectual, scientific and aesthetic standards of the Israelite aristocratic society. They taught the children, including those of the royal family; they became advisors to the king and were often the chief foreign policy strategists and economic planners.

It would appear that the sages used the early collections of the accumulated wisdom of the ways of the royal court, combined with older collected sapiential reflections—the Tribal Wisdom—not as a guidebook for the sages themselves (presumably they had internalized these directions) but as a kind of drill book for Israelite youth.

This type of wisdom produces advice that is much more cautious and reserved than what is found among the tribal elders. The writings urged extreme care when navigating the dangerous world of royal politics, in which supporting the wrong faction could lead to one's execution. The advice is cautious and state-supportive. The Wise advised the prospective royal functionaries to keep their mouths shut and to listen to their elders, while making their way up the administrative ladder.

Philosophical Wisdom. The sages produced another type of literature, as well, called Philosophical Wisdom. Although this type of Wisdom is most commonly associated with the Books of Job and Ecclesiastes, it also finds a place in the Book of Proverbs. This literature reflects upon the deep issues of life, the problems of evil and innocent suffering, for instance, or the absence and the darkness of God.

Structure

Proverbs, as it has appeared in versions for the last twenty centuries, divides into several different collections, with some overlap. Each collection can be distinguished by a noted and obvious prologue that introduces what follows and distinguishes it from what came before. To a lesser degree, the collections appear to divide on the basis of genre or style. A new collection is often characterized by a new type of literature.

The first collection, 1:1–9:18, is one of the most philosophical. It begins, *The proverbs of Solomon, son of David, king of Israel*, and consists of lengthy poems on the importance of following the elders' advice. Most notably, two strong women appear in this collection, often designated Dame Folly and Dame Wisdom. Each in her own way contrives to seduce a sexually innocent young man.

The second collection, 10:1–22:16, is the lengthiest and, according to many, the oldest collection in the book. It begins with the ascription, *The proverbs of Solomon*. It mainly consists of short pithy sayings, most akin to what we think of by the English word PROVERB. The Hebrew word has a much wider range of meaning, including parable, riddle, and fable. Short proverbs, like compressed pills of accumulated wisdom, are sometimes collected according to similarity of topic; more commonly, however, they are strung together quite randomly.

The remaining collections are briefer and will be grouped as follows: the third (22:17–24:22) is introduced by the phrase *The words of the wise*. Included with this section is a small group of proverbs introduced by the words: *These also are sayings of the wise* (24:23-34). The fourth, traced to *the officials of King Hezekiah* who served as copyists, is found in 25:1–29:27. The fifth, *the words of Agur* (30:1-33) and *the words of King Lemuel* (31:1-9), will be handled together, along with a lengthy acrostic poem about the *capable wife* (31:10-31). The commentary, therefore, will divide into five unequal sections.

In the outline and commentary the material is arranged topically within the several sections of the book. Readers should read through the indicated sections first and then turn to the discussion of the topics. In this way readers will gain a clearer picture of the social world of the Wise and also a better understanding of their counsel to their age and to any age.

In the outline readers will find references to the most important texts in the relevant sections of the Book of Proverbs dealing with the subject listed.

For Further Study

In the *Mercer Dictionary of the Bible*: ORACLE; PROVERB; PROVERBS, BOOK OF; RIDDLE; SOLOMON; WISDOM IN THE OT; WISDOM LITERATURE.

In other sources: S. H. Blank, "Proverbs, Book of," IDB; J. Crenshaw, *Old Testament Wisdom, Prolegomena to the Study of Wisdom*, "Proverbs, Book of," AncBD, and *Wisdom in the Old Testament*; C. R. Fontaine, "Proverbs," HBC; T. P. McCreesh, "Proverbs," NJBC; R. Murphy, *The Tree of Life*; G. von Rad, *Wisdom in Israel*; R. N. Whybray, "Proverbs, Book of." IDBSup.

Commentary

An Outline

I. The First Collection:
   Dame Wisdom and Dame Folly, 1:1–9:18
   A. Introduction, 1:1-6
   B. The Fear of the LORD, 1:7
   C. Two Strong Women
      Woo the Hapless Youth, 7:1–9:18
   D. The Law of Retribution, 1:18-19
   E. The Ethical Inscriptions, 3:27-30
   F. Keep Your Heart, 4:23
II. The Second Collection:
   The Proverbs of Solomon, 10:1–22:16
   A. Parenting, 10:1
   B. Riches and Poverty, 10:2, 16; 11:4; 18:9-11
   C. The Speech of the Wise and Foolish,
      18:21; 14:5, 25; 16:23-30
   D. Sacrifice and Worship, 15:8, 29
   E. The Law of Retribution, 11:3-8, 21
   F. Commerce, 11:1, 4; 16:11
   G. Court Politics, 16:10, 15
   H. Women and Wives, 12:4; 21:19
   I. Individual Human Emotions, 13:12; 14:13
   J. Theology and the Mystery of the Divine,
      15:3, 11; 21:1
III. The Third Collection:
   The Words of the Wise, 22:17–24:34
   A. The Poor, 22:22-23; 24:10-12
   B. Anger, 22:24-25

C. Pledges, 22:26-27
D. Ancient Landmarks, 22:28; 23:10
E. Work Ethic, 22:29
F. Taking Care of Business, 24:27
G. Story of a Lazy Man, 24:32-34
H. Courtly Behavior, 23:1-3, 6-8
I. Legal Behavior, 24:23b-29
J. Child Rearing and Parenthood,
   23:13-14, 22-25
K. Envy, 23:17
L. Wine, 23:29-35
M. Strange Woman, 23:26-28
N. Importance of Wisdom, 23:22-25; 24:3-7
O. Law of Retribution, 24:15-16
IV. The Fourth Collection:
   Other Proverbs of Solomon, 25:1–29:27
   A. The Mystery of God, 25:2; 27:1
   B. Court Politics, 25:4-5; 29:12
   C. Legal Behavior, 25:7b-10
   D. Speech, 25:13, 25; 26:20-21; 29:19-20
   E. Social Advice, 25:16; 27:7
   F. The Behavior of Fools, 25:19; 26:6, 10-11
V. The Fifth Collection:
   The Words of Agur and Lemuel, 30:1–31:31
   A. The Words of Agur, 30:1-33
   B. The Words of King Lemuel, 31:1-9
   C. The Capable Wife, 31:10-31

The First Collection: Dame Wisdom and Dame Folly, 1:1–9:18

Introduction, 1:1-6

For the attribution of the collection to King SOLOMON, see the introduction. Verses 2-6 express the purpose of the book, explaining the results for the diligent listener, the one who obeys these words, and what is to be gained from the study of wisdom. The passage introduces the first collection, 1:1–9:18, although it could have been written later to introduce the entire Book of Proverbs. The section functions to explain the reason for the writing that follows. It claims: "What I am about to say is important—it ought to be attended to very carefully."

Note that very little in this opening section speaks of the kind of life the sage leads, nor does it indicate why someone would want to live a life according to wisdom. The catalogue of benefits for the one who listens to these words consists of synonyms. Interpreters have attempted to develop fine points of distinction among the terms, but they are better treated as synonyms.

The whole might be summarized, "Read this and be wise," or perhaps more properly, "Learn this and know what the wise ones are talking about." The Book of Proverbs is an introduction to a particular kind of technical discussion or discourse used by an interpretive community. We here meet groups of people with shared language and values, for whom various words and descriptions mean the same thing. Skillful and knowledgeable use of these words makes a separation between those who use them and those who do not. It is as though the reader is presented with a codebook for entrance into the community of the wise. Those who enter will know *the words of the wise and their riddles* (v. 6).

The Fear of the LORD, 1:7

In a few texts we are presented with a particular activity that is identified as the beginning of wisdom. In this section, the first one occurs in 1:7 (and again in 9:10), where the text ascribes the honor of the first place to *the fear of the LORD* (see also Ps 111:10 for the same expression). In 4:7, the first thing is to simply *Get wisdom.* The word *beginning* implies primacy, either in importance, or foundationally, or temporally. That is, "Before you can gain any wisdom, you must do this first."

Fear implies a kind of relationship to superior power. One never fears (using this Hebrew word) anything that lacks authority over others. But beyond that, the particular content remains to be defined, it is defined in various ways. We are told that *the fear of the LORD* is "to hate evil" (8:13), or that it consists of *instruction in wisdom* (15:33). The results of this fear are wonderful. The fear of the Lord *prolongs life* (10:27); (gives) *strong confidence* (14:26); and *is a fountain of life* (14:27). We learn that it is better to have *a little* with this fear than to be fantastically wealthy (15:16). It enables one to avoid evil (16:6). It brings success.

We might therefore conclude regarding these words, first, that wisdom is a language, a discourse by which to understand the world. This discourse is mastered only through careful attention to the teachings of the wisdom tradition, and the teachings of the established sages. Second, fear characterizes this movement. Wisdom is not a secular notion in Proverbs. It admonishes its members to maintain a vague and undefined attitude of piety toward the Israelite God, promising success to all who do so.

Two Strong Women Woo the Hapless Youth, 7:1–9:18

There are three voices present in this series of long, somewhat related poems. First there is the voice of the parent, identified as father or mother. The entire passage (1:8–9:18) can be understood as the voice of this parent, giving important counsel to a child. This parent presents the child with an allegorical story of a youth torn between two conflicting desires. One voice entices the youth to participate in wickedness. This voice comes first in caricature. An evil gang entices the innocent young person to go out on a raid to steal someone's wealth. This gang seeks among themselves consciously and willfully to excel one another in evil (4:16).

The parental voice admonishes the youth to avoid such people because their way leads to a terrible, painful death. The cartoon-like way the gang is depicted leaves readers without a clue as to their identity. We are not likely to know anyone so utterly evil and destructive.

Although the *loose woman* (2:16-19) is patently dangerous, the description of her is sexually enticing. She is a sexual fantasy, like Mrs. Robinson in the film *The Graduate*: older, experienced, taking charge. It is all the poor young fool can do to keep out of her clutches, for she tempts him with a night of pleasure that, without her, no one can possibly discover. But the youth *goes like an ox to the slaughter* (7:22). In an earlier poem on this *loose woman*, we are told that to follow her causes one to lose honor (5:9), lose wealth (5:10), and to become sick in old age (5:11) and regretful (5:12).

Finally, we hear the voice of Dame Wisdom, who cries in the street, seeking to bring her charges to her home. Our first contact with her (1:20) is more prophetic and didactic than seductive. But in chapter five (vv. 15-20) we encounter dame wisdom in an openly erotic appeal to marital fidelity, the fountain serving as a vaginal image. *May her breasts satisfy you at all times; may you be intoxicated always by her love* (5:19). Such texts function simultaneously on two levels, first to persuade the youth against the erotic appeal of the dangerous and forbidden, that is, to demystify cheating on one's spouse; and second as an exhortation to a life married to wisdom.

Although we will encounter wise women in subsequent collections, we have in this section the fullest and most suggestive figure of Dame Wisdom, who looks more like a wisdom goddess than a virtuous Israelite woman (chap. 8). This lyrical poem divides into three sections. The first (8:1-21) corresponds to the seductive story of Dame Folly, the woman who seduces a young student, inviting him to a secret encounter in her house after her husband had gone away (7:6-20). In contrast, Dame Wisdom persuades her charges by means of a public invitation to a feast. Her proclamation reminds one of Second Isaiah crying out in Yahweh's voice,

Ho, everyone who thirsts, come to the waters;
and you that have no money, come, buy and eat! (Isa 55:1)

We also think of the great nobleman who invited all the poor and dispossessed to his feast, because those of his own class refused to attend (Matt 22:1-10).

Dame Wisdom invites all the simple. The sages classified many stages and kinds of ignorance that prevented one from understanding the wise. "Simple" is the most innocent kind of stupidity. Here they are the directionless, those without rudder who blunder through life with no idea of what is going on. If only they will eat at Wisdom's table they will gain life! She has prepared for them as carefully as the adulterous woman (Dame Folly) prepared her bedchamber (chap. 7). Here we do not have that wanton sexuality, but rather a coy invitation nonetheless. The reader is left with anxiety as to which woman the simple person will choose to follow.

In the next section of the poem (8:22-31) we encounter an ancient biblical text in which an entirely different religious sensibility bursts in, like a shaft of a different-colored light. The language is beautiful, even touching, but the picture of the divine realm that is disclosed must have alienated many Israelites. It alienates many modern interpreters as well. Wisdom is depicted as a little girl, divinely begotten, the first creation in all the universe. She sits at the feet of the divine creator and delights in his presence. Her power somehow focused YHWH's creative energy, it seems, enabling him to produce the world. The creative activity of these two bears similarities to what is termed a theogony, where a male and a female deity procreate and produce the world.

But the words *daily his delight, rejoicing before him always* (8:30) remain an undiminished burst of joy, maintaining its intensity over the centuries. It was joy that brought the universe into being, not power. Such a message continues to stir the reader, whether one regards Dame Wisdom here as a polytheistic vestige of an old non-Israelite tale, or a symbolical device representing an idea. She sits at God's feet as either *a master worker* or "little child" (NRSV mg.) depending on the way the Hebrew is translated.

She is not the mature woman waiting at her banquet hall for the simple to come. Rather, we note her childhood. When she was a child, the firstborn of YHWH, she played at his feet. And there is no one in creation with primacy over her. The author of the Epistle to the Colossians described the Christ using similar terms, "The firstborn of all creation . . . in him all things . . . were created, . . . through him were all things made" (Col 1:15-16). Had the gender not been changed, one would naturally think that the author was describing the same divine, supernatural person. One may wonder how such a figure got past the late Israelite and Rabbinical censors. Perhaps there were no censors, and the picture of God in late postexilic or early Hellenistic times was far more diverse and perplexing than we usually imagine.

The Israelites thought deeply and developed varied answers to the ultimate questions. Somehow, the late Israelite period brought these differing perspectives together into single works that others read as unitary. The diverse perspectives of Proverbs provide one example. The sages and editors collected in a single book many conflicting ways of answering the same questions.

The final section of this extended poem (8:32–9:18) draws the contrast more explicitly, describing again Dame Wisdom preparing her table for the simple, while Dame Folly sits at the door of her house and invites the simple to stolen water and secret bread. Augustine, the fifth century theologian, reflected upon the added attraction that the word "stolen" contributes to the value of the item. For him, stolen apples carried their appeal into his old age. Folly knows this about people instinctively. The invitations differ so profoundly that the narrative clarifies for the innocent student the immensity of the moral choice that she or he inescapably confronts.

Thus, this extended narrative (chaps. 8–9) exerts a hortatory, persuasive influence. It functions as a sermon does in some modern religious meetings. The sermon lays out a decision in the starkest contrast, with the speaker depicting one choice as unmistakably superior. In the biblical poem the writer shows great skill in depicting the evil choice in persuasive and attractive terms. But what is the choice? The student who chooses Dame Wisdom chooses a certain way to look at the world, choosing at the same time a certain group of people who share these common beliefs. In modern terms we might describe them as distinct interest group within a society.

In religious terms, the sages shared many of the same symbols with the rest of Israel, but they invested these symbols with dramatically different meanings. They also employed different ways of arguing in favor of those meanings. The sages argued, for example, in favor of the law of retribution from a different perspective than did the prophets. Dame Wisdom, then, functions as the personification of this group, the community of wisdom, and also at the same time, as a manifestation of their understanding of and approach to the divine realm. The poem reveals their theology. For some modern Christians, the virgin Mary functions similarly.

This woman, the personification of wisdom, appears later writings as well. She inspires sages such as Ben Sira, the authors of the Wisdom of Solomon, and of the wisdom poem in Baruch, and she is widely believed to have strongly influenced the Hellenistic notion of the *logos* in Jewish philosophy and in the Gospel of John. Such a powerful symbol, while not competing with descriptions of the Israelite God, powerfully tempers the radical MONOTHEISM of later Jewish and Christian theology. Dame Wisdom challenges later interpreters to widen their notions of divine influence and spiritual insight.

The Law of Retribution, 1:18-19

This collection vehemently teaches what is commonly called the law of retribution. The maxims depict the wicked as destined for a terrible fate (1:18–19, 31). Concerning the foreign, strange, or loose woman, *her way leads down to death* (2:18). The good, on the other hand, enjoy rich rewards for their righteousness (2:21). Therefore, the youth is exhorted by the wise parental figures to *trust in the LORD with all your heart* (3:5), which will result in *healing for your flesh* (3:8). Wisdom *will exalt you* (4:8), *place on your head a fair garland* (4:9) and grant you life (4:22) and *healing* (3:8; 4:22). Therefore, being wise involves both *trust in the LORD* (3:5) and giving generously in support of cultic sacrifice (3:9), with the result being full barns and full vats of wine (3:10).

We are told that following Dame Folly leads to horrible destruction but following the path of wisdom (as now described) leads to financial reward (3:10). Following wisdom also leads to a happy life, for *her income is better than silver, and her revenue better than gold* (3:14), and security (3:23). The confidence in God's governance of the world is undiminished in this wisdom collection:

> *The LORD's curse is on the house of the wicked*
> *but he blesses the abode of the righteous.* (3:33)

The Ethical Inscriptions, 3:27-30

In the third chapter we find the first truly ethical teaching in Proverbs, the first hint that wisdom is found in just action. The object of this attention is not specified: *to whom it is due* (v. 27), or more specifically, *your neighbor* (v. 28). These texts refer to specific situations in which a person (here no longer a youth) holds a position of power and is thus able to exercise authority over another. The sage is exhorted not to withhold money (v. 28) or security (v. 29); neither should the sage withhold peace (v. 30) from one who has not harmed him.

Keep Your Heart, 4:23

This passage speaks well to the modern condition, but it is difficult to articulate. *Keep your heart* (see also 4:24-26) seems to refer to strictly controlled speech and behavior. It also has an internal sense, that from which speech and behavior proceeds. The Hebrew term *leb* usually refers more to the thinking processes than to the emotions. *Keep your heart* might then suggest the importance of controlling one's thoughts.

The second part of the verse appears not to represent an elaborate anthropology—i.e., different "humors" pulsing out of the circulatory muscle—but is rather a poetic way of saying, "The heart is very important." Mental discipline provides a key to success.

One must not rest on laurels of privilege, but work hard at internal discipline or control. The old tell the young to exert discipline toward the mastery of an internal skill. It is one thing to have available the accumulated wisdom of previous generations, even to assent to its reliability. It is quite another to employ these insights in the practical living of life.

The Second Collection: The Proverbs of Solomon, 10:1–22:16

This section has a common style that reflects PARALLELISM or parallel couplets, and common concerns (see below), but does not have any discernible structure that is distinctive. If one rearranged these proverbs in a random order, that would not appreciably change the impact of the whole. The section is only delineated by an introductory phrase, *The proverbs of Solomon* (10:1), and by a dramatic shift in style after 22:16, which suggests the probability that the collection ends there. Besides that, there is no development of themes from beginning to end, and no significant thematic or topical arrangement, although there are occasional clusters of two or three couplets with similar topics. Therefore, the passages within this collection will be interpreted topically.

Parenting, 10:1

As with references to mothers and fathers in the first collection (1:1–9:18), here too there remains an ambiguity as to whether the references are to biological parents raising their children or to teachers in the schools. In the case of this collection, the writer probably intends actual parents. This is indicated by references to inheritance and by the intense way that the happiness of the parents is bound up with the success of the child.

The collection makes three separate points regarding the complex relationship between parent and child: (1) A child's character not only reflects upon the character of the parents; it also determines the ultimate happiness of the parents (v. 1). (2) Children should listen to the advice of their parents. Children who reject their parents and parental counsel suffer destruction (20:20). Note the following typical statements: *A fool despises a parent's instruction* (15:5), or, most blatantly: *the one who hates a rebuke will die* (15:10). (3) The sage exhorts the parents to discipline their children, including physical punishment (13:24). This advice opens up into a general exhortation (similar to the statements in the first collection) to obey instruction and advice from elders. The collection glorifies the dignity and wisdom inherent in old age: *the beauty of the aged is their gray hair* (20:29; cf. 19:20). Proverbs 10:1; 13:1, 24; 15:20; 19:13, 18, 26-27; 20:20; 22:6; 22:15 also exhibit further instances of parental instruction.

Riches and Poverty, 10:2, 16; 11:4; 18:9-11

Whereas the collection presents a single consistent, strongly authoritarian position regarding parenting, the notion of wealth and its lack appears to be a point of significant controversy among the sages. Virtually every societal attitude towards the accumulation of property can be gleaned from the text.

The messages are given to the upper classes and consist of various exhortations to live responsibly with wealth and to understand the role of wealth in society; even so, there is no unanimity. The following positions may be isolated.

(1) Wealth without righteousness will not endure. *Treasures gained by wickedness do not profit, but righteousness delivers from death* (10:2). See also, for example, 10:16; 11:4, 18, 28; 16:8, 16, 19; 17:1; 19:1; 22:1-2.

(2) The righteous will be or become wealthy, while the wicked are invariably poor (10:3). See also 12:27; 13:6, 18, 22-23; 19:10.

(3) Poverty is a result of laziness, get-rich-quick schemes and devotion to pleasure rather than diligent hard work. *The lazy person does not plow in season; harvest comes, and there is nothing to be found* (20:4). See also 10:4, 5, 26; 11:16b; 12:11-12, 24, 27; 13:4, 11; 14:23; 15:19; 18:9-11; 19:15, 24; 20:13, 21; 21:5, 17, 25; 22:13.

(4) Riches are good in that they provide security. Poverty produces a miserable existence. Therefore, it is much better to be rich. *The wealth of the rich is their fortress; the poverty of the poor is their ruin* (10:15). *The poor are disliked even by their neighbors, but the rich have many friends* (14:20). See also 15:15; 18:23; 19:4, 7; 22:7.

(5) It is the sacred responsibility of the rich to care for the poor through generosity and fairness. *Those who oppress the poor insult their Maker, but those who are kind to the needy honor him* (14:31). See also 11:24-26; 19:17; 21:13; 22:9, 16.

(6) There is a bare suggestion that poverty might in fact be the result of injustice in society and not the laziness of the poor themselves. *The field of the poor may yield much food, but it is swept away through injustice* (13:23).

The Speech of the Wise and Foolish, 18:21; 14:5, 25; 16:23-30

Death and life are in the power of the tongue; and those who love it will eat its fruits (18:21). The question that greatly troubled the sage concerned the power and proper use of speech. If we were to oversimplify and divide into two neat categories (a common practice in wisdom literature itself), we might ask, "What are the characteristics of the speech of the wise?" and "What are the characteristics of the speech of the foolish and/or the wicked?" Approached in this way, the material in this section of Proverbs yields the following results.

The speech of the wise is characterized by: (1) Truthfulness. There is no willful effort on the part of the speaker to create the wrong impression. *A faithful witness does not lie* (14:5). *A truthful witness saves lives, but one who utters lies is a betrayer* (14:25).

(2) Aptness. Their words are not spoken thoughtlessly, at an inopportune time. *To make an apt answer is a joy to anyone, and a word in season, how good it is!* (15:23).

(3) Health. Words of the righteous bring healing, both to the speaker and to the community. Wise speakers, through their speech, defuse conflict and promote reconciliation. *The mouth of the righteous is a fountain of life . . .* (10:11a). *The lips of the righteous feed many . . .* (10:21a). *The words of the mouth are deep waters; the fountain of wisdom is a gushing stream* (18:4; see also 12:6).

(4) Kindness. The speech of the wise does not seek the destruction of another individual through desire for personal gain or spite. More positively, wise speech is a source of life to the community. *A soft answer turns away wrath* (15:1a).

(5) Pleasantness. Such speech is pleasant to listen to, aesthetically pleasing, and thereby persuasive.

> *The mind of the wise makes their speech judicious,*
> *and adds persuasiveness to their lips.*
> *Pleasant words are like a honeycomb,*
> *sweetness to the soul and health to the body.* (16:23-24)

Wicked or foolish speech, in contrast, might be described as: (1) desiring to conceal and deceive, fundamentally untrustworthy. *The mouth of the wicked conceals violence* (10:6). *One who winks the eyes plans perverse things; one who compresses the lips brings evil to pass* (16:30).

(2) The intention of evil speech is the unlawful gain of the speaker, often achieved through the promotion of violence. *The getting of treasures by a lying tongue is a fleeting vapor and a snare of death* (21:6).

(3) Wicked speech leads to destruction. It leads, first, to the violent destruction of others through the intention of the speaker. *The babbling of a fool brings ruin near* (10:14b; see also 11:9; 16:27). But ultimately, wicked speech leads to the destruction of those who speak it. *The evil are ensnared by the transgression of their lips* (12:13a).

Although godly speech is prescribed in this section of Proverbs, one must also note the importance of godly silence. A wise person, according to Proverbs is one who speaks seldom. *Whoever belittles another lacks sense, but an intelligent person remains silent. . . . one who is trustworthy in spirit keeps a confidence* (11:12-13). See also 12:23a; 14:17, 29-30; 15:18; 16:32; 17:27-28; 19:11, 19.

In our world of pundits, where we pay experts dearly to speak their knowledge in every conceivable forum, this notion of the silent sage might seem unusual. However, according to the Egyptian model, which was very influential on Israelite wisdom, silence bespeaks a confidence and self-mastery seldom seen in our society.

Sacrifice and Worship, 15:8, 29

It has often been noted that references to "cult," that is, to outward, ritualized, communal religious observances, are sparse in the wisdom literature in general and in Proverbs in particular. The unique "secular" concerns of the sages might perhaps have caused this surprising omission in the literature of an ancient people for whom sacrifice and offering were central. The few references to cult in this section of Proverbs would seem to suggest that, for the sage, purity of purpose and motive were far more important than getting the forms and rituals exactly right (15:8; 15:29; 21:3, 27). In this, the sages agreed with the Israelite prophets throughout the biblical period, who were appalled at the moral laxity of worshipers, those who sang heartily to YHWH and offered expensive sacrifice, while oppressing the poor and the powerless (see for instance Amos 5:21-24). It is interesting to note that these two groups in Israel, whose concerns coincide infrequently, here take up a common cause for justice within the Israelite community.

Also, the writer admonishes the student to be prudent, thoughtful and reflective in worship, as in all other aspects of life. *It is a snare for one to say rashly, "It is holy," and begin to reflect only after making a vow* (20:25).

The Law of Retribution, 11:3-8, 21

The authors of this collection seem to have little difficulty with the notion that evildoers will suffer in their wickedness, while the righteous will be rewarded. What interests us here are the various ways that the punishments and rewards are meted out. That all get exactly what they deserve is never questioned! First, the wicked are thought to suffer punishment in the present, that is, during their lifetimes (11:31; 12:21; 17:13).

Second, punishment will also come at some time in the future, although the notion of some eternal punishment in the afterlife is not present in Proverbs. In the future, the reputation of the wicked will be blotted out (10:7), their hopes will be dashed (11:7), and they and their house will suffer trouble and death (10:25). See also 11:19; 12:21; 17:13. The sufferings of the wicked are caused by their own foolish choices (11:3-8; 11:27; 14:32a). But sometimes the wrath and condemnation of an enforcing deity will destroy the wicked: *Those who devise evil [YHWH] condemns* (12:2; see also 11:21a).

The arguments in this section are so strenuous and insistent that one can only suspect that they are in reaction to a deeply perceived threat to the law of retribution within the sapiential community. The future orientation of most of the punishments implies that at the present time the wicked appear to prosper. Further, there are strong rhetorical flourishes seeking to comfort those deeply troubled by the present state of affairs. *Be assured, the wicked will not go unpunished* (11:21, emphasis added).

Finally, there is a bare hint at more troubling details, the acknowledgement that the actual situation is not as it appears in this confident collection. It seems evident that, in fact, the evil are doing quite nicely. The teacher is desperate to assure that the present sweetness of the evil behavior is only temporary. *Bread gained by deceit is sweet*, we are told, *but afterward the mouth will be full of gravel* (20:17, emphasis added). It remains for the later sections of Proverbs to grapple more fully with this incomplete and misleading doctrine, and for the books of Job and Ecclesiastes to demolish it completely.

Commerce, 11:1-4; 16:11

Characteristic of Proverbs are some very secular comments on conduct in the arena of commerce. For the most part, they are ethically driven. Then, as now, there were ample opportunities to cheat and be cheated when exchanging objects of value. Two areas of trade are highlighted in this section. In the first, the sages focus on honesty. The second is more complex, dealing with issues such as power, naivete, and the consequences of foolish economic choices.

(1) False balances. Before the invention of MONEY (probably around 700 BCE) the exchange of commodities (barter) was replaced by a system of WEIGHTS AND MEASURES of useful and/or precious metals. Their value was determined by balance against fixed weights. It would be relatively easy—and no doubt was common practice—for a merchant to possess two sets of stones, one (heavier) for when he was buying and another (lighter) for selling. Thus he would pay less for purchases, but get higher payment for goods offered for sale. The authors of Proverbs strongly condemned this practice (11:1; see also 16:11, 20:10 and 20:23). The seriousness of the theological explanation for such an economic injunction (*abomination to the LORD* [11:1]) indicates how dependent ancient peoples were on trust to maintain the continuance of the economic system.

Ultimately, these admonitions were not successful. The invention of stamped metal coins, which assured both the purity and the weight of the pieces, replaced balances of weights, because coins were more difficult to counterfeit. The governments themselves then asserted the accuracy of the metallic value objects. In any case, the Bible places responsibility upon the merchant to maintain scrupulous standards; it does not endorse the Latin proverb *caveat emptor* ("Let the buyer beware!").

(2) Frequently, when buyers did not have sufficient value to procure needed commodities they would offer something of value as pledge or surety. Presumably, if at some appointed time the buyer was not able to redeem this pledged object, it would revert to the seller in lieu of the agreed purchase price. For instance, if an individual desired to buy a donkey at the agreed price of three shekels (a unit of weight) of silver, but did not have the silver, the buyer might offer a milk cow as surety until the debt was paid. If after the agreed time, the purchaser did not have the silver, the cow would revert to the one who had made the loan.

The buyer might further complicate the situation by asking a friend to provide the surety. It is here that the sages step in and offer their advice. From their perspective, providing surety for a neighbor or a stranger is the height of foolishness and self-destruction (11:15; 17:18). The language is strong. The writers characterize such dealings as trouble-causing and senseless, but no reason is given. It should be obvious, however, that such economic transactions produce division and hostility within the community.

The sages go one step further and suggest that anyone foolish enough to engage in this kind of economic suicide is "fair game." *Take the garment of one who has given surety for a stranger; seize the pledge given as surety for foreigners* (20:16). The ethical injunctions of caring for the poor and powerless seem not to apply in such situations. It is "found" money, and the person who suffers such loss clearly deserves to lose everything.

We may note some other general points about commerce in Proverbs. There is a category of proverbs that appears simply to observe economic behavior without comment, without judgment. These Proverbs have a faintly ironical and humorous slant on the vagaries of human nature, as if to say, "Aren't we silly, the ways we do things?" Note the following examples: *Some pretend to be rich, yet have nothing; others pretend to be poor, yet have great wealth* (13:7); *"Bad, bad," says the buyer, then goes away and boasts* (20:14; see also 16:26, 18:17).

Court Politics, 16:10, 15

We have already observed that the sages served as counselors to the royal household, serving as part of the palace bureaucracy. This collection within the larger works of the sages contains much advice as to how such royal officials are to regard the king and conduct themselves in the royal court. Such proverbs reflect the ambiguous relationship that Israelites had with their monarchs. On the one hand, they regarded them as the full representatives of God on earth, viewing them much as Egyptians and Babylonians regarded their monarchs (16:10, 15; 20:8). But on the other, the king was subject to YHWH who was the only true king over all Israel (21:1). Therefore, the sages enjoin the king to scrupulous honesty (17:7). The king's limitations required that he surround himself with loyal and intelligent counselors. Only then could he rule his kingdom successfully (15:22; see also 11:14; 20:18). The king's counselors, therefore, were exhorted to serve the king with diligence, loyalty and wisdom.

Ancient Near Eastern kings were enormously powerful; as a result, they were served and approached with great care (19:12; 20:2). Bribes have always been used to gain the ear of the well-connected, and to sway the king and officials towards a particular policy. Moderns call the practice "lobbying." The sages are ambivalent about the morality of bribing one's way to the inner sanctums of power. Its effectiveness is not in question! (18:16; see also 17:8, where a bribe is called *a magic stone*, and 19:6; 21:14). Only one verse raises an ethical objection: *those who hate bribes will live* (15:27).

The picture of the royal court, confirmed in much of the historical material in the Bible, is of a place fraught with danger and intrigue, where choosing the wrong side of an argument could mean imprisonment or execution. It was a place where the king, whether selfishly accumulating wealth and power or diligent to provide for the needs of his people, found himself in an extraordinarily lonely position. Sages looking out for the king's interest were therefore regarded as of the highest value (15:22; see also 11:14; 20:18).

Women and Wives, 12:4; 21:19

More will be said about the role of women in Proverbs when we examine subsequent sections. Here, the picture is clearly prejudicial against women. For the most part, in this section women are regarded as appendages and decorations for their husbands, either for good or ill. *A good wife is the crown of her husband, but she who brings shame is like rottenness in his bones* (12:4; see also 18:22; 19:13). Further, stereotypically, the sages regard women as prone to nagging and quarrelling to get their way, inflicting great misery upon their husbands: *A wife's quarreling is a continual dripping of rain* (19:13b; see also 21:9, 19).

Modern readers may be pleased to note the relative importance given to a woman's character and intelligence over her appearance: *The wise woman builds her house* (14:1); *A gracious woman gets honor* (11:16). But such a sentiment is framed in the most highly charged and offensive terms in one pronouncement: *Like a gold ring in a pig's snout is a beautiful woman without sense* (11:22). Although the comical image of swine jewelry effectively gets the message across, the association of this animal, regarded in Israel as highly unclean, with an unworthy woman is nothing less than abusive language.

We must ask exactly how a woman might be judged *without sense*. Are we speaking of women preoccupied with trivialities and superficialities, preferring the comforts of wealth over the just treatment of the poor? Amos described such women as the "cows of Bashan," who lie on their couches and ask their husbands to bring them drink (Amos 4:1). Or are we rather speaking of strong women who demand justice from their husbands, and for this reason are regarded as *contentious and fretful* (21:19)?

Individual Human Emotions, 13:12; 14:13

Some parts of Proverbs, as we have seen, are deeply grounded in the times in which they were produced, whether for good or ill. They share the prejudices and the common sense of an era that we have come to regard as unenlightened. Characteristic of the Israelite mentality is the notion of group ethos. Ancient peoples in general did not regard the individual as supremely important in relation to the desires and activities of the community. In modern Western society, individuals and their fulfillment are everything, it sometimes seems.

Even so, the insights of Proverbs on the complexities of *individual* emotional life are remarkable! There is a recognition that separate human persons have deep and important inner experiences that shape who they are. Such emotions work at profound levels, both to heal and to destroy. As one might imagine, the poetry that contains such insights is many times more complex than the average proverbial couplet in this section of Proverbs. A number of insights are gleaned from an examination of these passages: (1) Profound inner emotions are caused by outer developments, for example, by news that either fulfills expectations or dashes them! (13:12,17; see also 12:25).

(2) Emotions, by their very nature, will either heal or destroy the inner self. Their effect on the body is worse than physical illness. (18:14; 17:22; see 15:13b).

(3) Emotions, the way we truly feel inside, can never be fully shared with another: *The heart knows its own bitterness, and no stranger shares its joy* (14:10).

(4) Emotions, important as they are, are difficult to pin down. Can we ever really know exactly how we feel, or exactly what others are feeling? The sages wisely note the fundamental ambivalence of the world of human emotions: *Even in laughter the heart is sad, and the end of joy is grief* (14:13). Feelings are important, powerful, and yet impossible to understand.

Theology and the Mystery of the Divine, 15:3, 11; 21:1

We have already spoken of the "secular" nature of wisdom and of Proverbs in particular. Further, we have noted the relative inattention to cultic concerns on the part of the wise persons who assembled this collection. But there is a profound piety at the very heart of these reflections and in the sapiential sensibility as such. Proverbs bespeaks a profound sense of divine mystery. It displays a strong recognition that God is so wholly other as to be unapproachable and—more importantly— incomprehensible. Surprisingly, those supreme representatives of the intellectual tradition in Israel recognize the limitations of human wisdom. Perhaps this is the source of their sadness, their disappointment with the circumstances and possibilities of life.

The sages make many claims about their God; we note the following assertions.

(1) YHWH has unique and total insight into all aspects of the human psyche; for this reason the deity can effectively evaluate humans and refine their character (15:3, 11; 16:2; 17:3; 20:12, 27; 21:2).

(2) YHWH controls all things. This belief has three implications for the sage. First, it diminishes the importance of human intention and efforts (16:1; see also 16:9; 19:21; 20:24; 21:30-31.) Second, even the destructive side of creation is attributed to divine activity (16:4). Third, this divine control provides a basis for divination, telling the future through the operation of sacred LOTS, something like flipping a coin (16:33).

Further, divine control of the human will provides a key theological understanding of the courtier's ways with a king. The sage must recognize that the will of the king is not absolute: *The king's heart is a stream of water in the hand of the LORD; he turns it wherever he will* (21:1). Therefore, the sage must focus on conforming to the discerned will of the divine king rather than to that of the human king.

(3) The sage must depend upon God, considering the deity's power and control over all things. Faith characterizes the inner life of the sage (16:3). Note the tension

between the notion of God's control and the importance of faith. Looked at in one way, it does not matter what one does, for God is in control and will do whatever the deity wills. But some texts indicate that God's control requires human response by commitment to God's ways (16:3).

(4) *The rich and the poor have this in common: the* LORD *is the maker of them all* (22:2). This text implies an important ethical injunction that has enormous implications for the personal life of the sage, who is identified with the richer classes. This verse implies that the high and the low, the rich and the poor, the powerful and the dispossessed are not greatly different in the eyes of this God; accordingly, they *should* not treat each other as if the differences were significant. Certainly, many or perhaps most sages did not follow this injunction; even so, the idea presents itself, and the truly wise must act accordingly.

Therefore humility is enjoined. Pride and arrogance are not characteristic of the sage. And in true and consistent retributive fashion, the haughty are declared to be doomed by means of some unspecified moment of great reversal (16:5). Mary reflects a similar confidence in her joyful song, the MAGNIFICAT: "He has scattered the proud in the thoughts of their hearts. He has brought down the powerful from their thrones, and lifted up the lowly" (Luke 1:51-52; see also the Song of Hannah, 1 Sam 2:1-10).

The Third Collection: The Words of the Wise, 22:17–24:34

The Poor, 22:22-23; 24:10-12

The student is commanded not to rob the poor because YHWH pleads their cause. This section of Proverbs is more pious than the earlier sections. It claims an active role for God in enforcing the demands of wisdom. Yet it appeals to a sense of enlightened self-interest. One may not oppress the poor because they have a very powerful protector who will avenge injustice (22:22-23). A second passage (24:10-12) takes another tack. One is obligated not only to *avoid* taking advantage of the weak, but also to *rescue* those oppressed by others (*those taken away to death*). If one fails to help the powerless who are in danger of imminent destruction, God will know. God will exact a price because of one's failure to intervene to help the weak and the oppressed.

Anger, 22:24-25

Avoid a person whose emotions and behavior are uncontrolled, one who is capable of breaking out unpredictably against others. Avoid them and do not be like them. Such behavior is regarded as a snare or a means by which others might gain advantage over one, one's goals and even one's life, one's family and property. Also, in a more spiritual sense, such behavior hinders one's development as a full human being.

Pledges, 22:26-27

This passage offers greater detail about the consequences of such foolish action. Those who make foolish pledges will soon be sleeping on the floor, having lost their bed.

Ancient Landmarks, 22:28; 23:10

The sages commend the importance of a social conscience. One must not remove a neighbor's landmark. See the discussion above, on the treatment of the poor. The warrant is the same here. The redeemer is strong and will come to the owner's defense. The terms used in this case are legal: the "redeemer" is the "next of kin" (Heb. *go'el*); the case at law is a "complaint," (Heb. *rib*). The arena has shifted from robbing the poor and crushing the afflicted at the gate to moving the ancient landmarks. Someone, presumably a wealthy landowner, desires a neighboring field owned by a poorer family, which field is described as *fields of orphans* (23:10). In Israelite thought, a child missing only one parent was regarded as an orphan. The wealthy landowner moves the landmarks at night in order to include a choice field as part of his property, taking it from the poor family. The notion of legality, which would normally work in favor of the wealthy and well-connected landowner, works, in this schema, in favor of the widow and her children. She has a powerful *go'el* (redeemer) working on her behalf. The sage does not need to say that the *go'el* is YHWH.

We enjoy accounts of a great reversal. The poor, for whom the legal system usually does not work, in this case find themselves to be the most powerful. Their defender (God) equalizes all inequities.

Work Ethic, 22:29

The term "work ethic" is not used in the Bible. Rather, the sages speak of those who are skillful in their work, who apply themselves with diligence to the tasks at hand. The skilful person serves kings and not common people. There is a strong sense of class distinction in this verse, a distinction also found elsewhere in Proverbs. The sages imply that it is better to serve kings than commoners, implying also that those who serve the common people are the less skillful, while the ones who are worthy to serve kings are the more skillful.

Such a distinction may be understandable and simply a commonplace. But there is also an ethic here that is troubling. Working for the poor and disenfranchised is not regarded as a worthy occupation for a skilful worker. Such a view is the exact opposite of the idea found elsewhere that one honors God by helping the poor (14:31; 11:24-26; 19:17; 21:13; 22:9, 16). The mandate that gives preference to the poor, although occasionally present in Proverbs, does not dominate. To articulate the position most frequently expressed in Proverbs: the ruling elite deserve the best, and everyone else receives the leftovers.

Riches are ephemeral (23:4-5), and people who are rich often lose their wealth in sudden and unexpected ways. The sages imply that the pursuit of wisdom has more enduring value. Being rich is not criticized here, but rather the sages attack the notion that one must make great efforts in order to become rich. Such effort does not often succeed. Some people pursue wealth with unalloyed zeal and yet remain poor. Others, through no effort of their own, have riches thrust upon them. The patriarch Job, for instance, lost his wealth suddenly, although he did nothing to deserve his sudden poverty. He regained it just as easily.

In the light of this passage, then, how might we regard riches? The diligent worker will not necessarily become rich, but will become well-connected. Riches are not worth pursuing, because they are easily lost. The implication is that one must pursue things that are not so easily lost. A similar sentiment finds expression in the NT: "Do not store up for yourselves treasures on earth, . . . but store up treasures for yourself in heaven" (Matt 6:19-21).

Taking Care of Business, 24:27

This passage advises putting one's own comfort, security and well living last, after one has taken care of necessary business, that is those things that when neglected cause an entire enterprise to collapse. This sentiment represents "Tribal Wisdom" (see introduction), the wisdom that comes from small agricultural communities. However, it has been included in this collection characterized as primarily "Royal Wisdom" because its counsel was recognized as applicable within the royal courts even to individuals who never worked in a field.

Story of a Lazy Man, 24:32-34

This is a more lengthy reflection than we have seen in the second or the third collection. It is a little story or parable based on observation. Again it is agricultural and probably originates among the tribes. A lazy man's field is overgrown and in disrepair. The sage infers that the man's laziness caused his poverty. The last line further implies that just a *little* laziness causes a great deal of poverty. There is a significant contrast between the *little sleep* and the *little slumber,* and the *little folding of the hands to rest,* on the one hand, and poverty, which comes swiftly and destructively like a marauding army.

Poverty is depicted as an aggressive conquering force, waiting for any sign of weakness to sweep in with destruction. Only through constant diligence may one keep away the marauding hordes of poverty. The sages picture life as fraught with extreme insecurity and threat. Such is the life of an agricultural community: it is totally dependent on the chaotic forces of nature, forces over which the community has no control.

Courtly Behavior, 23:1-3, 6-8

Do not give free reign to your appetite when in the presence of royalty, the sage warns, not because it will create a bad impression, but because such fare is *deceptive food* (v. 3). Do not trust the king's friendship. Here we find a very cynical view of the court. One who depends upon the king's generosity and patronage will regret it, for the king serves only himself. Those who live for the "perks" that come from access to the centers of power will regret the trouble that is sure to come.

The sages here do not emphasize manners. Rather, they describe the court as a very dangerous setting. Trust no one! It is a very negative view of the monarchy, written for the benefit of those who will actually work for the monarchy, and written by those who have ample experience of how kings behave.

In 23:6-8 we have an interesting variation on the previous passage. Again the advice is, *Do not eat.* In this case, however, the dangerous hosts are not royalty but *the stingy.* In the first passage there is no reference to the consequences of eating with a ruler, but only a warning that the situation is dangerous. In the second passage, the consequences are graphically recorded: *You will vomit up the little you have eaten, and you will waste your pleasant words* (v. 8). The food is "wasted," that is, vomited out. It affords no nourishment, and it provides minimal pleasure. And the pleasant words too are wasted, presumably because *the stingy* are unable to appreciate or are unwilling properly to applaud the pleasant speech.

It remains to discuss the relationship between these two passages. They are placed moderately close in the collection, and they offer comment upon each other. Together, these writings are remarkably antiestablishment, antiauthority, and anti-wealth. Their tone is considerably different from what we find in the previous collections. Although warnings about the dangers of wealth and its responsible use might be found in the earlier collections, here these points are made much more forcefully.

This third collection of Proverbs develops a powerful theological critique of its society. It tends to be more pious, using theological justifications to support the advice: Don't do this, or you will suffer divine punishment. Further, this collection expresses hostility towards the avenues leading to wealth and power.

Proverbs 24:21-22 seeks to bridge the tension discussed above, between the power of the king and the power of YHWH, although it does not do so successfully. It urges fear of *both* the king and YHWH. It bases its argument on practical and self-serving considerations. Fear these kings, the earthly and the divine king, not because they are worthy of respect, loyalty and obedience, but rather because they are both capable of destroying you. This is a continuation of the advice to put a knife to one's throat when in the presence of a king. The point is clear: if you don't, the king will put a knife to *your* throat! The passage diminishes YHWH. YHWH rules and deserves to be respected only because he is brutal and vicious and may destroy you. YHWH is a dangerous and unpredictable king, an evil monarch. If you don't do things exactly right the deity will see that you are killed. Surely there are better reasons to devote oneself to God.

Legal Behavior, 24:23b-29

The sage urges honesty in the legal courts. First, this text speaks against those who unfairly favor the guilty, presumably because they are friends, or because they have been offered bribes. The sages condemn class loyalty (taking care of friends) when it interferes with others' rights.

In 24:17-20 the legal system is not at issue, but rather a circumstance in which one's enemy experiences a misfortune, presumably not as a result of any effort on the part of the sage's student. We are told, "Don't be happy about it." If God's anger is diverted towards *you* rather than your enemy, your enemy's suffering will be reduced, and you will lose the satisfaction of seeing your opponent suffer.

The consequence of favoring the wicked in the legal system is that *you . . . will be cursed by peoples, abhorred by nations* (v. 24). Cursing has much more serious overtones then a stained reputation. YHWH fulfills the curse by visiting destruction upon those who violate the moral order. Rather, the sage commands that the powerful person *rebuke the wicked* (v. 25). The person who stands against corruption will enjoy delight and *good blessing*.

Child Rearing and Parenthood, 23:13-14, 22-25

Here we find advice regarding child rearing, addressed first to the parents and then to the children. The message to the parents, repeating what has been said in the second collection, urges corporal punishment as a means to enforce parental authority. The sage tells the parents that such punishment will not result in the death of the child. There must have been some people who condemned corporal punishment. They might have suggested that physical discipline results in injury, and proposed alternate means of discipline. The sage here argues, however, that if you discipline your children physically you will save their lives.

The advice to the children (23:22-25) corresponds to the advice given previously to the parents, who have been told to assert their control over their children. Parents who do not discipline the young, harm or even kill their children. The advice to the children in *this* passage is to submit to the discipline (in this case discipline refers to the wisdom of the parents). The physical threat is not present here, but rather the promise that if the children obey, they will make their father and mother glad. The parents are told to discipline their children in order to save their (the children's) lives, while the children are told to submit to the parents' discipline because it will make the parents happy.

In all these child rearing passages, one finds an unspoken assumption that the well-being of society depends upon the maintenance of the rigid hierarchy between parents and children, and by extension, between those older ones who support the social order (and are in turn supported by that order) and the younger members of society. Probably, this injunction is directed toward those who are being groomed to take over the reins of power. The weak must be protected by the paternal efforts of those in power. If young people want to advance, they must be taught to respect the institutions of society, such as the schools, the temples, and the royal court.

Envy, 23:17

When the righteous were tempted to envy sinners, it was because the "righteous" were not doing as well the wicked. That is the only reason why sinful behavior would seem attractive. Envying sinners contrasts with continuing in the fear of the LORD. We are told not to envy the wicked because (in what seems like a tautology) they are so bad that *their minds devise violence, and their lips talk of mischief* (24:2).

Wine, 23:29-35

Why are certain kinds of immoderate behaviors strongly forbidden to the budding sage? Part of the reason relates to the work ethic, as we have seen above. Simple observation will suggest that those who indulge their appetites do not have the energy or motivation to make their way in a world that requires hard work and persistence if one is to achieve success.

In this passage the sages compose a funny story in order to ridicule unacceptable behavior. A drunken person has lost complete control, but he does not have the slightest idea of his present condition. "Why would anyone want to be like that?" the teacher implies. The student is urged not to envy the wicked. Here the pleasure-seeking style of the libertine appears at the outset very attractive, but it quickly results in disaster.

Strange Woman, 23:26-28

Here are further warnings against the danger of consorting with loose women. Two words are used, referring to different aspects of what is regarded as the same problem. The prostitute, one who sells her body, and the adulterous person, one who is unfaithful to her husband, are here lumped together (although the social dynamics of each is quite different). They pose a similar danger to the student. The sage argues that one must never associate with such wicked women for to do so can only result in harm.

Importance of Wisdom, 23:22-25; 24:3-7

The child is urged to obey the parent, regarded as the source and fount of wisdom. Further, the parent provides the reason and incentive for pursuing wisdom. The student (son) should buy wisdom in order to make the parents glad. In this instance, the metaphor is commercial. Wisdom is regarded as a valuable commodity, one that should be purchased at any cost, and never sold for any other commodity. One finds similar themes in several NT passages, (e.g., the pearl of great price, Matt 13:45-46; the treasure in the field, Matt 13:44; see also Matt 16:26). Each of these texts also uses some kind of commercial metaphor. There are many things that one may "purchase" in this life at the price of one's character, or one's soul. When persons make such a purchase, thereby sacrificing their character, the soul shrinks. Rather, one should spend all of one's personal capital to gain "wisdom."

Such efforts of elders to control the young contributed continuity and stability to the structures of society. Elders gained insight through living their lives actively self-reflective and aware. Usually, it is wise to pay careful heed to the counsel of the more experienced in society. We expect children to learn from their parents, a process that need not cease when an individual reaches maturity.

In 24:3-7 the claim is made that wisdom brings blessings, here understood to include the building and establishment of houses and the accumulation of wealth.

Further, the writer claims that wisdom is *better* than strength. By contrast, much contemporary thinking regards wisdom as stable, something homogenized and warmed over. Contemporary psychological analyses hardly ever use the term. But the sages understood wisdom as a significant element in society. They preferred wisdom to the accumulation of military might. Though they were not anti-military, the sages believed that their insight gleaned through wisdom was the most important aspect of military preparedness. In the historical narratives, sages often made the difference between military victory or disastrous defeat (e.g., Ahithophel and Hushai, 2 Sam 16:14–17:23).

The sages declare wisdom to be too high for fools. In the gate, fools do not speak with authority. Be wise, we are told, because fools contribute little to the common good. No one respects them. In the villages and rural communities the elders delivered legal decisions at the gate; in the more urbanized situations, judgment was rendered by the king or the king's representatives. Fools have no authority, no weight in such environments.

In 24:13-14 the sage leaves the commercial and legal metaphors, employing instead a metaphor of eating. Wisdom is like honey, sweet, pleasant, pleasurable. Just as the body delights in honey, the soul takes delight in wisdom. And in the last analysis, the sage reminds us, those who commit themselves to wisdom have a future, while those who don't, have their hope cut off.

Law of Retribution, 24:15-16

In 24:15-16 the sage affirms strongly the doctrine of divine retribution on the unjust and reward for the righteous, despite the many chaotic, random disasters of life. Righteous people fall seven times and rise again, unlike the wicked. The sage is arguing that the righteous recover from such blows more consistently and more rapidly than will the wicked.

The Fourth Collection: Other Proverbs of Solomon, 25:1–29:27

The maxims here are collected in larger units, usually made up of four or five related proverbs arranged according to similar concerns, structure or vocabulary.

The Mystery of God, 25:2; 27:1

Proverbs 25:2 compares God and the king, but not in the same way as in the previous collections, which saw the king and God as nearly the same. They are both a source of life, and both hold the power of life and death over their subjects. They both rule. They both exercise power with dangerous, unpredictable force. But in this collection the king and the deity contend over control of information. God remains hidden and conceals the divine plan. Therefore, an individual can have no access to the future. The king, however, in order to rule effectively, must uncover the concealed layers of information hidden by God in the world. In this conception, the king is not God, does not function as God, and is not to confuse his role with divine functions.

In 27:1, the sage, in a very sober and practical way, recognizes the limitations of wisdom: even with wisdom and careful observation, one cannot know the future.

Court Politics, 25:4-5; 29:12

The material in this collection regarding politics can be divided into two subtopics: The first surveys advice to the king and observations concerning the nature of kingship and rule. The second contains advice to the royal counselor and observations concerning the role of the royal counselor.

The king is given strong and practical advice about the way he is to conduct his rule. The proverbs warn him regarding the limitations of his authority and of his critical need for sound moral principles and honest advice so that he might accomplish the true aims of the state. He must strive to create a just and happy kingdom. The sages urge the king (or potential king) to surround himself with wise counselors. The writer compares wicked counselors to *the dross* that the metalsmith must remove when refining the silver (25:4-5). Conversely, a king who is surrounded by courtiers who tell him only what he wants to hear will surely pervert justice (29:12).

An "intelligent" king should expect to rule firmly, but will share his responsibility and authority with no one. The proverbs opt for strong, centralized government, something akin to the Davidic monarchy (28:2). An intelligent king promotes justice and righteousness in the kingdom (28:12, 15-16, 28; 29:2, 16). He must not oppress the poor (28:3; 29:14) or make *heavy exactions* (29:4). Although a wise king possesses absolute power, he must use that power to defend the weak, the poor, and the powerless. One who so rules causes the people to rejoice and find security (28:12).

Wise counselors must dedicate themselves to promoting such qualities of intelligence in the king. Such a counselor is humble, lacking obvious ambition (25:6-7), exercising persuasion with careful and courteous talk, and not exerting undue pressure (25:15). Wise counselors must treat fellow courtiers shrewdly and with suspicion. They are not to *give way* (25:26) before the wicked, and should mistrust those who compete with them for the king's attention (26:25; see 26:23-28). These passages paint a picture of the royal court as a struggle between the honest counselors who seek to steer the king toward just and unselfish practices that benefit the people, and manipulative flatterers who seek to win the king's attention through lies, telling the king only what he wants to hear.

The sages are careful to recognize both the limitations of the king and their own limitations. Justice, it is recognized, comes ultimately not from the king but from YHWH (29:26). The sage need not fear losing the king's ear to flatterers, because ultimately the divine presence in the kingdom will steer things in the right direction. Finally, we are given an enigmatic statement: *Where there is no prophecy, the people cast off restraint, but happy are those who keep the law* (29:18). "Prophecy," or more properly "vision," the communication of the divine will through direct revelation, seems to run exactly counter to the impulse of the sages who emphasize observation and critical reflection. The sages here acknowledge that other sources of information remain vital for the continuance of the work of the kingdom.

"Prophecy" restrains the people. The sages recognize that *their* type of information, while acceptable within the higher courts of royal power, does not function well in the popular realm (although the writer of Ecclesiastes probably saw things differently). "Vision" is necessary to mobilize the people to support the royal house and the king's initiatives. Clearly an examination of the written history of the kingdoms of Israel and Judah would demonstrate that the people were more likely to be swayed by prophets who claimed supernatural inspiration than by the sober advice of a wise person. For the sages, however, this would not be a problem in a well-balanced society that recognizes the need for many categories of persuasion.

Prophecy is juxtaposed with keeping the law, which again is a source of authority that differs from that of the sages. *Torah* or "law" has many meanings, but often is understood, as here, to represent the authority of the priests. The sages, wise in the extreme, recognize once again the limitations of their own efforts; they see their need to share authority with the other institutions of power in Israel. They should not seek to dominate the king by excluding those who do not share their outlook and method for understanding the divine will.

Legal Behavior, 25:7b-10

This section contains two comments about the legal system in Israel. The first one advises that one avoid excessive litigation. The advice here is based on the eventuality that one may not have all the information in the case so that, if additional information comes out subsequently, one will look foolish. Secondly, it is not fitting or seemly to air one's neighbor's secrets in public. It is far better for the offended party to take care of things privately and avoid a public scene. Again, to disobey this advice results in public shame, not for one's opponent but for oneself. Similar counsel appears in Matt 5:25; 18:15-17, and 1 Cor 6:1-8.

The second legal pronouncement, although couched in the form of advice, seems to comment on actual provisions found in the Torah itself. It refers to the individual carrying "bloodguilt" (BLOOD IN THE OT is a powerful symbol). In the ancient Near Eastern legal codes, such an individual must be avenged by the family or the community of the murdered victim. The sages command that no help or assistance be offered to such a fugitive. They are to be hounded until they are killed, and thus balance and harmony will be restored in the land (28:17).

Speech, 25:13, 25; 26:20-21; 29:19-20

The sages contrast wise speech to both speech that is ineffective and speech that is damaging. Wise and positive speech accomplishes its intention and provides health to the community. Another kind of speech does not do damage but has no real or no significant effect. A third kind of speech has an effect, but it is a damaging effect; it creates divisions within the community. These three must be distinguished if one is to understand the Israelite philosophy of rhetoric.

Positive speech is described as aesthetically pleasing (*apples of gold in a setting of silver* [25:11], a stunning image of beauty!), bringing refreshment, fruitfulness and agricultural abundance (25:13, 25).

Ineffective speech consists of words that accomplish little. The promise of a gift undelivered is compared to *clouds and wind without rain* (25:14). Words of rebuke to a servant are wasted words (29:19-20). The writer regards servants (slaves) as naturally lazy. They resist cooperation with their masters. To treat them as responsible human beings, that is, to tell them what is required in a simple and respectful manner, has no effect. Rather, the words must be accompanied by action, presumably with the threat or actual deliverance of physical punishment. This expresses the sentiment of wealthy members of society who feel that "the help" are fundamentally unreliable and must be dealt with as recalcitrant children. Words to such individuals have no effect, and are thus pointless and wasted.

In 26:2 we see how far the wise sometimes go in breaking with what they considered to be credulity or superstition. Many in the ancient world believed that words uttered in sacred curses or blessings took on a magical power that broke free and acted independently of any intention of the speaker. Because of such a concept of CURSE AND BLESSING extraordinary care must be used in choosing words, considering the damage they might do. The third commandment refers to this: "You shall not make wrongful use of the name of the LORD your God, for the LORD will not acquit anyone who misuses his name" (Exod 20:7). Use of the sacred name of God to empower a curse was forbidden, for the power of the divine name was simply too dangerous to unleash.

Contrary to this understanding, the sage here asserts that an ill directed curse remains ineffective. It *goes nowhere* (26:2). This is consistent with the sages' attitude that internal intentions hold more weight than external actions. In a similar way, we are told that cultic actions have no meaning unless accompanied by the correct internal attitude (15:8, 29; 21:3, 27).

This attitude of disparagement of ritual is seductive; it accords well with the contemporary Western notion that considers ritual and symbolic activity to be of little real importance. Only that which is done with intellectual understanding and proper emotional attitude has any value. For example, the ritual of marriage is often regarded as invalid if the two people find out later that they were not "in love," or if they are no longer "in love." One must affirm, however, that the sages are writing at a time when there might have been excessive emphasis on getting the exact ritual correct, without regard to internal attitudes or understanding. We might identify our culture as taking the opposite extreme. Therefore, the sage's counsel to our own day might well be to give greater weight to ritual than our society tends to give.

As for damaging speech, there are many words that, although neither wise nor just, are all too effective in that they tear apart the community that God has established. Such words are compared to *a war club, a sword, or a sharp arrow* (25:18), depicting a violent attack of one person on the neighbor. Such words destroy like a fire (26:20-21). Their effect is sure (25:23). Damaging speech ruins the community.

We are reminded of the many ways that speech might wound and divide. The last includes *false witness* (25:18; see also 26:28), *backbiting* (25:23), meddling in another's quarrel (26:17), malicious, deceptive joking (26:18-19), *whispering* (26:20-21 probably referring to concealed, malicious gossip), flattery (29:5), scoffing (29:8), *hasty . . . speech* (29:20), all of them examples of damaging speech.

Why does hurtful talk find such ready practitioners in the Israelite community? The writer suggests a powerful psychological explanation: *The words of a whisperer are like delicious morsels; they go down into the inner parts of the body* (26:22). Inexplicably, it feels good to tear down another person.

Social Advice, 25:16; 27:7

Here we have assembled the various maxims regarding human behavior. Two subcategories emerge that are uniquely characteristic of the wisdom point of view. The first has to do with appetite and self-control. The image of *honey* appears frequently. Sometimes it refers to the food itself. These comments provide some insight into the ways of appetite and physical well-being. In a world in which natural sweetness was not commonly available except in the form of fruit, honey when discovered was consumed enthusiastically. It caused Samson to willingly plunge his hands into the dead carcass of a lion, thereby defiling himself and breaking his vow (Judg 14:8-9). The possibility of excess was likely. The sage is warned to curb the appetite for sweets as well as other appetites indulged into excess.

Further, if one is full, honey loses its appeal. If one is starving, even the bitter appears sweet. In either case, one's judgment is skewed by appetite; appetite renders judgment unreliable. Honey also functions as a symbol for honor, reputation or standing in the community (25:27). Eating too much honey is compared with seeking too much honor. The passage enjoins humility in other contexts as well (27:2; 29:1).

Thus self-control becomes a ruling principle (25:28). Self-control counteracts the deceptive nature of appetite. It enables one to respect the boundaries of social relationships, not presuming on another's hospitality (25:17). Sages control their appetites, thereby not grabbing inappropriately for reputation, for gratification of appetite for food, or taking advantage of neighbors.

The second category of social advice is that which enjoins support for the institutions of power, and expects one's social behavior to submit to and uphold these institutions (27:8, 10; 28:24). The sages who assembled this collection highly valued the institutions of home, friendship, parents. These social constructions that hold a society together are valued highly in this collection.

Finally, the fundamental division between two groups within Israel is encouraged and maintained: *The unjust are an abomination to the righteous, but the upright are an abomination to the wicked* (29:27). The wicked, presumably those who oppose the institutions of Israel, are declared outsiders in the community, and eternal enmity is observed and commanded.

The Behavior of Fools, 25:19; 26:6, 10-11

Proverbs frequently create an imaginary group, seemingly recognizable in the constructed world of the sages but not quite so obvious in the actual lived world—a group known as or characterized as "fools." Fools possess exactly the opposite qualities of those that the sages find admirable. Fools are recognized as a terrible pain to those who depend upon them (25:19; 26:6, 10), persons not worthy of honor (26:1, 8), sluggards who only accomplish something when beaten (26:3), individuals not worthy of engaging in any kind of serious discourse:

Do not answer fools according to their folly,
  or you will be a fool yourself.
Answer fools according to their folly,
  or they will be wise in their own eyes. (26:4-5)

Although these two passages appear to contradict one another, in either case the notion is that fools are not capable of serious conversation. Fools also are incapable of wise communication, that is, they do not know how to communicate by using the categories of wisdom (26:7, 9), and finally, they are incapable of changing (26:11).

Other passages, not in this particular cluster of descriptions, build on the description of the fool. These references point out that the anger of fools is dangerous (27:3), that they do not know enough even to escape from danger (27:12), and that they make a mess out of the legal system (29:9).

As bad as the condemnation of fools appears, this cluster of negative descriptions is marshalled to support a different point that the sage is making. As bad as the fool appears to be, there is one quality commonly found in the sage that is even worse. This is the point the writer wants to make:

Do you see persons wise in their own eyes?
  There is more hope for fools than for them. (26:12)

The writer describes two kinds of fools, the second less obviously so, because they appear to be wise. A self-confident, independent sage is *a greater fool* than the hapless figure described in the preceding verses. This is an admirable moment of self-criticism on the part of the sages. In 28:26, walking in wisdom is contrasted with trusting one's own wits. Presumably, the sage expects the wise person to depend on wisdom that is external, either in the tradition or from some invisible divine source, rather than wisdom that proceeds only from raw, self-contained intellect.

The Fifth Collection: The Words of Agur and Lemuel, 30:1–31:31

Because of the unique nature of this section, I will treat its material differently. Section five consists of three lengthy, coherent poems that are very philosophical and literary. They are Philosophical or Theological Wisdom (see introduction) and have much in common with the other samples of philosophical wisdom, including the poems about Dame Wisdom and Dame Folly in the first section, as well as the Books of Job and Ecclesiastes. *The words of Agur* (30:1-33), *The words of King*

Lemuel (31:1-9), which include a distinct literary piece, and the Song of the Capable Wife (31:10-31), will be treated in order, since they represent coherent treatises.

The Words of Agur, 30:1-33

There exists no independent attestation regarding Agur. Although the name occurs in the ancient Near East, there is no figure with that name recorded in the Hebrew Bible. He must remain an anonymous scribe, although his profound reflections deserve our careful attention.

He introduces his thoughts as an ORACLE, *hammassa'* (often translated "the burden of . . ."), and also by the formula *thus says* (*ne'um*; more literally "utterance of . . ."). Both terms in Hebrew are standard, almost stereotypical introductions to prophetic speech. But the utterance here is not ascribed to YHWH as is customary in prophetic speech, or even to the king (often messengers would assume the prophetic formula when they delivered messages from the king). Instead, the utterance is attributed to *the man* (*hageber*). There is no clear precedent for this use of prophetic formulas; it creates an entirely unique space for the discourse that follows, one that is decidedly at home in the wisdom tradition. The utterance here is not from God, or from God's representatives, but is from the camp of mortality, from *the man*.

As we read on, we will note that this utterance is world-weary, from an individual who has given up on the normal sources of authority and information. He despairs of the entire wisdom enterprise, and finds himself in a deep pit of hopelessness and ennui. *I am weary, O God . . . Surely I am too stupid to be human . . . I have not learned wisdom* (vv. 1-3). Although he has identified himself as *the man*, in the next few verses he distances himself from normal human capabilities; these are no longer available to him. *I do not have human understanding* (v. 2).

Following his declaration of ignorance and inability, he asks a series of rhetorical questions, the answer to which is obviously "God." *Who has ascended to heaven and come down? . . . Who has established all the ends of the earth?* (v. 4). Agur does not know the answer, but he challenges the reader to answer the question. The tone mocks the presumption of the readers who think that they do know the answers. The questions are reminiscent of the questions that YHWH asks Job in the frightening climax to that book (Job 38–41). In Job, the questions are framed, "Can you do these things?" Of course, these questions silence Job, for only God can do these things and Job knows it. But here, the speaker denies even the ability of anyone to know who can do such magnificent deeds.

The following verses do not share the cynical tone of the opening lines. From a historical perspective, we might suggest that these subsequent verses originate from a different source, and were simply added here to fill out the collection. That certainly remains a possibility, but the placement of what follows after such a painful introduction, skews the reading and compels us to question the confident statements we find.

These positive words began as follows: *Every word of God proves true; he is a shield to those who take refuge in him* (v. 5). But has not Agur just told us how unavailable such a word might be in the world *he* inhabits? This weary sage does not even attempt to find such a word, but speaks from the heart of his own limited, damaged human experience. One might then understand this confident pronouncement as one half of a dialogue opposed to the cynicism of Agur. Here an individual finds refuge in God's word and expresses supreme confidence in the ability to remain true and unchanging through all the exigencies of life. Who then are we to believe, given this confluence of conflicting voices?

The tension here embodied expresses the struggles of faith in the wisdom enterprise. Wisdom, committed to the reliability of observation, looks upon the pain of the world, the stupidity and cruelty of humans, and despairs. In response, the pious believer declares confidence in what God has spoken, warning the intellectual regarding the danger of adding to the divine words. With ruthless honesty and confidence in the reader's ability to navigate this theological swamp, the sages place both expressions side by side. We must assert that both are expressions of faith, although we must enlarge our idea of faith in order to include both of them.

What follows in the Agur collection fits somewhere in between the two other pronouncements. The speaker recognizes the fundamental limitations of the human perspective. Poverty and riches both may turn a person away from God. The rich may deny YHWH, while the poor may profane God's name through violation of the moral order (theft). What is left is a kind of moderation, a safe mean where it may be possible to serve the LORD. The speaker makes two requests: the first, for deliverance from falsehood, and the second, for economic moderation. Both requests are characteristic of a sage who is committed to integrity in speech and mastery of appetites.

Not all proverbial statements affirm this notion of economic moderation. Some are rather supportive of rich people, regarding them as the uniquely blessed of the Lord. Here, however, riches are seen not as a blessing but rather as a snare that can drive someone from the divine path.

One finds here a unique sensitivity to the struggles faced by the poor, struggles that place them in moral dilemmas. The rich remain blissfully unaware of such dilemmas, according to this portrayal. Put very simply, issues of survival can easily overshadow efforts to "do the right thing."

In vv. 10-14 we have a list of various activities that are regarded as wicked. They include slander of a servant, cursing of parents, moral hypocrisy, and the oppression of the poor. It might be significant that the litany of negative behaviors concludes with a pronouncement concerning the poor, which relates this passage to the previous one (vv. 7-9). The first in the list of bad behaviors deals with persons who are marginalized by their profession, the servants; the last speaks of those who *devour the poor . . . [and] the needy* (v. 14).

Such a structure is called a CHIASM, where the beginning and the end of the poem reflect similar concerns, while the middle provides some comment on the whole. In this case, the frame speaks of subservient individuals oppressed by the rulers, of the poor devoured by the rich, while the middle verses refer to the moral hypocrisy of the proud. We note a profound criticism of the moral wickedness of the rich who, while *pure in their own eyes . . . are not cleansed of their filthiness* (v. 12). Perhaps throughout we are presented with a single sin, a boastful pride that shows no regard for those less powerful.

How can we relate any of these statements to the disillusioned pronouncements of the sage Agur? Perhaps we cannot. But a few connections appear possible. First, throughout most of these early poems of the chapter we note a profound disappointment in and distrust of the social structures of ancient Israelite society, which traditionally had regarded the rich as rightfully in first place, not only in power, but also in moral and spiritual blessedness. Historically, the sages tended to come from this group of the elite, and in their professional efforts they normally would support the structures that maintained this social division.

Agur has despaired of the wisdom enterprise. In the prayer that follows (vv. 7-9), the sage asks the Lord to keep him from riches because (contrary to the conventional wisdom) they breed forgetfulness of divine priorities. Poverty is regarded here not as a punishment but rather as a state that compels desperate measures for survival.

Finally, a picture of society is created in which the servants and the poor are oppressed horribly by the lofty, those who devour the weak and the powerless. The writer offers a twofold societal criticism, first, of the rich, and second, of the institution of the sages who are produced by the ruling class and in turn support its hold on power in society.

There follows a series of numerical proverbs that come close to pure natural observation without comment or wider application. They are similar in structure to v. 7 (*Two things I ask of you . . .*) but unlike v. 7 seem to contain no moral judgment.

It is difficult to determine whether the whole point of the numerical series found in vv. 18-19 is contained in the final item, or whether the list lacks any logical or literary arrangement. What does the sage mean exactly by *too wonderful for me*? Certainly there is an admission, present in the early statements of Agur, that there are some things that even the wisest sage cannot figure out, no matter how long and complex one's observation may have been. Scientific understanding of snakes or eagles does not in any way make the observations of their behavior any less wonderful. The last item, *the way of a man with a girl*, speaks of the mystery of romance. What makes men act the way they do? The sages shake their heads and confess bewilderment.

This last example, from the human community rather than from the world of nature, is meant to correspond to the others, but what qualities create this correspondence? What do the three descriptions have in common? In each case, a kind of movement appeared to have no external motive force—the movement seems to happen by itself. Romance and sexual attraction partake of this mysterious movement. It must also be pointed out that the last item functions as a kind of punchline, and in its original context it probably evoked laughter.

In v. 20, a powerful image describes the adulteress. Every time this woman appears in Proverbs the allusion is to Dame Folly. The image of sexual seduction communicated through eating makes this connection more intense. The woman wipes her mouth and cravenly claims her innocence. How better to express the cold and calculating picture of unrepentant evil? The verse seems to hang loose in this final collection, connected to nothing. Who is this woman? Is it simply a warning to the student against compromising his commitment to wisdom because of a hedonistic devotion to sexual experience? Or is it rather part of the teacher's continuing polemic against false doctrine and the teachers of such doctrine? We must suspend judgment until we get to the final poem in the collection, which deals with the *capable wife* (31:10).

What kinds of things make the earth tremble? The answer is given in vv. 21-23. Earthquakes shake the very foundations of a community, and in this case the writer challenges not physical structures but the very social fabric that maintains the human communal web. Trembling is negative, a fear at things shaken that were always believed stable and secure. Slaves will become kings. Fools will no longer be poor, but rather *glutted with food* (v. 22), and a maid will usurp her mistress. In each case relations between the classes break down, and that causes the sage to tremble with dread. The song of Mary in the NT regards the same reversal but with great joy. She sings:

> He has brought down the powerful from their thrones,
> and lifted up the lowly;
> he has filled the hungry with good things,
> and sent the rich away empty. (Luke 1:52-53)

See also the Song of Hannah: "He raises up the poor from the dust . . . to make them sit with princes and inherit a seat of honor" (1 Sam 2:8). In these verses in Proverbs however, that same reversal becomes a cause for terror and insecurity.

How does the reference to *an unloved woman when she gets a husband* (v. 23) fit the context? There appears to be a sense of appropriateness that certain women by virtue of their station deserve to remain lonely, and if such a woman finds companionship, it too threatens the communal ethos. What a mean-spirited series of pronouncements we find here! This writer acknowledges the same moral and intellectual collapse as Agur had portrayed in the first four verses. This person reacts differently, regarding the rise of the banished classes with horror, as a threat to the desirable status quo.

In vv. 24-28, the writer offers a list of things small but wise, all occurring in nature. We might want to find allegorical significance in the observations regarding the ants, the badgers, the locusts and the lizards, but the meaning is plain, more transparent than the sense of the preceding numerical series. The weak and the powerless, by virtue of their unique gifts and abilities, are able to compensate for their lack of power and thereby accomplish great things. These verses constitute a direct attack on the effectiveness and meaningfulness of the social order that is designed to keep people in their proper place. A lizard's place, for instance, is not in the king's palace, and yet, in spite of its seeming defenselessness, it frequents the domain of the royal family. In a similar fashion, the poor can move from their place to the place of privilege.

The next passage, vv. 29-31, by itself might express approval for the stately stride of the lion, the rooster, and the king, but juxtaposed with the earlier series, these descriptions take on a more mocking, ironic tone. Although we might admire the lion, the description of the king follows the image of a strutting rooster, thus allowing the possibility of its farcical intent. Lizards find access to king's houses, the social order is mocked (or reversed as in the previous series [vv. 21-23]) and so the strutting of the rooster/king takes on a rather comic or ludicrous aspect.

We conclude that these various passages in the chapter did not originate from a single hand. They represent different political and theological perspectives, frequently at odds with each other. However, when placed together, they take on a significance that none of them would have by itself. Agur begins the collection with his world-weary attitude, despairing of the ability of wisdom to solve humanity's problems or to answer humanity's questions. He raises significant doubts about the social and political structures that supported the institution of the sages. Therefore the later passages, which alternately support or question those social structures, come to be understood in the context of the original questions raised by Agur. The chapter, read as a whole, creates the impression of a world in turmoil, its stability shaken to the core. It remains for the reader to determine the possibilities of the new world that might yet be created.

The Words of King Lemuel, 31:1-9

Although these words are placed in the mouth of a king, a masculine figure, they claim to originate with the king's mother: *An oracle that his mother taught him* (v. 1). The queen mother advises the young monarch about life. The pronouncement takes the form of a series of prohibitions regarding behavior considered inappropriate to a king. They are introduced with a resounding threefold No!: *No, my son! No, son of my womb! No, son of my vows!* (v. 2). Stronger language can hardly be imagined.

The first prohibition is a warning once more, against the predatory woman who will rob the strength of a young man. How ironic that this warning against women comes from the mouth of a well-placed feminine figure. Were women ever as dangerous and soul-destroying as those portrayed in the Book of Proverbs? Although claiming to be a woman's admonition, must we characterize the text as typical patriarchal propaganda?

Or might this warning, like many others, be a warning against a rival theological perspective, personified here as the ravenous woman, frequently appearing as an alternate rendering of Dame Folly. The warning does not stand alone, however, but is first in a series. Kings must not consort with strange women; kings should not drink wine. The warrant for the command concerning women is that such women will rob the king of his strength and destroy him. Strong drink causes kings to forget their decrees and *pervert the rights of all the afflicted* (v. 5).

Strong drink is dangerous because under its influence the king might not protect the poor, which is his chief responsibility!

The themes of strong drink and poverty are then treated from a different perspective. *Give strong drink to one who is perishing* (v. 6), but not to a king. A king should not drink because it will cloud his moral judgment. Poor persons should drink to forget their misery. Lemuel's mother again directs the discourse towards the king, giving him strong advice regarding his treatment of the poor.

> *Speak out for those who cannot speak,*
> *   for the rights of all the destitute.*
> *Speak out, judge righteously,*
> *   defend the rights of the poor and needy.* (vv. 8-9)

The Capable Wife, 31:10-31

What follows in the chapter functions as the counterpart to the warning against the ravenous woman in 31:3. Lemuel's mother speaks of a *capable wife* (v. 10). What qualities make her so capable, so desirable to her husband, qualities that are *far more precious than jewels*? There are many passages throughout Proverbs that picture women who cause their husband misery. We have reflected upon some of the implications of these passages and what they say concerning the roles of women in the ancient world. Here we have their opposite figure.

How is she described? Why is she so good? Her efforts bring economic advantages to her husband and her family. She trades in fibers (v. 13), she imports necessities for her household (v. 14), and she works hard and long hours to direct and provide for them (v. 15). She increases her holdings and wields considerable economic power, acting with considerable autonomy.

The second section (vv. 17-24) regards specifically her manual labor. *She girds herself with strength* (v. 17). *She puts her hands to the distaff* (v. 19). *She makes herself coverings* (v. 22). It is mentioned that *she opens her hand to the poor, and reaches out her hands to the needy* (v. 20). We have here an example of an attitude common in this final collection of Proverbs. Strength and authority always bring with them responsibility to provide for the needs of the poor. "Survival of the fittest" does not function in this economy of the wise.

The third section of the poem about the capable wife (vv. 25-31) addresses the reputation of the woman and her husband, first in the community and then in the smaller family unit. *Her husband is known in the city gates, taking his seat among the elders of the land* (v. 23). Presumably, the husband has time to engage in civic activities because his wife cares for the more "material" needs of the household. Frequently, this passage has been regarded as one that empowers women more than most others in the Bible. However, the division of the labor, which here gives the woman a surprising degree of authority, nonetheless places the husband in the superior position.

The sage continues the description: those who surround the woman recognize and admire her qualities. *Her children rise up and call her happy; her husband too, and he praises her* (v. 28). Her husband compliments her: *Many women have done excellently, but you surpass them all* (v. 29). Finally, the woman's speech is marked by wisdom: *She opens her mouth with wisdom, and the teaching of kindness is on her tongue* (v. 26, lit. "a *torah* of steadfast love"). Note that wisdom here is associated with kindness.

We find, therefore, that women are capable of wisdom and of exercising significant economic freedom within the constraints of the ancient society. Therefore, at the close of the entire book, we confront once again the essential paradox at the heart of the wisdom enterprise: wisdom liberates; it opens up the possibilities of being human regardless of gender or economic status. But on the other hand, wisdom takes on the shape of the social structures in which it finds itself, and thereby assumes traditional prejudices that have always oppressed the powerless.

At the conclusion of this study, therefore, we are left with the necessity of making our own choice. *We may listen* to wisdom when it liberates, when it challenges us to break the boundaries and chains that hurt and restrict human potential. *We may listen* when the wisdom tradition protects us from accepting every trend or fashion that seems exciting and new but ultimately damages. But we will need to *reject* the teachings of the sages when they maintain and support the oppressive social structures that continue to plague our culture. So wisdom ultimately demands the exercise of *our* wisdom—as it always has.

Work Cited

Hassler, Jon. 1990. *North of Hope.*

Ecclesiastes

James L. Crenshaw

Introduction

Ecclesiastes may be the strangest book in the Bible. Its author, who bears the unusual name Qoheleth, considers life futile, even absurd. He questions the advantage of virtuous conduct and identifies death as the culprit. Nevertheless, he urges youth to seize the moment and to enjoy the positive things God has bestowed on humankind, reminding them of unwelcome days yet to come.

The author presents his reflections arising from close scrutiny, the ego remaining dominant throughout the book. Both form and content link his thoughts with Proverbs, Job, Sirach, Wisdom of Solomon, and a few of the Psalms (e.g., 49, 73, 37, 34). Modern interpreters label these works WISDOM LITERATURE, yet Ecclesiastes alone denies the power of wisdom to benefit human existence.

Authorship

The author identifies himself as *Qoheleth* (1:1; NRSV, *Teacher*), a feminine form construed as masculine, and claims to have been a ruler in Jerusalem (1:12). A colophon in 1:1 makes the claim specific, linking the book with Solomon. A major literary unit, 1:12–2:26, purports to be a royal testament, an experiment so grand that it recalls the Deuteronomistic portrayal of Solomon's vast wealth and achievements. Other parts of Ecclesiastes are written from the perspective of a subject rather than a king, and Qoheleth observes that oppression of the weak is a fact of life.

The language of the book indicates a considerably later period than the tenth century, confirming modern scholars' skepticism about the historicity of Solomonic authorship. Clearly, the author wished to alert readers to the literary fiction at work. Why else would he have referred to Solomon's kingship as a past event (1:12), a curiosity that prompted a later rabbinic suggestion that the king was deposed?

Like many books in the Bible, Ecclesiastes has been submitted to editorial activity. Qoheleth's teachings consist of 1:12–12:8, with possible glosses in 2:26; 3:17; 8:12-13 which contradict his understanding of divine judgment. A superscription (1:1) and two epilogues (12:9-12, 13-14) refer to Qoheleth in third-person narrative (vv. 9-10, perhaps also in v. 11, *one shepherd*: Solomon) and introduce traditional piety at odds with Qoheleth's views.

A thematic statement in 1:2 recurs in 12:8 and forms an inclusion for his teachings. It may derive from Qoheleth, or it may represent an astute editorial summary of his thoughts.

Contradictions in the book have evoked several different explanations. Some early Christian commentators suggested that the author employed a Greek device, diatribe, to emphasize the dialogic nature of reality. Qoheleth thus entered into debate with himself or with imagined disputants. Some modern critics think he cites opponents' views, without any indication of quoting, which he then proceeds to challenge in toto or in part.

Other interpreters consider Qoheleth's teachings a sort of notebook with entries from different periods and circumstances, hence contradictory in character. Still others distinguish between the author and his persona, while stressing both Qoheleth's honesty and life's ambiguities that led to opposing conclusions.

In short, Qoheleth describes life, which seldom accommodates the desire for tidiness. Some interpreters suggest the modern concern for consistency did not apply to ancient logic. However one understands the contradictions in the book, the fact stands that more than one author is responsible for its final form.

Historical Context

Like Proverbs and Job, Ecclesiastes lacks historical references that would enable critics to ascertain its date of composition. To be sure, a few allusions (4:13-16; 8:2-4; 9:13-15; 10:16-17) have seduced interpreters into considerable speculation, but such effort has borne little if any fruit.

The story of a poor person who emerged from prison to rule the land was a literary topos, recalling the Joseph episode, and the same goes for the ambiguous anecdote about a little city that was rescued (might have been spared?) by a poor wise man who was forgotten. The reference to a king may actually connote any local Persian authority. Two Persian loan words, *pardes* (garden) and *pitgam* (decree) occur in the book, and the Aramaizing language most resembles that of other biblical books from the transitional period before rabbinic Hebrew came to prominence.

Qoheleth seems to have fallen under minimal Hellenistic influence, but nothing suggests that he lived during or after the momentous events of the Maccabean revolt in the second century. His emphasis on entrepreneurial enterprises, wealth, mercantile ventures, and investments fits into the age reflected by the remarkable Zenon business records from Egypt which describe the economic situation in Syria-Palestine. A mid-third-century date for Qoheleth is therefore likely. Fragments of 5:13-17; 6:3-8; and 7:7-9 discovered at Qumran and dating from the middle of the second century BCE do not permit a date for Qoheleth much later than the third century.

Ecclesiastes was probably written in JERUSALEM, although a few interpreters opt for EGYPT or PHOENICIA as place of origin. Certain features indicate a Judean environment: the references to clouds and rain (11:3; 12:2), a farmer's preoccupation with

ECCLESIASTES 231

changes of the wind (1:6; 11:4), use of wells and cisterns (12:6), the almond tree (12:5), and mention of temple and sacrifice (5:1; 9:2).

Style and Structure

Qoheleth's style is rich in literary forms. Besides the reflection based on personal observation (I saw, I said, I turned, I considered, I know, I concluded) and royal fiction, he drew on traditional wisdom. One finds short sayings, admonitions, exemplary story, parable, antitheses, better sayings, statements of existence (there is . . .), lists, and autobiographical narratives. His special antitheses, variously described as polar opposites or *zwar/aber* statements (yes . . . but), engage the mind by recognizing relative truths.

Use of preferred phrases, refrains, and special words hammers away at resistance to the content of Qoheleth's teaching. Life is futile, indeed absurd; all effort amounts to chasing after or feeding on (shepherding) the wind; there is nothing better than to enjoy life. Favorite expressions (under the sun) and words (futile, toil, work, profit, chance, time, gift, portion, death, evil, good, etc.) echo through the corridors of the mind.

Neither the structure nor the form of discourse is clear. The lines between poetry and prose have thus far eluded critics, who cannot agree as to which of these best characterizes the book. Similar controversy surrounds the attempt to identify a structure.

Most interpreters agree that Qoheleth's teachings are enclosed by a colophon and by one or two epilogues, while poems prominently featuring nature's rhythm (1:4-11) precede and conclude (11:7–12:7) his insights. Beyond these indications of structure, scholars have identified formal linkages (refrains; polar expressions) and have sought the book's structure in its content (a palindrome or mirror image; unity of tone and spirit). Perhaps part of the difficulty derives from the inadequacy of the Hebrew language to convey abstract philosophical observations of the sort Qoheleth wished to advance.

Theology

Interpreters are divided over the nature of Qoheleth's teachings. Some critics think he champions the cause of joy and protects divine freedom. Others argue that Qoheleth announces the bankruptcy of wisdom with respect to its mastery of life and its faith in divine benevolence. Whether the ambiguity rests in the text or in its readers, the fact remains that Qoheleth's teachings continue to fascinate moderns and to compel them to ask the same questions he did more than two millennia ago.

Given the presence of death's shadow, does life have any purpose? Enjoyment, when possible, certainly seemed an appropriate response to Qoheleth, but was it sufficient to offset the terrible silence or indifference of God? Qoheleth's oft-mentioned divine gift softened the concept only if human beings controlled this good, which they did not. Chance determined everything, irrespective of worth. Such a message, however accurate, offers little basis for joy, even while encouraging efforts to live as fully as possible before old age and death put an end to all hope.

For Further Study

In the *Mercer Dictionary of the Bible*: ECCLESIASTES, BOOK OF; WISDOM IN THE OT; WISDOM LITERATURE.

In other sources: J. L. Crenshaw, *Ecclesiastes,* OTL; *Old Testament Wisdom*; and "Qoheleth in Current Research," *HAR* 7 (1984):41–56; M. V. Fox, *Qohelet and his Contradictions*; R. Gordis, *Koheleth—the Man and his World*; A. Lauha, *Kohelet,* BZAW; J. A. Loader, *Polar Structures in the Book of Qohelet*; N. Lohfink, *Kohelet,* DNEB; R. Murphy, *Ecclesiastes,* WBC; G. Ogden, *Qoheleth*; G. von Rad, *Wisdom in Israel*; C. F. Whitley, *Koheleth*; R. N. Whybray, *Ecclesiastes,* NCB.

Commentary

An Outline

I. Introductory Framework, 1:1-11
  A. A Colophon, 1:1
  B. Thematic Statement, 1:2-3
  C. Nothing New under the Sun, 1:4-11
II. Qoheleth's Teachings
  Enclosed by the Envelope Structure, 1:12–11:6
  A. A Royal Experiment, 1:12–2:26
  B. Events and Their Times, 3:1-15
  C. The Tears of the Oppressed, 3:16–4:3
  D. Some Proverbial Insights, 4:4-6
  E. Advantages of Companionship, 4:7-12
  F. The Fickle Crowd, 4:13-16
  G. Religious Duties, 5:1-9 [MT 4:17–5:8]
  H. The Disappointments of Wealth,
    5:10–6:9 [MT 5:9–6:9]

  I. A Transitional Unit, 6:10-12
  J. A Collection of Proverbs, 7:1-14
  K. On Moderation, 7:15-22
  L. Seeking and Finding, 7:23-29
  M. Rulers and Subjects, 8:1-9
  N. The Mystery of Divine Activity, 8:10-17
  O. Death's Shadow, 9:1-10
  P. Time and Chance, 9:11-12
  Q. Wasted Wisdom, 9:13-18
  R. Another Collection of Proverbs, 10:1-20
  S. The Element of Risk, 11:1-6
III. Concluding Framework, 11:7–12:14
  A. Youth and Old Age, 11:7–12:7
  B. Thematic Statement, 12:8
  C. Two Epilogues, 12:9-14

Introductory Framework, 1:1-11

A Colophon, 1:1

As in so many biblical texts (e.g., Prov 1:1; 30:1; Amos 1:1; Jer 1:1), an editor identifies the author. The name Qoheleth, otherwise unattested outside this book, occurs seven times (1:1, 2, 12; 7:27; 12:8, 9, 10), twice with a definite article (7:27; 12:8). The participle form indicates a function, like similar terms for a scribe and binder of gazelles in Ezra 2:55, 57 and Neh 7:59, respectively. In light of the reference to Davidic lineage, the verb *qahal* (to assemble) may allude to Solomon's actions recorded in 1 Kgs 8:1-2, and by extension to his assembling of wives and proverbs.

Alternatively, the name Qoheleth is taken to be a personal name, a pen name, and an acronym. The name is also explained as haranguer, as in a diatribe, and as a personification of sayings in the way wisdom and folly were personified in Prov 8 and 9. In the Latin Vulgate, Jerome equated the Greek translation of the word *ecclesiastes* with an official function of speaking in an assembly, which gave rise to Luther's "Der Prediger" and English renderings such as "the Preacher" (NRSV, *the Teacher*).

Thematic Statement, 1:2-3

A thematic statement and its elaboration set the tone of the book. The expression, often translated "vanity of vanities," is a superlative, meaning the ultimate futility—like "Song of Songs," the most excellent song. The word *hebel* (NRSV, *vanity*), which Qoheleth uses thirty-eight times, expresses brevity and insubstantiality, ephemeral like breath and a nonentity like idols. The repetition underlines the absurdity of everything, as does the question, which functions as negation. One achieves nothing from toil on earth.

Nothing New under the Sun, 1:4-11

A remarkable poem leads into Qoheleth's royal experiment and increases the irony of such endeavor. Some critics think Qoheleth borrowed the poem, which uses several stylistic devices to maximum effect—*generations* with respect to the heavenly bodies and human beings, *goes* as a euphemism for death, withholding of the subject *wind* until the latest possible moment, achieving a sense of totality by referring to the four compass points, and imitating life's monotony by dull repetition. Movements in nature and society have no discernible results except to exhaust the participants; the glorious sun (god) pants, like his steed, and the everflowing rivers do not make any permanent difference in the depth of the sea. In society ceaseless speech, ears eager to hear, and insatiable eyes engage in a frustrated search for something new. Forgetfulness alone provides an illusion of novelty, and the human wish to be remembered is declared to have no basis in reality.

Qoheleth's Teachings Enclosed by the Envelope Structure, 1:12–11:6

A Royal Experiment, 1:12–2:26

1:12-18. Qoheleth's conclusions. Qoheleth claims to have been *king . . . in Jerusalem* (v. 12), and boasts about surpassing all previous rulers there. Both comments expose the author's literary fiction, for neither actually applies to SOLOMON, although the tradition about his exceptional wisdom gave rise to the remark here.

Qoheleth assesses life as an unpleasant preoccupation and shepherding (or chasing) the wind. Two proverbs reinforce his point. The first saying asserts that the crooked (back?) cannot be straightened and what is missing cannot be counted. Ancient educators in Egypt used the former notion differently; they insisted that carpenters could indeed straighten a crooked stick and that teachers could educate reluctant students. Qoheleth sets the proverb in the context of divine determinism, which none could alter. The second proverb also derives from an educational context. It acknowledges the unwelcome aspects of increased knowledge.

2:1-11. Pleasure examined. The purpose of the royal fiction becomes evident in this section, for only a king had the means and the power to put pleasure to the ultimate test. A curious feature of this text is Qoheleth's insistence that his intellect remained in control, which arguably skewed the results, but one must not forget that a wise man speaks here. Qoheleth examines pleasure and dismisses it as futile; is this a commentary on his subsequent admonitions to enjoy life? Here he calls pleasure a profitless endeavor. The other royal activities are typical in the ancient Near East. The king built monuments to his greatness— houses, vineyards, gardens, parks—and acquired unlimited possessions, precious metals—gold and silver—and slaves for sexual pleasure. He did what he desired, in the end concluding that the entire experiment only highlighted life's futility and profitlessness, indeed reinforced the image of chasing the wind.

2:12-23. The life of the intellect. Now Qoheleth puts wisdom to the test and concedes that it is relatively superior to stupidity. He uses a proverb to make this point: the eyes of intelligent people are open, whereas ignorant people walk in darkness. Ancient Sumerian teachers referred to their school as the place to which students came with closed eyes and from which they departed with open eyes. Qoheleth notes, however, that a common end awaits the wise and the fool, making all his own efforts to be wise wasted energy. Death cancels all supposed benefits, and short memories exacerbate matters. Such unpleasant thoughts prompt Qoheleth to reach the astonishing conclusion, at least for a sage, that he *hated life* (v. 17).

His subsequent remarks take up another irksome reality, one connected with the earlier observation about death's leveling power. No one can be certain that the person who inherits will act intelligently, thus the one slight comfort for those who cannot take their possessions with them is effectively canceled.

2:24-26. What then? Qoheleth concludes that nothing is better than the ordinary pleasures of eating, drinking, and working. One need not be a king to enjoy these things; however, Qoheleth observes that God determines who can find such joy. The language lacks moral connotations; the one who pleases God simply means "the lucky person," and the sinner is "the unlucky person." Of course, such arbitrary treatment of human beings occurs in an absurd universe where people feed on the wind.

Events and Their Times, 3:1-15

3:1-9. A list of times. In form, this brief section resembles Prov 30:11-14 and 18-19, where the words "generation" and "way" unite short lists of related things. Qoheleth uses a poem, which some interpreters think antedates him, to demonstrate life's profitlessness. The chiastic form sets vv. 1-8 off from Qoheleth's concluding question; v. 1 refers to birth and death, whereas v. 8 mentions love and hate, war and peace.

Fourteen antitheses appear here, each introduced by the word *time*. The rhythm is noteworthy, and in several instances the first and third verb are related, as are the second and fourth (e.g., weeping and laughing, mourning and dancing). This practice favors an erotic understanding of "casting stones" (NRSV, *throw*) as some rabbinic interpreters recognized. Other explanations for this image appeal to counting procedures in commerce, agricultural efforts to clear land for tilling, and mythological concepts for repopulating the earth after a flood. The poem spans the course of human events, beginning on the personal level and ending in the public domain.

3:10-15. God's relationship to time. This section begins positively, only to end on a somber note. God made everything appropriate for its occasion and concealed something within the human intellect—perhaps a sense of mystery or a yearning for eternity—but rendered the gift useless. The word translated frequently as "eternity" (v. 11, ASV, RSV, NJV, TLB, NIV, NKJV, NASV; NRSV, REB, *a sense of past and future*) means "hiddenness" if vocalized differently, which makes sense of futile searching from A to Z (by astrologers claiming to know the times?). The divine purpose is said to be educative—to instill fear in human beings, a curious idea when juxta-posed alongside the image of God chasing past events (cf. Sir 5:3).

The Tears of the Oppressed, 3:16–4:3

3:16-22. A single fate for human beings and animals. The prevalence of injustice provokes an explanation: that God has surely fixed a time for judging deeds—if the principle behind 3:1-8 holds true.

Qoheleth ventures still another justification for divine inactivity, the posing of a test to show people that they do not differ essentially from beasts. They breathe the same air and then die, returning to dust (cf. Gen 3:9; Job 10:9; 34:15). With this observation Qoheleth rejects the emerging belief in survival after death as more substantial than a shadowy existence in SHEOL. The *who knows . . . ?* (v. 21) functions as a strong denial: no one knows what happens to human breath at death. This ignorance again prompts Qoheleth to urge enjoyment in toil.

4:1-3. Undried tears. Qoheleth witnessed oppression and looked in vain for comforters. The repetition of the pitiful words "and there was none to comfort them" may indicate how deeply Qoheleth felt their pain. If the observer were really King Solomon, he could punish offenders promptly; instead, Qoheleth notes that power belonged to the oppressors. He thinks of the unborn as luckier than the living and the dead, for they are spared such sights.

Some Proverbial Insights, 4:4-6

Qoheleth views envy as an invigorating passion that forces people to waste time competing for nothing. One can never know the result of an action, for a fool remains idle and lives off accumulated fat or has ample food in spite of laziness. The final aphorism seems to imply that a morsel is preferable to the ceaseless struggle for something more.

Advantages of Companionship, 4:7-12

An observation about the absurd striving to accumulate wealth by one who has no dependents gives rise to a rare concession that something is better than the much-prized individualism of sages. In companions one finds a measure of security against robbers, accidental falls, and the night's chill. Qoheleth clinches the point with an aphorism about the strength of a threefold cord, a saying also current in ancient MESOPOTAMIA. The ego remains supreme in this acknowledgment that com-panions make life more comfortable and safe, for Qoheleth thinks about what others can do for him. The same heightened ego had come to expression in the royal experiment, which frequently uses the words "for myself."

The Fickle Crowd, 4:13-16

The section echoes the JOSEPH story, although somewhat erratically. The praise of youth contrasts markedly with earlier wisdom and may signify Greek influence. Older attitudes to the poor often implied fault, a laziness that contributed to poverty. That understanding necessarily followed from the optimistic claim that good people mastered their lives by using wisdom and therefore earned wealth, honor, progeny, and longevity. A poor but wise youth was almost an anomaly, but so was much of what Qoheleth taught. Wise counselors worked closely with Egyptian kings, and DAVID is said to have had two advisors, Ahithophel and HUSHAI. A king who refused to take advice, or one who heeded foolish counsel, was headed for disaster. In Qoheleth's anecdote, the youth supplanted the king and was subsequently replaced, it seems, amply demonstrating the fickleness of society.

Religious Duties, 5:1-9 [MT 4:17–5:8]

5:1-7. Prayer, dreams, and vows. This section advises against rash speech in the holy place, presumably the TEMPLE. Qoheleth thinks of a great distance separating worshipers and God, both spatially and essentially. Fear is the appropriate attitude for human beings, who should speak sparingly lest the sacrifice of fools (insincere praise?) prompt an angry reaction from on high. Qoheleth's distrust of religious dreams was more consistent than SIRACH's, perhaps owing to the necessity of interpreting them. The advice against reneging on religious vows echoes Deut 23:21, but Qoheleth goes further when advising against the taking of vows in the first place. The term for unwitting offenses (v. 6, *mistake*) is a technical expression in biblical legal codes. The *messenger* is either a priestly emissary or the death angel, which Egyptian wisdom also mentions.

5:8-9. A hierarchy of responsibility. Qoheleth probably alludes to the complex Persian system of officials in Judah, which complicated matters greatly when one endeavored to locate blame for injustice. The prophetic outcry on behalf of victims has made no impression on Qoheleth, who merely registers awareness that such cruelty happens and none can put a stop to it. Does he think of God as ultimately at fault? The obscure comment about the advantage of a king with fields may imply that even a corrupt monarch at least keeps a semblance of order (contrast Judg 19–21).

The Disappointments of Wealth, 5:10–6:9 [MT 5:9–6:9]

5:10-12. Money's unwelcome companions. The third century witnessed a rise in acquisitiveness and the resultant disparity between rich and poor. Fortunes were won and lost overnight, particularly those resulting from investments at sea. Qoheleth observes that money never brings satisfaction, for people invariably want more. Furthermore, increased holdings require additional laborers, who inflate expenditures, and add to one's worry about loss through an ill-advised venture or robbery. Perhaps Qoheleth refers to sleeplessness resulting from overeating, a problem seldom affecting day laborers who fall asleep from exhaustion.

5:13-20. An object lesson. Qoheleth is moved by an instance in which a man loses everything as a result of a bad venture, although that man has a son who hopes to inherit the wealth. Both father and son will depart empty-handed; the allusion to the sentiment otherwise expressed in Job 1:21 can hardly be missed. Neither the man's toil nor his resentment made any appreciable difference. Qoheleth concludes that people should accept their lot as God dispenses it, knowing that they will little remember the joys with which God occupies their minds (or afflicts them with thoughts of how things ought to be). This section introduces the notion of DARKNESS, which will come to prominence in 11:7–12:7. The present reference seems to suggest a miserly lifestyle in which the person is too stingy to light a lamp during evening meals (v. 17).

6:1-9. Divine irony. Qoheleth recognizes the irony in circumstances where individuals prosper mightily but lack the ability to enjoy such largess. The usual signs of divine approval often deceive, for someone may have numerous children and lengthy existence without the honor associated with a proper burial. Qoheleth sees that one's ability to enjoy life and one's burial depend on others, God in the first instance and people in the second. He considers a stillborn luckier than a person who has a long life but lacks power to enjoy it, for an untimely birth quickly attained rest (cf. Job 3:11-19).

A Transitional Unit, 6:10-12

The mention of the first human creature, ADAM, in a context denying anything new is nicely ironical. Qoheleth seems to refer to JOB who multiplied words in the colossal struggle with one more powerful than he. The principal aim of ancient wisdom has been summed up in the words "what is good for men and women?" By denying that anyone can actually know the answer, Qoheleth calls into question the fundamental premise of the sages. In doing so he returns to the earlier notion, often repeated, that life is futile. He also introduces a new image, that of a lengthening shadow. Many interpreters think these three rhetorical questions bring the first half of the book to a close.

A Collection of Proverbs, 7:1-14

Ancient sages tried to weigh the relative merits of various things, often using "better proverbs" to state their findings. This unit effectively uses alliteration, for example, in the Hebrew words for *name* and oil (*ointment*), *thorns, pot,* and *laughter* (v. 6). Qoheleth indicates a preference for life's darker features; he chooses death over birth, the house of mourning over one of feasting, sorrow over laughter. Nevertheless, he values wisdom more than folly, comparing the advantage of knowledge to that of wealth, which offers a measure of security. Once more he quotes the traditional saying about the impossibility of straightening out what God *has made crooked* (v. 13). This time it is introduced by an invitation to examine God's work. In v. 14 Qoheleth repeats the earlier observation (3:11) that God has concealed the future from humankind.

On Moderation, 7:15-22

An instance of gross injustice—wicked persons who prosper and virtuous people who perish—leads to Qoheleth's radical conclusion that one should not try to be a model of piety, like legendary Job, or for that matter a master villain. Presumably, Qoheleth fears that either extreme might call God's attention to the person and bring misfortune. At least one critic thinks this section has nothing to do with moderation but attacks self-righteousness. Another interpreter compares its teaching to the Chinese concept of a median way instead of the more obvious Greek parallel.

Seeking and Finding, 7:23-29

This section emphasizes the limits imposed on human knowledge, an insight familiar to earlier sages. It also focuses that limitation precisely where some older proverbs do: on the mystery of eros. In the Book of Proverbs the foreign woman—by action or by nationality—constituted a threat to young men. Qoheleth appears to generalize that threat to include all women. He may cite a popular aphorism with which he disagrees, or he may simply relativize its point by indicating that men are only 1/1,000th more reliable than women. The text probably plays on Solomon's reputation for having a thousand wives and concubines, and it thereby offers a subtle clue to the meaning of "the Qoheleth" (v. 27, *the Teacher*). He gathers women in search of the *sum* (profit?) but ends up with a huge zero, nay a minus, for evil women are *more bitter than death* (v. 26; or stronger than death, like love in Cant 8:6).

Rulers and Subjects, 8:1-9

This unit begins by citing an obscure saying that praises the perspicacity of the wise, which may allude to the previous mystery about women, then moves on to treat an equally potent threat. Qoheleth cautions those who come in contact with rulers to keep a safe distance when unpleasant matters come up, for kings do as they please. Royal power as depicted in 1 Esd 4:1-12 is eclipsed by that of woman (1 Esd 4:13-32). Qoheleth mentions death as the power to which everyone must submit, kings and women (cf. 1 Esd 4:37). This advice about conduct before rulers does not seem to be aimed at courtiers, like the "men of Hezekiah" (Prov 25:1, RSV) who probably disappeared in Judah with the collapse of the monarchy.

The Mystery of Divine Activity, 8:10-17

Qoheleth reports on a particularly galling incident involving evil persons whose guilt was hidden even in death. Praise instead of rebuke accompanied their burial. Delay in divine judgment encourages such conduct. Without warning, the text suddenly affirms God's justice in the face of contradictory evidence (vv. 12-13). Many interpreters consider this statement out of character and attribute it to a later editor, particularly since vv. 14-15 go on to talk about the absence of divine justice as grounds for seeking pleasure.

Qoheleth has no patience with sages who claim to have access to the truth about what God is doing. For them a single response suffices: they are mistaken. This sharp attack may be directed against emerging apocalyptic movements and their leaders, the sort of mantic wisdom reflected in the Book of Daniel.

Death's Shadow, 9:1-10

This section lumps all people together in a common fate; it makes no difference whether they have been good or bad. Such a state of affairs strikes Qoheleth as indication that one cannot determine whether God's disposition toward human beings is favorable or unfavorable. Qoheleth employs a powerful rhetorical device to suggest death: he simply breaks off the sentence in the middle—like life itself. The traditional saying that *a living dog is better than a dead lion* (v. 4) probably derives from another setting, one justifying marriage to a person of lower social status. Here the saying reeks with irony: if the only advantage that the living possess over the dead is the knowledge that they must die, then the "hope" is hollow to the core.

Qoheleth's counsel in v. 7 is liberating to persons who possess a scrupulous conscience, but it probably only means that if one can do something then it follows that God has approved the action. The advice in vv. 8-10 resembles Siduri's counsel to Gilgamesh ("Death is decreed for mortals, eternal life is reserved for the gods"), although one need not think of direct literary influence. Qoheleth's syntax—"a woman you love"—is unusual if *wife* (as in KJV–NRSV) is intended.

Time and Chance, 9:11-12

In Qoheleth's opinion, chance governs human lives. The outcome of actions has no direct correlation with the effort expended. Such a view stands in opposition to older wisdom, which insisted that by careful mastery of the passions and by wise action, human beings could assure certain desirable consequences. According to the Book of Proverbs danger certainly existed, but one could escape its clutches by taking care. Qoheleth abandons such optimism, for he thinks none can avert disaster, which falls unexpectedly like a fishnet.

Wasted Wisdom, 9:13-18

An example illustrates society's low estimate of wisdom. The incident may be hypothetical. When a mighty ruler attacked a tiny village, a poor wise man saved it but was promptly forgotten, or he might have saved the city had anyone thought to consult him. Qoheleth still considers wisdom superior to force, although he concedes that one wicked person can cause considerable harm.

Another Collection of Proverbs, 10:1-20

Such unassimilated sayings as these frustrate all attempts to discover a consistent structure in the book. A few words in these sayings occur elsewhere in Qoheleth's thought, but much of the material would be equally at home in the Book of Proverbs. The sayings give voice to the ancient tendency to attribute moral connotations to right and left, express dismay when reversals occur within society (slaves riding horses, princes walking), alert those who do domestic chores to some inherent dangers, and praise eloquence (a frequent subject in ancient wisdom). The final warning against useless curses has a parallel in Egyptian wisdom (v. 20).

The Element of Risk, 11:1-6

Qoheleth recognizes that life always carries risk, whether in commercial ventures or in agricultural pursuits. He advises action despite the danger and warns against a cautious attitude that paralyzes one. The advice to throw bread on the water, which has a parallel in the Egyptian *Instructions of 'Onkhsheshonqy* (19.10), probably refers to mercantile investments. Qoheleth notes that the mystery of life does not surrender to human investigation any more than does God's activity, so people should sow seed at opportune times.

Concluding Framework, 11:7–12:14

Youth and Old Age, 11:7–12:7

This exquisite poem describes the collapse of a house during a storm as a symbol of a wasting human body. The verbs *remember* and *rejoice* and the nouns *darkness* and *light* unite the poem, which juxtaposes youth and old age. Three times the word *before* points beyond the formula to unwelcome occurrences culminating in death. The domestic images for death are not exactly clear, but they refer to the breaking of a cord that holds a lamp and the shattering of a pitcher as a result of a faulty pulley at the well. A puff of dust and the release of God's breath signal the end and evoke Qoheleth's solemn remark that both have returned to their source. The translation *creator* in 12:1 does not fit the context. The unusual word may allude to one's wife ("well" in Prov 5:15-19) and grave. The warning of divine *judgment* in 11:9 also seems strange; it may be a gloss.

Thematic Statement, 12:8

This verse serves as an inclusion with 1:2.

Two Epilogues, 12:9-14

Two editors comment on Qoheleth's teachings. The first, vv. 9-12, speaks admiringly of his honesty, trustworthiness, and aesthetic sense. This editor identifies Qoheleth as a sage who taught the people, not just young boys, and concedes that his words were at times demanding, indeed exhausting. The second editor submits Qoheleth's radical teachings to traditional piety: fear God and keep the commandments, for a judgment day is coming (vv. 13-14).

Song of Solomon

Mona West

Introduction

Song of Solomon is unique in all the literature of the Hebrew Bible. It contains erotic poetry that celebrates human love and the joy of sex. Neither of these, in the Song, leads to marriage or procreation. There is no mention of God or of any event of Israel's salvation history. The primary speaker of the poems is a woman, who is free to express sexuality and mutuality in advances toward the male beloved.

Early Jewish and Christian interpretations allegorized and spiritualized the Song, stripping the book of its sensual, bodily focus. Currently, theologians are reaffirming the book's emphasis on the erotic. In an age when we as human beings feel alienated from the world, God, each other, and our own bodies, Song of Songs can help us celebrate our sexual selves and rejoice in our physical bodies.

The lovers in the Song show us the goodness of sex without shame, domination, or alienation. The poetry of the Song challenges us to embrace and encounter God and the world with the same senses and passion used in sexual intercourse.

Authorship and Date

The opening verse, along with the references of 3:7-11 and 8:11-12, indicate King SOLOMON may have been the book's author. However, it is unlikely he actually wrote the poems found in the Song. Because he was known for his poetic compositions (1 Kgs 4:32-33) and his love of women (1 Kgs 11:3), Solomon was associated with the book's composition.

In reality the majority of the poems are spoken by a woman. One commentator has noted, "the protagonist in the Song is the only unmediated female voice in scripture" (Weems 1992, 156). One must not rule out the possibility that the author(s) may have been female. Even so, her identity remains anonymous.

The timeless nature of love poetry makes it difficult to assign a specific date to the book. The nature of some of the poetry would indicate a time in Israel's history (postexilic) when lovers were compelled to affirm their right to love whomever they chose regardless of class, ethnicity (1:5-6; 6:13), or societal or family approval (5:7; 8:1-4, 8-9).

History of Interpretation

While there is no scholarly consensus on how to construe the Song, interpretations generally fall into one of two categories: a unified work with intentional design, or an anthology of independent poems.

Dominant interpretive theories that assume some type of unity include: (1) an allegory of God's relationship to Israel (Jewish) and Christ's relationship to the Church (Christian), (2) a drama with two or three characters and a chorus, (3) a liturgy celebrating the sacred marriage of a fertility god and goddess, (4) a cycle of wedding songs sung during the wedding feast.

Anthological readings of the Song will vary concerning the number of poems found within the book, the criteria used to delineate the poetic units, and the relationship of the poems to one another. Scholars who view the Song as a collection of independent poems are willing to admit some "surface structure" based on the repetition of key words (e.g., lilies, stags, and *gazelles* in 2:1, 2, 7, 9, 16, 17), refrains (*I adjure you . . .* in 2:7; 3:5; 5:8; 8:4), and characters (*daughters of Jerusalem* in 1:5; 2:7; 3:5, 10; 5:8, 9; 6:1; 8:4). This "surface structure" could be the result of skillful editing and/or the recurrence of stock phrases used in the love poetry of ancient Israel.

More recently, feminists have offered their interpretation of the Song. Emphases include the possibility of female authorship; positive cultural reflection of the role of women (assertive, sexual without the strictures of patriarchal marriage or procreation); mention of the mother's house and the mother as images of the woman's autonomy in lovemaking.

Literary Unity

The outline and commentary that follow are attempts to preserve the independent nature of the poems. However, readers encounter the Song as a "book" of the Bible and its repetitions invite efforts to group the poems into meaningful subunits.

Thirty-three distinct poetic units are identified in the outline (but not all of the units receive extended treatment). The criteria used for determining these poetic units were: a change in speaker, tone, content, or context; repetition of words, phrases and refrains; a general sense of an ending or beginning.

These units can be grouped into five categories. The categories are an effort to aid the reader by assigning labels that indicate how the poems function within the book.

Poems of *description* can be of the lover (the woman) or the beloved (the man). They are physical descriptions of beauty, incorporating a variety of images, usually made by one lover of the other. However, there is one instance in which a group of people describe the woman (7:1-5). Other descriptions include the power of love (8:6-7) and Solomon's marriage processional (3:6-11).

The *wasf* is the most distinctive poem of description. It is a type of Arabic poetry that describes parts of the female or male body beginning from top to bottom (head to feet), or the reverse. Images from nature, architecture, and the military are used to create a sensory (most often visual) picture of the lover or the beloved. The *wasf* can be found in 4:1-7; 5:10-16; 6:4-10; 7:1-5.

Encounter poems depict the sexual meetings of the lovers. These can be present (1:12-14; 5:1) or past (2:4-7). Often their lovemaking is depicted with imagery of eating and drinking (2:4-7; 5:1).

In *seeking* poems lovers search for one another in the contexts of pastures (1:7-8) and city streets (3:1-5; 5:2-8). Sometimes the lovers find one another; sometimes they do not. Another type of seeking occurs in 8:1-4 when the woman seeks the approval of her love by society.

Related to seeking and encounter, poems of *beckoning* are made by both male and female. Often desire is expressed and lovemaking is described (2:8-15; 4:8-11). In one instance a group beckons the woman (6:13).

Poems of *affirmation* fall into three subcategories: self affirmation (1:5-6; 8:10); mutual affirmation (1:15-17; 2:1-3); general statement of affirmation (6:1-3; 7:10-13; 8:11-12). Affirmation poems usually occur within the context of objection (1:5-6) or competition (6:1-3).

The polemical tone of the book may be yet another way to make sense of the individual poems. Much of the poetry seems to focus on the lovers' right to their relationship regardless of societal and family pressures. This polemic provides an organizing principle for reading the poems as part of a larger whole.

When society will not affirm the lovers' relationship because of race, class, and sex-role stereotypes, the lovers' affirm each other with descriptions of beauty and lovemaking (1:5-6, 9-11, 12-14, 15-17; 5:2-8, 9-16; 8:1-4, 5, 6-7). The woman continues to assert her right to love when family members attempt to discourage her (1:5-6, 7-8; 8:8-9, 10). The fact that the lovers are continually seeking and beckoning one another in hopes of lovemaking indicates their determination to be together whatever the cost (1:7-8; 2:8-15; 3:1-5; 4:8-11, 16; 5:2-8; 8:13-14).

Related to the argumentative tone of these poems is the theme of barriers: barriers that prevent or threaten love; barriers that invite or protect love. Race, class and family would be barriers that prevent love (see above). Barriers that provide an opportunity for love are the countryside (2:8-15); the beloved's chambers and banqueting house (1:2-4; 2:4-7); the mother's house (3:1-4).

For Further Study

In the *Mercer Dictionary of the Bible*: FEMINIST HERMENEUTICS; LOVE IN THE NT; LOVE IN THE OT; SOLOMON; POETRY; SONG OF SONGS; WOMEN IN THE NT; WOMEN IN THE OT.

In other sources: A. Brenner, *The Song of Songs*; M. Falk, *Love Lyrics from the Bible: A Translation and Literary Study of The Song of Songs;* M. D. Goulder, *The Song of Fourteen Songs*; M. H. Pope, *Song of Songs*, AncB; P. Trible, *God and the Rhetoric of Sexuality*.

Commentary

An Outline

I. Introduction, 1:1-4
   Title, 1:1
   Encounter, 1:2-4
II. Love that Transcends Class and Race, 1:5-17
   Self-affirmation, 1:5-6
   Seeking the Beloved, 1:7-8
   Description of the Lover, 1:9-11
   Encounter, 1:12-14
   Mutual Affirmation, 1:15-17
III. Love in Springtime, 2:1-17
   Mutual Affirmation and Encounter, 2:1-3
   Encounter, 2:4-7
   Beckoning the Lover, 2:8-15
   Statement of Affirmation, 2:16-17
IV. Love's Couches, 3:1-11
   Seeking the Beloved, 3:1-5
   Description of Solomon's
      Marriage Processional, 3:6-11
V. Description and Desire, 4:1–5:1
   Description of the Lover, 4:1-7
   Beckoning the Lover, 4:8-11
   Description of the Lover, 4:12-15

   Beckoning the Beloved, 4:16
   Encounter, 5:1
VI. Dialogue with Jerusalem's Daughters, 5:2–6:3
   Seeking the Beloved, 5:2-8
   Description of the Beloved, 5:9-16
   Statement of Affirmation, 6:1-3
VII. Description and Encounter, 6:4-12
   Description of the Lover, 6:4-10
   Encounter, 6:11-12
VIII. Dance of the Shulammite, 6:13–7:13
   Beckoning the Shulammite, 6:13
   Description of the Lover, 7:1-5
   Description of the Lover, 7:6-9
   Statement of Affirmation, 7:10-13
IX. The Triumph of Love, 8:1-14
   Seeking Approval, 8:1-4
   Encounter, 8:5
   Description of Love, 8:6-7
   Description of the Lover, 8:8-9
   Self Affirmation, 8:10
   Statement of Affirmation, 8:11-12
   Mutual Beckoning, 8:13-14

Introduction, 1:1-4

Title, 1:1

The book's title in the Hebrew Bible comes from the phrase in 1:1 which is translated, *The Song of Songs*. This phrase can be rendered in a number of ways, including "A song made up of many songs," and "The most sublime or best song." Because the book has traditionally been associated with SOLOMON, the title, "Song of Solomon," will occur in some English translations.

Encounter, 1:2-4

The first poem serves as an introduction. It is a poem of encounter but contains imagery and themes that are repeated throughout the book: physical love (kiss), sensual imagery (wine, oil, fragrance), the presence of others (maidens), barriers that protect love (beloved's chambers).

Love that Transcends Class and Race, 1:5-17

The woman's self-affirmation in 1:5-6 is the first indication that not all is well with the love expressed in the Song. The identity of the woman is uncertain. She is different from the *daughters of Jerusalem* (v. 5) in two ways. Her skin is dark as a result of working in the fields, which may indicate her lower socioeconomic status. (Her darkness implies the fairer skin of the *daughters of Jerusalem* who stayed indoors.) There is also the possibility that her skin color may denote a different ethnic background than the Jerusalem daughters. The claims she makes about herself are not apologetic, but boastful: *I am black and beautiful* (v. 5).

The woman is also different in that she is experienced sexually. She indicates her brothers were angry because she had not kept her vineyard (vines and vineyards are symbols for lovemaking throughout the Song, cf. 2:15; 7:12). Her remarks to the daughters of Jerusalem elsewhere in the Song are words of advice from an experienced lover to the unexperienced (2:7):

> *I adjure you, O daughters of Jerusalem,*
> *by the gazelles or the wild does;*
> *do not stir up or awaken love until it is ready!*

The poems that follow in the remainder of this section indicate that regardless of the strictures of class, race, family, or societal norms lovers will continue to seek out one another and claim their right to relationship. While the daughters of Jerusalem may stare and brothers may be angry, lovers mutually affirm the beauty of their love and are content with each other (vv. 15-17).

Love in Springtime, 2:1-17

Images of flowers, fruit, and animals are interwoven in the poems of this section as the lovers single out one another for encounter and speak of their love as a banquet. The woman claims that she is one flower among many, yet the man claims her for his own (vv. 1-2, 16). Likewise, out of all the trees of the wood, the woman claims the man for her own (v. 3). Their encounter is described as a banquet at which they feast on the fruit of love (vv. 3-6).

In vv. 8-15 the woman recalls a spring visit by her beloved. The beloved is described as *a gazelle or young stag* who invokes the rite of spring in his beckoning of the female lover. In the midst of the beauty and promise of spring, a note of caution still surrounds the lovers with a reference to *the foxes that ruin the vineyards* of their love.

The section closes with a statement of affirmation in which the images of *lilies, gazelle, stag*, and *mountains* are repeated (vv. 16-17).

Love's Couches, 3:1-11

In dream or reality the woman puts herself at considerable risk seeking the beloved in the city streets in the middle of the night. The search climaxes in lovemaking with advice to the *daughters of Jerusalem* concerning the hazards of this kind of meeting (vv. 1-5).

Juxtaposed to the nighttime lovemaking of the woman and man is the description of Solomon's marriage processional (vv. 6-11). King Solomon is symbol for the double standards the lovers face in overcoming the barriers to their love. Solomon, the king associated with class structure in Israel. Solomon, who had many foreign women, sanctioned by marriage, but how many for love and how many for political expediency?

The juxtaposition is carried further with the images of two couches for love: the lovers' secret rendezvous in the chamber of the house of the woman's mother, presumably upon a couch or bed (cf. v. 1); Solomon's marriage processional, which consists of a fortified couch (v. 7) whose interior is *inlaid with love* (v. 10).

Description and Desire, 4:1–5:1

Poems of description and beckoning alternate as the man and woman express their desire for one another, which culminates in an encounter of lovemaking. The *wasf* is used by the man to describe the woman in 4:1-7. To the modern reader it may not seem complimentary to compare one's hair to a *flock of goats, moving down the slopes*, or one's teeth to a *flock of shorn ewes that have come up from the washing, all of which bear twins, and not one of them is bereaved* (vv. 1, 2). But the visual image is striking if the graceful, curved, flowing, movement of goats coming down a mountain from a distance is considered for the hair. Likewise, ewes shorn smooth and washed white, evenly matched, none broken, are fitting imagery for healthy white teeth in a society that did not know about fluoride or preventative dentistry.

The words *sister* and *bride* in 4:8, 9, 10, 11, 12 and 5:1 are not to be taken literally. *Sister* was a term of endearment used in Egyptian love poetry (Falk 1982, 122). Here the words are metaphors for the love relationship. The words may also be an allusion to the boundaries of acceptability against which the lovers struggle.

In vv. 12-15 the woman is described as a locked garden and sealed fountain, indicating her fidelity, or her inaccessibility. The images of garden and fountain also allude to the woman's sexuality and fecundity. The woman invokes the north and south winds to blow the fragrance of her garden abroad, beckoning her beloved to *come to his garden and eat its choicest fruits* (v. 16). In 5:1 the beloved comes to his garden, eats his honeycomb, and drinks his wine and milk.

Dialogue with Jerusalem's Daughters, 5:2–6:3

The seeking poem of 5:2-8 is parallel to 3:1-5. Both take place at night with a thin line between dream and reality. In chap. 3 the woman had gone in search of her beloved; in chap. 5 the beloved comes to her. The scene is suggestive, the language titillating.

The beloved knocks on the woman's door in the middle of the night and says, *"Open to me, my sister, my love . . . , for my head is wet with dew . . ."* (5:2).

The woman claims, *My beloved thrust his hand into the opening, and my inmost being yearned for him* (5:4).

She is slow in her response and finds the beloved gone when she finally opens the door. As in chap. 3, she searches for him in the city streets. By contrast with chap. 3, she is beaten by the sentinels of the city (cf. 5:7 and 3:3) and does not find her beloved. (This may indicate societal objection to her assertiveness.) As in 3:5, *the daughters of Jerusalem* are adjured; this time, however, she says, *If you find my beloved, tell him this: I am faint with love* (5:8).

This variation on the repeated refrain to the daughters of Jerusalem leads to a dialogue. In 6:9 the daughters ask the woman why her beloved is so special that she entreats them in this way. She responds to their question with a *wasf* in which she describes her beloved with images of precious metals and stones (vv. 10-16).

After this description, the daughters are interested in searching for the beloved, too. The poetry takes on a competitive tone when the woman replies with a statement of affirmation: *I am my beloved's and he is mine* (v. 3a).

Description and Encounter, 6:4-12

The dialogue with the daughters of Jerusalem is followed by a *wasf* in which the man describes the woman (vv. 4-10). It is essentially the same *wasf* found in 4:1-7, framed by the phrase, *terrible as an army of banners* vv. 4, 10). The phrase denotes the awesomeness of gazing upon the lover.

The encounter in vv. 11-12 presents some difficulties. The speaker of the poem is ambiguous and the Hebrew in v. 12 is virtually untranslatable (Falk 1982, 126). Since the man has been speaking in the previous poem, it is assumed that he is the one recalling this encounter. The word translated *prince* could be rendered "princely people." The whole line seems to be alluding to the ecstasy of lovemaking.

The Dance of the Shulammite, 6:13–7:13

A crowd beckons the woman at the beginning of this group of poems. The designation, *Shulammite*, is uncertain. It probably refers to the woman's distinctiveness (cf. 1:5-8). There is a hint of voyeurism when the crowd pleads, *Return . . . that we may look upon you*, to which she replies, *Why should you look upon the Shulammite, as upon a dance before two armies?* (6:13; MT 7:1). The meaning of this last phrase is debatable, but the earlier context of competition (6:4-12), as well as the alternating descriptions that follow (7:1-5; 7:6-9), indicate that the woman dances before two parties, a crowd and her beloved.

The crowd describes the woman and her dance with a *wasf* (vv. 1-5). This *wasf* differs from the others in that it starts with the feet and moves upward. It is also complete. (The others describe only half of the body, the upper torso.)

The man in turn describes the woman and expresses his desire for her (vv. 6-9).

Just as the woman's description of her beloved and the dialogue with the daughters of Jerusalem (5:9-16; 6:1-3) ended with a statement of affirmation, *I am my beloved's and he is mine* (6:3), so too, *the dance before two armies* and alternating descriptions (6:13; 7:1-5; 7:6-9) culminate in the statement of affirmation found in 7:10-13.

The Triumph of Love, 8:1-14

Themes from previous poems are repeated in this last section of the Song: longing for approval (vv. 1-4); the mother and the mother's house (vv. 1, 2, 5); the *daughters of Jerusalem* (v. 4); encounter under a fruit tree (v. 5); the disapproving brothers (vv. 8-9); King Solomon (vv. 11, 12); vineyards and gardens (vv. 11, 12, 13).

In the midst of all these images that recall the struggles of lovers, there is a strong statement and description of the power of love. It is strong as death, fierce as the grave, unquenchable, without price (vv. 6-7).

The Song has an open ending of mutual beckoning (vv. 13-14) indicating the triumph of love. In the face of whatever adversity, lovers will continue to listen for one another's voice, bounding unfettered upon mountains of spices.

Works Cited

Falk, Marcia. 1982. *Love Lyrics from the Bible: A Translation and Literary Study of the Song of Songs.*

Weems, Renita J. 1992. "Song of Songs" in *The Women's Bible Commentary.*